to: Bill Penn

May your new Colorado home bring you much joy & many happy times with family & friends —

Love,

Ted & Sharon Jackson

Ken Gire

BETWEEN HEAVEN AND EARTH

Prayers and Reflections
that Celebrate an
Intimate God

BETWEEN
HEAVEN
AND
EARTH

Compiled and Edited by
KEN GIRE

HarperSanFrancisco
An Imprint of HarperCollins*Publishers*

BETWEEN HEAVEN AND EARTH: *Prayers and Reflections that Celebrate an Intimate God.* Copyright © 1997 by Ken Gire. Printed in the United States of America. No part of this book may be used or reproduced in any manner whatsoever without written permission except in the case of brief quotations embodied in critical articles and reviews. For information address HarperCollins Publishers, 10 East 53rd Street, New York, NY 10022.

HarperCollins,® ♨,® and HarperSanFrancisco™
are trademarks of HarperCollins Publishers Inc.
HarperCollins Web Site: http://www.harpercollins.com
FIRST EDITION

Library of Congress Cataloging-in-Publication Data

Between heaven and earth : prayers and reflections that celebrate an intimate God / compiled and edited by Ken Gire. — 1st ed.
Includes bibliographical references and index.
ISBN 0–06–063046–9 (cloth)
1. Prayer—Christianity. 2. Prayers. I. Gire, Ken.
BV210.2 B497 1997
248.3'2—dc20   96–36699

97 98 99 00 01 ❖RRDH 10 9 8 7 6 5 4 3 2 1

The soul is like a bird,
shaken from its peaceful roost by the inclement
     circumstances of life,
where windblown branches
and sudden gusts from darkening horizons
thrust it into weather that is wild and uncertain.
And sometimes, however hard we beat our wings,
we can't seem to overcome the elements galing against us.
We are thrashed about in the air,
windsheered and weary,
wondering if our cries for help are reaching God.
But then the tempest subsides,
for a while anyway,
and the updrafts of God's Spirit lift us to new heights,
above the wind, above the rain, above the earth.
And, for a moment,
we soar.

KEN GIRE

CONTENTS

ACKNOWLEDGMENTS

I would like to acknowledge my profound appreciation and indebtedness to Lee Hough, the managing editor on this project, and to Howard Baker, the consulting editor. Without their long hours of hard work, dedication, and prayer, this project could not have been accomplished.

BETWEEN HEAVEN AND EARTH

PREFACE

Between heaven and earth lies the firmament of our prayers.

In one sense, the firmament is ethereal as air. In another sense, it is substantial as atmosphere. In a sense, it is a mere wisp of who we are. In another sense, it is rich with the elements of life, gritty with the dust of our humanity.

Within this ever-changing sky funnels a maelstrom of faith and doubt. Turbulent at times. Galing with emotion. Wild and windswept and full of fury. A swirling vortex of questions, arguments, and confusion.

But that is not all there is to the weather of the heart.

There are calm days, too. Serene as a sunset. A tinting of thankfulness on the horizon. A billowing of praise. And, thank God, for most of us, there are more blue skies than storms.

Between Heaven and Earth is less an anthology of prayer and more a sampling of the atmosphere. As a weather balloon gathers samples in its ascent, we have tried to gather prayers and reflections of every age and every walk of life from around the world and across the centuries. Some of the prayers have been sighed into the heat of day. Others have been shivered into the cold loneliness of night. Together they make up the atmosphere.

And together they celebrate an intimate God.

A God who walked in the garden with our first parents . . . and who walks with us still. A God who befriended the first patriarch . . . and who befriends us still. A God who listened and spoke, cleaving all of human history with a word.

Immanuel.

God with us.

It is, I think, an expression of our deepest longing. Unspoken syllables tearfully ascending an expansive sky. Snowflaking into a word. And coming down.

Something beautiful from heaven, coming down.

Glistening with grace and truth. Settling on our shoulders. Touching us with wonder. And love. And hope.

Immanuel.

Perhaps it is more than a name.

Perhaps in the firmament between heaven and earth
        it is both a prayer
                and an answer to prayer.

PART ONE

WHAT IS PRAYER?

INTRODUCTION

What is prayer?
Prayer is the conversation we have with God.

As in any conversation, sometimes we communicate what's in our heart with great articulation, even eloquence. Other times we find only a toy box of childish expressions. Still other times we grope for words the way a newborn gropes for its mother's breast.

But the expression of our longing is not as important as the longing itself.

For prayer is nothing more than the soul's longing for God—and the words nothing more than a child's attempt to describe them.

Now I lay me down to sleep.
I pray the Lord my soul to keep.
If I should die before I wake,
I pray the Lord my soul to take.
If I should live for other days,
I pray the Lord to guide my ways.

The stitchwork prayer of a child being tucked into bed. A simple prayer with simple words. Not much different than the simple prayer with simple words whispered so many years ago—"Father, into thy hands I commit my spirit"—as another weary child lay himself down to sleep.

James Montgomery, *What Is Prayer?*

(1771–1854) Hymnwriter from Scotland. Montgomery wrote four hundred hymns, many of which, like the following classic, are still sung today.

Prayer is the soul's sincere desire,
Unuttered or expressed,
The motion of a hidden fire
That trembles in the breast.

Prayer is the burden of a sigh,
The falling of a tear,
The upward glancing of the eye,
When none but God is near.

Prayer is the Christian's vital breath,
The Christian's native air,
His watchword at the gates of death;
He enters heaven with prayer.

Prayer is the contrite sinner's voice,
Returning from his ways,
While angels in their songs rejoice
And cry, "Behold, he prays!"

O Thou by whom we come to God,
The life, the truth, the way,
The path of prayer Thyself hast trod:
Lord, teach us how to pray.

—∞∞—

George MacDonald

(1824–1905) Poverty-stricken Scottish pastor, poet, and novelist whose works profoundly influenced C. S. Lewis.

"O God," I said, and that was all. But what are the prayers of the whole universe more than expansions of that one cry? It is not what God can give us, but God that we want.

—∞∞—

C. S. Lewis, *The World's Last Night*

(1898–1963) Christian apologist, Oxford scholar, and author.

Prayer is either a sheer illusion or a personal contact between embryonic, incomplete persons (ourselves) and the utterly concrete Person. Prayer in the sense of petition, asking for things, is a small part of it; confession and penitence are its threshold, adoration its sanctuary, the presence and vision and enjoyment of God its bread and wine.

—∞∞—

O. Hallesby, *Prayer*

(1879–1961) Norwegian theologian and leader in the resistance against the Nazis. He was arrested and sent to a concentration camp that was liberated in 1945.

Prayer is something deeper than words. It is present in the soul before it has been formulated in words. And it abides in the soul after the last words of prayer have passed over our lips.

———∞∞———

E. M. Bounds

(1835–1913) Methodist minister and devotional writer who served as a pastor in the American South and became a POW during the Civil War.

Prayer is the easiest and the hardest of all things; the simplest and the sublimest; the weakest and the most powerful; its results lie outside the range of human possibilities—they are limited only by the omnipotence of God. *Few Christians have anything but a vague idea of the power of prayer; fewer still have any experience of that power.* The Church seems almost wholly unaware of the power God puts into her hand; this spiritual carte blanche on the infinite resources of God's wisdom and power is rarely, if ever, used—never used to the full measure of honoring God. It is astounding how poor the use, how little the benefits. Prayer is our most formidable weapon, but the one in which we are the least skilled, the most averse to its use. We do everything else for the heathen save the thing God wants us to do; the only thing which does any good—makes all else we do efficient.

———∞∞———

Howard Macy, *Rhythms of the Inner Life*

Prayer has less to do with getting things than with knowing God. It is more concerned with loving God than with lists of prayer requests. Asking for assistance and knowing God are related, of course, but coming into intimacy with the Holy One is the principal purpose and context of prayer.

———∞∞———

Friedrich Heiler

(1892–1967) German theologian who taught comparative religious history and was a leader in the liturgical movement in the church.

Prayer appears in history in an astonishing multiplicity of forms; as the calm collectedness of a devout individual soul, and as the ceremonial liturgy of a great congregation; as an original creation of a religious genius, and as an imitation on the part of a simple, average religious person; as the spontaneous expression of upspringing religious experiences, and as the mechanical recitation of an incomprehensible formula; as bliss and ecstasy of heart, and as painful fulfillment of the law; as the involuntary discharge of an overwhelming emotion, and as the voluntary concentration on a religious object; as loud shouting and crying, and as still, silent absorption; as artistic poetry, and as stammering speech; as the flight of the spirit to the supreme Light, and as a cry out of the deep distress of the heart; as joyous thanksgiving and ecstatic praise, and as humble supplication for forgiveness and compassion; as a childlike entreaty for life, health, and happiness, and as an earnest desire for power in the moral struggle of existence; as a simple petition for daily bread, and as an all-consuming yearning for God Himself; as a selfish wish, and as an unselfish solicitude for a brother; as wild cursing and vengeful thirst, and as heroic intercession for personal enemies and persecutors; as a stormy clamor and demand, and as joyful renunciation and holy serenity; as a desire to change God's will and make it chime with our petty wishes, and as a self-forgetting vision of and surrender to the Highest Good; as the timid entreaty of the sinner before a stern judge, and as the trustful talk of a child with a kind father; as swelling phrases of politeness and flattery before an unapproachable King, and as a free outpouring in the presence of a friend who cares; as the humble petition of a servant to a powerful master, and as the ecstatic converse of the bride with the heavenly Bridegroom.

E. M. Bounds

Praying is spiritual work; and human nature does not like taxing, spiritual work. Human nature wants to sail to heaven under a favoring breeze, a full, smooth sea. *Prayer is humbling work. It abases intellect and pride, crucifies vain glory and signs our spiritual bankruptcy, and all these are hard for flesh and blood to bear.* It is easier not to pray than to bear them. So we come to one of the crying evils of these times, maybe of all times—little or no praying. Of these two evils, perhaps little praying is worse than no praying. Little praying is a kind of make-believe, a salve for the conscience, a farce and a delusion.

Howard Macy, *Rhythms of the Inner Life*

Talking to God personally differs entirely from trying to put the Almighty under our thumbs with prayers born of magic and ritual. Yet many people, ancient and modern, have treated prayer more as incantation than dialogue. Many of ancient Israel's neighbors, certainly, tried to sway the will of the gods by spreading sumptuous banquets for them in their temples and by flawlessly reciting prescribed prayers. Israel herself fell into this trap at times, but was sharply rebuked for presuming that God is more interested in formal phrases, fasts, and festivals than in loyal love toward God and neighbor . . . Israel, at her best, knew that prayer is not manipulation and hocus-pocus.

Modern Christians, at their best, know that, too, but practices of prayer akin to magic persist widely in the Christian movement. For example, some pray as if they will be heard the better for their flowery language or impassioned style. Others insist that certain postures, patterns, and phrases must be used if prayer is to be effective. Still others presume on grace, thinking that by "laying claim" to "promises" they find in Scripture, they put God under obligation to do as they ask. In such sub-Christian and unbiblical expressions of prayer, what once may have been vital has degenerated into idle form. Biblical prayer is personal, not magical; dialogue, not demand.

Brennan Manning, *Abba's Child*

Jeffrey D. Imbach, in *The Recovery of Love*, wrote, "Prayer is essentially the expression of our heart longing for love. It is not so much the listing of our requests but the breathing of our own deepest request, to be united with God as fully as possible."

Augustine

(354–430) Bishop of Hippo in North Africa. Philosopher and Church Father whose ideas greatly influenced the Protestant Reformation.

True, whole prayer is nothing but love.

John Piper, *The Pleasures of God*

Prayer is the walkie talkie on the battlefield of the world. It calls on God for courage (Eph. 6:19). It calls in for troop deployment and target location (Acts 13:1–3). It calls in for protection and air cover (Matt. 6:13; Luke 21:36). It calls in for fire power to blast open a way for the Word (Col. 4:3). It calls in for the miracle of healing for the wounded soldiers (James 5:16). It calls in for supplies for the forces (Matt. 6:11; Phil. 4:6).

And it calls in for needed reinforcements (Matt. 9:38). This is the place of prayer—on the battlefield of the world. It is a wartime walkie talkie for spiritual warfare, not a domestic intercom to increase the comforts of the saints. And one of the reasons it malfunctions in the hands of so many Christian soldiers is that they have gone AWOL.

Donald Whitney, *Spiritual Disciplines for the Christian Life*

To abandon prayer is to fight the battle with our own resources at best, and to lose interest in the battle at worst.

Eugene Peterson, *Working the Angles*

Prayer is a daring venture into speech that juxtaposes our words with the sharply alive words that pierce and divide souls and spirit, joints and marrow, pitilessly exposing every thought and intention of the heart (Heb. 4:12–13; Rev. 1:16). If we had kept our mouths shut we would not have involved ourselves in such a relentlessly fearsome exposure. . . .

That is why so many of the old masters counsel caution: Be slow to pray. This is not an enterprise to be entered into lightly. . . .

Praying puts us at risk of getting involved in God's conditions. Be slow to pray. Praying most often doesn't get us what we want but what God wants, something quite at variance with what we conceive to be in our best interests. And when we realize what is going on, it is often too late to go back. Be slow to pray.

Billy Graham

Praying is simply a two-way conversation between you and God. It is not the body's posture but the heart's attitude that counts when we pray. Prayer is not our using of God; it more often puts us in a position where God can use us.

Oswald Chambers, *My Utmost for His Highest*

(1874–1917) *Scottish minister who was converted to Christianity through the preaching of Charles Spurgeon. Best known as a devotional writer.*

When a man is born from above, the life of the Son of God is born in him, and he can either starve that life or nourish it. Prayer is the way the life of God is nourished. Our ordinary views of prayer are not found in the New Testament. We look upon prayer as a means of getting things for ourselves; the Bible idea of prayer is that we may get to know God Himself.

W. Bingham Hunter, *The God Who Hears*

Faith is not a magical force which has direct action on the creation. People, from the biblical viewpoint, are not healed *by* faith, they are healed by God. Prayer, contrary to almost everything written about it, is not the most powerful force in the universe. God is. . . . More has been wrought *by God* in response to faith expressed through prayer than this world imagines. The point is not just a matter of semantics or an example of theological hair-splitting. It concerns a common and fundamentally mistaken conception about what prayer is and the role faith plays in it.

Roberta Bondi, *To Pray and to Love*

Living in an intentional relationship with God in prayer is like living in a happy marriage. When a person is first in love, the beloved is constantly on the mind, and time spent in the other person's presence can have an almost hallucinatory quality. The one in love has a heightened sense of the self and the lover in which every minute counts, and the other's every word and gesture seem full of meaning. It is magical while it lasts, and it is always remembered. If this initial love is to grow into the nourishing and long-term love of a good marriage, however, the way lovers come to be together on a day-to-day basis has to change of itself. The intensely focused times continue, but the two come to spend far more time together when nothing productive appears to be happening; they read the paper together, do the dishes, eat a meal, and this shared, very ordinary, everyday time becomes a fundamental and very necessary part of the precious foundation of the marriage, in which love infuses all that the lovers do together.

For many people, beginning to pray regularly is like falling in love, and prayer for them often also has a very focused, very intense quality to it. Like first falling in love, it is wonderful. Nevertheless, if you believe that what you "get out of" prayer depends on having an intense experience in prayer, when that focused quality begins to fall away, you may come to believe that you are no longer truly praying when just the opposite is probably true: You are entering into the deep and solid life of everyday prayer that is equivalent to the precious ordinary time in marriage.

———⊶⊷———

Leonard Cohen

Prayer is translation. A man translates himself into a child asking for all there is in a language he has barely mastered.

———⊶⊷———

Hans Urs von Balthasar, *Prayer*

Prayer is something more than an exterior act performed out of a sense of duty, an act in which we tell God various things he already knows, a kind of daily attendance in the presence of the Sovereign who awaits, morning and evening, the submission of his subjects. Even though Christians find, to their pain and sorrow, that their prayer never rises above this level, they know well enough that it should be something more. Somewhere, here, there is a hidden treasure, if only I could find it and dig it up—a seed that has the power to grow into a mighty tree bearing abundant flowers and fruits, if only I had the will to plant and cultivate it. Yet this duty of mine, though dry and bitter, is pregnant with a life of the fullest freedom, could I once open and give myself up to it. We know all this or, at least, have some inkling of it, through what we have occasionally experienced, but it is another matter to venture further on the road which leads into the promised land. Once again, the birds of the air have eaten the seed that was sown, the thorns of everyday life have choked it and all that remains is a vague feeling of regret. And if that feeling becomes, at times, a pressing need to converse with God otherwise than in stereotyped formulas, how many know how to do so? It is as if they had to speak in a language whose rules they had never learnt; instead of fluent conversation, all they can manage are the disjointed, disconnected phrases of a foreigner unacquainted with the language of the country; they find themselves as helpless as a stuttering child who wants to say something and cannot.

———⊶⊷———

E. M. Bounds

Prayer is no fitful, short-lived thing. It is no voice crying unheard and unheeded in the silence. It is a voice which goes into God's ear and it lives as long as God's ear is open to holy pleas, as long as God's heart is alive to holy things. God shapes the world by prayer. Prayers are death-less. The lips that utter them may be closed in death, the heart that felt them may have ceased to beat, but the prayers live before God, and God's heart is set on them. Prayers outlive the lives of those who uttered them; outlive a generation, outlive an age, outlive a world.

Eddie Askew, *A Silence and a Shouting*

There is a description of prayer that is more of a poem and meditation than anything else. Here it is:

> The important thing about prayer is that it is almost indefinable. You see, it is: hard and sharp, soft and loving, deep and inexpressible, shallow and repetitious, a groaning and a sighing.
>
> A silence and a shouting, a burst of praise digging deep down into loneliness, into me. Loving. Abandonment to despair, a soaring to heights which can be only ecstasy, dull plodding in the grayness of mediocre being—laziness, boredom, resentment.
>
> Questing and questioning, calm reflection, meditation, cogitation. A surprise at sudden joy, a shaft of light, a laser beam. Irritation at not understanding, impatience, pain of mind and body hardly uttered or deeply anguished.
>
> Being together, the stirring of love shallow, then deeper, then deepest. A breathless involvement, a meeting, a longing, a loving, an inpouring. . . .

> It sounds exciting, put like that.
> It sounds **real.** An exploration.
> A chance to do more than catalogue
> and list the things I want,
> to an eternal Father Christmas.

> The chance of meeting you,
> of drawing close to the love that made me,
> and keeps me, and knows me.
> And, Lord, it's only just begun.
> There is so much more of you,
> of love, the limitless expanse of knowing you.
> I could be frightened, Lord, in this wide country.
> It could be lonely, but you are here, with me.

The chance of learning about myself,
of facing up to what I am.
Admitting my resentments,
bringing my anger to you, my disappointments, my frustration.
And finding that when I do,
when I stop struggling and shouting
and let go
you are still there.
Still loving.

Sometimes, Lord, often—
I don't know what to say to you.
But I still come, in quiet
for the comfort of two friends
sitting in silence.
And it's then, Lord, that I learn most from you.
When my mind slows down,
and my heart stops racing.
When I let go and wait in the quiet,
realizing that all the things I was going to ask for
you know already.
Then, Lord, without words,
in the stillness
you are there . . .
And I love you.

Lord, teach me to pray.

Howard Macy, *Rhythms of the Inner Life*

As William Penn counsels, "Do not think to overcome the Almighty by the best material put in the aptest phrase. No. One groan, one sigh from a wounded soul, excels and prevails with God." The sublimest prayers of all must not blind us to the fact that real prayer is simple.

William Law, *A Serious Call to a Devout and Holy Life*

(1686–1761) Puritan devotional writer who influenced the lives of such men as George Whitefield, the Wesleys, and Samuel Johnson.

Prayer is the nearest approach to God, and the highest enjoyment of Him, that we are capable of in this life.

It is the noblest exercise of the soul, the most exalted use of our best faculties, and the highest imitation of the blessed inhabitants of Heaven.

Oswald Chambers, *My Utmost for His Highest*

We think rightly or wrongly about prayer according to the conception we have in our minds of prayer. If we think of prayer as the breath in our lungs and the blood from our hearts, we think rightly. The blood flows ceaselessly, and breathing continues ceaselessly; we are not conscious of it, but it is always going on. We are not always conscious of Jesus keeping us in perfect joint with God, but if we are obeying Him, He always is. Prayer is not an exercise, it is the life.

Tilden Edwards, *Living in the Presence*

Authentic prayer is opening to God's gracious presence with all that we are, with what Scripture summarizes as our whole heart, soul, and mind (Matt. 22:37). Therefore prayer is more of a way of *being* than an isolated act of doing.

Larry Dossey, M.D., *Healing Words*

What *is* prayer? "Prayer" comes from the Latin *precarious,* "obtained by begging," and *precari,* "to entreat"—to ask earnestly, beseech, implore. This suggests two of the commonest forms of prayer—*petition,* asking something for one's self, and *intercession,* asking something for others. There also are prayers of *confession,* the repentance of wrongdoing and the asking of forgiveness; *lamentation,* crying in distress and asking for vindication; *adoration,* giving honor and praise; *invocation,* summoning the presence of the Almighty; and *thanksgiving,* offering gratitude. But like the 108 names for the Ganges in Hinduism, the classification of prayer can seem endless; theologian Richard J. Foster describes twenty-one separate categories.

The complex ways in which prayer manifests in the human psyche have been eloquently describe by theologian Ann Ulanov and Professor Barry Ulanov. Prayer, they state, is the most fundamental, primordial, and important "language" humans speak—"primary speech," they call it. "Prayer starts without words and often ends without them," they say.

"It knows its own evasions, its own infinite variety of dodges. It works some of the time in signs and symbols, lurches when it must, leaps when it can, has several kinds of logic at its disposal. . . ."

Prayer may be individual or communal, private or public. It may be offered in words, sighs, gestures, or silence. Prayer may be a conscious activity, of course, but as we shall see, it may flow also from the depths of the unconscious. Prayer may even emerge in dreams, completely bypassing our waking awareness.

In researching the role of prayer in healing, I was surprised that so many authorities on prayer failed to define it in their books and papers on the subject. Now I think I know why. If prayer has its roots in the unconscious, we can never fully grasp its nature. This means that a complete definition of prayer can never be given.

The primary reason to focus on the role of prayer in healing is not to prove its effectiveness scientifically—although this can be done, I feel. . . . The best reason goes deeper: *Prayer says something incalculably important about who we are and what our destiny may be.*

—⊗⊗⊙—

Arthur Hertzberg, *Judaism*

The focus of prayer is not the self. A man may spend hours meditating about himself, or be stirred by the deepest sympathy for his fellow man, and no prayer will come to pass. Prayer comes to pass in a complete turning of the heart toward God, toward His goodness and power. It is the momentary disregard of our personal concerns, the absence of self-centered thoughts, which constitute the art of prayer. Feeling becomes prayer in the moment in which we forget ourselves and become aware of God. . . . The thought of personal need is absent, and the thought of divine grace alone is present in his mind. Thus, in beseeching Him for bread, there is *one* instant, at least, in which our mind is directed neither to our hunger nor to food, but to His mercy. This instant is prayer.

—⊗⊗⊙—

Brother David Steindl-Rast, *Gratefulness, the Heart of Prayer*

Every human being knows prayer from experience. Have we not all experienced moments in which our thirsting heart found itself with surprise drinking at a fountain of meaning? Much of our life may be a wandering in desert lands, but we do find springs of water. If what is called "God" means in the language of experience the ultimate Source of Meaning, then those moments that quench the thirst of the heart are moments of prayer. They are moments when we communicate with God, and that is, after all, the essence of prayer.

But do we recognize these meaningful moments as prayer? Here, the answer is often "no." And under this aspect we cannot presume that everyone knows what prayer is. It happens that people who are in the habit of saying prayers at certain set times have their moments of genuine prayer precisely at times when they are not saying prayers. In fact, they may not even recognize their most prayerful moments as prayer. Others who never say formal prayers are nourished by moments of deep prayerfulness. Yet, they would be surprised to learn that they are praying at all.

———— ⚬∞⚬ ————

Don Postema, *Space for God*

Prayer is taking time to let God recreate us, play with us, touch us as an artist who is making a sculpture, a painting, or a piece of music with our lives. . . .

———— ⚬∞⚬ ————

James Houston, *The Transforming Power of Prayer*

I used to think that prayer was a spiritual exercise—something that needed to be worked at, like running or vaulting. But I was never any good at sports, and perhaps I would never be any good at prayer either.

After years of feeling useless and guilty, I began to realize the truth of a comment made by one of the early Fathers of the church, Clement of Alexandria. He said that "prayer is keeping company with God." This began to give me a new focus on prayer. I began to see prayer more as a friendship than a rigorous discipline. It started to become more of a relationship and less of a performance.

———— ⚬∞⚬ ————

C. S. Lewis, *Letters to Malcolm*

Now the moment of prayer is for me—or involves for me as its condition—the awareness, the re-awakened awareness, that this "real world" and "real self" are very far from being rock-bottom realities. I cannot, in the flesh, leave the stage, either to go behind the scenes or to take my seat in the pit; but I can remember that these regions exist. And I also remember that my apparent self—this clown or hero or super—under his grease-paint is a real person with an off-stage life. The dramatic person could not tread the stage unless he concealed a real person: unless the real and unknown I existed, I would not even make mistakes about the imagined me. And in prayer this real I struggles to speak, for once, from his real being, and to address, for once, not the other actors, but—what shall I call Him? The Author, for He invented us all? The Producer, for He controls all? Or the Audience, for He watches, and will judge, the performance?

Ruth Senter, *I Don't Believe in Prayer If . . .*

I don't believe in prayer if
Prayer is JUST a magic charm.
But that's how some people pray. They pray
only so they'll be safe when they go on vacation, or
when someone they love goes on vacation.
only so their day will go smoothly.
only so their family will stay happy and healthy.
only so they will get the lucky breaks.
But I don't believe in that kind of prayer.

I don't believe in prayer if
Prayer is JUST a way to "place my order" with God.
But that's how some people pray. They pray
only because they'd like to have something they
don't have.
only because they'd rather not have something they
do have.
only because someone is bugging them
and they need to
have God straighten that person out.
only because they don't want to have to go through
hard times.
But I don't believe in that kind of prayer.

I don't believe in prayer if
Prayer is JUST a tranquilizer.
But that's how some people pray. They pray
only because they feel so much better when they do.
only because they're more relaxed
and at peace with the world when they pray.
only because they're easier to be

around when they pray and they want
people to like being around them.
But I don't believe in that kind of prayer.

I don't believe in prayer if it's only a matter of what I can get from God.

But

I do believe in prayer if
Prayer is a conversation with someone I love.
And that's just how some people pray. They pray
because they want to show God how much they love
him (and spending time with him is a way
to show him).
because they want to tell God how wonderful they
think he is.
because they want to let God know how they're
feeling and what they need him to do
for them and for others.
because they want to say thank you to God.
because they want to say, "I'm sorry."

I do believe in prayer if
Prayer is a window that lets me see into God's heart. (This does not
     mean I will always understand what he's doing, but I will understand
     . the kind of God
he is—that he is loving and kind, for example.)
And that's just how some people pray. They pray
so they can listen to God.
so they can know what he wants them to do.
so they learn what to ask for and what not
to ask for.
so they understand him better.

I don't believe in prayer if prayer is only a matter of what I can get
     from God.

But

I do believe in prayer if prayer is a matter of what I can give to God—my
love, my admiration, my trust.

PART TWO

WHAT DO OTHERS
SAY ABOUT PRAYER?

INTRODUCTION

What do other people say about prayer?

That depends on the people. And the time in which they lived. And the place.

And yet, when you stand back from the times and places of other people's lives, it's remarkable how similar are the things they say about prayer. Almost as if prayer has been the melting pot out of which a new nation of people has been formed, a nation that transcends all natural boundaries, all cultural boundaries, all regional and racial ones, too.

One nation. Under God. Indivisible.

We're not talking about America. But we are talking about a land of immigrants, people who came to a foreign land with hopes and dreams. Hopes of a new start. Dreams of a wonderful future. Land of the free, the truly free. Home of the brave, the truly brave. A place where they were now citizens.

Each received their citizenship speaking his or her own language. But syllable by syllable, word by word, sentence by sentence, they learned a common language.

That language was the language of prayer. Full of the light vowels of joy and the low gutterals of sorrow, the gliding consonants of faith and the hard consonants of doubt. Punctuated with question marks and exclamation marks.

Prayer is the language that unites us. And maybe that is why we feel such a kinship with those in this chapter and with what they have to say.

James Houston, *The Transforming Power of Prayer*

Homesickness for God is a mark of the life of prayer.

Augustine

(354–430) Bishop of Hippo in North Africa. Philosopher and Church Father whose ideas greatly influenced the Protestant Reformation.

If you would never cease to pray, never cease to long for it. The continuance of your longing is the continuance of your prayer.

Elizabeth Gray Vining, *The World in Tune*

There are many ways to pray, and each soul must find its own. The important, the essential thing, is to pray.

———∞∞∞———

Bill Huebsch, *A New Look at Prayer*

In prayer
    we gather together,
    all the fragments of our lives,
    and we find in them
        the hand of God,
        molding us as a potter.
In prayer
    we take what is divided,
        ruptured,
        scattered in our lives
            and give it to God
                who folds it all together
                to form beautiful vessels.

———∞∞∞———

E. M. Bounds, *Power Through Prayer*

(1835–1913) Methodist minister and devotional writer who served as a pastor in the American South and became a POW during the Civil War.

Talking to men for God is a great thing, but talking to God for men is greater still.

———∞∞∞———

A. W. Tozer, *Of God and Men*

(1897–1963) Without any formal education, Tozer became one of America's most well-known pastor-theologians.

Prayer is never an acceptable substitute for obedience. The sovereign Lord accepts no offering from His creatures that is not accompanied by obedience. To pray for revival while ignoring or actually flouting the plain precept laid down in the Scriptures is to waste a lot of words and get nothing for our trouble.

Jeremy Taylor, *The Rule and Exercises of Holy Living*

(1613–1667) Anglican bishop and writer.

Whatsoever we beg of God, let us also work for it.

———⊗∞⊗———

Augustine

Do what you can and then pray that God will give you the power to do what you cannot.

———⊗∞⊗———

Benjamin Franklin, *Poor Richard's Almanac*

(1706–1790) American statesman, inventor, and writer.

Work as if you were to live a hundred years,
Pray as if you were to die tomorrow.

———⊗∞⊗———

David McCasland, *Oswald Chambers: Abandoned to God*

William Quarrier, founder of the Orphan Homes of Scotland, was a great man of faith and prayer. His homes for children, like those of George Müller in Bristol, England, operated by faith, making no financial appeals. . . .

In addition to faith, Quarrier was a man of action who never expected God to do for him what he could do for himself. While driving a visiting preacher to the railway station in Bridge of Weir, Quarrier and the clergyman spotted the train rapidly approaching. The preacher, fearing he would miss the train, shouted, "Don't you think we should pray about it, Mr. Quarrier?"

"No, not yet," Quarrier said as he cracked the reins. "Wait till we see what the horse can do."

———⊗∞⊗———

Charles Finney, *Lectures on Revivals of Religion*

(1792–1875) American revivalist.

Some men will spin out a long prayer telling God who and what He is, or they pray out a whole system of divinity. Some people preach, others exhort the people, till everybody wishes they would stop and God wishes so, too, most undoubtedly.

———⊗⊗⊗———

Samuel Taylor Coleridge, *The Ancient Mariner*

(1772–1834) English poet.

He prayeth well, who loveth well
Both man and bird and beast.
He prayeth best, who loveth best
All things both great and small;
For the dear God who loveth us,
He made and loveth all.

———⊗⊗⊗———

C. S. Lewis, *Letters to Malcolm*

(1898–1963) Christian apologist, Oxford scholar, and author.

If God had granted all the silly prayers I've made in my life, where should I be now?

———⊗⊗⊗———

Samuel Chadwick

(1860–1932) Reverend Chadwick served as the superintendent of the Leeds Mission for sixteen years and as the president of the National Council of Free Churches.

The one concern of the devil is to keep the saints from prayer. He fears nothing from prayerless studies, prayerless work, prayerless religion. He laughs at our toil, mocks at our wisdom, *but trembles when we pray.*

———⊗⊗⊗———

Carlo Carretto, *Letters from a Desert*

Prayer is the sum of our relationship with God. We are what we pray. The degree of our faith is the degree of our prayer. Our ability to love is our ability to pray.

———⊗⊗⊗———

Arthur Hertzberg, *Judaism*

In the palace of the king there are many rooms and there is a key for each room. An axe, however, is the passkey of passkeys, for with it one can break through all the doors and all the gates.

Each prayer has its own proper meaning and it is therefore the specific key to a door in the Divine Palace, but a broken heart is an axe which opens all the gates.

Oswald Chambers

(1874–1917) Scottish minister who was converted to Christianity through the preaching of Charles Spurgeon. Best known as a devotional writer.

Prayer is not a preparation for work, it *is* work.
Prayer is not a preparation for the battle, it *is* the battle.

Motto of the Benedictine Order

(Mid-sixth century) Oldest and premier form of organized monastic life in the Western Church dedicated to prayer, work, and moderation in all things.

Orare est laborare, laborare est orare.
[To pray is to work, to work is to pray.]

Fulton J. Sheen, *Lift Up Your Heart*

(1895–1979) American Roman Catholic archbishop who authored some fifty books and is best remembered for his radio and television sermons.

See where I stand at the door, knocking; if anyone listens to my voice and opens the door, I will come in to visit him, and take my supper with him, and he shall sup with me. (Rev. 3:20)

This text reverses the order that many people think to be the law of prayer. They assume that when we pray we ring God's doorbell and ask for a favor. Actually, it is He Who rings our bell.

John Allen Lavender, *Why Prayers Are Unanswered*

To ask rashly is foolish. To seek selfishly is dangerous. To knock flippantly is audacious. But when in dogged faith you persistently pray that God's will may be your own, the sheer daring of prayer becomes glorious. All God has is yours—exceedingly abundant above all you can ask or think.

A. W. Tozer, *God Tells the Man Who Cares*

Almost anything associated with the ministry may be learned with an average amount of intelligent application. It is not hard to preach or manage church affairs or pay a social call. . . .

But prayer—that is another matter. . . . There the lonely man of God must wrestle it out alone, sometimes in fasting and tears and weariness untold. There every man must be an original, for true prayer cannot be imitated.

————

Abraham Lincoln

(1809–1865) Sixteenth president of the United States.

I have been driven many times to my knees by the overwhelming conviction that I had nowhere else to go. My own wisdom, and that of all about me, seemed insufficient for the day.

————

Dwight D. Eisenhower

(1890–1969) Thirty-fourth president of the United States.

Addressing a crowd of college students, Eisenhower ended his forty-minute speech by saying, "Prayer is still the mightiest force in the world and, when used by dedicated men and women, nothing in this world remains impossible."

————

Henri Nouwen, *Reaching Out*

Sometimes it seems as if the Christian community is "so busy" with its projects and plans that there is neither the time nor the mood to pray. But when prayer is no longer its primary concern, and when its many activities are no longer seen and experienced as part of prayer itself, the community quickly degenerates into a club with a common cause but no common vocation.

————

George MacDonald

(1824–1905) Poverty-stricken Scottish pastor, poet, and novelist whose works profoundly influenced C. S. Lewis.

So long as we have nothing to say to God, nothing to do with Him, save in the sunshine of the mind when we feel Him near us, we are poor creatures, willed upon, not willing.

———∞∞———

Abraham Heschel, *The Prophets*

(1907–1972) Jewish scholar, philosopher, and author.

In prayer we shift the center of living from self-consciousness to self-surrender. God is the center toward which all forces tend. He is the source, and we are the flowing of His force, the ebb and flow of His tides.

———∞∞———

Herman Wouk, *This Is My God*

Huckleberry Finn prayed for a fishing pole, and got a pole and no hooks, whereupon he gave up religion as an economic recourse. It is a perfect parable. Nevertheless Moses prayed and Miriam was cured of her leprosy. Whether she would have been cured without the prayer, there is no earthly way of knowing. If you believe in fatality, prayer is nothing. If you believe in God, the prayer of a man is an event; not necessarily a decisive event, or we would all have our fishing poles with hooks when we wanted them . . .

———∞∞———

D. L. Moody

(1837–1899) American evangelist and founder of Moody Bible Institute.

The Christian on his knees sees more than the philosopher on tiptoe.

———∞∞———

A. W. Tozer, *The Divine Conquest*

It is well that we accept the hard truth now: *the man who would know God must give time to Him.* He must count no time wasted which is spent in the cultivation of His acquaintance. He must give himself to meditation and prayer hours on end. So did the saints of old, the glorious company of the apostles, the goodly fellowship of the prophets and the believing members of the holy Church in all generations. And so must we if we would follow in their train.

Corrie ten Boom

(1892–1983) Imprisoned by the Nazis for sheltering Jews. Corrie survived Ravensbruck concentration camp and her life and ministry became the embodiment of Christ's forgiveness.

Is prayer your steering wheel or your spare tire?

———————

John Bunyan

(1628–1688) English pastor and author of Pilgrim's Progress.

When thou prayest, rather let thy heart be without words than thy words be without heart.

———————

St. John Chrysostom

(ca. 344/354–407) Bishop of Constantinople nicknamed "Golden Mouth" for his preaching.

No one should give the answer that it is impossible for a man occupied with worldly cares to pray always. You can set up an altar to God in your mind by means of prayer. And so it is fitting to pray at your trade, on a journey, standing at a counter or sitting at your handicraft.

———————

St. Francis de Sales

(1567–1622) Bishop of Geneva best known for his work Introduction to the Devout Life.

Every Christian needs an half hour of prayer each day, except when he is busy, then he needs an hour.

———————

Abraham Heschel

Prayer takes the mind out of the narrowness of self-interest, and enables us to see the world in the mirror of the holy.

———————

C. S. Lewis, *Letters to Malcolm*

We must lay before Him what is in us, not what ought to be in us.

———————

Rabbi Phineas Shapiro, *The Koretzer Rebbe*

(1726–1791) Hasidic rabbi who emphasized the special value of prayer.

It is the nature of gold and silver that they are refined through the heat of fire.

If we, after we have prayed, do not feel that we have been refined and improved then maybe the reason is that we are made of a baser metal or our prayer was not filled with enough fire.

— ✺ —

St. Cyril of Jerusalem

(ca. 310–386) Bishop of Jerusalem who sold church property during a famine to feed the poor.

Take courage, toil and strive zealously, for nothing will be lost.
Every prayer you
make, every psalm you sing is recorded; every alms, every fast
is recorded.

— ✺ —

E. M. Bounds

The possibilities of prayer are the possibilities of faith. Prayer and faith are Siamese twins. One heart animates them both. Faith is always praying. Prayer is always believing.

— ✺ —

Frederick Buechner, *Now and Then*

A great deal of public prayer seemed to me a matter of giving God something that he neither needed nor, as far as I could imagine, much wanted.

— ✺ —

E. M. Bounds

Woe to the generation of sons who find their censers empty of the rich incense of prayer, whose fathers have been too busy or too unbelieving to pray.

— ✺ —

Henri Nouwen, *Reaching Out*

Prayer, therefore, is far from sweet and easy. Being the expression of our greatest love, it does not keep pain away from us. Instead, it makes us suffer more since our love for God is a love for a suffering God and our entering into God's intimacy is an entering into the intimacy where all of human suffering is embraced in divine compassion. To the degree that our prayer has become the prayer of our heart we will love more and suffer more, we will see more light and more darkness, more grace and more sin, more of God and more of humanity.

Andrew Murray, *Abide in Christ*

(1828–1917) Known for his deep devotional life, Murray was also the most influential leader of the nineteenth-century South African Dutch Reformed Church.

Believer, abide in Christ, for there is the school of prayer—mighty, effectual, answer-bringing prayer. Abide in Him, and you shall learn what to so many is a mystery: *That the secret of the prayer of faith is the life of faith*—the life that abides in Christ alone.

Tilden Edwards, *Living in the Presence*

It is no accident then that the Latin root of our word prayer is *precaria,* "precarious." In the heart of prayer we are vulnerable, and our trust that God is good is vital if we are to abide there.

Hudson Taylor

(1832–1905) Physician, evangelist, and visionary who founded the China Inland Mission.

The guiding precept of Hudson Taylor's ministry: To move man, through God, by prayer alone.

A. W. Tozer, *Jesus, Our Man in Glory*

I am reminded that one old saint was asked, "Which is the more important: reading God's Word or praying?" To which he replied, "Which is more important to a bird: the right wing or the left?"

Elton Trueblood, *The New Man for Our Time*

The man who supposes that he has no time to pray or to reflect, because the social tasks are numerous and urgent, will soon find that he has become fundamentally unproductive, because he will have separated his life from its roots.

Dr. Thomas Guthrie

The first true sign of spiritual life, prayer, is also the means of maintaining it. Man can as well live physically without breathing, as spiritually without praying. There is a class of animals—the cetaceous, neither fish nor seafowl—that inhabit the deep. It is their home, they never leave it for the shore; yet, though swimming beneath its waves, and sounding its darkest depths, they have ever and anon to rise to the surface that they may breathe the air. Without that, these monarchs of the deep could not exist. And something like what is imposed on them by a physical necessity, the Christian has to do by a spiritual one. It is by ever and anon ascending up to God, by rising through prayer into a loftier, purer region for supplies of divine grace, that he maintains his spiritual life. Prevent these animals from rising to the surface, and they die for want of breath; prevent the Christian from rising to God, and he dies for want of prayer.

Edith Schaeffer, *Common Sense Christian Living*

Prayer is as natural as breathing, as necessary as oxygen.

A. W. Tozer, *The Root of the Righteous*

It is written of Moses that he "went in before the Lord to speak with him . . . and he came out, and spake unto the children of Israel." This is the Biblical norm from which we depart to our own undoing and to the everlasting injury of the souls of men. No man has any moral right to go before the people who has not first been long before the Lord. No man has any right to speak to men about God who has not first spoken to God about men. And the prophet of God should spend more time in the secret place praying than he spends in the public place preaching.

Thomas à Kempis

(ca. 1380–1471) German monk and mystic whose writings were profoundly devotional as best exemplified in the classic The Imitation of Christ.

The man of God ought to be more at home in his prayer chamber than before the public.

———❦———

Victor Hugo, *Les Miserables*

(1802–1885) Hugo revolutionized French literature with his poems, plays, and novels. At his death, two million Frenchmen followed his pauper's hearse to its final resting place in the Panthéon.

There are thoughts which are prayers. There are moments when, whatever the posture of the body, the soul is on its knees.

———❦———

Arthur Hertzberg, *Judaism*

Prayer is an act of daring. Otherwise it is impossible to stand in prayer before God. When imagining the greatness of the Creator, how else could one stand in prayer before Him?

PART THREE

WHO PRAYS?

INTRODUCTION

Who prays?

In a word, everybody.

Or almost everybody. People who pray come from all ages and all walks of life. From the very young to the very old. From teenagers to parents of teenagers. From monks to married couples. From Jews to Christians. From Catholics to Protestants. Popes to prostitutes. American Indians to agnostics.

Yes, agnostics. Even atheists. Surveys indicate that nearly one in five of them prays daily. Hedging their bets, maybe. Or perhaps they are drawn to prayer by a tidal pull on the ragged shores of their soul, a pull so irresistible it overcomes even the seawalls of their own unbelief.

The more appropriate question, maybe, is not who prays . . . but who doesn't?

Since the dawn of time people have prayed for all kinds of reasons and to all kinds of deities. They have prayed to Amon Ra, the Egyptian sun God, and to the pantheon of petty and capricious gods of the Greeks and Romans. Some have prayed to the earth; others to the sky. Some have prayed to Baal, the Canaanite deity; others to Yahweh, the God of the Old Testament. Some have prayed to Allah; others to Jesus. Some have prayed to a "higher power"; others to patron saints. Some, to angels; others to Mary, mother of God.

And though the object of their prayers differs, sometimes dramatically, the subject of their prayers doesn't. Not substantially, anyway. Regardless of their faith, or lack of it, all people seem to realize the tenuousness of their humanity and their dependence on someone or something greater than themselves.

Who of us, however faithful or faithless, doesn't pray in a moment when the lump on the breast turns out to be malignant? Or in another moment when an officer calls to report an accident in which a loved one has been critically injured? Who of us doesn't pray at the birth of a child? Or at the death of a parent? At the bar mitzvah of a son or at the wedding of a daughter? Who of us doesn't pray when a radio bulletin tells a nation its president has been shot or when a television broadcast tells a community that one of its children has been kidnapped? Who of us doesn't pray when the young men and women of our country are sent into battle? Or when a baby has a temperature of 106?

Who of us doesn't pray then?

What follows is a sampling of prayers, some of which were wept in the foxholes of life; others, whispered in the serenity of a spring day.

Some were spoken in innocence; others in repentance. Some, in faith; others in doubt.

The prayers are as diverse as the people who pray them, but together they reflect a universal longing for God.

BELIEVERS

Thomas Aquinas

As told by Peter Calo

Brother Reginald . . . exclaimed with many tears: "My brothers, while he was still in life, my Master forbade me to disclose the admirable things concerning him whereof I have been witness. One of these things was that he had acquired his science not by human industry but by the merit of prayer, for whenever he wished to study, discuss, read, write, or dictate, he first had recourse to prayer in private, and poured forth his soul with tears in order to discover the divine secrets, and by the merits of this prayer his doubts were removed and he issued therefrom fully instructed."

George Müller

As told by Colin Whittaker

This was something [Müller] constantly shared wherever he went, that the believer's first business at the beginning of the day was to get their soul into a state of happiness with the Lord. Müller also took to walking and praying—with his New Testament in his hand—when conditions were suitable. On occasions he made this his early morning devotions, walking, reading a New Testament in large type, meditating and praying, as he walked in the fields for between an hour or two hours before breakfast. Both his physical and spiritual health benefited from this method.

In George's journal he had the courage to bare his soul on many occasions, revealing that he was a man of similar passions to the rest of us and subject to his "off days" when he was irritable with his wife, or with visitors who outstayed their welcome; he too had his battle with doubts and fears. His great secret was that he learned not only to pray but never to give up praying.

A Farmer

As told by Edith Schaeffer

I know a farmer who used to be a L'Abri worker. He writes that he now prays as he works on his tractor. He carries the prayer list with its page of verses and another page of requests. . . . Even as his hours are spent raising quantities of mint, his hours are also being used to affect what is going on thousands of miles away.

Fyodor Dostoyevski

Be not forgetful of prayer.

Every time you pray, if your prayer is sincere, there will be new feeling and new meaning in it, which will give you fresh courage, and you will understand that prayer is an education.

Madame Chiang Kai-shek

One of my strongest childhood experiences is of Mother going to a room she kept for the purpose on the third floor to pray. She spent hours in prayer, often beginning before dawn. When we asked her advice about anything, she would say, "I must ask God first."

David Brainerd

As told by Colin Whittaker

He spent a great deal of time in prayer and frequently set aside days for prayer and fasting. He loved to retire into the nearby woods for solitude and there, alone with God, he poured out his soul in earnest and intense intercession. More and more he found himself with a great burden for the conversion of the heathen. He drew near to God and God drew near to him in such a beautiful and inspiring way that he felt himself overwhelmed by the divine nearness. . . .

He celebrated his twenty-fifth birthday by setting it aside as a day of prayer and fasting. It turned out to be a celebration of the highest order, for he recorded in his diary, "God was with me of a truth. Oh, it was blessed company indeed! God enabled me to agonise in prayer so that I was quite wet with perspiration, though in the shade, and the wind cool. My soul was drawn out very much from the world, for multi-tudes of souls."

Martin Luther

As told by E. M. Bounds

One of Melancthon's correspondents writes of [Martin] Luther's pray-ing: "I cannot enough admire the extraordinary cheerfulness, consis-tency, faith and hope of the man in these trying and vexatious times. He constantly feeds these gracious affections by a very diligent study of the Word of God. *Then not a day passes in which he does not employ in prayer at least three of his very best hours.* Once I happened to hear him at prayer. Gracious God! What spirit and what faith is there in his ex-pressions! He petitions God with as much reverence as if he were in the divine presence, and yet with as firm a hope and confidence as he would address a father or a friend. 'I know,' said he, 'Thou art Father and our God; and therefore I am sure that Thou wilt bring to naught the per-secutors of Thy children. For shouldest Thou fail to do this, Thine own cause, being connected with ours, would be endangered. It is entirely Thine own concern. We, by Thy providence, have been compelled to take a part. Thou therefore wilt be our defense.' *Whilst I was listening to Luther pray in this manner, at a distance, my soul seemed on fire within me,* to hear the man address God so like a friend, yet with so much grav-ity and reverence; and also to hear him, in the course of his prayer, in-sisting on the promises contained in the Psalms, as if he were sure his petitions would be granted. . . ."

Martin Luther said, "If I fail to spend two hours in prayer each morn-ing, the devil gets the victory through the day. I have so much business I cannot get on without spending three hours daily in prayer."

Giants of the Faith

As told by Warren Wiersbe

When John Knox grasped all Scotland in his strong arms of faith, his prayers terrified tyrants. George Whitefield, after much holy, faithful close-pleading, went to the Devil's fair and in one day took more than a thousand souls out of the paw of the lion. See a praying Wesley turn more than ten thousand souls to the Lord! Look at the praying Charles Finney, whose prayers, faith, sermons, and writings shook this country and sent a wave of blessing through two continents.

———— ∞∞ ————

Dr. Hoste

As told by Edith Schaeffer

My first observation of perfectly natural and conscientious prayer came when I was a very little girl in Shanghai. One morning I went skipping along beside Dr. Hoste, at that time the director of the China Inland Mission (he had followed Hudson Taylor). He didn't turn me away, but simply said, "Edith, I am praying now, but you may come along if you wish."

I walked with him a number of times, holding his hand and being very quiet and impressed as he prayed aloud. It was his custom to walk when he prayed, and he counted it his first responsibility for the mission to pray four hours a day. He prayed for each missionary in the China Inland Mission, and for each of their children by name. He had the list with him, and he went through it. It was not just a recitation of names; he cared about each person and knew something of their needs. He felt this was his work.

"All right, walk with me and pray," he would say in his peculiarly high voice. The impression that penetrates my memory is the respect I received for the *work* of prayer. I know it meant more than any series of lectures in later life could mean.

———— ∞∞ ————

Moses

As told by E. M. Bounds

The Lord was very wroth with Aaron also, and to Moses He said, "Let me alone that I may destroy them." But Moses prayed, and kept on praying; day and night he prayed forty days. He makes the record of his prayer struggle. "I fell down," he says, "before the Lord at the first forty days and nights; I did neither eat bread nor drink water because of your sins which ye sinned in doing wickedly in the sight of the Lord to provoke him to anger. For I was afraid of the anger and hot displeasure wherewith the Lord was hot against you to destroy you. But the Lord hearkened to me at this time also. And the Lord was very angry with Aaron to have destroyed him, and I prayed for him also at the same time." Men like Moses knew how to pray and to prevail in prayer. Their faith in prayer was no passing attitude that changed with the wind or with their own feelings and circumstances. . . . And thus these men, strong in faith and in prayer, "subdued kingdoms, wrought righteousness, obtained promises, stopped the mouths of lions, quenched the violence of fire, escaped the edge of the sword, from weakness were made strong, waxed mighty in war, turned to flight the armies of the aliens."

Richard Foster, *Prayer*

A student of mine, Jung-Oh Suh—a Korean pastor on a study sabbatical—learned of my research on prayer and brought me a newspaper article (complete with his excellent translation, for it was written in Korean) that describes the story of the Myong-Song Presbyterian Church, located in the southeastern part of Seoul. The Korean churches are well known for their early morning prayer meetings, but even so this story is unusual. This is a group that began about ten years ago with forty people, and today twelve thousand gather each morning for three prayer meetings—at 4:00 A.M., 5:00 A.M., and 6:00 A.M. Jung-Oh explained to me that they must shut the doors at 4:00 A.M. to begin the first service, and so if people arrive a little late, they must wait until the 5:00 A.M. meeting. Then he added, "This is a problem in my country because it gets cold in the winter! So everyone brings a little pot of tea or coffee to keep warm while they wait for next service." This is organized, corporate, intercessory prayer.

There are indications that, as we approach the twenty-first century, the greatest prayer movement in living memory is already under way. In much smaller but still significant ways the story of Myong-Song Presbyterian Church can be repeated many times over. One congregation I know has forty prayer meetings per week involving a total of a thousand people. I am acquainted with churches in which anywhere from 15 to 24 percent of the congregation are engaged in organized, corporate, intercessory prayer weekly. I have met with national prayer leaders, and none of them has seen anything like what is now beginning to occur. It is too early to tell how significant this new awakening toward prayer will be, but the signs are encouraging.

John Wesley

As told by E. M. Bounds

John Wesley spent two hours daily in prayer. He began at four in the morning. Of him, one who knew him well wrote: "He thought prayer to be his business more than anything else, and I have seen him come out of his closet with a serenity of face next to shining."

⸻⸻

John Wesley

As told by Warren Wiersbe

One of the most moving experiences of my own life was stepping from John Wesley's bedroom in his London house into the little prayer room adjacent. Outside the house was the traffic noise of City Road, but in that prayer chamber was the holy hush of God. Frankly, I am not one who is easily moved by atmosphere, but in that little room I was moved. The only furnishings are a walnut table with a Greek Testament and a candlestick, a tiny prayer stool, and a chair. It was here that Wesley would come early each morning (when he was in London), read God's Word, and pray. "This little room was the powerhouse of Methodism," the guide whispered.

⸻⸻

Giants of the Faith

As told by E. M. Bounds

William Wilberforce, the peer of kings, said: "I must secure more time for private devotions. I have been living far too public for me. The shortening of private devotions starves the soul; it grows lean and faint. I have been keeping too late hours." . . .

Samuel Rutherford, the fragrance of whose piety is still rich, rose at three in the morning to meet God in prayer. . . .

David Brainerd said: "I love to be alone in my cottage, where I can spend much time in prayer."

William Bramwell is famous in Methodist annals for personal holiness and for his wonderful success in preaching and for the marvelous answers to his prayers. For hours at a time he would pray. He almost lived on his knees. He went over his circuits like a flame of fire. The fire was kindled by the time he spent in prayer. He often spent as much as four hours in a single season of prayer in retirement.

Sir Henry Havelock always spent the first two hours of the day alone with God. If the encampment was struck at six A.M., he would rise at four.

Robert Louis Stevenson

As told by his wife

In every Samoan household the day is closed with prayer and the singing of hymns. The omission of this sacred duty would indicate not only a lack of religious training in the house chief but a shameless disregard of all that is reputable in Samoan social life. . . .

With my husband, prayer, the direct appeal, was a necessity. When he was happy he felt impelled to offer thanks for that undeserved joy; when in sorrow, or pain, to call for strength to bear what must be borne.

Dwight D. Eisenhower

(1890–1969) Thirty-fourth president of the United States.

Personal prayer, it seems to me, is one of the simplest necessities of life, as basic to the individual as sunshine, food and water—and at times, of course, more so.

SEEKERS FROM ALL WALKS OF LIFE

Frederick Buechner, "Breaking the Silence," *The Magnificent Defeat*

I think of the waiting room of a railroad station late at night, or a large gallery in a museum just before closing time, or the corridor of a hospital after the patients are all asleep—some neutral, public kind of place where the light is dim and where there is an air of great stillness, isolation, a vague sense of expectancy. The place is empty except for two people, and they are standing or sitting some distance apart waiting for something, passing the time, in that strange, suspended state where time seems almost to stop because nothing is happening to mark its passage. Let us say that one of the people is you, and the other is a stranger. The silence between you is very deep, so deep that you can almost hear it, but there is no convention that says you must speak to a stranger in a public place, so it is not an embarrassing silence like the silence on occasions where humans beings are expected to speak. In fact the truth of it is that for you the stranger is hardly a human being; he is a face dimly seen, a dark shape sitting on a bench or leaning against the wall. The silence, the emptiness, the preoccupation with your own thoughts and your own waiting, separate you from him as fully as light-years of space separate stars. The mystery of who you are—your loves and fears and dreams—are as hidden from him as the mystery of who he is, is hidden from you; and if somebody asked you later if there was anyone else there with you, you might say, "No. At least I don't think so. I'm not sure."

Then maybe, on impulse, you speak—"Hi . . . It's a long wait. . . ." Some silly word. Something. A very small miracle. What made you speak? God knows. Maybe a sudden pang of loneliness. A sudden desire to be known, to know. Maybe you need the sound of your own voice to bring you back to reality again from the shadow world of our introspection. But whatever the reason, you do speak; for some combination of reasons, you have to break the silence. To a stranger you reveal some part of the mystery of who you are: not just the silly words that you speak but the sense of some kind of human need that breathes behind your words. In some partial, tentative way, you open yourself to the stranger's knowing. Does he hear you? Does he answer you? If he does, a little bridge is built, and you can meet on the bridge. But does he? Is there really a person there at all, or is it just a trick of shadows?

This is what I think, in essence, prayer is. It is the breaking of silence. It is the need to be known and the need to know. Prayer is the sound made by our deepest aloneness. I am thinking not just of formal prayers that a religious person might say in church or in bed at night, but of the kind of vestigial, broken fragments of prayer that people use without thinking of them as prayers: something terrible happens, and you might say, "God help us" or "Jesus Christ"—the poor, crippled prayers that are hidden in the minor blasphemies of people for whom in every sense God is dead except that they still have to speak to him if only through clenched teeth. Prayer is a man's impulse to open up his life at its deepest level. People pray because they cannot help it. In one way or another, I think, all people pray.

And God, of course, is the stranger. Does he listen? Does he answer? Does he exist at all? The light is so dim, and we are so caught up in ourselves, that sometimes it is hard to be sure whether the stranger is really there or just the shadow cast by our own starved longing for him.

Joan Bel Geddes, *Are You Listening God?*

DEAR GOD (if there is a God):
Please help me (if you can).
I need help but don't know where to find it.

If you exist, God, I apologize for ignoring you until now,
and beg your forgiveness and help.
If you *don't* exist, I won't be any worse off for talking to Nothingness
than I have been trying to maintain a heroic silence and indepen-
dence.

I'm going to try to talk to you, God, and I'm going to try to get you to talk
to me.
After all, why not gamble when there's nothing—except despair—to
lose?

I'm turning to you out of some kind of blind, primitive instinct, in a
burst of hope against hope, a sort of reversion to childishness . . .
even though I am not at all sure that you're there or that, if you are,
you are powerful enough to help me or interested enough in me to
want to help me.
People are supposed to function with brains and education, not with
blind instinct—but instinct serves animals and birds pretty well, and
I've always said human beings are animals, so maybe I should trust
this instinct.

I've always been skeptical—and I've always thought that skepticism was
a virtue, a sign of sophistication and intelligence, because it protects
people from believing in nonsense and superstition. It does, of
course. But maybe it also "protects" people from believing in *true*
things.
Skepticism is like a high wall that keeps things from entering the mind,
good ideas as well as bad—so I'm going to knock down that wall for a
while, and invite in whatever thoughts want to come. My new "open
door policy."

It makes me feel awfully foolish—in fact, it's rather spooky!—to find
myself trying to talk seriously to someone I'm not even sure is there.
However, if nobody is there then at least nobody will hear me making a
fool of myself!
So I can forget about being embarrassed and just pour my heart out
freely hoping it will do some good. That's what I'm going to do. . . .

I've spent most of my life ignoring or turning away from God, and then considering the fact that I couldn't see God or hear God and knew nothing about God as evidence that God wasn't there.

I guess that's a bit like being blind and therefore concluding that color is nonexistent, or being deaf and therefore refusing to believe in the existence of music. Or like being illiterate and then taking that fact as proof that there's no such thing as literature.

It's not very logical. Rather unimaginative! Even a bit pigheaded? Is it too late for me to change? . . .

Is there any way you can help me find you, God, if you *do* exist? And if you do, can you really help me to be a stronger and better and happier person than I am?

Please do whatever you can!

Maybe prayer is just a sort of self-hypnosis. You're not actually talking to anyone except yourself but you convince yourself that you are. However, I suppose that, if the things you say to yourself are constructive, it can still be a useful procedure.

But I really do hope that I'm talking to Somebody other than just myself, because I'm looking for a source of strength and understanding that is much, much greater than any I possess on my own.

Is hoping one form of praying? If so, maybe I've already begun to learn to pray!

Is my reaching out for a God that I could get to know and love and trust a prelude to faith, or the actual first step in faith? I long to believe in and to get to know and love and count on God the way a thirsty soldier lost in a desert longs to find, and to drink, and to be refreshed by water! If I keep searching for God will I discover God (or only a mirage)?

Francis Thompson

(1859–1907) English poet.

In his *Study of Francis Thompson's "Hound of Heaven"* (1912), Mr. J. F. O'Conner says: "As the hound follows the hare, never ceasing in its running, ever drawing nearer to the chase . . . so does God follow the fleeing soul by his Divine grace."

THE HOUND OF HEAVEN

"Whom wilt thou find to love ignoble thee
　　Save Me, save only Me?

All which I took from thee I did but take,
    Not for thy harms,
But just that thou might'st seek it in My arms.
    All which thy child's mistake
Fancies as lost, I have stored for thee at home;
    Rise, clasp My hand, and come!"

"Ah, fondest, blindest, weakest,
I am He Whom thou seekest!"

———

Howard Macy, *Rhythms of the Inner Life*

The seeking for God that is born of discovery has a houndlike quality. Once we've caught the scent and, perhaps, broken the leash, we'll eagerly follow the trail, wherever it might lead, nose down, through field and bramble, water and shrub, in the hope of cornering our quarry. To have come to know God at all is to have been given the scent, and though we know well that we will hardly tree the Holy One, we also know that this is the trail we must follow. So we rush on as fast as our noses will take us, and we would do well to bay with excitement as we go.

Those who recall Francis Thompson's haunting image of God as the Hound of Heaven, pursuing us down the halls of time, might well ask who, in fact, is the hound and who the quarry, whether we seek God or whether we are sought. If we try to answer the question on those terms, however, we stray into theological foolishness. What we discover, instead, is that all the while we have been pursing God, he has been rushing toward us with reckless love, arms flung wide to hug us home. God aches for every person, for every creature, indeed, for every scrap of life in all creation to be joined again in the unity that was its first destiny. So while we are crying out, "Where are you, God?" the divine voice echoes through our hiding places, "Where are you?" Indeed, the story of the Garden of Eden reminds us that it is God who calls out first, and to this we answer. God's yearning for us stirs up our longing in response. God's initiating presence may be ever so subtle—an inward tug of desire, a more-than-coincidence meeting of words and events, a glimpse of the beyond in a storm or in a flower—but it is enough to make the heart skip a beat and to make us want to know more.

———

C. S. Lewis, *Surprised by Joy*

(1898–1963) Christian apologist, Oxford scholar, and author.

The fox had been dislodged from Hegelian Wood and was now running in the open, "with all the wo in the world," bedraggled and weary, hounds barely a field behind. And nearly everyone was now (one way or another) in the pack; Plato, Dante, MacDonald, Herbert, Barfield, Tolkien, Dyson, Joy itself. Everyone and everything had joined the other side. . . .

You must picture me alone in that room in Magdalen, night after night, feeling, whenever my mind lifted even for a second from my work, the steady, unrelenting approach of Him whom I so earnestly desired not to meet. That which I greatly feared had at last come upon me. In the Trinity Term of 1929 I gave in, and admitted that God was God, and knelt and prayed: perhaps, that night, the most dejected and reluctant convert in all England. I did not then see what is now the most shining and obvious thing; the Divine humility which will accept a convert even on such terms.

Twenty-Four-Year-Old Prostitute in White Pine County, Nevada

As told to Life *magazine, March 1994*

I don't talk about my feelings a lot. Instead I lie in my bed and think onto Him. I meditate because sometimes my words don't come out right. But He can find me. He can find what's inside of me just by listening to my thoughts.

Prisoner

As told by Mark Link

Piri Thomas was a convict, a drug addict, and an attempted killer. One night he felt an overwhelming desire to pray. But he was sharing his cell with another prisoner called "the thin kid." So he waited until the kid was asleep. Then he got out of bed, knelt on the cold concrete, and prayed aloud. He writes:

> I told God what was in my heart. . . . I talked to him plain . . . no big words. . . . I talked to him of my wants and lacks, of my hopes and disappointments. . . . I felt like I could even cry . . . something I hadn't been able to do for years.

After Piri finished his prayer, a voice said, "Amen." It was "the thin kid." "There we were," Piri said, "he lying down, head on bended elbows, and I still on my knees." No one spoke for a long time. Then the kid whispered, "I believe in *Dios* also."

The two young men talked a long time. Then Piri climbed back into his bunk. "Good night, Chico," he said. "I'm thinking that God is always with us. It's just that we aren't always with him."

Haing Ngor

(1941–1996) Cambodian physician who suffered greatly under the regime of the Khmer Rouge, which destroyed his country and slaughtered more than a million of his countrymen. He survived four years of torture amidst mindless genocide to escape from Cambodia and migrate to the United States. He is best known for his Oscar-winning performance in the film The Killing Fields. *Haing dedicated all his energies, his fame and fortune, to providing relief for other refugees like himself. On February 25, 1996, however, he was shot and killed outside his home in Los Angeles. In his book,* A Cambodian Odyssey, *Haing retells the horrors of those days and the tortures he endured. Once, while being roasted alive, he prayed this desperate prayer.*

You gods—any gods who can hear. Hindu gods. Jesus. Allah. Buddha. Spirits of the forests and the rice fields. Spirits of my ancestors. Hear me, gods: I never killed anyone. Never, never, never. I saved lives. I was a doctor and I saved the lives of Lon Nol soldiers and Viet Cong and didn't care who they were. So why make me suffer?

Spirits of the wind, I prayed. If the gods cannot hear, then carry the news to them. To any god who has power. Tell the gods what is happening to me.

Norman Lear

Film producer best known for creating the sitcoms All in the Family, Maude, *and* Sanford and Son. *He also produced the movies* Stand by Me, The Princess Bride, *and* Fried Green Tomatoes. *In 1980 he co-founded the constitutional-liberties organization People for the American Way.*

On my treadmill, every morning of my life, I have the Saint Francis of Assisi prayer, which, to me, says just about everything.

Lord, make me a channel of thy peace,
That where there is hatred, I may bring love;
That where there is wrong, I may bring the spirit of forgiveness;
That where there is discord, I may bring harmony;
That where there is error, I may bring truth;
That where there is doubt, I may bring faith;
That where there is despair, I may bring hope,

That where there are shadows, I may bring light;
That where there is sadness, I may bring joy.
Lord, grant that I may seek to comfort rather than to be comforted;
To understand than to be understood;
To love than to be loved.
For it is in giving that we are received,
It is by forgiving that we are forgiven,
And it is by dying that we awaken to eternal life.

Those are the best words I have found for prayer. What I love about
it is it isn't asking for anything except to be a better person. It's the essence, I think, of what Jesus asked of his disciples and what the Buddha
talks about. It seems to me the essence of everything. I would never
consider praying to ask for anything, either for myself or anybody else.
All I can expect of it is to let me serve, to be the kind of person who
can give as close to 100 percent of myself as I can.

Saint Francis's prayer is all about relationships. Let me bring love
and forgiveness and harmony. And these words are the best prescription
for living: "Grant that I may seek to comfort rather than to be comforted."
It's happened that I've come back from a writer's meeting pretty unhappy;
we didn't come up with anything new, and the script or the scene was in
trouble, and I became deeply unhappy. And then suddenly, in the middle
of the night or on the way home, I'll say, "Wait a second. I went into that
meeting wishing to hear *from them* that everything was going to be okay,
that they had the answers. I basically wanted to leave the meeting having
been assured and convinced by my cohorts that everything was going to
be okay. So, I was seeking to be comforted rather than to comfort others.
When the prayer says, "By dying . . . we awaken to eternal life," it isn't re-
ferring to literal death, but to the death of the self. Only when one dies in
the self does one awaken to eternal life.

Frederick Buechner, "Prayer," *Wishful Thinking*

Everybody prays whether he thinks of it as praying or not. The odd silence you fall into when something very beautiful is happening or something very good or very bad. The ah-h-h-h! that sometimes floats up out
of you as out of a Fourth of July crowd when the sky-rocket bursts over
the water. The stammer of pain at somebody else's pain. The stammer of
joy at somebody else's joy. Whatever words or sounds you use for sighing
with over your own life. These are all prayers in their way.

SEEKERS FROM ACROSS THE CENTURIES

Larry Dossey, M.D., *Healing Words*

The urge to pray seems so constant and widespread throughout history,
it appears to be innate.

Hymn to the Sun God, Amon Ra

(?—*1580 B.C.*) *Seventeenth Dynasty papyrus at Giza.*

Hail to Thee, Amon Ra, who dwellest in the sanctuary of Karnak;
Prince of heaven, Heir of earth, Lord of all things that exist,
Maker of things below and of things above!
He illumineth the Two Lands of Egypt, He traverseth the sky in peace.
Great One of valour, Lord of awe; the gods gather as dogs at His feet,
    they recognize His majesty as their Lord.
Great of soul, lordly in manifestations, acclamations to Thee who dost
    upraise the sky and lay down the ground!

Babylonian Prayer for the City of Ur

(*ca. 669–626 B.C.*) *Tablet of Ishtar-shuma-eresh, Chief Scribe of Asshur-bani-pal, King of
the Universe.*

Father Nannar, Lord of the firmament, Lord of the gods, Merciful One,
Begetter of the universe, who foundeth among living creatures His illus-
trious seat; Father, long-suffering and full of forgiveness, whose hand
upholdeth the life of all mankind;

Lord, Thy divinity, like the far-off heaven, filleth the wide sea with
fear; First-born, Omnipotent, whose heart is immensity, and there is
none who may discover it.

Who dost march in glory from the horizon to the zenith, opening
wide the doors of heaven, and establishing light in the world; the
Ordainer of the laws of heaven and earth, whose command may not
be broken; Thou holdest the rain and the lightning, Defender of all living things.

In heaven, who is great? Thou alone. On earth who is exalted? Thou alone. When Thy voice resoundeth in heaven, the very gods fall prostrate. When Thy voice resoundeth on earth, the spirits kiss the dust.

Thy will is seen in stall and stable; it increaseth all living things. Thy word hath created law and justice, so that mankind hath established law.

King of Kings, whose divinity no god resembleth, where Thine eye doth glance there cometh harmony; where Thou dost grasp the hand there cometh salvation; look with favour on Thy temple! Look with favour on Thy city Ur.

Socrates

About 400 B.C., Phaedrus and Socrates are seated beneath a spreading tree in a spot sacred to the gods, where they have been in thought-provoking discussion through the heat of the day.

Phaedrus: But let us depart . . . as the heat of the day is over.

Socrates: Were it not better to offer up a prayer to these gods before we go? Beloved Pan, and all ye other gods who haunt this place, give me beauty in the inward soul; and may the outward and inward man be as one.

Lacedaemonian Prayer to Zeus

(*Fourth century* B.C.)

Give us, O Zeus, what is good, whether we pray for it or not; and avert us from the evil, even if we pray for it.

Prayer by Muhammad

(*ca. 632* A.D.)

O God, I take refuge with Thee from laziness and from the weakness of old age and from debt and from that which causeth me to sin.

O God, verily I take refuge with Thee from the punishment of the fire and the calamity of the fire, and from the calamity of the grave and the punishment of the grave, and from the evil and seduction of riches, and from the evil and affliction of poverty.

O God, wash my sins in snow-water and hail-water, and purify my heart as a white garment is cleansed from impurity, and place a distance between me and my sins as Thou hast placed a distance between the East and the West.

Native American Prayer

O Great Spirit,
Whose voice I hear in the winds,
And whose breath puts life into all things,
hear my prayer!

I am small and weak,
I need your wisdom, and your strength.

Let me walk in beauty, and let me revere the red and purple sunset.
Make my hands respect all things you have made and my ears sharp to hear your voice.
Make me wise so that I may understand the things you have taught my people.
Let me find the lessons you have hidden in every leaf and rock.
I ask you for strength, not to be greater than another, but to oppose my greatest
enemy—myself.

Make me always ready to come to you with clean hands and straight eyes.
So when life fades, like the dwindling daylight,
my spirit may come to you without shame.

PEOPLE OF ALL AGES

C. S. Lewis, *Letters to Malcolm*

Those who do not turn to God in petty trials will have no *habit* or such resort to help them when the great trials come, so those who have not learned to ask Him for childish things will have less readiness to ask Him for great ones. We must not be too high-minded. I fancy we may sometimes be deterred from small prayers by a sense of our own dignity rather than of God's.

Stuart Hample and Eric Marshall,
Children's Letters to God, "The New Collection"

Dear God,

Is it true my father won't get in heaven if he uses his bowling words in the house?

Anita

Did you really mean Do Unto Others As They Do Unto You, because if you did then I'm going to fix my brother.

Darla

Dear God,

My brother is a rat. You should give him a tail. Ha. ha.

Danny

God: the bad people laughed at Noah—you make an ark on dry land you fool. But he was smart he stuck with you. That's what I would do.

Eddie

Dear God,

I bet it is very hard for you to love all of everybody in the whole world. There are only 4 people in our family and I can never do it.

Nan

Dear God,

Maybe Cain and Abel would not kill each so much if they had their own rooms. It works with my brother.

Larry

Dear God,

It rained for are whole vacation and is my father mad! He said some things about you that people are not supposed to say, but I hope you will not hurt him anyway.

Your friend, but I am not going to tell you who I am.

Stuart Hample and Eric Marshall, *Children's Letters to God*

Dear God,

If you do all these things you are pretty busy. Now here's my question. When is the best time I can talk to you? I know you are always listening but when will you be listening hard in Troy, New York.

Sincerely Yours,
Allen

———— ⚬⚬⚬ ————

Bill Adler, *Dear Lord*

Dear Lord,

How do I know that you hear my prayers?
Could you please give me a sign like leaving me a $10 bill under my pillow?

Gloria

———— ⚬⚬⚬ ————

Norman C. Habel, *For Mature Adults Only*

DID YOU EVER FAIL, LORD?, by David (a teenager)

No one pays any attention to me
or what I say, Lord.
I'm nobody, I guess.
I haven't done anything important
or made anything
or won anything.
No one listens when I talk,
no one asks my opinion.
I'm just there
like a window
or a chair.

I tried to build a boat once,
but it fell apart.
I tried to make the baseball team,
but I always threw past third base.
I wrote some articles
for our school paper,
but they didn't want them.

I even tried out for the school play,
but the other kids laughed
when I read my lines.
I seem to fail
at everything.

I don't try anymore
because I'm afraid to fail.
And no one likes to fail
all the time.

If only there was something I could do,
something I could shout about,
something I could make
that was my work,
only mine.
And people would say,
"David did that!"
And my parents would say,
"We're proud of you, son!"

But I can't do anything.
Everyone else is so much better
at everything
than I am.
The more I fail
the more it eats away at me
until I feel weak inside.
I feel like I'm nothing.

Lord,
the world seems full of heroes
and idols and important people.
Where are all the failures?
Where are they hiding?
Where are people like me?
Did you ever fail, Lord?
Did you?
Do you know how I feel?

Do you know what it's like
when everyone looks up at you and says:
"He's a failure."

Sallie Smith, "Some Prayers of Slave Children"

Aunt Sallie, what did you and your brother decide upon in the woods!

O, we wandered about in the woods, I don't know how long. We would pick berries to eat, and would get any thing we came upon. I told Warren about my dream of our mother, and that I saw her come up to me, and that I had been praying every night on my moss bed. I wanted to get him to pray too. I said to him, "Warren, you know how our poor mother used to pray way before day in the morning, and how we used to hear her cry and say, 'O, Daniel's God, have mercy on me!' And it makes me feel glad every time I pray, Warren; and now let us pray every time before we go to sleep." Warren said, "Well, let us pray to Daniel's God just like our poor mother did." And we did every night before we went to sleep, after wandering all through the woods all day. Me and Warren would pray. We prayed low and easy; we just could hear each other. Warren used to pray, "O, Daniel's God, have mercy on me and Sallie. Mother said you will take care of us, but we suffer here; nobody to help us. Hear us way up in heaven and look down on us here." Madam, we did not know hardly what to say, but we had heard mother and other people praying, and we tried to do the best we could.

Jo Carr and Imogene Sorley,
Plum Jelly and Stained Glass & Other Prayers

Lord,
why is it that even with my own children I get tongue-tied—and can't say the things that are aching to be said?
All I can get said is "Good-bye" and "Have a good trip!" and "Take care." And they are gone—perhaps without even knowing the love in which they are held—the pride I have in them—the faith. The memories of a thousand shared joys—aches—problems—crazy moments of fun— are there
. . . but all I can say is "Take care."
Maybe there aren't any words. But, dear Lord, let my message get through to them, somehow. Help them understand that some things are beyond saying. Some moments are more than tongue can tell—or heart can hold in silence. And the meaningless words I manage to say are fraught with love.
I guess they know, Lord,
. . . even as I know, through *their* tongue-tied good-bye and unsaid affection,

the bond of love that continues to unite us. I'm grateful, Lord, that it doesn't
have to depend on words.
 Bless us with thy unspoken word—
  thy unspoken love.
   Amen.

———∽∞∞∽———

Michael Leunig, *The Prayer Tree*

We give thanks for our friends.
Our dear friends.
We anger each other.
We fail each other.
We share this sad earth, this tender life,
 this precious time.
Such richness. Such wildness.
Together we are blown about.
Together we are dragged along.
All this delight.
All this suffering.
All this forgiving life.
We hold it together.
Amen.

———∽∞∞∽———

Lee Hough, "Houghs' Residence, Lee Speaking"

A pause . . .
 Heads bowed.
 Everyone's dutifully silent.
 Then I begin,
 Houghs' residence, Lee speaking.
 Another pause . . .
 This time for a brief moment of confusion.
 Then laughter, table-slapping, teary-eyed belly laughs.
 I had just opened my prayer for the family dinner with the rote jingle
my parents had taught me for answering the phone.
 "Houghs' residence, Lee speaking."
 Well, it kinda worked.
 Embarrassed, I laughed too.

But I was just a child then and God seemed distant. Not in a hurtful
way, I mean, it's just that life was so carefree and kick-the-can fun.

Now I'm a husband and a father—and unemployed. Life's real now, hard, and I'm the one who feels like he's getting kicked. God seems distant again, too. But this time it hurts.

God help me, please!
Please don't humiliate me again,
not before my friends
not before my wife
not before my children
not before my parents

"Hello, Dad? . . . I'm good, yes, Deb and the kids are fine. (*I wish I were*) Listen, Dad," (*This is your stupid son, the one who can't keep a job*) "I wanted to let you know, I, last week, uhmm," (*This is the screw up calling*) "well, I got laid off" (*fired, jobless, clueless*).

Father,
What's helping find me a job compared to the power it takes You to run this world for even one day?
Nothing!
If a sparrow doesn't fall without You noticing, why aren't You noticing me? Why are You tending millions of beautiful flowers that bloom today and are gone tomorrow but You won't tend to me, Your child? One nod, one word from You and a door would open. Why are You humiliating me?
Houghs' residence, Lee speaking—hello? Are you there God?

I prayed alone all day on the mountain, offering thanks, confessing, seeking a word from Him. I listened. But there was no word.
So,
I prayed alone during the next day at the Academy. Still no word.
I walked alone during the next day on the Santa Fe Trail. Still no word.
I walked alone the next morning and found a quiet woods. Still no word.
I prayed alone the next night at the Academy. Still no word.
I feel tired, spiritually exhausted. Alone.
Jesus,
I don't know any more words. I have no more words. Does Your silence mean, No, You won't help? Does it mean, wait?

How long?
I'm listening, Lord. Straining to hear.
I'm calling, Lord, with all my heart. Please, let me laugh again, help me find my reason for getting up in the mornings, take away this humiliation that slaps me in the face all day, every day.

Houghs' residence, Lee speaking . . . yes, I'll hold. But please God, don't let it be much longer.

——— ∞∞∞ ———

Michel Quoist, *Prayers*

This afternoon I went to see a patient at the hospital.

From pavilion to pavilion I walked, through that city of suffering, sensing the tragedies hardly concealed by the brightly painted walls and the flower-bordered lawns.

I had to go through a ward; I walked on tiptoe, hunting for my patient.

My eyes passed quickly and discreetly over the sick, as one touches a wound delicately to avoid hurting.

I felt uncomfortable,

Like the non-initiated traveler lost in a mysterious temple,

Like a pagan in the nave of a church.

At the very end of the second ward I found my patient,

And once there, I could only stammer. I had nothing to say.

Lord, suffering disturbs me, oppresses me.

I don't understand why you allow it.

Why, Lord?

Why this innocent child who has been moaning for a week, horribly burned?

This man who has been dying for three days and three nights, calling for his mother?

This woman with cancer who in one month seems ten years older?

This workman fallen from his scaffolding, a broken puppet less than twenty years old?

This stranger, poor isolated wreck, who is one great open sore?

This girl in a cast, lying on a board for more than thirty years?

Why, Lord?

I don't understand.

Why this suffering in the world

    that shocks,

       isolates,

       revolts

       shatters?

Why this hideous suffering that strikes blindly without seeming cause,

Falling unjustly on the good, and sparing the evil;

Which seems to withdraw, conquered by science, but comes back in another form, more powerful and more subtle?

I don't understand.
Suffering is odious and frightens me.
Why these people, Lord, and not others?
Why these, and not me?

Attributed to an Aged Seventeenth-Century Nun

Lord, you know better than I know myself that I am growing older, and will someday be old. Keep me from getting talkative, and particularly from the fatal habit of thinking that I must say something on every subject and on every occasion.

Release me from craving to straighten out everybody's affairs. Make me thoughtful but not moody; helpful but not bossy. With my vast store of wisdom it seems a pity not to use it all, but you know, Lord, that I want a few friends at the end. Keep my mind from the recital of endless details—give me wings to come to the point.

I ask for grace enough to listen to the tales of others' pains. But seal my lips on my own aches and pains—they are increasing, and my love of rehearsing them is becoming sweeter as the years go by. Help me to endure them with patience.

I dare not ask for improved memory, but for a growing humility and a lessening cocksureness when my memory seems to clash with the memories of others. Teach me the glorious lesson that occasionally it is possible that I may be mistaken.

Keep me reasonably sweet. I do not want to be a saint—some of them are so hard to live with—but a sour old woman is one of the crowning works of the devil.

Give me the ability to see good things in unexpected places, and talents in unexpected people. And give me, O Lord, the grace to tell them so.

Marjorie Holmes, *I've Got to Talk to Somebody, God*

Oh, God, dear God, I'm showing my age.

I'm not young and beautiful any more, the way my heart imagines. When I look in the mirror I could cry. For I look just what I am—a woman growing older.

And I protest it, Lord. Perhaps foolishly, I am stricken.

"Vanity, vanity, all is vanity," the Bible says. But is vanity truly such a fault? You, who made woman with this instinctive hunger to hang onto personal beauty, must surely understand.

Dear God, if this be vanity, let me use it to some good purpose.

Let it inspire me to keep my body strong and well and agile, the way you made it in the beginning. May it help me to stay as attractive as possible for as long as possible—out of concern for other people as well as myself. For you, who made women, also know that when we feel attractive we're a lot easier to live with.

But oh God, whatever happens to my face and body, keep me always supple in spirit, resilient to new ideas, beautiful in the things I say and do.

If I must "show my age" let it be in some deeper dimension of beauty that is ageless and eternal, and can only come from you.

Don't let me be so afraid of aging, God. Let me rejoice and reach out to be replenished; I know that each day I can be reborn into strength and beauty through you.

PEOPLE FROM AROUND THE WORLD

Zimbabwe

In Mbereshi is a girls' school, founded by Miss Mabel Shaw and noteworthy for the way in which the African heritage has been conserved, enriched and ennobled through the spirit of Christ. Here Christianity is not a western faith, but has the feel and flavor of Africa. The school is a "tribe" in miniature, centered around an invisible chief whose commandment of love is the tribal law. The following prayer is taken from Miss Shaw's fascinating book *God's Candlelights*—a prayer voiced one evening by a little girl.

O Thou Great Chief, light a candle in my heart that I may see what is therein, and sweep the rubbish from thy dwelling place.

China

After a four months' refugee Bible class in which a number of illiterate women had learned to read, the day came when they were returning to their homes. At the meeting before parting one of the women prayed:

We are going home to many who cannot read. So, Lord, make us Bibles so that those who cannot read the Book can read it in us.

Alaskan Eskimo

To thee, the God of truth, of light and of love, to thee I speak, thou who art highest and holiest and noblest. I know that there is bad about me; when thou seest it, forget. I am like others of mine own people—of the spirits we were afraid. Our chief thought was to get food and fur to make our bodies comfortable. In this we were like the beasts—they want only a warm place in which to lie down with a full stomach.

From the beginning we lived in fear, in ignorance, and in darkness, but now from afar we see light arising; but alas! in the faint light we see the filth of our lives.

We understand that thou art our great father whose heart is filled with love for us; that thou dost love all truth and mercy and light and cleanness and goodness, and that thou dost hate the false and the dark and the cruel and the dirty and the bad. So we pray—make the light brighter that we may see more clearly and learn more of thee. Cause us to hate that which thou dost hate and to love that which thou dost love.

Father, I and my people will be strong for thee; we will fight against the bad; we will fight for the good; we will use our heads and our hearts and our hands and our feet and our tongues and all that we have to follow the truth to gratify and please thee.

Kenya

From the cowardice that dare not face new truth
From the laziness that is contented with half truth
From the arrogance that thinks it knows all truth,
Good Lord, deliver me.

Hassan Dehqani-Tafti of Iran

A father's prayer upon the murder of his son:

O God
We remember not only our son but also his murderers;
Not because they killed him in the prime of his youth and made our
    hearts bleed and our tears flow,
Not because with this savage act they have brought further disgrace
    on the name of our country among the civilized nations of the
    world;

But because through their crime we now follow thy footsteps more
closely in the way of sacrifice.
The terrible fire of this calamity burns up all selfishness and posses-
siveness in us;
Its flame reveals the depth of depravity and meanness and suspicion,
the dimension of hatred and the measure of sinfulness in human
nature;
It makes obvious as never before our need to trust in God's love as
shown in the cross of Jesus and his resurrection;
Love which makes us free from hate towards our persecutors;
Love which brings patience, forbearance, courage, loyalty, humility,
generosity, greatness of heart;
Love which more than ever deepens our trust in God's final victory
and his eternal designs for the Church and for the world;
Love which teaches us how to prepare ourselves to face our own day
of death.

O God
Our son's blood has multiplied the fruit of the Spirit in the soul of our
souls;
So when his murderers stand before thee on the day of judgment
Remember the fruit of the Spirit by which they have enriched our
lives.
And forgive.

———— ◦◦◦◦ ————

Japan

For many Japanese an unspoken prayer often underlies their marked
appreciation of the beauties of nature. In flowers, trees, mountains,
rivers, fish, they see certain qualities of character which they wish to
emulate. So strong is the instinctive feeling of the Japanese for nature
that when Christ points to the beauty of the lily of the field; when he
lifts his eyes to the birds of the air; when he calls our attention to the
evening glow, the soil by the roadside, the wheat, the tares, the fig
tree and the lamb, the Japanese leap to an understanding of his
meaning. . . .

Just after the Cherry Blossom Festival a Japanese pastor was heard
to pray:

As the cherry blossoms quickly fall and are forgotten, so in thy boun-
teous mercy grant that our sins may be shed and remembered no more.

Japan

This prayer, by Dr. Toyohiko Kagawa, was written for Japanese children.

OUR FATHER, we thank thee for the beauty of this New Year's Day. We thank thee for the New Year's decoration of pine, bamboo and plum placed at each gateway. They turn our thoughts to thee for they have been chosen from thy generous store of natural beauty.

Teach us this year to learn their meaning and their message to us. Like the pine may we be unchangingly steadfast. Like the bamboo may we bend without breaking during the storms and when the storm has passed may we be straighter and stronger. Like the inconspicuous plum flower blooming among the falling flakes of snow may we bloom courageously and give fragrance to the air about us reminding men that spring is near.

As thou art in the trees giving life and strength and beauty, be in our hearts that we may glorify thy Son, our Savior Jesus Christ in whose name we pray. Amen.

Elizabeth Gray Vining, *The World in Tune*

Be still, my heart, these great trees are prayers.
Rabindranath Tagore

I think I know the very trees that Tagore had in mind when he wrote this, for many of the poems in his volume *Stray Birds* were said to have been written at the place in Karuizawa where I spent the summer holidays during my four years in Japan. The house was surrounded by great balsam trees, and the clear pure mountain air was tangy with their fragrance. In the early mornings long shafts of sunlight came slanting through their purplish trunks and green branches, and cuckoos called in the distance. In the hush and the freshness, one's heart was filled with that wonder and awe which comes when nature silences us with beauty like a trumpet call. Something more explicit than words, higher than thought, deeper than feeling, seemed to be expressed by those majestic trees, as if they were indeed prayer made visible.

Northern Ireland

Between 1969 and today, tens of thousands of people—children and adults, Protestants and Catholics—have been killed or brutally in-

jured in a savage civil war. This is one child's prayer from that war-
torn region.

> Father God, some of us know
> what it is to be afraid to talk to people
> of a different religion.
> We are afraid because of what our
> parents will say or do to us.
> We are afraid because of what our
> neighbors will say or do to us.
> Give us courage.
> Teach children and grown-ups in this
> and every land
> to show love to people
> no matter what color they are
> or by what name they are called.
> Amen.

―――

Cameroon

A little boy leading prayer at the opening of school:

> Our hearts are like a book full of mistakes. Take thy eraser . . .
> Lord, and erase all our faults.

―――

Puerto Rico

A child's prayer:

> I give thanks to God
> because he has not left me alone in the world,
> that I have a family that I love very much
> and that they love me also.
> I would like it if everyone in the world
> had a family and that being together
> could feel the warmth of love and care
> the same as I feel.
> Almighty God, I would like that there would be
> no more hungry children in the world,
> that people would stop thinking of killing
> and would help the people that are so poor.
> Amen.

PEOPLE FROM ACROSS THE CENTURIES

Psalm 90 (NIV)

A prayer by Moses:

> Lord, you have been our dwelling place
> > throughout all generations.
> Before the mountains were born
> > or you brought forth the earth and the world,
> > from everlasting to everlasting you are God.
>
> You turn men back to dust,
> > saying, "Return to dust, O sons of men."
> For a thousand years in your sight
> > are like a day that has just gone by,
> > or like a watch in the night.
> You sweep men away in the sleep of death;
> > they are like the new grass of the morning—
> though in the morning it springs up new,
> > by evening it is dry and withered.
>
> We are consumed by your anger
> > and terrified by your indignation.
> You have set our iniquities before you,
> > our secret sins in the light of your presence.
> All our days pass away under your wrath;
> > we finish our years with a moan.
> The length of our days is seventy years—
> > or eighty, if we have the strength;
> yet their span is but trouble and sorrow,
> > for they quickly pass, and we fly away.
>
> Who knows the power of your anger?
> > For your wrath is as great as the fear that is due you.
> Teach us to number our days aright,
> > that we may gain a heart of wisdom.
>
> Relent, O Lord! How long will it be?
> > Have compassion on your servants.
> Satisfy us in the morning with your unfailing love,
> > that we may sing for joy and be glad all our days.
> Make us glad for as many days as you have afflicted us,
> > for as many years as we have seen trouble.

May your deeds be shown to your servants,
    your splendor to their children.

May the favor of the Lord our God rest upon us;
    establish the work of our hands for us—
    yes, establish the work of our hands.

—⊶∞⊷—

Psalm 139:1–17a (NIV)

A prayer by David:

O Lord, you have searched me
    and you know me.
You know when I sit and when I rise;
    you perceive my thoughts from afar.
You discern my going out and my lying down;
    you are familiar with all my ways.
Before a word is on my tongue
    you know it completely, O Lord.

You hem me in—behind and before;
    you have laid your hand upon me.
Such knowledge is too wonderful for me,
    too lofty for me to attain.

Where can I go from your Spirit?
    Where can I flee from your presence?
If I go up to the heavens, you are there;
    if I make my bed in the depths, you are there.
If I rise on the wings of the dawn,
    if I settle on the far side of the sea,
even there your hand will guide me,
    your right hand will hold me fast.

If I say, "Surely the darkness will hide me
    and the light become night around me,"
even the darkness will not be dark to you;
    the night will shine like the day,
    for darkness is as light to you.

For you created my inmost being;
    you knit me together in my mother's womb.
I praise you because I am fearfully and wonderfully
    made;

your works are wonderful,
    I know that full well.
My frame was not hidden from you
    when I was made in the secret place.
When I was woven together in the depths of the
    earth,
    your eyes saw my unformed body.
All the days ordained for me
    were written in your book
    before one of them came to be.

How precious to me are your thoughts, O God!
    How vast is the sum of them!
Were I to count them,
    they would outnumber the grains of sand.

Matthew 6:9–13 (KJV)

A prayer by Jesus:

Our Father which art in heaven,
Hallowed be thy name.
Thy kingdom come.
Thy will be done in earth,
as it is in heaven.
Give us this day our daily bread.
And forgive us our debts,
as we forgive our debtors.
And lead us not into temptation,
but deliver us from evil:
For thine is the kingdom,
and the power,
and the glory,
for ever.
Amen.

Jesus Christ

As told by E. M. Bounds

The praying of Christ was real. . . . Prayer pressed upon Him as a
solemn, all-imperative, all-commanding duty, as well as a royal privilege

. . . alluring and absorbing. Prayer was the secret of His power, the law of His life, the inspiration of His toil, and the source of His wealth, His joy, His communion and strength. To Christ Jesus prayer occupied no secondary place, but was exacting and paramount, a necessity, a life, the satisfying of a restless yearning, and a preparation for heavy responsibilities.

Closeting with His Father in council and fellowship, with vigour and indeed joy, all this was His praying. Present trials, future glory, the history of His Church, and the struggles and perils of His disciples in all times and to the very end of time—all these things were born and shaped by His praying. Nothing is more conspicuous in the life of our Lord than prayer.

Cyprian of Carthage

(ca. 200–258) Bishop in that North African city until arrested and beheaded during the Valerian persecution.

We believe and trust, Lord, that at the time of terrible persecution, you will hear and answer our prayers with the utmost urgency. We pray with all our hearts that you will give us courage to remain true to the gospel, and proclaim your name right up till the moment of death. Then may we emerge from the snares of this world with our souls unscathed, and rise from the darkness of the world into your glorious light. As we have been linked together by love and peace, and together we have endured persecution, may we rejoice together in the kingdom of heaven.

Ambrose of Milan

(ca. 339–397) Fearless church leader who influenced Augustine and whose first act as bishop was to distribute his great wealth among the poor.

Jesus, I wish you would let me wash your feet, since it was by walking about in me that you soiled them. I wish you would give me the task of wiping the stains from your feet, since it was my behaviour that put them there. But where can I get the running water I need to wash your feet? If I have no water, at least I have tears. Let me wash your feet with my tears, and wash myself at the same time.

Jesus, you called me to the priesthood from the noisy wranglings of the law courts and the daunting responsibilities of public administration. In my former life I pursued my own interests, without thought of you. But you decided that you could re-shape me to be of service to you and your Church. You forgave my sins, and made me what I am. I was a lost soul when you called me; help me not to become a lost priest as well.

As a priest let me always remember the depth of sin in which I used sto dwell; and in this way let me sympathize with those who still dwell in sin, and so help to draw them up to your love. May I show compassion to anyone who falls into sin. Instead of reproving him, may I grieve and lament with him. Instead of looking upon him with contempt, may I weep for him, that through me he may know your mercy.

Augustine

(354–430) Bishop of Hippo in North Africa. Philosopher and Church Father whose ideas greatly influenced the Protestant Reformation.

You are great, Lord, and greatly to be praised. Great is your power, and of your wisdom there is no end. And man, who is part of what you have created, desires to praise you. Yes, even though he carries his mortality wherever he goes, as the proof of his sin and testimony of your justice, man desires to praise you. For you have stirred up his heart so that he takes pleasure in praising you. You have created us for yourself, and our hearts are restless until they rest in you.

Thomas Aquinas

(ca.1225–1274) Italian philosopher and theologian who became the most influential monk of the medieval period. Nevertheless, Aquinas came to view his prodigious theological works as valueless when compared to a direct encounter with God.

Most merciful God, order my day so that I may know what you want me to do, and then help me to do it. Let me not be elated by success or depressed by failure. I want only to take pleasure in what pleases you, and only to grieve at what displeases you. For the sake of your love I would willingly forgo all temporal comforts. May all the joys in which you have no part weary me. May all the work which you do not prompt be tedious to me. Let my thoughts frequently turn to you, that I may be obedient to you without complaint, patient without grumbling, cheerful without self-indulgence, contrite without dejection, and serious without solemnity. Let me hold you in awe without feeling terrified of you, and let me be an example to others without any trace of pride.

Thomas à Kempis

(1380–1471) German monk and mystic whose writings were profoundly devotional as best exemplified in the classic The Imitation of Christ.

Grant me, O Lord, to know what is worth knowing,
to love what is worth loving,
to praise what delights you most,
to value what is precious in your sight,
to hate what is offensive to you.
Do not let me judge by what I see,
nor pass sentence according to what I hear,
but to judge rightly between things that differ,
and above all to search out and to do what pleases you,
through Jesus Christ our Lord.

———— ∞ ————

Martin Luther

(1483–1546) Theologian, teacher, and writer who ignited the Reformation.

Behold, Lord, an empty vessel that needs to be filled. My Lord, fill it.
I am weak in the faith; strengthen thou me. I am cold in love; warm me
and make me fervent that my love may go out to my neighbour. I do not
have a strong and firm faith; at times I doubt and am unable to trust
thee altogether. O Lord, help me.

———— ∞ ————

Michelangelo

(1475–1564) Italian painter, sculptor, architect, and poet.

Lord, make me see your glory in every place:
If mortal beauty sets my heart aglow,
Shall not that earthly fire by thine burn low
Extinguished by the great light of thy grace?

Dear Lord, I cry to thee for help, O raise
Me from the misery of this blind woe,
Thy spirit alone can save me: let it flow
Through will and sense, redeeming what is base.

Thou hast given me on earth this godlike soul,
And a poor prisoner of it thou hast made
Behind weak flesh-walls; from that wretched state

How can I rescue it, how my true life find?
All goodness, Lord, must fail without thy aid:
For thou alone hast power to alter fate.

———∞∞———

Teresa of Ávila

(1515–1582) Spanish nun whose mental and physical sufferings finally gave way to a deep spiritual life and the founding of a new Carmelite order with John of the Cross.

A side to Teresa's character which may be related to humility is her incredible sense of humor. . . .

There is her famous dialogue with the Lord when, fighting with a river crossing in her advanced age, she complained to the Lord that she had a sore throat and high temperature. She added, therefore, that this prevented her from enjoying the incidents of the journey as she might. The Lord was alleged to have said, "But that is how I treat My friends," to which she readily replied: "Yes, my Lord, and that is why Thou hast so few of them."

———∞∞———

Abraham Lincoln

(1809–1865) Sixteenth president of the United States.

O, God, we have been recipients of the choicest blessings of heaven. We have been preserved, these many years, in peace and prosperity. We have grown in numbers, wealth and power as no other nation has ever grown; but we have forgotten God. We have forgotten the gracious hand which preserved us in peace, and multiplied and enriched and strengthened us; and we have vainly imagined, in the deceitfulness of our hearts, that all these blessings were produced by some superior wisdom and virtue of our own. Intoxicated with unbroken success, we have become too self-sufficient to feel the necessity of redeeming and preserving grace, too proud to pray to the God that made us.

It behooves us, then, to humble ourselves before the offended Power, to confess our national sins, and to pray for clemency and forgiveness.

———∞∞———

Fyodor Dostoyevski, *The Brothers Karamozov*

Young man, be not forgetful of prayer. Every time you pray, if your prayer is sincere, there will be new feeling and new meaning in it, which will give you fresh courage, and you will understand that prayer is an education. Remember, too, every day, and whenever you can, repeat to yourself, "Lord, have mercy on all who have appeared before Thee to-day." For every hour and every moment thousands of men leave life on this earth, and their souls appear before the Lord. And how many of them depart in solitude, unknown, sad, dejected, because no one mourns for them or even knows whether they have lived or not. And behold, from the other end of the earth perhaps, your prayer for their rest will rise up to God though you knew them not nor they you. How touching it must be to a soul standing in dread before the Lord to feel at that instant that, for him, too, there is one to pray, that there is a fellow creature left on earth to love him, too.

Mother Teresa

Lord, open our eyes,
That we may see you in our brothers and sisters.
Lord, open our ears,
That we may hear the cries of the hungry, the cold, the frightened, the
   oppressed.
Lord, open our hearts,
That we may love each other as you love us.
Renew in us your spirit,
Lord, free us and make us one.

Aleksandr Solzhenitsyn

How easy for me to live with you, O Lord!
How easy for me to believe in you!
When my mind parts in bewilderment or falters,
when the most intelligent people see no further
than this day's end
and do not know what must be done tomorrow,
You grant me the serene certitude
that you exist and that you will take care
that not all the paths of good be closed.
Atop the ridge of earthly fame,
I look back in wonder at the path
which I alone could never have found,

a wondrous path through despair to this point
from which I, too, could transmit to mankind
a reflection of your rays.
And as much as I must still reflect
You will give me.
But as much as I cannot take up
You will have already assigned to others.

PART FOUR

WHY DO WE PRAY?

INTRODUCTION

Why do we pray?

For reassurance, sometimes, because it's an uncertain world and each of us needs our spirit bolstered from time to time. For guidance, sometimes, because it's an uncharted way we travel, and we need all the direction we can get. For help, other times, because the way is long and almost always uphill and sometimes perilous.

We pray for our daily bread and our yearly physical. We pray when we wake up in the morning and when we go to bed at night. We pray when we're confused. Or lonely. Or sad. We pray when we're happy, too. And when we're grateful. Grateful for seeing a hummingbird up close or a double-rainbow off in the distance. Grateful for a good friend who was there when we needed someone to listen . . . or there when we needed someone to speak.

We pray for reasons as slight as a sudden feeling of appreciation for a cloud that shades us from the sun to one as serious as a lingering sense of abandonment in the face of some personal tragedy.

Partly, though, at least, we pray to find the part of us that is missing. Like the missing piece of a jigsaw puzzle that draws attention to itself by its absence. Like the empty space on a wall that calls out to be filled with a picture or a piece of furniture. Like the bare spot in a lawn that yearns for grass.

Prayer is a cry from the bare spot in our lives, from the empty space, from the part of us that is missing. It is the wounded part seeking to be healed, the missing part seeking to be found, the now-dry clay of the sculpture seeking the hands that first touched it, first caressed it, first loved it.

BECAUSE WE NEED HELP—PETITION

Max Lucado, *The Applause of Heaven*

Being a parent is better than a theology course.

Two ten-year-old boys walked up to my five-year-old daughter on the bus yesterday, scowled at her, and demanded that she scoot over.

When I came home from work, she told me about it. "I wanted to cry, but I didn't. I just sat there—afraid."

My immediate impulse was to find out the names of the boys and punch their dads in the nose. But I didn't. I did what was more important. I pulled my little girl up into my lap and let her get lost inside my arms and told her not to worry about those old bullies because her daddy was here, and I'd made sure if any thugs ever got close to my princess they'd be taking their lives in their own hands, yessir.

And that was enough for Jenna. She bounded down and ran outside.

She came back a few minutes later, crying. Her elbow was scraped.

I picked her up and carried her into the bathroom for first aid. She tried to tell me what happened.

"I"—sniff, sniff—"was turning in circles"—sniff, sniff—"like a helicopter"—sniff, sniff—"and then I fell doaaaaawwwn," she wailed.

"It's gonna be OK," I said as I set her on the bathroom counter.

"Can I have a Band-Aid?"

"Of course."

"A big one?"

"The biggest."

"Really?"

I stretched the adhesive bandage over the scrape and held her arm up in the mirror so she could see her badge of courage.

"Wow. Can I go show Mommy?"

"Sure." I smiled.

And that was enough for Jenna.

"Daddy."

The voice was coming from another world—the world of the awake. I ignored it and stayed in the world of slumber.

"Daddy." The voice was insistent.

I opened one eye. Andrea, our three-year-old, was at the edge of my bed only a few inches from my face.

"Daddy, I'm scared."

I opened the other eye. It was three in the morning.

"What's wrong?"

"I need a fwashwight in my woom."

"What?"

"I need a fwashwight in my woom."

"Why?"

"Cause it's dark."

I told her the lights were on. I told her the night light was on and the hall light was on.

"But Daddy," she objected, "what if I open my eyes and can't see anything?"

"Say that again."

"What if I open my eyes and can't see anything?"

Just as I was about to tell her that this was not the best time for questions on affliction, my wife interrupted. She explained to me that there was a power failure around midnight and Andrea must have awakened in the dark. No night light. No hall light. She had opened her eyes and had been unable to see anything. Just darkness.

Even the hardest of heart would be touched by the thought of a child waking up in a darkness so black she couldn't find her way out of her room.

I climbed out of bed, picked Andrea up, got a flashlight out of the utility room, and carried her to her bed. All the while, I told her that Mom and Dad were here and that she didn't need to be afraid. I tucked her in and gave her a kiss.

And that was enough for Andrea.

My child's feelings are hurt. I tell her she's special.

My child is injured. I do whatever it takes to make her feel better.

My child is afraid. I won't go to sleep until she is secure.

I'm not a hero. I'm not a superstar. I'm not unusual. I'm a parent. When a child hurts, a parent does what comes naturally. He helps.

And after I help, I don't charge a fee. I don't ask for a favor in return. When my child cries, I don't tell her to buck up, act tough, and keep a stiff upper lip. Nor do I consult a list and ask her why she is still scraping the same elbow or waking me up again.

I'm not brilliant, but you don't have to be to remember that a child is not an adult. You don't have to be a child psychologist to know that kids are "under construction." You don't have to have the wisdom of Solomon to realize that they didn't ask to be here in the first place and that spilled milk can be wiped up and broken plates can be replaced.

I'm not a prophet, nor the son of one, but something tells me that in the whole scheme of things the tender moments described above are infinitely more valuable than anything I do in front of a computer screen or congregation. Something tells me that the moments of comfort I give my child are a small price to pay for the joy of someday seeing my daughter do for her daughter what her dad did for her.

Moments of comfort from a parent. As a father, I can tell you they are the sweetest moments in my day. They come naturally. They come willingly. They come joyfully.

If all of that is true, if I know that one of the privileges of fatherhood is to comfort a child, then why am I so reluctant to let my heavenly Father comfort me?

Why do I think he wouldn't want to hear about my problems? ("They are puny compared to people starving in India.")

Why do I think he is too busy for me? ("He's got a whole universe to worry about.")

Why do I think he's tired of hearing the same old stuff?

Why do I think he groans when he sees me coming?

Why do I think he consults his list when I ask for forgiveness and asks, "Don't you think you're going to the well a few too many times on this one?"

Why do I think I have to speak a holy language around him that I don't speak with anyone else?

Why do I think he won't do in a heartbeat to the Father of Lies what I thought about doing to the fathers of those bullies on the bus?

Do I think he was just being poetic when he asked me if the birds of the air and the grass of the field have a worry? (No sir.) And if they don't, why do I think I will? (Duh. . . .)

Why do I not take him seriously when he questions, "If you, then, though you are evil, know how to give good gifts to your children, how much more will your Father in heaven give good gifts to those who ask him!"

Why don't I let my Father do for me what I am more than willing to do for my own children?

I'm learning, though. Being a parent is better than a course on theology. Being a father is teaching me that when I am criticized, injured, or afraid, there is a Father who is ready to comfort me. There is a Father who will

hold me until I'm better,
help me until I can live with the hurt,
and who won't go to sleep when I'm afraid of
waking up and seeing the dark.
Ever.
And that's enough.

Richard Foster, *Prayer*

Do you know why the mighty God of the universe chooses to answer prayer? It is because his children ask. God delights in our asking. He is pleased at our asking. His heart is warmed by our asking. . . .

When our asking is for ourselves it is called petition; when it is on behalf of others it is called intercession. Asking is at the heart of both experiences.

We must never negate or demean this aspect of our prayer experience. Some have suggested, for example, that while the less discerning will continue to appeal to God for aid, the real masters of the spiritual life go beyond petition to adoring God's essence with no needs or requests whatever. In this view our asking represents a more crude and naive form of prayer, while adoration and contemplation are a more enlightened and high-minded approach, since they are free from any egocentric demands.

This, I submit to you, is a false spirituality. Petitionary Prayer remains primary throughout our lives because we are forever dependent upon God. It is something that we never really "get beyond," nor should we even want to. In fact, the Hebrew and Greek words that are generally used for prayer mean "to request" or "to make a petition." The Bible itself is full of Petitionary Prayer and unabashedly recommends it to us.

Eric Marshall and Stuart Hample, *Children's Letters to God*

DEAR GOD,

I WOULD LIKE THESE THINGS.

a new bicycle

a number three chemistry set

a dog

a movie camera

a first baseman glove

IF I CAN'T HAVE THEM ALL I WOULD LIKE HAVE MOST OF THEM.
YOURS TRULY,
ERIC

P.S. I KNOW THERE IS NO SANTA CLAUS.

Norman C. Habel, *For Mature Adults Only*

By Stevie (a teenage girl):

Do you know what it's like
to be a clown?
Do you know what it's like
to suffer
from too many laughs?
Do you know what it's like
for a girl

to be born a circus act?
Do you know what it's like
to have a funny bone
for a brain?
Do you?

I don't have any white paint
on my face
but I wear a mask.
I have a silly smile
that never changes.
It's always there
and everyone expects it
to be there.
They like it that way.
They enjoy a clown
and they use a clown
because they think
a clown doesn't care
about anything.
I can't enjoy a bad mood
with other people.
That's a strange luxury.
I have to be a clown.
Whenever people tease me
I turn into an act,
a fool standing on my head.
Then I look up
and I see a world full
of upside-down people
trying to be
what they aren't.

I see so many people
wearing strange colorless makeup,
and the longer they wear it
the harder it is to discover
what kind of people they really are,
underneath.

I'm waiting for someone
to step behind my face

and find me!
Not Stevie, but me!

Lord,
when will this Stevie
be free
to be me?

Marjorie Holmes, *I've Got to Talk to Somebody, God*

Dear God, as I iron these clothes for my family, please make me aware not what a chore it is, but what a blessing:

That we have so many clothes to keep them warm. So many clothes to make them happy—pretty dresses, bright plaid shirts. Let me be thankful even for the trousers, hard as they are to press. Let me be thankful for having sons.

Thank you for this iron, with its simple yet marvelous power—heat and steam. Thank you for this sturdy ironing board. Thank you for spray starch, which has cut down my dampening time and makes everything so sweetly crisp. Thank you for this tumbled treasury of garments and tablecloths and pillow slips.

Thank you for the strength to make them smooth. And for all the hours of my life that I have been able to do this job, however I have dreaded it or put it off.

Give me the patience, please, to teach my own daughters this ancient art that every woman should know. And to teach my sons, as well, so that they, if they ever have to, can do their own.

And dear Lord, give me a spiritual strength to match this strength I bring to the smoothing of these clothes. As you have equipped my hands to guide this iron, please equip me with the wisdom to guide my children, to smooth out the wrinkles in their lives as well.

Charles Spurgeon

As told by an unknown Christian

Spurgeon once said: "There is no need for us to go beating about the bush, and not telling the Lord distinctly what it is that we crave at His hands. Nor will it be seemly for us to make any attempt to use fine language; but let us ask God in the simplest and most direct manner for just the things we want. . . . I believe in business prayers. I mean prayers in which you take to God one of the many promises which He has given us in His Word, and expect it to be fulfilled as certainly as we look for the money to be given us when we go to the bank to cash a check. We should not think of going there, lolling over the counter chartering with the clerks on every conceivable subject except the one thing for which we had gone to the bank, and then coming away without the coin we needed; but we should lay before the clerk the promise to pay the bearer a certain sum, tell him in what form we wished to take the amount, count the cash after him, and then go on our way to attend to other business. That is just an illustration of the method in which we should draw supplies from the Bank of Heaven.

Stuart Hample and Eric Marshall, *Children's Letters to God*

Dear God,

I wrote you before do you remember? well I did what I promised. But you did not Send me the horse yet. What about it?

Lewis

Henri Nouwen, *With Open Hands*

When it comes to prayer, it seems that we do more asking than hoping. This is not surprising, since we pray mostly when very specific and often momentary circumstances ask for it. When there is war, we pray for peace; when there is drought, we pray for rain; when we go on vacation, we pray for nice weather; when a test is coming, we pray that we'll pass; when friends are sick, we pray that they will get well; and when they die, we pray for their eternal rest. Our prayer emerges in the midst of our lives and is interwoven with everything else which busies our day. Whatever fills the heart is what the mouth pours forth. This is also true of prayer.

Our hearts are filled with many concrete, tangible desires and expectations. A mother hopes her son will come home on time. A father hopes he'll get a promotion. A boy dreams of the girl he loves, and the child thinks of the bicycle she was promised. Often our thoughts are no further than a couple of hours, a couple of days, a couple of weeks ahead of us, seldom as much as a couple of years. We can scarcely let ourselves think too far in advance, for the world we live in requires us to focus our attention on the here and now. If we pray, and really pray, we can hardly escape the fact that our cares for the moment, big and small, will fill our prayer and often make it nothing but a long list of requests.

Often this prayer of petition is treated with a certain disdain. Sometimes we regard it as less noble than prayer of thanksgiving and certainly less noble than prayer of praise. Prayer of petition is supposedly more egocentric because we are putting our own interest first and trying to get something for ourselves. The prayer of thanksgiving, it is said, is directed more toward God, even if it is in connection with gifts that God has given us. The prayer of praise is supposedly directed completely to God, independently of anything we may or may not have received.

But the question is whether this distinction helps us understand what prayer is. The important thing about prayer is not whether it is classified as petition, thanksgiving or praise, but whether it is a prayer of hope or of little faith. . . .

The prayer of little faith is filled with wishes which beg for immediate fulfillment. This kind of prayer has a Santa Claus naiveté about it and wants the direct satisfaction of very specific wishes and desires. When this prayer is not heard, that is, when we don't get the presents we wanted, there is disappointment, even hard feelings and bitterness.

It is understandable, therefore, that this prayer of little faith carries a great deal of fear and anxiety with it. If you pray with little faith for health, success and advancement, for peace or whatever else, then you get so set on the concrete request that you feel left out in the cold when the expected answer doesn't come. You even say to yourself: "See what I told you, it doesn't work anyway. . . ."

With this prayer, your petition is aimed at getting what you ask for, any way you can, instead of being directed toward the person who might or might not make that wish come true. People of little faith pray like children who want a present from Santa Claus. . . . All the attention is on the gift and none on the one who gives it. . . .

When we live with hope we do not get tangled up with concerns for how our wishes will be fulfilled. So, too, our prayers are not directed toward the gift, but toward the one who gives it. Our prayers might still contain just as many desires, but ultimately it is not a question of having a wish come true but of expressing an unlimited faith in the giver of all good things. You wish that . . . but you hope in . . .

In the prayer of hope, there are no guarantees asked, no conditions posed and no proofs demanded. You expect everything from the other without binding the other in any way. Hope is based on the premise that the other gives only what is good. Hope includes an openness by which you wait for the promise to come through, even though you never know when, where or how this might happen. . . .

Thus, every prayer of petition becomes a prayer of thanksgiving and praise as well, precisely because it is a prayer of hope. In the hopeful prayer of petition, we thank God for God's promise and we praise God for God's faithfulness.

Our numerous requests simply become the concrete way of saying that we trust in the fullness of God's goodness. Whenever we pray with hope, we put our lives in the hands of God. Fear and anxiety fade away, and everything we are given and everything we are deprived of is nothing but a finger pointing out the direction of God's hidden promise which one day we shall taste in full.

> *Dear God,*
> I am full of wishes,
> full of desires,
> full of expectations.
> Some of them may be realized, many may not, but in the
>   midst of all my satisfactions and disappointments,
> I hope in you.
> I know that you will never leave me alone
> and will fulfill your divine promises.
> Even when it seems that things are not going my way,
> I know that they are going your way
> and that in the end your way is the best way for me.
> O Lord, strengthen my hope,
> especially when my many wishes are not fulfilled.
> Let me never forget that your name is Love.
> Amen.

St. Thomas More

(1478–1535) Lord Chancellor of England who, because of his allegiance to the Church, was beheaded by Henry VIII.

> Lord. . . .
> Let me not be too concerned
>   with the bothersome thing
>   I call "myself."

Queen Mary Stuart

(1542–1587) Queen of Scotland.

Keep us, O God, from all pettiness,
Let us be large in thought, in word, in deed.
Let us be done with faultfinding
    and leave off all self-seeking.
May we put away all pretense and meet each
    other face to face,
    without self-pity and without prejudice.
May we never be hasty in judgment,
    and always generous.
Let us always take time for all things,
    and make us grow calm, serene and gentle.
Teach us to put into action our better
    impulses,
    to be straightforward and unafraid.
Grant that we may realize
    that it is the little things of life that create
    differences,
    that in the big things of life
    we are as one.
And, O Lord God, let us not forget to be kind!

C. R. Findley

Answers to prayer often come in unexpected ways. We pray, for instance, for a certain virtue; but God seldom delivers Christian virtues
all wrapped in a package and ready for use. Rather he puts us in situations where by his help we can develop those virtues. Henry Ward
Beecher told of a woman who prayed for patience, and God sent her
a poor cook. The best answers to prayer may be the vision and strength
to meet a circumstance or to assume a responsibility.

C. S. Lewis

(1898–1963) Christian apologist, Oxford scholar, and author.

"Thy will *be done.*" But a great deal of it is to be done by God's creatures;
including me. The petition, then, is not merely that I may patiently suffer

God's will but also that I may vigorously do it. I must be an agent as well as a patient. I am asking that I may be enabled to do it. . . . "Thy will be *done*—by me—now" brings one back to brass tacks.

— ⁂ —

Phillips Brooks, "Going up to Jerusalem," *Sermons*

(1835–1893) American preacher and bishop who wrote the carol "O Little Town of Bethlehem."

Do not pray for easy lives. Pray to be stronger men! Do not pray for tasks equal to your powers. Pray for powers equal to your tasks.

— ⁂ —

Archbishop Anthony Bloom, *Beginning to Pray*

God gives us strength but we must use it. When, in our prayers, we ask God to give us strength to do something in His Name, we are *not* asking Him to do it *instead* of us because we are too feeble to be willing to do it for ourselves.

The lives of the saints are enlightening in this respect, and in the life of St. Philip Neri just such an occasion is described. He was an irascible man who quarreled easily and had violent outbursts of anger and of course endured violent outbursts from his brothers. One day he felt that it could not go on. Whether it was virtue or whether he could no longer endure his brothers his *Vita* does not tell us. The fact is that he ran to the chapel, fell down before a statue of Christ and begged Him to free him of his anger. He then walked out full of hope. The first person he met was one of the brothers who had never aroused the slightest anger in him, but for the first time in his life this brother was offensive and unpleasant to him. So Philip burst out with anger and went on, full of rage, to meet another of his brothers, who had always been a source of consolation and happiness to him. Yet even this man answered him gruffly. So Philip ran back to the chapel, cast himself before the statue of Christ and said "O Lord, have I not asked you to free me from this anger?" And the Lord answered "Yes, Philip, and for this reason I am multiplying the occasions for you to learn."

— ⁂ —

Anonymous Prayer for Grace

Deliver me Jesus
    from the desire of being loved;

from the desire of being honored;
from the desire of being praised;
from the desire of being preferred to others;
from the desire of being consulted;
from the desire of being approved;

from the fear of being humiliated;
from the fear of being despised;
from the fear of suffering rebuke;
from the fear of being forgotten;
from the fear of being wrong;
from the fear of being suspected.

And Jesus, grant me the grace to desire
that others might be loved more than I;
that others might be esteemed more than I;
that in the opinion of the world, others may increase and I decrease;
that others may be chosen and I set aside;
that others may be praised and I unnoticed;
that others may be preferred to me in everything;
that others may become holier than I, provided that I become as
holy as I should.

Henri Nouwen, *With Open Hands*

Dear God,
As you draw me ever deeper into your heart,
I discover that my companions on the journey
are women and men
loved by you as fully and as intimately as I am.
In your compassionate heart, there is a place for all of them.
No one is excluded.
Give me a share in your compassion, dear God,
so that your unlimited love may become visible
in the way I love my brothers and sisters.
Amen.

Mother Teresa, *Words to Love By*

I think if we can spread this prayer, if we can translate it into our lives,
it will make all the difference. It is so full of Jesus. It has made a great

difference in the lives of the Missionaries of Charity.

> Dear Jesus,
> Help us to spread your fragrance everywhere we go.
> Flood our souls with your spirit and life.
> Penetrate and possess our whole being so utterly
>   that our lives may only be a radiance of yours.
> Shine through us
> and be so in us
> that every soul we come in contact with
>   may feel your presence in our soul.
> Let them look up and see no longer us
> but only Jesus.
> Stay with us
> and then we shall begin to shine as you shine,
> so to shine as to be a light to others.
> The light, O Jesus, will be all from you.
> None of it will be ours.
> It will be you shining on others through us.
> Let us thus praise you in the way you love best
>   by shining on those around us.
> Let us preach you without preaching
>   not by words, but by our example
>   by the catching force
>   the sympathetic influence of what we do
>   the evident fullness of the love our hearts bear to you
> Amen.

—∞∞—

William Henry Channing

> To live content with small means;
> to seek elegance rather than luxury,
> and refinement rather than fashion;
> to be worthy, not respectable,
> and wealthy, not rich;
> to listen to stars and birds, babes and sages
> with open heart;
> to study hard;
> to think quietly, act frankly, talk gently
> await occasions, hurry never;
> in a word, to let the spiritual,

unbidden and unconscious,
grow up through the common—
this is my symphony.

———— ∞ ————

Reinhold Niebuhr

(1893–1971) German pastor, theologian who taught at Union Theological Seminary for thirty-two years.

God, grant me the
 Serenity to accept the things
 I cannot change;
 Courage to change the things I can; and
 Wisdom to know the difference.

Living one day at a time;
 Enjoying one moment at a time;
 Accepting hardship
 As the pathway to peace.

Taking as He did,
 This sinful world as it is
 not as I would have it.

Trusting that He will make
 all things right
 If I surrender to His will.

That I may be reasonably happy
 in this life,
 And supremely happy
 With Him forever in the next.

———— ∞ ————

Kelsey Tyler, *Heaven Hears Each Whisper*

[There is a story] about the highway patrol officer who tentatively pulls over an eighteen-wheeler on a dark, deserted desert highway. As he approaches the cab he realizes he has not radioed for backup and he hopes there will be no confrontation.

"Got a light out, back of the truck, left side," the officer states, noting that the trucker is a thousand miles from his home base. "No ticket this time. Just get it fixed."

The trucker's eyes narrow and he climbs down from the cab, staring strangely at the officer. "What'd you say?"

The officer shifts his weight uncomfortably and repeats himself.

The trucker is silent several seconds. Then he speaks. "You were in Vietnam, weren't you?" he asks, his eyes narrow, searching those of the officer.

"Yes." The officer is puzzled. "Why?"

Drifting back in time, the trucker narrates the incident clearly. His military unit was under heavy attack and he had been hit badly. The others were about to flee in a waiting helicopter and had wanted to leave him behind. But the commanding officer would not allow it. He worked over the bleeding soldier until he could be transferred to a gurney and lifted into the helicopter.

"I couldn't see you very well," the trucker says. "But I forced myself to remember your voice so that someday I could find you and thank you. I've prayed about this meeting every day since then. I begged God to let me meet you. You saved my life, and I couldn't imagine leaving this life without the chance to tell you thanks."

A trucker prays for the chance to thank the man who once saved his life. He's a thousand miles away from home when he's pulled over by the very man who rescued him. All because a tail-light was out.

Answered prayer? Can it be that God is listening if only we will ask?

BECAUSE OTHERS NEED HELP — INTERCESSION

Oswald Chambers, *My Utmost for His Highest*

(1874–1917) Scottish minister who was converted to Christianity through the preaching of Charles Spurgeon. Best known as a devotional writer.

In intercession you bring the person, or the circumstance that impinges on you before God until you are moved by His attitude towards that person or circumstance.

Albrecht Dürer

(1471–1528) German painter and engraver.

Albrecht Dürer, the artist who painted "Praying Hands," was the son of a Hungarian goldsmith who was born in Nuremburg, Germany. He was obliged to work at his father's trade while he was a young boy, because of a very large family and lack of money. Always he wanted to draw and paint. Finally he was allowed to leave home and to go away and study with a great artist. Because he was very poor, it was hard for him to study and make a living at the same time. During these days of struggle Albrecht (Albert) Dürer found a friend, a man somewhat older than himself, who also had a desire to become a great artist. The two of them decided to live together, and one day when the struggle to earn enough food had discouraged both of them almost to the point of giving up their dreams, Albert's friend made a suggestion.

"This way of working and trying to study," he said, "is intolerable. We are neither making a living nor are we mastering our art. Let us try another way. One of us could make the living for us both while the other continues to study. Then when the paintings begin to sell, the one who has worked may have his chance."

"True," answered Albert, thoughtfully, "but let me be the one to work."

"No, I must be the one to work, because I have already a place to work in the restaurant. I am older, and I have not so much talent. You must not waste your years. Let it be as I say."

So the older man had his way. Albert Dürer worked faithfully to master his art while his friend worked at any kind of labor he could find to buy them food and to pay for their mean little room. He served in the restaurant, washing dishes, and scrubbing floors to add to the small sum he was paid. His hours were long and the work was menial and hard, but he did it cheerfully because he was helping his young friend and looking forward to the time when he would be able to use his brush again.

At last the day came when Albert Dürer came home bringing the money which he had received for the sale of a wood-carving. It was sufficient to buy food and to pay their rent for a considerable length of time.

"Now," he said, "the time has come when I will be the breadwinner, and you shall go to your paints, my good friend. You need no longer work, but I will care for both of us."

So his good friend left his serving and dish-washing and scrubbing, and took up his brush. But something had happened in those days during which he had worked so hard with his hands. The hard work had stiffened his muscles, enlarged his joints, and twisted his fingers so that they could no longer hold the brush with mastery and skill. He worked long and hard, only to find that his art would have to be sacrificed forever.

When Albert learned what had happened to his friend, he was filled with a great sorrow. Of course he would always care for him and give him a friend's love, but he could not give him back his skill. One day Albert returned to his room unexpectedly and heard the voice of his friend in prayer. He entered softly, and seeing the work-worn hands folded reverently, a great thought came to him.

"I can never give back the lost skill of those hands," he thought. "But I can show the world the feeling of love and gratitude which is in my heart for his noble deed. I will paint his hands as they are *now*, folded in prayer, and the world shall know my appreciation for a noble, unselfish character. It may be that when people look at the picture they will remember with love and devotion all hands that toil for others and like me express in some beautiful way their appreciation for such beautiful service."

—◦◦◦◦—

Richard Foster, *Prayer*

If we truly love people, we will desire for them far more than it is within our power to give them, and this will lead us to prayer. Intercession is a way of loving others.

When we move from petition to intercession we are shifting our center of gravity from our own needs to the needs and concerns of others. Intercessory Prayer is selfless prayer, even self-giving prayer.

In the ongoing work of the kingdom of God, nothing is more important than Intercessory Prayer. People today desperately need the help that we can give them. Marriages are being shattered. Children are being destroyed. Individuals are living lives of quiet desperation, without purpose or future. And we can make a difference . . . if we will learn to pray on their behalf.

Intercessory Prayer is priestly ministry, and one of the most challenging teachings in the New Testament is the universal priesthood of all Christians. As priests, appointed and anointed by God, we have the honor of going before the Most High on behalf of others. This is not optional; it is a sacred obligation—and a precious privilege—of all who take up the yoke of Christ. . . .

There are as many ways to go about the work of intercession as there are people. Some like to keep lists of people they are concerned to pray for with regularity. I once visited a very holy lady who was confined to a bed. She showed me her "family album" of some two hundred photographs of missionaries and others she was concerned to hold before the throne of heaven. She explained how she worked her way through this entire album each week, flipping the pages and praying over the pictures. I was a teenager at the time, but even at that young age I knew that the place where I stood beside that bed was holy ground. Another approach comes from the great preacher and pray-er George Buttrick. He recommends that we begin with prayer for our enemies: "The first intercession is, 'Bless So-and-so whom I foolishly regard as an enemy. Bless So-and-so whom I have wronged. Keep them in Thy favor. Banish my bitterness.'" He next encourages us to go on to leaders in "statecraft, medicine, learning, art, and religion; the needy of the world, our friends at work or play, and our loved ones." The great value of Buttrick's counsel is that it keeps us moving beyond our provincial little concerns and into a broken and needy world.

Augustine

(354–430) Bishop of Hippo in North Africa. Philosopher and Church Father whose ideas greatly influenced the Protestant Reformation.

Tend your sick ones, O Lord Christ.
Rest your weary ones,
bless your dying ones,
soothe your suffering ones,
pity your afflicted ones,
shield your joyous ones,
and all for your love's sake. Amen.

Edith Schaeffer, *Common Sense Christian Living*

As we pray for the needy around us, God may open our eyes to what *we* can do to help in that immediate need. He may use *us* as an answer to our own prayers.

As we pray for the need of education of falsely informed people concerning abortion, one answer may be that, along with others in our church, we do something practical about it such as having an educational series, or purchasing a house to open as a crisis pregnancy center. As we pray for families with older people or handicapped children to care for, we may need to prepare a place where perhaps one day or more a week these children could come to play or to have a special treat such as wheelchair races or whatever your imagination can think up! What skills do you have? . . .

The essential thing for each of us to discover is that prayer is *not* an isolationist activity. Prayer involves us in what is going on around us, both locally and in the world.

Kelsey Tyler, *Heaven Hears Each Whisper*

David Hunter received the call just after nine on a Saturday evening in 1986 while on patrol with the sheriff's department in Knox County, Tennessee. A woman was weeping loudly in a corner booth at the Raccoon Valley Truck Stop. Several patrons had grown concerned and contacted the sheriff's department.

Hunter sighed and turned his patrol car in the direction of the truck stop. As a veteran officer of eight years, he had seen so much pain in the lives of people that he could only imagine what might cause a woman to weep aloud in a truck stop. . . .

Not sure what he would find, Hunter entered the truck stop cafe and immediately spotted the woman, still weeping, her face covered with her hands. Nearby sat two frightened little blond girls, ages about four and five.

Hunter's face softened as he approached the children.

"What seems to be the matter, girls?" he asked them. The older child turned to look at him, and Hunter could see she had tears in her eyes, too.

"Daddy left us," she said. "He put our stuff out of the car while we was in the bathroom."

Hunter's heart sank. He studied the woman, and gently placed a hand on her shoulder. Then he looked at the girls and smiled a warm, comforting smile. "Well, now, is that so?"

The children nodded.

"In that case I want you two to climb on those stools over there and order something to eat."

Reluctantly the girls walked away from their mother and took separate stools along the counter. Hunter signaled the waitress and asked her to get the girls whatever they wanted from the menu.

With the children out of earshot, the officer sat down across from the woman. She looked up from her hands and stared sadly at Hunter, her eyes filled with heartbreak.

"What's the problem?" Hunter asked quietly.

"Just what my girl said," the woman replied, wiping her eyes. "My husband's not cruel. Just at the end of his rope. We're flat broke, and he figured we'd get more help alone than if he stayed. I've been sitting here praying about what to do next, but I don't even have the money for a phone call. I just want to know God is listening, you know?"

Hunter nodded, his eyes gentle and empathetic. And silently he added his own prayer, asking God to show him a way to help this woman and her little children. He touched the gold St. Michael medallion he always wore around his neck. Although most police officers didn't spend a great deal of time talking about religion, Hunter knew few who did not rely on their faith. Many officers wore the St. Michael medallion under their uniforms because the archangel was recognized as the patron saint of warriors. Hunter believed with all his heart that God had indeed used angels to protect him in the line of duty on more than one occasion.

She needs an angel about now, Lord, he prayed silently. *Please help her out.*

Hunter broke the silence between the woman and him. "Do you have family?"

"The nearest is in Chicago."

Hunter thought a moment, and then suggested several agencies that could help her. As they spoke, the waitress brought hot dogs and french fries to the children, and the officer stood up and moved toward the counter. He took out his wallet to pay the bill.

"The boss says no charge," the waitress said. "We know what's going on here."

Hunter smiled at the woman and nodded his thanks. Then he stooped down to ask the girls how they liked their food. As he did, a trucker stood up from his table and approached the waitress. He mumbled something to her, and then she took him by the arm and led him to Hunter.

It was unusual for a truck driver to approach Hunter on his own. Typically truck drivers and police officers had something of a natural animosity for each other. Most truck drivers tended to see the police as cutting into their earnings by writing them tickets, while the police saw truckers as reckless people who placed their potential earning before safety. The truth, of course, was somewhere in the middle, but still, Hunter couldn't remember a time when he'd been approached by a truck driver outside of the line of duty.

The trucker wore jeans, a T-shirt, and a baseball cap. He walked up to the counter and stood alongside Hunter. The officer noticed that the normal buzz of conversation and activity had stilled and the cafe was silent. Most of the patrons—nearly all of them long-distance truckers—were watching the conversation between the trucker and the officer.

"Excuse me, officer," the man said. "Here."

The trucker reached out his hand and gave the officer a fistful of bills. He cleared his throat.

"We passed the hat. There ought to be enough to get the woman and her girls started on their way."

Back when he was a boy, Hunter had learned that cops don't cry, at least not in public. So he stood there, speechless until the lump in his throat disappeared and he was able to speak.

Then Hunter shook the man's hand firmly. "I'm sure she'll appreciate it," he said, his voice gruff from covering up his emotion. "Can I tell her your name?"

The trucker raised his hands and backed away from the officer. "Nope. Just tell her it was from folks with families of their own."

Hunter nodded, and thought of the fiercely loyal way in which people in Tennessee looked out for each other. When the trucker walked away, Hunter counted the money and was again amazed. A small room of truck drivers had in a matter of minutes raised two hundred dollars, enough money for three bus tickets to Chicago and food along the way.

The officer walked back to the booth and handed the money to the woman, at which point she began to sob again.

"He heard," she whispered through her tears.

"Ma'am?" Hunter looked confused, wondering who the woman was talking about.

"Don't you see?" she said. "I came here completely desperate, hopeless. And I sat in this booth and asked God to help us, to give us a sign that he still loved us and cared for us."

Hunter felt chills along his arms and remembered his own prayer, how he had asked God to send help and provide this woman with angelic assistance. The truck drivers certainly didn't look like a textbook group of angels, but God had used them all the same. "You know, ma'am, I think you're right. I think he really did hear.". . .

Hunter . . . radioed dispatch.

"The situation's resolved," he said.

Then he walked toward his patrol car and climbed inside. When he was safely out of sight he let the tears come, tears that assured him he would never forget what happened that night in the truck stop. As a patrol officer he had almost always seen the worst in people around him. But that night, he'd been reminded that kindness and love do exist among men. And Hunter had learned something else. Sometimes God answers prayer by using nothing more than a dozen big-hearted truckers sharing coffee at a truck stop in East Tennessee—and playing the part of angels.

Oswald Chambers

In a letter dated February 16, 1907.

I want to tell you a growing conviction with
me, and that is that as we obey the leadings of
the Spirit of God, we enable God to answer the
prayers of other people. I mean that our lives,
my life, is the answer to someone's prayer,
prayed perhaps centuries ago. . . .
I have the unspeakable knowledge that my life
is the answer to prayers, and that God is blessing
me and making me a blessing entirely of His
sovereign grace and nothing to do with my merits,
saving as I am bold enough to trust His leading
and not the dictates of my own wisdom and common
sense.

———◇∞◇———

William Barclay

*(1907–1978) Scottish minister and scholar best known for his New Testament commentary
series, The Daily Study Bible.*

O God our Father, we ask you to bless those for
whom there will be no sleep tonight . . .
. . . those who this night will not sleep because of the
pain of their body or the distress of their mind;
those in misfortune, who will lie down in hunger
and in cold;
those who are far from home and far from friends,
and who are lonely as the shadows fall.
Grant that in our own happiness and comfort we
may never forget the sorrow and the pain, the
loneliness and the need of others in the slow,
dark hours. This we ask for your love's sake.

———◇∞◇———

Susan Stanford

Susan Stanford, a psychologist and well-known speaker and workshop
leader, tells about a very difficult time in her life when she was suffering
deep depression and physical back pain and was contemplating suicide.

Though not a Christian herself, she had taken a short vacation with a Christian friend, who was sensitive to Susan's hesitancy to share her problems. In seeking to minister to Susan, her friend offered to pray, and her prayer style is a model of simplicity and sincerity.

Upstairs, I sprawled on top of my sleeping bag. Jeanie came in, knelt down beside me on the floor, and started to knead the painful knots around my lower and middle back.

"Susan," she said, a little timidly, "would you mind if I said a prayer for you?"

I was surprised. Accusations ricocheted inside me. *Don't you know, Jeanie? I'm lower than dirt. What God would listen to a prayer for a sinner like me?* But I replied, "Sure, if you want."

Clearing her throat as her hands continued to knead, Jeanie started to speak in a soft voice.

"Dear Jesus, I'm not sure of what to say. But I come to You in prayer for my friend Susan."

As I lay there listening I was amazed at the simplicity of her words. Even more amazing was her childlike confidence that God was actually listening to her prayers. . . . Jeanie's prayer went on for five or ten minutes, interspersed with times of silence while she continually rubbed my back. There was such gentleness, depth of spirit.

As I grew drowsy I heard her conclude: "Susan is hurting badly, Lord. Reach down and touch her. Let her know that *You* are the solution. Let her not despair. She is my good friend, and I care about her so much. I know that You are the Almighty. You can do all things. And You can help her."

Then she leaned forward, gave me a hug, and said goodnight. Switching off the light, she quietly slipped from the room.

John F. DeVries, "Prayer Can Change a City, One Neighborhood at a Time," *Pray!* magazine

Modesto, CA, USA—A Baptist church decides to "use prayer" to change a low-income apartment complex of 200 units. They rent an apartment and move one of their couples into it for the specific purpose of setting up a neighborhood house of prayer to serve the other 199 apartments.

The couple prays for a few weeks, and then with the help of teams from the church, contacts all the other units, asking residents if they have prayer requests. All seem to be excited about the idea of having a house of prayer in their complex. Sixty percent invite the teams into their homes, and some break down weeping at the thought that someone would pray for them.

Violence and vandalism are lowered to the point that the owners of the complex offer to give the apartment free of charge and offer other free apartments in similar complexes! Within two years very effective social ministries are spawned by this house of prayer.

Richard Foster, *Prayer*

There is a religious word for what I have been describing: *supplication*. Supplication means to ask with earnestness, with intensity, with perseverance. It is a declaration that we are deadly serious about this prayer business. We are going to keep at it and not give up. John Calvin writes, "We must repeat the same supplications not twice or three times only, but as often as we have need, a hundred and a thousand times. . . . We must never be weary in waiting for God's help."

This is an important teaching to hear, for we live in a generation that eschews commitment. One of the old cardinal virtues was fortitude, but where today do we find such courageous staying power? We must admit that it is in short supply everywhere we look. Jesus, however, makes it foundational to real effectiveness in Intercessory Prayer.

Sojourner Truth, "Always Pray"

(1799–1883) Former slave, abolitionist, itinerant preacher. Champion of women's rights and one of the most well-known women of the nineteenth century, and yet she was illiterate.

While, in deep affliction, [Isabella] labored for the recovery of her son, she prayed with constancy and fervor; and the following may be taken as a specimen:—"Oh, God, you know how much I am distressed, for I have told you again and again. Now, God, help me get my son. If you were in trouble, as I am, and I could help you, as you can me, think I wouldn't do it? Yes, God, you *know* I would do it. Oh, God, you know I have no money, but you can make the people do for me, and you must make the people do for me. I will never give you peace till you do, God. Oh, God, make the people hear me—don't let them turn me off, without hearing and helping me."

Edwin Robertson, *The Shame and the Sacrifice*

On 1 July 1937, Martin Niemöller [German clergyman and leader in the anti-Nazi Confessing Church] was arrested, and although at the time it looked like one more irritation from which the Church leader would be released, the imprisonment lasted until the end of the war in Europe, 1945. Niemöller had been arrested before in 1935, when together with five hundred other pastors he spent three days in prison. In the autumn of 1936, he expected to be arrested and calmly waited, but it was a false alarm. In the spring of 1937, he was told that the public prosecutor had forty charges against him, still he remained untouched. Then it came.

It was the first day of the school holidays. His two oldest boys had already left on their bicycles; Mrs. Niemöller had just returned from seeing off the girls on an early train for the Baltic; Niemöller himself, after a late night at a church conference, was not yet dressed, but playing with his youngest son, Martin. The Gestapo arrived at 8.30 A.M. and asked him to come for interrogation. He dressed and went, thinking he would return a little later. These interrogations had happened before and they were always in the same place, the police headquarters in Alexander Platz. But this time he waited for hours. There was no interrogation. He was put in a prison, without charge, for the next eight years.

The Church never forgot him during that long imprisonment. In the little mission church of St. Anne, attached to Niemöller's parish church, from the day after his arrest until the day after the end of the war, intercession services were held regularly—at first twice a week and then daily. These services were always well attended, especially by the women. Gradually other names were added and it became an intercession service for the martyrs of the Confessing Church. During the summer of 1937 the Gestapo tried to stop the services by mass arrests. The simple courage of the people outdid them. The more they arrested the more came, and at last they gave up.

Leslie Weatherhead

(1883–1975) Pastor of the Congregationalist City Temple in London for thirty years. Best-known work is The House of Prayer.

Almighty and merciful God, we lift up our hearts to thee for all who are the prey of anxious fears, who cannot get their minds off themselves, and to whom every demand brings the feeling that they cannot cope with what is required of them. Give them the comfort of knowing that this is illness, not cowardice; that millions have felt as they feel; that there is a way through this dark valley, and light at the end of it. Lead them to those who can show them the pathway to health and happiness. Sustain them by the knowledge that the Savior knows and understands all our woe and fear; and give them enough courage to face each day, and to rest their minds in the thought that thou wilt see them through.

———⊗⊗⊙———

Eugene Peterson, *Answering God*

The last word on the enemies is with Jesus . . . "Love your enemies and pray for them that persecute you."

Our hate is used by God to bring the enemies of life and salvation to notice, and then involve us in active compassion for the victims. Once involved we find that while hate provides the necessary spark for ignition, it is the wrong fuel for the engines of judgment; only love is adequate to sustain these passions.

But we must not imagine that loving and praying for our enemies in love is a strategy that will turn them into good friends. Love is the last thing that our enemies want from us and often acts as a goad to redoubled fury. Love requires vulnerability, forgiveness, and response; the enemies want power and control and dominion. The enemies that Jesus loved and prayed for killed him.

———⊗⊗⊙———

Anselm of Canterbury

(1033–1109) Archbishop, scholar, and writer.

Almighty and tender Lord Jesus Christ,
Just as I have asked you to love my friends
So I ask the same for my enemies.
You alone, Lord, are mighty.
You alone are merciful.
Whatever you make me desire for my enemies,
Give it to them.
And give the same back to me.
If I ever ask for them anything
Which is outside your perfect rule of love,
Whether through weakness, ignorance or malice,
Good Lord, do not give it to them
And do not give it back to me.

You who are the true light, lighten their darkness.
You who are the whole truth, correct their errors.
You who are the incarnate word, give life to their souls.
Tender Lord Jesus.
Let me not be a stumbling block to them
Nor a rock of offense.
My sin is sufficient to me, without harming others.
I, a slave to sin,
Beg your mercy on my fellow slaves.
Let them be reconciled with you,
And through you reconciled to me.

―――∞∞∞―――

C. S. Lewis

The practical problem about charity (in one's prayer) is very hard work,
isn't it? When you pray for Hitler and Stalin, how do you actually teach
yourself to make the prayer real? The two things that help me are (a)
A continual grasp of the idea that one is only joining one's feeble little
voice to the perpetual intercession of Christ who died for these very
men. (b) A recollection, as firm as I can make it, of all one's own cruelty; which might have blossomed under different conditions into
something terrible. You and I are not at bottom so different from these
ghastly creatures.

BECAUSE WE NEED FORGIVENESS—CONFESSION

Ken Gire, "An Instructive Moment about Humility," *Instructive Moments
with the Savior*

Scripture (Luke 18:9–14)

To some who were confident of their own righteousness and looked
down on everybody else, Jesus told this parable:

"Two men went up to the temple to pray, one a Pharisee and the
other a tax collector. The Pharisee stood up and prayed about himself;
'God, I thank you that I am not like other men—robbers, evildoers, adulterers—or even like this tax collector. I fast twice a week and give a
tenth of all I get.'

"But the tax collector stood at a distance. He would not even look up to heaven, but beat his breast and said, 'God, have mercy on me, a sinner.'

"I tell you that this man, rather than the other, went home justified before God. For everyone who exalts himself will be humbled, and he who humbles himself will be exalted."

Meditation

Tax collectors are the dung on the sandals of the Jewish community. The stench is particularly repugnant to Jewish nostrils because the tax collectors are fellow Jews.

Licensed by the Roman government, they put tolls on roads, tariffs on imports, and taxes on anything they can get away with. Every time you turn around they have their hands in your pockets. And if you resist, they resort to force or threaten to turn you over to the Romans.

It's understandable, then, why the Jews detest any contact with them. Understandable, too, why it furrowed a few brows when Jesus reached into this mound of dung to mold one of his disciples.

Jesus went out and saw a tax collector by the name of Levi sitting at his tax booth. "Follow me," Jesus said to him, and Levi got up, left everything and followed him.

Then Levi held a great banquet for Jesus at his house, and a large crowd of tax collectors and others were eating with them. But the Pharisees and the teachers of the law who belonged to their sect complained to his disciples, "Why do you eat and drink with tax collectors and 'sinners'?"

Didn't Jesus know that you can't walk through a pigpen without getting manure on your sandals? He should have been scraping these people off his feet, but instead he sat next to them at their dinner table, eating and drinking and—God help him—enjoying their company. Why? What was it about the riff-raff that attracted him?

"It is not the healthy who need a doctor," Jesus explained, "but the sick. I have not come to call the righteous, but sinners to repentance."

That call was heard by one of the tax collectors sitting at Levi's table. It troubled him all night, and it kept troubling him all the next morning. By noon he couldn't take it anymore, and he responded to the call.

That hour happens to be an hour of prayer, one of the appointed times when every devout Jew goes to the temple to pray. A steady stream of petitioners flows through the western gate, past the outer courtyard of the Gentiles, and into the inner courtyard of the Israelites. The tax collector finds himself caught in a current of that stream and is swept along with them.

Once he is inside the temple grounds, his steps grow timid. This is unfamiliar ground to him, this holy ground. The noonday sun makes him even more self-conscious, and he retreats to the shadows of the marble columns bordering the courtyard.

In the safety of those shadows his eyes pool. His head falls forward, and remorse spills from his soul to spot the stone floor beneath him.

A Pharisee also comes this hour to pray. He comes every day at each of the four appointed hours of prayer. He stops and takes his position somewhere in the center of the courtyard, his usual spot.

As he prays, he looks neither upward in worship nor downward in remorse but sideways in comparison to the others who have gathered there. His eyes skim the scrawl of sins written so legibly across their faces. He is pleased with the comparison.

"God, I thank you that I am not like other men—robbers, evildoers, adulterers—or even like this tax collector. I fast twice a week and give a tenth of all I get."

The Pharisee's posture is erect. He is proud he has stood resolute against the temptations that have ruined lesser men. And he is proud he has stood as an example to others. He fasts twice a week, which is above the requirements of the Law. He gives a tenth of all his income, which is beyond the practices of his peers.

Taking inventory, the Pharisee is satisfied with the account of his life. The tax collector, however, is not.

"God, have mercy on me, a sinner."

He stands in the distance, sobbing. He is painfully aware of the sins levied against him, but he is too ashamed to list them. He knows the greed. He knows the deceit. He knows the ledger of injustices credited to his account.

That's why his eyes are downcast. That's why he beats his fists against his chest. And that's why he stands in a corner of the courtyard; his only companions, the shadows cast by columns of cool and indifferent stone.

But God sees the tax collector slumped in those shadows. His heart overflows with mercy for the man, and his eyes glisten with approval.

In that same city a couple of generations later when the esteemed teacher rabbi Eliezer ben Hyrcanus was on his deathbed, his disciples asked him to teach them the ways of life. His last words to them were: "When you pray, realize before whom you stand."

In that courtyard at that hour of prayer, both the Pharisee and the tax collector realized *where* they stood.

Only one of them realized before *whom*.

That is what humbled the tax collector. And that is what lifted him from being the dung on everybody's sandals to become the delight in the eyes of the Almighty.

Brennan Manning, *The Ragamuffin Gospel*

Lord Jesus, we are silly sheep who have dared to stand before you and try to bribe you with our preposterous portfolios. Suddenly we have come to our senses. We are sorry and ask you to forgive us. Give us the grace to admit we are ragamuffins, to embrace our brokenness, to celebrate your mercy when we are at our weakest, to rely on your mercy no matter what we may do. Dear Jesus, gift us to stop grandstanding and trying to get attention, to do the truth quietly without display, to let the dishonesties in our lives fade away, to accept our limitations, to cling to the gospel of grace, and to delight in your love. Amen.

Thomas Cranmer, *The Book of Common Prayer*

(1489–1556) English Reformer and Archbishop of Canterbury; chief compiler of The Book of Common Prayer. *Later condemned by Queen Mary for heresy and burned at the stake.*

Before Holy Communion

Almighty God, Father of our Lord Jesus Christ, Maker of all things, Judge of all men; We acknowledge and bewail our manifold sins and wickedness, Which we, from time to time, most grievously have committed, By thought, word, and deed, Against thy Divine Majesty, Provoking most justly thy wrath and indignation against us. We do earnestly repent, And are heartily sorry for these our misdoings; The remembrance of them is grievous unto us; The burden of them is intolerable. Have mercy upon us, Have mercy upon us, most merciful Father; For thy Son our Lord Jesus Christ's sake, Forgive us all that is past; And grant that we may every hereafter serve and please thee In newness of life, To the honour and glory of thy Name; Through Jesus Christ our Lord. Amen.

Anthony de Mello, *Taking Flight*

It is the custom among Catholics to confess their sins to a priest and receive absolution from him as a sign of God's forgiveness. Now all too often there is the danger that penitents will use this as a sort of guarantee, a certificate that will protect them from divine retribution, thereby placing more trust in the absolution of the priest than in the mercy of God.

This is what Perugin, an Italian painter of the Middle Ages, was tempted to do when he was dying. He decided that he would not go to confession if, in his fear, he was seeking to save his skin. That would be sacrilege and an insult to God.

His wife, who knew nothing of the man's inner disposition, once asked him if he did not fear to die unconfessed. Perugin replied, "Look at it this way, my dear: My profession is to paint and I have excelled as a painter. God's profession is to forgive and if he is as good at his profession, as I have been at mine, I see no reason to be afraid."

Augustine, *Confessions*

The house of my soul is too small for you to come to it. May it be enlarged by you. It is in ruins: restore it. In your eyes it has offensive features. I admit it, I know it; but who will clean it up? Or to whom shall I cry other than you? "Cleanse me from my secret faults, Lord, and spare your servant from sins to which I am tempted by others" (Ps. 31:5).

Edward Rowland Sill, *The Fool's Prayer*

(1841–1887) Poet and essayist of indomitable spirit who was orphaned young and suffered poor health.

The royal feast was done; the King
    Sought some new sport to banish care,
And to his jester cried: "Sir Fool,
    Kneel now, and make for us a prayer!"

The jester doffed his cap and bells,
    And stood the mocking court before;
They could not see the bitter smile
    Behind the painted grin he wore.

He bowed his head, and bent his knee
    Upon the monarch's silken stool;

His pleading voice arose: "O Lord,
  Be merciful to me, a fool!

"No pity, Lord, can change the heart
  From red with wrong to white as wool:
The rod must heal the sin: but, Lord,
  Be merciful to me, a fool! . . .

"These clumsy feet, still in the mire,
  Go crushing blossoms without end;
These hard, well-meaning hands we thrust,
  Among the heart-strings of a friend.

"The ill-timed truth we might have kept—
  Who knows how sharp it pierced and stung?
The word we had not sense to say—
  Who knows how grandly it had rung?

"Our faults no tenderness should ask,
  The chastening stripes must cleanse them all;
But for our blunders—oh! in shame
  Before the eyes of Heaven we fall.

"Earth bears no balsam for mistakes;
  Men crown the knave, and scourge the tool
That did his will; but Thou, O Lord!
  Be merciful to me, a fool!"

The room was hushed; in silence rose
  The King, and sought his garden cool,
And walked apart, and murmured low,
  "Be merciful to me, a fool!"

George MacDonald

(1824–1905) Poverty-stricken Scottish pastor, poet, and novelist whose works profoundly influenced C. S. Lewis.

If I felt my heart as hard as a stone; if I did not love God, or man, or woman, or little child, I would yet say to God in my heart, "O God, see how I trust Thee, because Thou art perfect, and not changeable like me. I do not love Thee. I love nobody. I am not even sorry for it. Thou seest how much I need Thee to come close to me, to put Thy arm round me, to say to me, *my child:* for the worse my state, the greater my need of my

Father who loves me. Come to me, and my day will dawn; my love will come back, and, oh! how I shall love Thee, my God! and know that my love is Thy love, my blessedness Thy being."

---∞∞∞---

Matthew 6:12, 14–15 *(The Living Bible)*

Forgive us our sins, just as we have forgiven those who have sinned against us. . . . Your heavenly Father will forgive you if you forgive those who sin against you; but if *you* refuse to forgive *them*, *he* will not forgive *you*.

---∞∞∞---

Robert Louis Stevenson, *Prayers*

(1850–1894) Scottish author best known for his work Treasure Island.

After all work and meals were finished, the "pu," or war conch, was sounded from the back veranda and the front, so that it might be heard by all. I don't think it ever occurred to us that there was any incongruity in the use of the war conch for the peaceful invitation to prayer. In response to its summons the white members of the family took their usual places in one end of the large hall, while the Samoans—men, women, and children—trooped in through all the open doors, some carrying lanterns if the evening were dark, all moving quietly and dropping with Samoan decorum in a wide semicircle on the floor beneath a great lamp that hung from the ceiling. The service began by my son reading a chapter from the Samoan Bible. . . .

On [one] occasion the chief himself brought the service to a sudden check. He had just learned of the treacherous conduct of one in whom he had every reason to trust. That evening the prayer seemed unusually short and formal. As the singing stopped he arose abruptly and left the room. I hastened after him, fearing some sudden illness. "What is it?" I asked. "It is this," was the reply; I am not yet fit to say, "Forgive us our trespasses as we forgive those who trespass against us."

---∞∞∞---

Psalm 32:1–5 (NASB)

A psalm of David:

> How blessed is he whose transgression is forgiven,
>> Whose sin is covered!
> How blessed is the man to whom the Lord does not impute iniquity,

And in whose spirit there is no deceit!
When I kept silent about my sin, my body wasted away
Through my groaning all day long.
For day and night Thy hand was heavy upon me;
My vitality was drained away as with the fever heat of summer.
I acknowledged my sin to Thee,
And my iniquity I did not hide;
I said, "I will confess my transgressions to the Lord";
And Thou didst forgive the guilt of my sin.

Psalm 51:1–17 (NIV)

A psalm of David that voices his confession after the prophet Nathan confronted him concerning his adulterous relationship with Bathsheba:

Have mercy on me, O God,
according to your unfailing love;
according to your great compassion
blot out my transgressions.
Wash away all my iniquity
and cleanse me from my sin.

For I know my transgressions,
and my sin is always before me.
Against you, you only, have I sinned
and done what is evil in your sight,
so that you are proved right when you speak
and justified when you judge.
Surely I was sinful at birth,
sinful from the time my mother conceived me.
Surely you desire truth in the inner parts;
you teach me wisdom in the inmost place.

Cleanse me with hyssop, and I will be clean;
wash me, and I will be whiter than snow.
Let me hear joy and gladness;
let the bones you have crushed rejoice.
Hide your face from my sins
and blot out all my iniquity.

Create in me a pure heart, O God,
and renew a steadfast spirit within me.
Do not cast me from your presence

or take your Holy Spirit from me.
Restore to me the joy of your salvation
    and grant me a willing spirit, to sustain me.

Then I will teach transgressors your ways,
    and sinners will turn back to you.
Save me from bloodguilt, O God,
    the God who saves me,
    and my tongue will sing of your righteousness.
O Lord, open my lips,
    and my mouth will declare your praise.
You do not delight in sacrifice, or I would bring it;
    you do not take pleasure in burnt offerings.
The sacrifices of God are a broken spirit;
    a broken and contrite heart,
    O God, you will not despise.

Ken Gire, *Intimate Moments with the Savior*

Prayer for forgiveness upon reflecting on the woman caught in adultery in John 8.

Dear Lord Jesus,

I confess with shame that there are times I have stood in the midst, condemned. And there are times I have stood in the crowd, condemning.

There are times my heart has been filled with adultery. And there are times my hands have been filled with stones.

Forgive me for a heart that is so prone to wander, so quick to forget my vows to you. Forgive me, too, for my eagerness in bringing you the sins of others. And my reluctance in bringing you my own. Forgive me for the times I have stood smugly Pharisaic and measured out judgment to others. Others I am not qualified to judge. Others, who you, though qualified, refuse to.

Help me to be more like you, Jesus—full of grace and truth. Help me to live not by Law but by grace, by the spirit of compassion you showed to that woman so many mornings ago.

Give me, I pray, the pierced conscience of the older ones in regard to the stumblings of others so my hands may be first to drop their stones, and my feet, first to leave the circle of the self-righteous.

Thank you for those sweet words of forgiveness; "Neither do I condemn you." Words that flow so freely from your lips. Words that I have heard so often when I have stumbled. And in the strength of those unmerited words, help me to go my way and sin no more. . . .

C. S. Lewis, *Letters to Malcolm*

I really must digress to tell you a bit of good news. Last week, while at prayer, I suddenly discovered—or felt as if I did—that I had really forgiven someone I have been trying to forgive for over thirty years. Trying, and praying that I might. When the thing actually happened—sudden as the longed-for cessation of one's neighbour's radio—my feeling was "But it's so easy. Why didn't you do it ages ago?" So many things are done easily the moment you can do them at all. But till then, sheerly impossible, like learning to swim. There are months during which no efforts will keep you up; then comes the day and hour and minute after which, and ever after, it becomes almost impossible to sink. . . .

The important thing is that a discord has been resolved, and it is certainly the great Resolver who has done it. Finally, and perhaps best of all, I believed anew what is taught us in the parable of the Unjust Judge. No evil habit is so ingrained nor so long prayed against (as it seemed) in vain, that it cannot, even in dry old age, be whisked away.

Matthew 18: 21–35 (NIV)

Then Peter came to Jesus and asked, "Lord, how many times shall I forgive my brother when he sins against me? Up to seven times?"

Jesus answered, "I tell you, not seven times, but seventy-seven times.

"Therefore, the kingdom of heaven is like a king who wanted to settle accounts with his servants. As he began the settlement, a man who owed him ten thousand talents was brought to him. Since he was not able to pay, the master ordered that he and his wife and his children and all that he had be sold to repay the debt.

"The servant fell on his knees before him. 'Be patient with me,' he begged, 'and I will pay back everything.' The servant's master took pity on him, canceled the debt and let him go.

"But when that servant went out, he found one of his fellow servants who owed him a hundred denarii. He grabbed him and began to choke him. 'Pay back what you owe me!' he demanded.

"His fellow servant fell to his knees and begged him, 'Be patient with me, and I will pay you back.'

"But he refused. Instead, he went off and had the man thrown into prison until he could pay the debt. When the other servants saw what had happened, they were greatly distressed and went and told their master everything that had happened.

"Then the master called the servant in. 'You wicked servant,' he said, 'I canceled all that debt of yours because you begged me to. Shouldn't you have had mercy on your fellow servant just as I had on you?' In anger his master turned him over to the jailers to be tortured, until he should pay back all he owed.

"This is how my heavenly Father will treat each of you unless you forgive your brother from your heart."

C. S. Lewis, *Letters to Malcolm*

To forgive for the moment is not difficult. But to go on forgiving, to forgive the same offense again everytime it recurs to the memory—there's the real tussle.

A Prayer of Forgiveness

During World War II, ninety-two thousand women and children died at the death camp Ravensbruck. Most of them were Jews. This prayer was found scrawled on a scrap of paper near a dead child.

Lord, remember not only the men and women of good will but also those of ill will. But do not only remember the suffering they have inflicted on us; remember the fruits we have brought, thanks to this suffering—our comradeship, our loyalty, our humility, the courage, the generosity, the greatness of heart which has grown out of all this, and when they come to judgment, let all the fruits we have borne be their forgiveness.

BECAUSE WE ARE GRATEFUL—THANKSGIVING

Don Postema, *Space for God*

To be grateful is to recognize the Love of God in everything He has given us—and He has given us everything. Every breath we draw is a gift of His Love, every moment of existence is a grace, for it brings with it immense graces from Him.

The realization may go deeper during a time of worship when you become aware that God's great gift of Jesus Christ was given not only for everyone, but for *you*. The covenant promises are not just for the child being baptized but also for you. *You* belong. God has made a space for you. Whether you live or die, you belong to the Lord. A joyous surge stirs in you and you want to bow in humble gratitude.

Gratitude is the appropriate response to belonging. Gratitude is certainly central to biblical Christian thought. . . .

People as diverse as Calvin and Merton agree.

God is justly honoured when he is acknowledged to be Author of all blessings; it thence follows that they all be received from his hand, as to be attended with unceasing thanksgiving; and that there is no other proper method of using the benefits which flow to us from his goodness, but by continual acknowledgement of his praise and unceasing expressions of our gratitude.

Thankfulness is "the chief exercise of godliness" in which we ought to engage during the whole of our life.

Gratitude is the heart . . . of the Christian life.

A thankful life is a response to seeing life as a gift from God and realizing that our lives belong to God. God is the Giver; we are thanksgivers.

But to recognize the gifts and the Giver we need to be alert and awake; to have our eyes, ears, minds, and hearts open to what is going on around us. We need to savor each moment as though it were a bowl of homemade soup prepared by someone who loves us very much.

Helen Steiner Rice

Thank You, God, for little things
    that often come our way—
The things we take for granted
    but don't mention when we pray—
The unexpected courtesy,
    the thoughtful, kindly deed—
A hand reached out to help us
    in the time of sudden need—
Oh make us more aware, dear God,
    of little daily graces

That come to us with "sweet surprise"
from never-dreamed-of places.

Gotthold Lessing

(1729–1781) German writer and dramatist.

A single grateful thought toward heaven is the most complete prayer.

Psalm 100 (NIV)

A psalm. For giving thanks.

Shout for Joy to the Lord, all the earth.
Worship the Lord with gladness;
come before him with joyful songs.
Know that the Lord is God.
It is he who made us, and we are his;
we are his people, the sheep of his pasture.
Enter his gates with thanksgiving
and his courts with praise;
give thanks to him and praise his name.
For the Lord is good and his love endures forever;
his faithfulness continues through all generations.

John Oxenham, "A Little Te Deum of the Commonplace"

(1852–1941) John Oxenham was the pen name of William Dunkerley, who was the son of a Manchester merchant. In 1913 he published at his own expense a book of poetry titled Bees in Amber. By the time he died in 1941, he had written forty novels.

For all the first sweet flushings of the spring;
The greening earth, the tender heavenly blue;
The rich brown furrows gaping for the seed;
For all thy grace in bursting bud and leaf . . .
For hedgerows sweet and hawthorn and wild rose;
For meadows spread with gold and gemmed with stars,
For every tint of tiniest flower,
For every daisy smiling to the sun;
For every bird that builds in joyous hope,
For every lamb that frisks beside its dam,
For every leaf that rustles in the wind,

For spring poplar, and for spreading oak,
For queenly birch, and lofty swaying elm;
For the great cedar's benedictory grace,
For earth's ten thousand fragrant incenses,
Sweet altar-gifts from leaf and fruit and flower . . .
For ripening summer and the harvesting;
For all the rich autumnal glories spread—
The flaming pageant of the ripening woods,
The fiery gorse, the heather-purpled hills,
The rustling leaves that fly before the wind
and lie below the hedgerows whispering;
For meadows silver-white with hoary dew;
For sheer delight of tasting once again
That first crisp breath, of winter in the air;
The pictured pane; the new white world without;
The sparkling hedgerows witchery of lace,
The soft white flakes that fold the sleeping earth;
The cold without, the cheerier warmth within . . .
For all the glowing heart of Christmas-tide,
We thank thee, Lord!

Corrie ten Boom, *The Hiding Place*

(1892–1983) Imprisoned by the Nazis for sheltering Jews. Corrie survived Ravensbruck con-centration camp and her life and ministry became the embodiment of Christ's forgiveness.

The move to permanent quarters came the second week in October. We were marched, ten abreast, along a wide cinder avenue and then into a narrower street of barracks. Several times the column halted while numbers were read out—names were never used at Ravens-bruck. At last Betsie's and mine were called: "Prisoner 66729, Prisoner 66730." We stepped out of line with a dozen or so others and stared at the long gray front of Barracks 28. . . . A door in the center let us into a large room where two hundred or more women bent over knitting needles. On tables between them were piles of woolen socks in army gray.

On either side doors opened into two still larger rooms—by far the largest dormitories we had yet seen. Betsie and I followed a prisoner-guide through the door at the right. Because of the broken windows the vast room was in semi-twilight. Our noses told us, first, that the place was filthy: somewhere plumbing had backed up, the bedding was soiled and rancid. Then as our eyes adjusted to the gloom we saw that there were no individual beds at all, but great square piers stacked three high, and wedged side by side and end to end with only an occasional narrow aisle slicing through.

We followed our guide single file—the aisle was not wide enough for two—fighting back the claustrophobia of these platforms rising everywhere above us. The tremendous room was nearly empty of people; they must have been out on various work crews. At last she pointed to a second tier in the center of a large block. To reach it we had to stand on the bottom level, haul ourselves up, and then crawl across three other straw-covered platforms to reach the one that we would share with—how many? The deck above us was too close to let us sit up. We lay back, struggling against the nausea that swept over us from the reeking straw. We could hear the women who had arrived with us finding their places.

Suddenly I sat up, striking my head on the cross-slats above. Something had pinched my leg.

"Fleas!" I cried. "Betsie, the place is swarming with them!"

We scrambled across the intervening platforms, heads low to avoid another bump, dropped down to the aisle, and edged our way to a patch of light.

"Here! And here another one!" I wailed. "Betsie, how can we live in such a place!"

"Show us. Show us how." It was said so matter of factly it took me a second to realize she was praying. More and more the distinction between prayer and the rest of life seemed to be vanishing for Betsie.

"Corrie!" she said excitedly. "He's given us the answer! Before we asked, as He always does! In the Bible this morning. Where was it? Read that part again!"

I glanced down the long dim aisle to make sure no guard was in sight, then drew the Bible from its pouch. "It was in First Thessalonians," I said. We were on our third complete reading of the New Testament since leaving Scheveningen. In the feeble light I turned the pages. "Here it is: 'Comfort the frightened, help the weak, be patient with everyone. See that none of you repays evil for evil, but always seek to do good to one another and to all. . . .'" It seemed written expressly to Ravensbruck.

"Go on," said Betsie. "That wasn't all."

"Oh yes: '. . . to one another and to all. Rejoice always, pray constantly, give thanks in all circumstances; for this is the will of God in Christ Jesus—'"

"That's it, Corrie! That's His answer. 'Give thanks in all circum-stances!' That's what we can do. We can start right now to thank God for every single thing about this new barracks!"

I stared at her, then around me at the dark, foul-aired room.

"Such as?" I said.

"Such as being assigned here together."

I bit my lip. "Oh yes, Lord Jesus!"

"Such as what you're holding in your hands."

I looked down at the Bible. "Yes! Thank You, dear Lord, that there was no inspection when we entered here! Thank You for all the women, here in this room, who will meet You in these pages."

"Yes," said Betsie. "Thank You for the very crowding here. Since we're packed so close, that many more will hear!" She looked at me expec-tantly. "Corrie!" she prodded.

"Oh, all right. Thank You for the jammed, crammed, stuffed, packed, suffocating crowds."

"Thank You," Betsie went on serenely, "for the fleas and for—"

The fleas! This was too much. "Betsie, there's no way even God can make me grateful for a flea."

"'Give thanks in *all* circumstances,'" she quoted. "It doesn't say, 'in pleasant circumstances.' Fleas are part of this place where God has put us."

And so we stood between piers of bunks and gave thanks for fleas. But this time I was sure Betsie was wrong. . . .

One evening I got back to the barracks late from a wood-gathering foray outside the walls. A light snow lay on the ground and it was hard to find the sticks and twigs with which a small stove was kept going in each room. Betsie was waiting for me, as always, so that we could wait through the food line together. Her eyes were twinkling.

"You're looking extraordinarily pleased with yourself," I told her.

"You know we've never understood why we had so much freedom in the big room," she said. "Well—I've found out."

That afternoon, she said, there'd been confusion in her knitting group about sock sizes and they'd asked the supervisor to come and settle it.

"But she wouldn't. She wouldn't step through the door and neither would the guards. And you know why?"

Betsie could not keep the triumph from her voice: "Because of the fleas! That's what she said, 'That place is crawling with fleas!'"

My mind rushed back to our first hour in this place. I remembered Betsie's bowed head, remembered her thanks to God for creatures I could see no use for.

Thomas Aquinas

(ca. 1225–1274) Italian philosopher and theologian who became the most influential monk of the medieval period. Nevertheless, Aquinas came to view his prodigious theological works as valueless when compared to a direct encounter with God.

Give us, O Lord,
thankful hearts which never forget
Your goodness to us.
Give us, O Lord, grateful
hearts, which do not waste
time complaining.

Wilfred A. Peterson, "The Art of Thanksgiving"

The art of thanksgiving is thanksliving. It is gratitude in action. It is applying Albert Schweitzer's philosophy: "In gratitude for your own good fortune you must render in return some sacrifice of your life for other life."

It is thanking God for the gift of life by living it triumphantly.

It is thanking God for your talents and abilities by accepting them as obligations to be invested for the common good.

It is thanking God for all that men and women have done for you by doing things for others.

It is thanking God for opportunities by accepting them as a challenge to achievement.

It is thanking God for happiness by striving to make others happy.

It is thanking God for beauty by helping to make the world more beautiful.

It is thanking God for inspiration by trying to be an inspiration to others.

It is thanking God for health and strength by the care and reverence you show your body.

It is thanking God for the creative ideas that enrich life by adding your own creative contributions to human progress.

It is thanking God for each new day by living it to the fullest.

It is thanking God by giving hands, arms, legs, and voice to your thankful spirit.

It is adding to your prayers of thanksgiving, acts of thanksliving.

BECAUSE OF WHO GOD IS — WORSHIP

Evelyn Underhill, *The Love of God*

(1875–1941) Scholar of mysticism and devotional writer for the Anglican Church.

If the first term of the spiritual life is recognition in some way or other of the splendour and reality of God, the first mood of prayer—the ground from which all the rest must grow—is certainly worship, awe, adoration; delight in that holy reality for its own sake. . . . Religion, as von Hügel loved to say, *is* adoration; man's humble acknowledgment of the Transcendent, the Fact of God—the awestruck realism of the seraphs in Isaiah's vision—the meek and loving sense of mystery which enlarges the soul's horizon and puts us in our own place. . . .

Adoration begins to purify us from egotism straight away. It may not always be easy—but it is realism; the atmosphere within which alone the spiritual life can be lived. . . .

The reason the saints are so winning and persuasive, and so easily bring us into the presence of God, is that their lives are steeped in this loving and selfless adoration.

Don Postema, *Space for God*

Being in the dazzling presence of God is a wondrous experience; realizing God's majestic, just, and compassionate action in the world and in our lives urges us to let all thanks break loose!

We come so often to God, if we come at all, as beggars. We ask and beg: give me; bless me; help me; guide me; grant me. And that's one necessary level of our existence.

But in thanksgiving and adoration we come to God not to ask but to give! We come not whimpering but shouting praise; not in guilt but in gratitude. We feel not distant from God but close to God. We are like a traveler who is home again at last, the prodigal at a banquet. Those moments may be seldom, but when they happen we know that we were created *for God.*

In a rare moment of happiness,

> when the past does not plague you,
>
> when the present is serene,
>
> when the future holds no threats,
>
> when life is not conditioned by all kinds of ifs,
>
> when you simply say "Thanks,"
>
> it all comes together for you. Your whole life is focused.

You leave all that held you bound—money and misery, sin and sickness—leave it all behind in doxology. There are only joy and cheers!

You experience that sometimes when you attend sporting events or concerts. All the people, thousands of them with worries about marriages and mortgages, sex and sin, God and gold, are all of one mind, all wrapped up. They become admirers, praise-shouters. That's something of a parable of what the goal of a thankful life is: with one voice people cheering and applauding God. . . .

For a moment, for eternity, we forget tears and struggles and all is joy! We know we are created for God!

We know that with certainty in those precious moments when we sing the Doxology with so much inner strength and conviction that we become the choir directors of the universe.

Thomas Ken

(1637–1711) Bishop of Bath and Wells.

PRAISE HYMN

Praise God, from whom all blessings flow,
Praise Him, all creatures here below;
Praise Him above, ye heavenly host,
Praise Father, Son and Holy Ghost.

Abraham Heschel, *God In Search of Man*

(1907–1972) Jewish scholar, philosopher, and author.

Awe, unlike fear, does not make us shrink from the awe-inspiring object, but, on the contrary, draws us near to it.

St. Francis of Assisi

As told by Johannes Jörgensen

Francis [became] disquieted, troubled, and bowed down with thoughts of the future. . . .

Francis understood that there was nothing for him but to suffer to the end, and that his days of good fortune were gone for ever. And he resigned himself to God's will.

In the night which followed, Francis could not sleep. In vain did he turn on his hard bed—in vain did he listen for the call of the Friars of La Verna, announcing the hour for saying matins. "All will be as it should be in heaven," Francis said to comfort himself; "there, at least, there is eternal peace and happiness!" And with these thoughts he fell asleep.

Then it seemed to him that an angel stood by his bed with violin and bow in hand. "Francis," said the shining denizen of heaven, "I will play for thee as we play before the throne of God in heaven." And the angel placed the violin to his chin and drew the bow across the strings a single time only. Then Brother Francis was filled with so great a joy, and his soul was filled with such living sweetness, that it was as if he had a body no longer, and knew of no secret sorrow. "And if the angel had drawn the bow down across the strings again," thus Francis told his Brothers the next morning—"then would my soul have left my body from uncontrollable happiness."

———∞∞———

Teresa of Ávila

(1515–1582) Spanish nun whose mental and physical sufferings gave way to a deep spiritual life and the founding of a new Carmelite order with John of the Cross.

May you be blessed forever, Lord, for not abandoning me when I abandoned you.

May you be blessed forever, Lord, for offering your hand of love in my darkest, most lonely moment.

May you be blessed forever, Lord, for putting up with such a stubborn soul as mine.

May you be blessed forever, Lord, for loving me more than I love myself.

May you be blessed forever, Lord, for continuing to pour out your blessings upon me, even though I respond so poorly.

May you be blessed forever, Lord, for drawing out the goodness in all people, even including me.

May you be blessed forever, Lord, for repaying our sin with your love.

May you be blessed forever, Lord, for being constant and unchanging, amidst all the changes of the world.

May you be blessed forever, Lord, for your countless blessings on me and on all your creatures.

Richard Foster, *Prayer*

To the extent we can draw a line of demarcation, praise lies on a higher plane than thanksgiving. In his classic work entitled simply *Prayer,* Ole Hallesby observes, "When I give thanks, my thoughts still circle about myself to some extent. But in praise my soul ascends to self-forgetting adoration, seeing and praising only the majesty and power of God, His grace and redemption."

The Bible is certainly packed with praise. The ancient law code startles us with its trenchant words: "He is your praise; he is your God" (Deut. 10:21). The Psalms reverberate with the tumult of praise: "Praise the Lord! Praise the Lord, O my soul! I will praise the Lord as long as I live; I will sing praises to my God all my life long" (Ps. 146:1–2); "I will bless the Lord at all times; his praise shall continually be in my mouth" (Ps. 34:1); "You who fear the Lord, praise him!" (Ps. 22:23); "He put a new song in my mouth, a song of praise to our God" (Ps. 40:3).

The writer to the Hebrews urges us to "continually offer a sacrifice of praise to God, that is, the fruit of lips that confess his name" (Heb. 13:15). And the writer of Revelation assures us that praise is the serious business of heaven: "I heard the voice of many angels surrounding the throne and the living creatures and the elders; they numbered myriads of myriads and thousands of thousands, singing with full voice 'Worthy is the Lamb that was slaughtered to receive power and wealth and wisdom and might and honor and glory and blessing!'" (Rev. 5:11–12).

Blessing is jubilant praise, praise raised to its highest point. "Bless the Lord, O my soul," enjoins the Psalmist, "and all that is within me, bless his holy name" (Ps. 103:1). Luke closes his Gospel with the enthralling words of blessing "and they were continually in the temple blessing God" (Luke 24:53). When we are brought into experiences of blessing God, the soul is enraptured in praise.

Who can question the significance of these twin activities of heart and mind? Together they help us exegete the meaning of adoration. May our hearts be stirred. May our minds be rejuvenated. May we ardently join with that ancient processional up the holy hill of Zion: "Enter his gates with thanksgiving, and his courts with praise. Give thanks to him, bless his name" (Ps. 100:4).

John Baillie, *A Diary of Private Prayer*

(1886–1960) Scottish theologian, writer, and apologist.

Eternal Father of my soul, let my first thought today be of Thee, let my first impulse be to worship Thee, let my first speech be Thy name, let my first action be to kneel before Thee in prayer.

For Thy perfect wisdom and perfect goodness:
For the love wherewith Thou lovest mankind:
For the love wherewith Thou lovest me:
For the great and mysterious opportunity of my life:
For the indwelling of Thy Spirit in my heart:
For the sevenfold gifts of Thy Spirit:
   I praise and worship Thee, O Lord.

Yet let me not, when this morning prayer is said, think my worship ended and spend the day in forgetfulness of Thee. Rather from these moments of quietness let light go forth, and joy, and power, that will remain with me through all the hours of the day. . . .

C. S. Lewis, *Letters to Malcolm*

William Law remarks that people are merely "amusing themselves" by asking for the patience which a famine or a persecution would call for if, in the meantime, the weather and every other inconvenience sets them grumbling. One must learn to walk before one can run. So here. We—or at least I—shall not be able to adore God on the highest occasions if we have learned no habit of doing so on the lowest. At best, our faith and reason will tell us that He is adorable, but we shall not have *found* Him so, not have "tasted and seen." Any patch of sunlight in a wood will show you something about the sun which you could never get from reading books on astronomy. These pure and spontaneous pleasures are "patches of Godlight" in the woods of our experience.

Archbishop William Temple

(1881–1944) Writer, theologian, and philosopher whose efforts focused primarily on the outworking of the Christian faith in social issues.

Worship is the submission of all our nature to God. It is the quickening of conscience by his holiness; the nourishment of mind with his truth; the purifying of the imagination by his beauty; the opening of the heart to his love; the surrender of will to his purpose—and all of this gathered up in adoration, the most selfless emotion of which our nature is capable and therefore the chief remedy of that self-centeredness which is our original sin and the source of all actual sin.

Isaiah 6:1–4 (NIV)

As told by the prophet Isaiah

In the year that King Uzziah died, I saw the Lord seated on a throne, high and exalted, and the train of his robe filled the temple. Above him were seraphs, each with six wings: With two wings they covered their faces, with two they covered their feet, and with two they were flying. And they were calling to one another:

"Holy, holy, holy is the Lord Almighty;
the whole earth is full of his glory."

At the sound of their voices the doorposts and thresholds shook and the temple was filled with smoke.

Teresa of Ávila

O Lord my God! I cannot speak to you at present without both tears of sadness and also overwhelming joy. You desire constantly to be present within me; and for that my soul is filled with gladness. Yet despite your wonderful love, I still so often do things which offend and upset you. Is it possible, Lord, for a soul which has received such blessings as you have bestowed on my soul, still to remain so hard and stubborn? Yes, I know it is possible, because I so frequently rebuff your advances and reject your blessings. Perhaps I am the only person alive who treats you so badly. I hope so, because I cannot bear the thought of others offending you in the same measure.

Teach me, Lord, to sing of your mercies. Turn my soul into a garden, where the flowers dance in the gentle breeze, praising you with their beauty. Let my soul be filled with beautiful virtues; let me be inspired by your Holy Spirit; let me praise you always.

———∞∞∞———

Revelation 4:1–11; 5:11–14 (NIV)

As told by the Apostle John

After this I looked, and there before me was a door standing open in heaven. And the voice I had first heard speaking to me like a trumpet said, "Come up here, and I will show you what must take place after this." At once I was in the Spirit, and there before me was a throne in heaven with someone sitting on it. And the one who sat there had the appearance of jasper and carnelian. A rainbow, resembling an emerald, encircled the throne. Surrounding the throne were twenty-four other thrones, and seated on them were twenty-four elders. They were dressed in white and had crowns of gold on their heads. From the throne came flashes of lightning, rumblings and peals of thunder. Before the throne, seven lamps were blazing. These are the seven spirits of God. Also before the throne there was what looked like a sea of glass, clear as crystal.

In the center, around the throne, were four living creatures, and they were covered with eyes, in front and in back. The first living creature was like a lion, the second was like an ox, the third had a face like a man, the fourth was like a flying eagle. Each of the four living creatures had six wings and was covered with eyes all around, even under his wings. Day and night they never stop saying:

"Holy, holy, holy
is the Lord God Almighty,
who was, and is, and is to come."

Whenever the living creatures give glory, honor and thanks to him who sits on the throne and who lives for ever and ever, the twenty-four elders fall down before him who sits on the throne, and worship him who lives for ever and ever. They lay their crowns before the throne and say:

"You are worthy, our Lord and God,
to receive glory and honor and power,
for you created all things,
and by your will they were created
and have their being.". . .

Then I looked and heard the voice of many angels, numbering thousands upon thousands, and ten thousand times ten thousand. They encircled the throne and the living creatures and the elders. In a loud voice they sang:

"Worthy is the Lamb, who was slain,
to receive power and wealth and wisdom and strength
and honor and glory and praise!"

Then I heard every creature in heaven and on earth and under the earth and on the sea, and all that is in them singing:

"To him who sits on the throne and to the Lamb
be praise and honor and glory and power,
for ever and ever!"

The four living creatures said, "Amen," and the elders fell down and worshiped.

Edith Schaeffer, *Common Sense Christian Living*

Appreciation can be expressed to God with spoken words in prayer, alone in one's "closet," or sitting on a stone in a field, or walking in the woods or on a city street. Appreciation can be written to God in your handwriting for His eyes alone, written in a private notebook or on the back of an envelope. Praise and thanksgiving can be in the form of a painting if that is a person's best medium of expression, or in song, or with a musical instrument. It doesn't always have to be verbal . . . nor heard by anyone else.

Prose, poetry, or musical instruments can be used by you alone to praise God, with only the sound of the rain adding anything to whatever sound you are making your communication. A dancer can dance with a heart full of adoration and appreciation being expressed directly to the Lord, as that person dances alone up and down a curving staircase, alone in the house, alone in a room, on the grass or field in the moonlight, with a string trio as the music comes from a record player . . . and no eyes watching except the Lord's.

Yussel's Prayer: A Yom Kippur Story

As re-told by Barbara Cohen

It was Yom Kippur, the Day of Atonement. All the people who lived in the village were on their way to the shul to pray. There they would remain for the entire day, fasting, beating their breasts, and asking God to forgive all their sins.

All the people, that is, except one. Yussel, the orphan boy who slept in Reb Meir's dairy barn, rose at dawn as usual. He didn't know much, for no one had ever taught him anything, but he knew that this was a special day.

He stood in the courtyard and waited for Reb Meir to come out of his great house. He didn't have to wait long. Reb Meir and his sons always left early for shul. They wore long black coats, lined with fur, and big fur hats.

Yussel tugged at Reb Meir's wide sleeve. "Excuse me, Reb Meir," he whispered.

From his great height, Reb Meir looked down at Yussel. "Yes?" he asked.

"Please, Reb Meir, may I go to shul today? May I go and pray like everyone else?"

"No," Reb Meir replied. His voice was not unkind, but it was very firm. "The cows must be taken to pasture today. The cows don't know it's Yom Kippur. You must do your job, as you do any other time."

"Besides," scoffed Reb Meir's eldest son, "what good would it do you to go to shul? You can't read. So how can you understand the prayer book? How can you pray?"

Reb Meir and his sons walked out through their wide gate. Yussel watched as they made their way down the street toward the shul. He watched until he could no longer see even a dot of black in the distance.

Then he returned to the barn. He called softly to the cows. They came when he called them, as they always did.

He picked up the little pipe he had made from a reed he had found growing by the river. Holding the pipe in his hand, he led the cows out to pasture. He didn't stop first at Reb Meir's kitchen to beg a piece of black bread from the cook, as he usually did. It was Yom Kippur, and if he couldn't pray, at least he could fast.

Reb Meir and his sons sat in the seats of honor, the seats by the eastern wall of the synagogue. Of all the people in the congregation, they were seated nearest their holy rabbi, who was known far and wide for his loving kindness and his deeds of charity. Some of the rabbi's followers even believed that he spoke directly to God, as had Abraham and Moses long ago.

Reb Meir's lips formed the words of the prayers. According to tradition, he beat his breast with his fist when he and everyone else in the room together confessed their sins. But his mind wasn't on the words he was saying, or the gestures he was making.

"If I can buy a thousand bushels of grain in Lublin next week," he was thinking as he said the prayers, "I can store it in my barns until deep winter sets in, and sell it then at a great profit. I wonder," his mind said as his fist struck his chest, "I wonder how much the farmers at the Lublin market will ask for their grain this year, and I wonder how much less I can give them than they ask."

Reb Meir's eldest son formed the words of the prayers too. He also beat his breast with his fist. But he wasn't thinking about the words of the Yom Kippur service either. He was thinking instead about asking his father to let him make a trip to Warsaw.

"It's so dull in this little town," he thought to himself. "In Warsaw there are fine shops and theaters and restaurants, and beautiful women everywhere. I think," his mind said as his fist struck his chest, "I think I'll go to Warsaw whether my father likes it or not!"

All day Reb Meir and his sons fasted and prayed. All day they prayed and fasted. The day seemed endless. There were many moments when instead of praying to God to forgive their sins they prayed for darkness to come.

At long last, through the window, they saw the sun sinking low in the west. Yom Kippur was almost over. Soon their holy rabbi would begin the final prayers. Then they could go home and break their day-long fast with herring and boiled potatoes. Their mouths watered. Already they could taste the black bread spread with yellow butter.

But, though the shadows deepened, though darkness grew nearer and nearer, the rabbi didn't begin the final prayers. He didn't begin the closing service. He didn't ask God to shut the gates of heaven to seal the congregation in the Book of Life.

Instead he chanted hymn after hymn and recited prayer after prayer, begging God to listen to the words of those gathered in the shul, to listen to the words of all those celebrating Yom Kippur everywhere.

Reb Meir began to get angry. What was the matter with the rabbi? Why didn't he end the service? It had gone on long enough. It was dark out. Then sun had long since sunk below the horizon. There were three stars in the sky. It was time to be done with Yom Kippur.

If the Rabbi didn't begin Ne'lah, the closing service, in two minutes, Reb Meir decided he and his sons were going to walk out of the shul anyway!

In the pasture, the day had been a long one too. The cows had grazed as usual, but Yussel had eaten nothing. He hadn't even gone down to the river to get a drink of water. He had sat in the sunshine, thinking. The evening drew near, and the shadows lengthened.

As the sun sank in the west, he picked up his reed pipe.

"O God," he cried, "I don't know any prayers. But I do know how to play the pipe. Since I can't give you any words, I give you this tune instead."

On his pipe, Yussel began playing a melody that he had made up himself.

While he played it, he gazed at the thick grass growing all around him, at the great sky above him, at the cows grazing peacefully before him, and he thought about the goodness of God.

His mind, his soul, his heart were all in the music he played for God as the sun set below the horizon and three stars appeared in the sky.

And at that moment, at that very moment, in the shul, the rabbi began to chant the Ne'lah prayers.

"Our Father, our King," he cried, his voice full of joy, "seal us in the Book of Life. Seal us there for a year of health and prosperity."

And then he picked up the shofar, the ram's horn, and blew a loud, clear blast that echoed in every corner of the room. Yom Kippur was over.

"Thank goodness," thought Reb Meir. "About time," thought his sons. But to each other, and to all the other members of the congregation, they murmured, "L'shana tova — a good year."

Reb Meir went forward to greet the rabbi. A crowd pressed around him, but they separated to make way for Reb Meir.

"L'shana tova, Reb Meir," said the rabbi.

"I have a question," Reb Meir said. He was the only one who dared to ask it, although the very same question was in the mind of every person in the shul.

"Why did you wait so long to begin Ne'lah? Why did you wait so long to bring Yom Kippur to an end?"

The rabbi looked straight into Reb Meir's eyes. "I had a vision," he said. "In my vision I saw that the gates of heaven were closed. Our prayers weren't reaching God. Our prayers weren't acceptable to Him.

"Why?" asked Reb Meir.

The rabbi shrugged. "I'm not sure," he said. "I think because they didn't come from the heart. And how could I end Yom Kippur when I felt that God wouldn't grant us forgiveness or mercy because He hadn't heard us ask for it?"

"But then you did," Reb Meir said. "Then you did end Yom Kippur."

The rabbi nodded. "I had another vision," he said. "I heard a melody, a simple melody played on a reed pipe. I saw the gates of heaven open up. All our prayers went in to God, because He had opened the gates to admit that melody."

"But why?" asked Reb Meir again. "Why just a tune on a reed pipe and not all the holy words we were saying?"

"Because," said the rabbi, "whoever sent that melody to God sent it with his whole heart. It was true prayer."

Head down, eyes thoughtful, Reb Meir left the shul, all his sons around him. On his way home, he met Yussel, coming back from the pasture with the cows. By the light of the moon that shone above them, Reb Meir saw the little reed pipe in Yussel's hand.

"L'shana tova, Yussel," said Reb Meir.

"L'shana tova, Reb Meir," Yussel replied. He could hardly believe that the great Reb Meir was wishing him a good year.

"Will you come into my house, Yussel?" Reb Meir asked. "Will you break the fast with me and my family?"

"Father!" exclaimed Reb Meir's eldest son. "He's so dirty and so ragged. How can you let him in the house?"

"Very easily," said Reb Meir. "Through the front door." He put his arm around Yussel's shoulders. Together they walked up the moonlit street, all of Reb Meir's sons and all of Yussel's cows trailing behind.

Reverend Canon Shuttleworth, *Self-Culture for Young People,* vol. X

Music . . . is the voice of the heart's aspiration toward God. It is the speech of the spirit, the language of the soul. What we cannot utter, but only dimly feel, that music seems to say for us. It is the voice of our un-shaped and unspoken prayers.

Duke Ellington

(1899–1974) Brilliant jazz composer, orchestra leader, and pianist.

Everyone prays in their own language, and there is no language that God does not understand.

Augustine

What are you, my God? What are you, but the Lord God himself? You are the highest, the most righteous and the most powerful being. You are the most merciful, and yet the most just. You are the most mysterious, and yet the most present. You are the most beautiful, and yet the strongest. You are stable, yet incomprehensible. You are unchanging, yet changing all things. You are never new and never old, yet you are constantly renewing all things. You are always working, yet always at rest. You create great riches on earth, yet you need nothing yourself. You support, nourish and protect all.

You love, and yet you are without passion. You are jealous, and yet have no fear. You recoil at our sin, and yet you do not grieve. You are angry, yet remain serene. You alter your plans in response to our actions, yet your law and purpose remain firm. You take as you find, yet never lose. You have no needs, yet you rejoice in all goodness. You have no envy, yet you require us to multiply the talents you have bestowed. You pay debts, yet owe nothing; you forgive debts, yet lose nothing.

What shall I say, O my God, my life, my holy joy? What can any man say when he speaks of you? Silence offers the greatest eloquence, yet woe to him who does not sing your praise.

Johann Freylinghausen

(1670–1739) His Spiritual Songbook *provided the popular music of the German Pietist movement, which urged people to enter a personal relationship with Jesus as their saviour. The words of his hymns are mostly directed to Jesus, and are charged with the passion of a lover for the beloved.*

Who is like you,
Jesus, sweet Jesus?

You are the light of those who are spiritually lost.
You are the life of those who are spiritually dead.
You are the liberation of those who are imprisoned by guilt.

You are the glory of those who hate themselves.
You are the guardian of those who are paralysed by fear.
You are the guide of those who are bewildered by falsehood.

You are the peace of those who are in turmoil.
You are the prince of those who yearn to be led.
You are the priest of those who seek the truth.

Psalm 148 (NASB)

Praise the Lord!
Praise the Lord from the heavens;
Praise Him in the heights!

Praise Him, all His angels;
Praise Him, all His hosts!
Praise Him, sun and moon;
Praise Him, all stars of light!
Praise Him, highest heavens,
And the waters that are above the heavens!
Let them praise the name of the LORD,
For He commanded and they were created.
He has also established them forever and ever;
He has made a decree which will not pass away.

Praise the Lord from the earth,
Sea monsters and all deeps;
Fire and hail, snow and clouds;
Stormy wind, fulfilling His word;
Mountains and all hills;
Fruit trees and all cedars;
Beasts and all cattle;
Creeping things and winged fowl;
Kings of the earth and all peoples;
Princes and all judges of the earth;
Both young men and virgins;
Old men and children.
Let them praise the name of the LORD,
For His name alone is exalted;
His glory is above earth and heaven.
And he has lifted up a horn for His people,
Praise for all His godly ones;
Even for the sons of Israel, a people near to Him.
Praise the LORD!

BECAUSE CHRIST IS LORD — CONSECRATION

Puritan Prayer

"SPIRITUS SANCTUS"

O Holy Spirit,
As the sun is full of light, the ocean full of water,
Heaven full of glory, so may my heart be full of Thee. . . .

Give me Thyself without measure,
    as an unimpaired fountain,
    as inexhaustible riches.
I bewail my coldness, poverty, emptiness,
    imperfect vision, languid service,
    prayerless prayers, praiseless praises.
Suffer me not to grieve or resist Thee.
Come as power,
    to expel every rebel lust, to reign supreme and keep me Thine;
Come as teacher,
    leading me into all truth, filling me with all understanding;
Come as love,
    that I may adore the Father, and love him as my all;
Come as joy,
    to dwell in me, move in me, animate me;
Come as light,
    illuminating the Scripture, molding me in its laws;
Come as sanctifier,
    body, soul and spirit wholly Thine;
Come as helper,
    with strength to bless and keep, directing my every step;
Come as beautifier,
    bringing order out of confusion, loveliness out of chaos;
Magnify to me Thy glory by being magnified in me,
    and make me redolent of Thy fragrance.

Martin Luther

(1483–1546) Theologian, teacher, writer who ignited the Reformation.

Ah, dearest Jesus, Holy Child,
Make thee a bed, soft, undefiled,
Within my heart, that it may be
A Quiet chamber kept for thee.

The Journals of Jim Elliot

(1927–1956) Missionary to Ecuador who was killed by the Auca Indians.

July 7 Psalms 104:4: "He makes his ministers a flame of fire." Am I ignitable? God deliver me from the dread asbestos of "other things."

Saturate me with the oil of the Spirit that I may be a *flame*. But flame is transient, often short-lived. Canst thou bear this, my soul, short life? In me there dwells the Spirit of the Great Short-Lived, whose zeal for God's house consumed Him, and He has promised baptism with the Spirit and with fire. "Make me Thy fuel, flame of God."

Celtic Prayer

The Celts inhabited the British Isles after the fall of the Roman Empire (ca. 450–700 A.D.). They had a rich artistic tradition particularly in sculpture and in the illumination of manuscripts.

Lord of my heart, give me vision to inspire me, that, working or resting, I may always think of you.

Lord of my heart, give me light to guide me, that, at home or abroad, I may always walk in your way.

Lord of my heart, give me wisdom to direct me, that, thinking or acting, I may always discern right from wrong.

Lord of my heart, give me courage to strengthen me, that, amongst friends or enemies, I may always proclaim your justice.

Lord of my heart, give me trust to console me, that, hungry or well-fed, I may always rely on your mercy.

Lord of my heart, save me from empty praise, that I may always boast of you.

Lord of my heart, save me from worldly wealth, that I may always look to the riches of heaven.

Lord of my heart, save me from military prowess, that I may always seek your protection.

Lord of my heart, save me from vain knowledge, that I may always study your word.

Lord of my heart, save me from unnatural pleasures, that I may always find joy in your wonderful creation.

Heart of my own heart, whatever may befall me, rule over my thoughts and feelings, my words and action.

Bonaventura

(1217–1274) Successor to St. Francis of Assisi as the leader of the Franciscans. Bonaventura gave theological form to Francis's teachings while continuing the founder's passion for Christ.

Crucifixion

O Lord, holy Father, show us what kind of man it is who is hanging for our sakes on the cross, whose suffering causes the rocks themselves to crack and crumble with compassion, whose death brings the dead back to life.

Let my heart crack and crumble at the sight of him. Let my soul break apart with compassion for his suffering. Let it be shattered with grief at my sins for which he dies. And finally let it be softened with devoted love for him.

Burial

O my God, Jesus, I am in every way unworthy of you. Yet, like Joseph of Arimathea, I want to offer a space for you. He offered his own tomb; I offer my heart.

Enter the darkness of my heart, as your body entered the darkness of Joseph's tomb. And make me worthy to receive you, driving out all sin that I may be filled with your spiritual light.

Howard Thurman

My ego is like a fortress.
I have built its walls stone by stone
To hold out the invasion of the love of God.

But I have stayed here long enough. There is light
Over the barriers. O my God—
The darkness of my house forgive
And overtake my soul.
I relax the barriers.
I abandon all that I think I am,
All that I hope to be,
All that I believe I possess.
I let go of the past,
I withdraw my grasping hand from the future,
And in the great silence of this moment,
I alertly rest my soul.

As the sea gull lays in the wind current,
So I lay myself into the spirit of God.
My dearest human relationships,
My most precious dreams,
I surrender to His care
All that I have called my own
I give back. All my favorite things
Which I would withhold in my storehouse
From his fearful tyranny,
I let go.
I give myself
Unto Thee, O my God. Amen.

St. Ignatius of Loyola

(1491–1556) Founder of the Society of Jesus (Jesuits) and author of Spiritual Exercises.

Dear Lord,
teach me to be generous:
teach me to serve you as you deserve;
to give and not to count the cost;
to fight and not to heed the wounds;
to toil and not to seek for rest;
to labor and not to ask for reward,
    save that of knowing that I am doing your will.

Augustine

Breathe in me, Holy Spirit, that all my thoughts may be holy.
Act in me, Holy Spirit, that my work, too, may be holy.
Draw my heart, Holy Spirit, that I may love only what is holy.
Strengthen me, Holy Spirit, to defend all that is holy.
Guard me, Holy Spirit, that I may always be holy.

Mother Teresa

The following is the daily prayer of [consecration for] the workers at the
Calcutta Orphanage. In 1948, this Yugoslavian teacher felt called out of
the convent to work among the poorest of Calcutta's poor. She started
a school for the impoverished children of the streets, and after the first

year, she was joined in the effort by some of her former students. These were the first Missionaries of Charity. In 1952, she picked up a dying woman in the street, half eaten by rats and insects, and cared for her, taking a former Hindu temple and converting it into a home for the dying.

Dearest Lord, may I see you today and every day in the person of your sick, and, whilst nursing them, minister unto you.

Though you hide yourself behind the unattractive disguise of the irritable, the exacting, the unreasonable, may I still recognize you, and say: "Jesus, my patient, how sweet it is to serve you."

Lord, give me this seeing faith, then my work will never be monotonous. I will ever find joy in humouring the fancies and gratifying the wishes of all poor sufferers.

O beloved sick, how doubly dear you are to me, when you personify Christ; and what a privilege is mine to be allowed to tend you.

Sweetest Lord, make me appreciative of the dignity of my high vocation, and its many responsibilities. Never permit me to disgrace it by giving way to coldness, unkindness, or impatience.

And O God, while you are Jesus my patient, deign also to be to me a patient Jesus, bearing with my faults, looking only to my intention, which is to love and serve you in the person of each one of your sick.

Lord, increase my faith, bless my efforts and work, now and forevermore. Amen.

BECAUSE WE DESIRE HIM — ABOVE ALL ELSE

Psalm 42:1–2a (NIV)

As the deer pants for streams of water,
so my soul pants for you, O God.
My soul thirsts for God, for the living God.

James S. Stewart

His prayer life was never at the mercy of moods. Changes of feeling Jesus certainly knew. He was no passionless Stoic. He knew joy and sorrow, smiles and tears, ecstasy and weariness. But through it all, His heart turned to prayer, like the compass to the north. Prayer meant communing with the One He loved best in heaven and earth. Jesus loved God His Father so utterly and so passionately that He could not bear to be away from Him, but used every opportunity the days and nights brought Him to go and speak to the God of His love again. This means that those failures in our own prayer life which we trace back to lack of mood are really, according to Jesus, a symptom of something deeper; they are a symptom of a breakdown of affection. Christ bids us go and give God our love.

Oswald Chambers, *My Utmost for His Highest*

Think of the last thing you prayed about—were you devoted to your desire or to God? Determined to get some gift of the Spirit or to get at God? "Your Father knows what you need before you ask him." The point of asking is that you may get to know God better. "Delight yourself in the Lord and he will give you the desires of your heart." Keep praying in order to get a perfect understanding of God Himself.

Brigid E. Herman, *Creative Prayer*

(1875–1923) Widowed at a young age, she gave herself to writing, especially in the field of theology.

At the beginning of our prayer life we are self-centered. Prayer means little more to us than "asking." We ask for personal favors, for blessings upon ourselves and those belonging to us. In our prayer vocabulary personal pronouns occupy a disproportionate place. It is *my* needs, *my* relations, *my* friends; and even when we go further afield and pray for those whom we have never seen, it is because their needs have been so presented to us as to stir our sympathies and appeal to our idiosyncrasies. In the last resort, we still make use of God in prayer. What altruism we have is temperamental, and remains uninformed by a deep view of God and man, and limited by our natural affinities; our prayer, in fact, remains essentially self-centered. And it belongs to the pathos of our spiritual pilgrimage that so many sincere and noble souls never seem to get beyond the prayer of self-regard and self-reference.

Moreover, many of the new methods of prayer which profess to deliver us from the prison house of self are seen, upon closer analysis, to be but subtle variations of the self-centered prayer. Not a few leaders of fashionable prayer cults make a point of insisting on complete concentration upon God as the prime condition of success. Human need, they urge, must be forgotten entirely. The devotee must, by intense mental abstraction and concentration, ascend to heavenly places, and think only of God in His inalienable omnipotence, indestructible peace, and inextinguishable joy. Only so shall His victorious and health-giving power be communicated to us, and through us to those for whom we pray. But all the time the motive of this "giving out of one-self into God" is to gain relief from trouble, sickness, or sin. No less than frankly self-centered prayer, these cults make God not an end, but a means to an end. They name God, and intend self.

But in the normal course of our spiritual growth, there comes a time when the center of prayer shifts from self to God. Petition, in its narrower sense, recedes. True, it is not excluded, for nothing that touches us can be indifferent to our Father in heaven; and our Lord Himself had a special love for plain, forthright, "unmystical" folk, who asked God for what they wanted, as simply and frankly as they would ask their neighbor to help them out in a domestic emergency. But petition will no longer be the pivot upon which prayer turns. The true motive power will now be to get nearer God, to know Him better, to experience His friendship, to enter more fully into His thoughts and purposes. . . .

We need devise no elaborate theory or method of God-centered prayer. There is only one "rubric"—*the lifting up to God of our honest desire to know Him and to be made one with Him*. . . .

The life of prayer is the life of conversion—a gradual, progressive turning from self to God. Potentially and ideally, that conversion is accomplished in the first genuine act of surrender, whereby the soul dissociates itself from sin and enters into its right relation with Eternal Love; actually it involves a lifetime of successive and growingly complete acts of daily self-denial and daily integration into Christ, a yielding up of the self that it may be filled with the fullness of God, a losing of life that it may be found again in Him.

George MacDonald

He who seeks the Father more than anything He can give, is likely to have what he asks, for he is not likely to ask amiss.

Psalm 63:1–8 (NIV)

A psalm of David when he was in the Desert of Judah:

O God, you are my God,
     earnestly I seek you;

my soul thirsts for you,
   my body longs for you,
in a dry and weary land
   where there is no water.

I have seen you in the sanctuary
   and beheld your power and your glory.
Because your love is better than life,
   my lips will glorify you.
I will praise you as long as I live,
   and in your name I will lift up my hands.
My soul will be satisfied as with the richest of foods;
   with singing lips my mouth will praise you.

On my bed I remember you;
   I think of you through the watches of the night.
Because you are my help,
   I sing in the shadow of your wings.
My soul clings to you;
   your right hand upholds me.

Andrew Murray, *With Christ in the School of Prayer*

(1828–1917) Known for his deep devotional life, Murray was also the most influential leader of the nineteenth-century South African Dutch Reformed Church.

We seek God's gifts: God wants to give us Himself first. We think of prayer as the power to draw down good gifts from heaven; Jesus as the means to draw ourselves up to God. We want to stand at the door and cry; Jesus would have us first enter in and realize that we are friends and children. Let us accept the teaching. Let every experience of the littleness of our faith in prayer urge us first to have and exercise more faith in the living God, and in such faith to yield ourselves to him. A heart full of God has power for the prayer of faith. Faith in God begets faith in the promise, in the promise too of an answer to prayer.

Therefore, child of God, take time, take time, to bow before *Him,* to wait on *Him* to reveal *Himself*. Take time, and let thy soul in holy awe and worship exercise and express its faith in the Infinite One, and as He imparts Himself and takes possession of thee, the prayer of faith will crown thy faith in God.

George Fox

(1624–1691) Founder of the Society of Friends (Quakers). Imprisoned as a blasphemer for six years, was released, and spent his later years promoting schools and campaigning for greater toleration.

Grant us, O Lord, the blessing of those whose minds are stayed upon Thee, so that we may be kept in perfect peace—a peace which cannot be broken. Let not our minds rest upon any creature, but only in the Creator: not upon goods, things, houses, lands, inventions of vanities or foolish fashions, lest our peace being broken, we become cross and brittle and given over to envy. From all such deliver us, O God, and grant us thy peace.

Richard of Chichester

(1197–1253) English bishop who fought to abolish the abuses common in the church of his day.

Thanks be to you, our Lord Jesus Christ,
for all the benefits that you have given us,
for all the pains and insults that you have borne for us.
Most merciful Redeemer, Friend, and Brother,
may we know you more clearly,
love you more dearly,
and follow you more nearly,
day by day.

Oswald Chambers

Whenever the insistence is on the point that God answers prayer, we are off the track. The meaning of prayer is that we get hold of God, not of the answer.

Anthony de Mello, *Taking Flight*

The Moghul Emperor, Akbar, was one day out hunting in the forest. When it was time for evening prayer he dismounted, spread his mat on the earth, and knelt to pray in the manner of devout Muslims everywhere.

Now it was precisely at this time that a peasant woman, perturbed because her husband had left home that morning and hadn't returned, went rushing by, anxiously searching for him. In her preoccupation she did not notice the kneeling figure of the Emperor and tripped over him, then got up and without a word of apology rushed farther into the forest.

Akbar was annoyed at this interruption, but being a good Muslim, he observed the rule of speaking to no one during the namaaz.

At just about the time that his prayer was over, the woman returned, joyful in the company of her husband, whom she had found. She was surprised and frightened to see the Emperor and his entourage there. Akbar gave vent to his anger against her and shouted, "Explain your disrespectful behavior or you will be punished."

The woman suddenly turned fearless, looked into the Emperor's eyes and said, "Your Majesty, I was so absorbed in the thought of my husband that I did not even see you there, not even when, as you say, I stumbled over you. Now while you were at namaaz, you were absorbed in One who is infinitely more precious than my husband. And how is it you noticed me?"

The Emperor was shamed into silence and later confided to his friends that a peasant woman, who was neither a scholar nor a Mullah, had taught him the meaning of prayer.

A. W. Tozer, *The Pursuit of God*

(1897–1963) Without any formal education, Tozer became one of America's most well-known pastor-theologians.

To have found God and still to pursue Him is the soul's paradox of love, scorned indeed by the too-easily-satisfied religionist, but justified in happy experience by the children of the burning heart. . . .

Come near to the holy men and women of the past and you will soon feel the heat of their desire after God. They mourned for Him, they prayed and wrestled and sought for Him day and night, in season and out, and when they had found Him the finding was all the sweeter for the long seeking.

St. John of the Cross

(1542–1591) Spanish mystic who wrote a number of prayers, but his most noted work is The Dark Night of the Soul.

I no longer want just to hear about you, beloved Lord, through messengers. I no longer want to hear doctrines about you, nor to have my emotions stirred by people speaking of you. I yearn for your presence. These messengers simply frustrate and grieve me, because they remind me of how distant I am from you. They reopen wounds in my heart, and they seem to delay your coming to me. From this day onwards please send me no more messengers, no more doctrines, because they cannot satisfy my overwhelming desire for you. I want to give myself completely to you. And I want you to give yourself completely to me. The love which you show in glimpses, reveal to me fully. The love which you convey through messengers, speak it to me directly. I sometimes think you are mocking me by hiding yourself from me. Come to me with the priceless jewel of your love.

A. W. Tozer, *Faith Beyond Reason*

We must be concerned with the person and character of God, not the promises. Through promises we learn what God has willed to us, we learn what we may claim as our heritage, we learn how we should pray. But faith itself must rest on the character of God.

Is this difficult to see? Why are we not stressing this in our evangelical circles? Why are we afraid to declare that people in our churches must come to know God Himself? Why do we not tell them that they must get beyond the point of making God a lifeboat for their rescue or a ladder to get them out of a burning building? How can we help our people get over the idea that God exists just to help run their businesses or fly their airplanes?

God is not a railway porter who carries your suitcase and serves you. God is God. He made heaven and earth. He holds the world in His hand. He measures the dust of the earth in the balance. He spreads the sky out like a mantle. He is the great God Almighty. He is not your servant. He is your Father, and you are His child. He sits in heaven, and you are on the earth.

Anselm of Canterbury

(ca. 1033–1109) Anselm, a monk, wrote a beautiful book called Proslogion, *designed to help unlearned people find God. The book contains this prayer:*

O Lord my God,
teach my heart where and how to seek you,
where and how to find you. . . .
You are my God and you are my Lord,

and I have never seen you.
You have made me and remade me,
and you have bestowed on me
all the good things I possess,
and still I do not know you. . . .
I have not yet done that
for which I was made. . . .

Teach me to seek you . . .
for I cannot seek you unless you teach me
or find you unless you show yourself to me.
Let me seek you in my desire,
let me desire you in my seeking.
Let me find you by loving you,
let me love you when I find you.

A. W. Tozer, *The Pursuit of God*

When religion has said its last word, there is little that we need other
than God Himself. The evil habit of seeking *God-and* effectively pre-
vents us from finding God in full revelation. In the *and* lies our great
woe. If we omit the *and* we shall soon find God, and in Him we shall
find that for which we have all our lives been secretly longing.

Anselm of Canterbury

I am desperate for your love, Lord.
My heart is aflame with fervent passion.
When I remember the good things you have done,
My heart burns with desire to embrace you.
I thirst for you,
I hunger for you,
I long for you,
I sigh for you.
I am jealous of your love.
What shall I say to you? What can I do for you?
Where shall I seek you?
I am sick for your love.
The joy of my heart turns to dust.
My happy laughter is reduced to ashes.

I want you.
I hope for you.
My soul is like a widow, bereft of you.
Turn to me, and see my tears.
I will weep until you come to me.
Come now, Lord, and I will be comforted.
Show me your face, and I shall be saved.
Enter my room, and I shall be satisfied.
Reveal your beauty, and my joy will be complete.

—⊗⊗—

Gregory Palamas

(ca. 1296–1359) Greek theologian, monk, and mystic.

It is of this [union of the mind with God] that the Fathers speak when
they say, "The end of prayer is to be snatched away to God."

—⊗⊗—

Olive Wyon, "The White Birds," *The School of Prayer*

There was once a man who had a waking dream. He dreamed he was in
a spacious church. He had wandered in to pray, and after his prayers
were finished, he knelt on, his eyes open, gazing around at the beauty of
the ancient building, and resting in the silence. Here and there in the
great building were quiet kneeling figures across the dim darkness of the
nave and aisles. Shafts of sunlight streamed into the church from upper
windows. In the distance a side door was open, letting in scents of summer air, fragrant with the smell of hay and flowers, and the sight of trees
waving in the breeze, and beyond, a line of blue hills, dim and distant as
an enchanted land.

Presently the man withdrew his eyes from the pleasant outdoor world
and looked again at the church. Suddenly, close to the spot where he
was kneeling, there was a gentle whir of wings and he saw a little white
bird fluttering about in the dim nave; it flew uncertainly hither and
thither, and once or twice he thought it would fall to the ground. But
gradually it gathered strength, rose toward the roof, and finally, with a
purposeful sweep of its wings, sped upward, and out through one of the
open windows into the sunshine.

The stranger looked down again at the kneeling men and women,
scattered singly throughout the building; and now he saw, what he had
not noticed before, that by the side of each worshiper there hovered,

close to the stone floor, a little white bird. Just then he saw another bird rise from the floor and try to reach the roof. But it, too, was in difficulties; it flew round and round in circles, occasionally beating its wings in a futile way against the great lower windows, rich with stained glass. Finally it sank down exhausted, and lay still. A little later another bird rose from the ground, with a swift and easy flight; for a moment it seemed that it would reach the open window and the open air beyond; but suddenly, it whirled round, fell helplessly over and over, and came to the ground with a thud, as if it had been shot. The man rose from his knees and went over to see what had happened; the little bird was dead.

He went back to his place and sat down on one of the chairs; then he noticed an ugly bird, its white feathers dirty and bedraggled, rise from the ground. At first this bird labored heavily, but it soon gathered speed, for it was strong, and it soared up and out into the sunlit world beyond the walls of the great church. More and more the man wondered what all this might mean. He looked again at the persons at prayer near him and he noticed one kneeling very reverently, by whose side lay a very beautiful bird, snowy white and perfectly formed. But when he looked at it more closely he saw that its eyes were glazed, its wings stiff, it was a lifeless shell. "What a pity," he murmured under his breath. At that moment, a gentle whir of wings a few feet away attracted his attention, another bird was rising from the ground, steadily and quietly, at first with some appearance of effort, but more and more easily and lightly as it gathered strength, this bird flew straight up, past the carved angels which seemed to be crying "Hallelujah" to one another across the dim spaces of the church, and out through the open window into the blue sky, where it was soon lost to sight.

Pondering on what he had seen, the man looked round again, and this time he saw standing close to him, an angel, tall and strong, with a face of great kindness, wisdom and compassion. It all seemed perfectly natural (as things do in dreams), and the man whispered to him, "Can you explain to me about these white birds?"

"Yes," said the angel, in a low voice, as he seated himself beside him, "for I am the guardian of this place of prayer. These white birds are the outward sign of the prayers of the people who come here to pray. The first bird, which found it difficult to rise, but then succeeded, is the prayer of a woman who has come here straight from a very busy life; she has very little time to herself; in fact she usually comes here in the midst of her shopping. She has a great many duties and claims, and her mind was full of distractions when she first knelt down and tried to pray. But she persevered, for her heart is right with God, and He helped her; her prayer was real and her will good, so her prayer reached God."

"And what about the bird that flew around in circles?" asked the man.

The angel smiled slightly, with a tinge of faint amusement. "That," he said slowly, "is the prayer of a man who thinks of no one but himself; even in his prayers he only asks for 'things'— success in his business and things like that; he tries to use God for his own ends . . . people think he is a very religious man . . . but his prayer does not reach God at all."

"But why did that other bird fall to the ground as if it had been shot?"

The angel looked sad as he replied: "That man began his prayer well enough; but suddenly he remembered a grudge against someone he knew; he forgot his prayer and brooded in bitter resentment, and his bitterness killed his prayer. . . . And the ugly bird," he went on after a moment's silence, "is the prayer of a man who hasn't much idea of reverence; his prayer is bold, almost presumptuous, some people might call it; but God knows his heart, and He sees that his faith is real: he does really believe God, so his prayer reaches Him."

"And the beautiful lifeless bird that never stirred from the ground at all?" said the man.

"That," said the angel, "is a beautifully composed prayer: the language is perfect, the thought is doctrinally correct; the man offered it with the greatest solemnity and outward reverence. But he never meant a word of it; even as he said the words his thoughts were on his own affairs, so his prayer could not reach God."

"And what about the last bird that flew upstairs so easily?"

The angel smiled. "I think you know," he said gently. "That is the prayer of a woman whose whole heart and will is set upon God. . . . Her prayer went straight to God."

———— ∞ ————

Psalm 73:25–26 (NASB)

A psalm of Asaph:

> Whom have I in heaven *but Thee?*
> And besides Thee, I desire nothing on earth.
> My flesh and my heart may fail,
> But God is the strength of my heart and my portion forever.

———— ∞ ————

W. Bingham Hunter, *The God Who Hears*

Understanding God's existence as personal spirit undergirds almost everything else which might be said about prayer. God's personalness is the factor which makes prayer voluntary interpersonal communication and communion rather than compulsory mechanical manipulation and exploitation. Not until we come to view God *himself* as our treasure in heaven are we likely to genuinely *desire* to pray. "For where your treasure is, there your heart will be also" (Matt. 6:21).

—∞∞—

Eugene Peterson, *Working the Angles*

It is with God with whom we have to do. People go for long stretches of time without being aware of that, thinking it is money, or sex, or work, or children, or parents, or a political cause, or an athletic competition, or learning with which they must deal. Any one or a combination of these subjects can absorb them and for a time give them the meaning and purpose that human beings seem to require. But then there is a slow stretch of boredom. Or a disaster. Or a sudden collapse of meaning. They want more. They want God.

—∞∞—

Dag Hammarskjöld

Secretary-General of the United Nations in 1953. He died in an airplane crash while flying to Northern Rhodesia to negotiate a cease-fire between United Nations and Katanga forces. He wrote the following prayer on July 19, 1961; it can be found in the posthumously published diary of his spiritual life, titled Markings.

Give me a pure heart—that I may see thee,
A humble heart—that I may hear thee,
A heart of love—that I may serve thee,
A heart of faith—that I may abide in thee.

PART FIVE

HOW DO WE PRAY?

INTRODUCTION

How do we pray?
In as many different ways as there are people.
Some of us pray with our eyes closed; others with our eyes
open. Some raise their hands; others lower their heads. Some stand;
others kneel. Some pray regularly; others sporadically. Some pray
formally; others spontaneously. Some pray throughout the day;
others bookend their day with morning and evening prayers. Some
pray out loud; others in silence. Some pray easily; for others, it
takes great effort.

We pray in our favorite chair with a hot cup of coffee and a quilt
thrown over our legs. We pray kneeling on the hardwood floor by the
bassinet of a sick baby. We pray standing in a phone booth. Sitting
in a park bench. Lying on a hospital bed.

We pray "Heavenly Father" or "Hail, Mary" or "Dear Jesus." And
though our theology may differ, our thoughts about prayer are remarkably similar. The thoughts on prayer by a twenty-four-year-old prostitute in Nevada (in the section, Seekers from Around the World), are
surprisingly similar to those of an 86-year-old Mother Teresa of Calcutta (in the section, Proven Methods: Silence—Listening to God).
And the way Norman Lear of Hollywood prays (in the section, Seekers
from Around the World), is surprisingly similar to the way St. Francis
of Assisi prayed almost eight hundred years earlier.

But along with the similarities are great diversities. Who's to say
why? Maybe it's cultural. Maybe it's individual. Or maybe . . . maybe
it's biblical. For when we look in the Bible we see people praying in
all sorts of ways.

Daniel prayed three times a day at a set time and in a set place.
David seems to have been more spontaneous. Moses made lengthy intercession for the Israelites. The publican in the Temple courtyard
made a short plea for only himself. Job called out to God in his anger
and despair. Mary called out to him in joy and exultation.

Some prayed in synagogues; others in streets. Some spoke with the
tongues of angels; others stammered. Some prayed in priestly robes;
others in sackcloth and ashes.

However they came with their prayers, they came. In their own
way. With their own words. Standing or kneeling, they came. Raising
their hands or clenching their fists, they came. Full of food or fasting,
they came.

> *And maybe there's something to be learned from that.*
> *Maybe it's not so important how we come . . .*
>   *but that we come.*

PERSONAL EXAMPLES

Jesus in Gethsemane

Walter Wangerin, *Reliving the Passion*

> Mark 14:35–36
> *And going a little farther, he fell on the ground and prayed that, if it were possible, the hour might pass from him. And he said, "Abba, Father, all things are possible to thee; remove this cup from me; yet not what I will, but what thou wilt."*

"Lord," the disciples had asked in an earlier, easier time, "teach us to pray." And Jesus had answered by teaching them certain words: "When you pray," he said, "say . . . "

The prayer he spoke then we call *The Lord's.*

But Jesus teaches the same thing twice. And the second lesson is not words only; deeds make up the prayer as well, and passion and experience—the whole person dramatically involved.

Words alone might be as hollow and irrelevant as ping-pong balls. But now the Lord reveals how prayer can be the expression of an event already in progress; it is human experience finding its voice—and by that voice directing itself wholly (the whole experience, action, emotion, thought, desire, body, and spirit) straight to God.

Behold: what takes place in the Garden of Gethsemane is the Lord's Prayer actually *happening,* as though the earlier words were a script and this is the drama itself:

> Jesus cries his deepest and desperate desire: that the hour, by the power of his Father, pass away from him. This is the living substance of the sixth petition: *Save us from the time of trial.*

> Jesus pleads three times, "remove this cup from me," the plea of the seventh petition: *Deliver us from evil.*

> But under every request of his own, he places an attitude of faithful obedience to his Father, saying, "Yet not what I will, but what thou wilt." Here is the third petition, which prepares us properly for any

answer God may give all other petitions: *Thy will be done on earth as it is in heaven.*

Implicit, hereafter, in his entering into "the hour" of trial after all is his personal conviction that "the time is fulfilled, and the kingdom of God is at hand." Jesus, now more than ever in his ministry, is the living embodiment of the second petition, *Thy kingdom come.* Right now, his acceptance of the Father's will *is* the coming of that kingdom here!

And he begins both prayers the same. But whereas the first might have seemed a formal address to "Our Father," this latter cry is a howl, a spontaneous, needful plea: "Abba, Father!" Here is a child who cannot survive apart from this relationship. By crying "Abba!" he hurls himself at the holy parent: he runs like a child; like a child he begs attention; but also like a perfect child he trusts his daddy to do right and well.

When Jesus teaches us to pray, he does not teach plain recitation. Rather, he calls us to a way of being. He makes of prayer a doing. And by his own extreme example, he shows that prayer is the active relationship between ourselves, dear little children, and the dear Father, *Abba.*

Who can pray The Lord's Prayer now with words and not with the heart's experience?

Chester P. Michael and Marie C. Norrisey, *Prayer and Temperament*

When asked how he prayed, a Southern rural minister replied: "I reads myself full; I thinks myself clear; I prays myself hot; I lets myself cool."

Billy Graham

My wife and I live in a very remote part of America in the mountains of North Carolina. There's a little place where I walk or run or jog, and it's about a tenth of a mile each way. We have two dogs who accompany me. One of them will go with me all the way, but the other has gotten so used to the routine that now he sits down in the middle and just watches me go both ways. That run is where I do a lot of praying and confessing. But I also have stated periods of prayer. My wife and I, for example, read the Bible every night before we go to bed and then we pray together. Then I usually get up around seven and am usually finished with breakfast by eight. I watch the news and then I have my devotional period. I read the Bible, and sometimes read a little commentary on it. As I read, I think of things to pray for—besides those things and individuals I already have on my prayer list.

———∞∞∞———

John Hyde

(1865–1912) Missionary to India nicknamed "Praying Hyde," who was known for his all-night prayer vigils.

Dr. Wilbur Chapman . . . wrote to a friend: "I have learned some great lessons concerning prayer. At one of our missions in England the audiences were exceedingly small. But I received a note saying that an American missionary . . . was going to pray God's blessing down upon our work. He was known as 'Praying Hyde.' Almost instantly the tide turned. The hall became packed, and at my first invitation fifty men accepted Christ as their Savior. As we were leaving I said, 'Mr. Hyde, I want you to pray for me.' He came to my room, turned the key in the door, and dropped on his knees, and waited five minutes without a single syllable coming from his lips. I could hear my own heart thumping and beating. I felt the hot tears running down my face. I knew I was with God. Then, with upturned face, down which the tears were streaming, he said 'O God!' Then for five minutes at least he was still again; and then, when he knew that he was talking with God . . . there came up from the depth of his heart such petitions for men as I had never heard before. I rose from my knees to know what real prayer was."

———∞∞∞———

Annie Dillard

As described by Eugene Peterson in The Contemplative Pastor

Writer Annie Dillard is an exegete of creation in the same way John Calvin was an exegete of Holy Scripture. The passion and intelligence Calvin brought to Moses, Isaiah, and Paul, she brings to muskrats and mockingbirds. She reads the book of creation with the care and intensity of a skilled critic, probing and questioning, teasing out, with all the tools of mind and spirit at hand, the author's meaning.

Calvin was not indifferent to creation. He frequently referred to the world around us as a "theater of God's glory." He wrote of the Creator's dazzling performance in arranging the components of the cosmos. . . .

Calvin knew all this, appreciated it, and taught it. But, curiously, he never seemed to have purchased a ticket to the theater, gone in, and watched the performance himself. He lived for most of his adult ministry in Geneva, Switzerland, one of the most spectacularly beautiful places on the earth. Not once does he comment on the wild thrust of the mountains into the skies. He never voices awe at the thunder of an avalanche. There is no evidence that he ever stopped to admire the gem flowers in the alpine meadows. He was not in the habit of looking up from his books and meditating before the lake loaded with sky that graced his city. He would not be distracted from this scriptural exegesis by going to the theater, even the legitimate theater of God's glory. . . .

Annie Dillard has a season ticket to that theater. Day after day she takes her aisle seat and watches the performance. She is caught up in the drama of the creation. *Pilgrim at Tinker Creek* is a contemplative journal of her attendance at the theater over the course of a year. She is breathless in awe. She cries and laughs, and in turn, she is puzzled and dismayed. She is no uncritical spectator. During intermissions, she does not scruple to find fault with either writer or performance. All is not to her liking, and some scenes bring her close to revulsion. But she always returns to the action and ends up on her feet applauding, "Encore! Encore!". . .

There are two great mystical traditions in the life of prayer, sometimes labeled kataphatic and apophatic. Kataphatic prayer uses icons, symbols, ritual, incense; the creation is the way to the Creator. Apophatic prayer attempts emptiness; the creature distracts from the Creator, and so the mind is systematically emptied of idea, image, sensation until there is only the simplicity of being. Kataphatic prayer is "praying with your eyes open"; apophatic prayer is "praying with your eyes shut."

At our balanced best, the two traditions intermingle, mix, and cross-fertilize. But we are not always at our best. The Western church is heavily skewed on the side of the apophatic. The rubric for prayer when I was a child was, "Fold your hands, bow your head, shut your eyes, and we'll pray." My early training carries over into my adult practice. Most of my praying still is with my eyes shut. I need balancing.

Annie Dillard prays differently: Spread out your hands, lift your head, open your eyes, and we'll pray. "It is still the first week in January, and I've got great plans. I've been thinking about seeing. There are lots of things to see, unwrapped gifts and free surprises." We start out with her on what we supposed will be no more than a walk through the woods. It is not long before we find ourselves in the company of saints and monks, enlisted in the kind of contemplative seeing "requiring a lifetime of dedicated struggle."

She gets us into the theater that Calvin told us about, and we find ourselves in the solid biblical companionship of psalmists and prophets who watched the "hills skip like lambs" and heard the "trees clap their hands," alert to God everywhere, in everything, praising, praying with our eyes open: "I leap to my feet; I cheer and cheer."

Annie Dillard, *Holy the Firm*

The world at my feet, the world through the window, is an illuminated manuscript whose leaves the wind takes, one by one, whose painted illuminations and halting words draw me, one by one, and I am dazzled in days and lost.

Psalm 19:1–6 (NASB)

A psalm of David:

> The heavens are telling of the glory of God;
>> And their expanse is declaring the work of His hands.
>> Day to day pours forth speech,
>> And night to night reveals knowledge.
>> There is no speech, nor are there words;
>> Their voice is not heard.
>> Their line has gone out through all the earth,
>> And their utterances to the end of the world.
>> In them He has placed a tent for the sun,
>> Which is as a bridegroom coming out of his chamber;
>> It rejoices as a strong man to run his course.
>> Its rising is from one end of the heavens,
>> And its circuit to the other end of them;
>> And there is nothing hidden from its heat.

Brother Lawrence

(ca. 1605–1691) Kitchen worker in a monastery of the Carmelite Order best known for the way he communed with God in the simple chores of daily life.

As described in The Practice of the Presence of God

God molded Brother Lawrence's character. It became so natural to him that he passed the last forty years of his life in continuous practice of the presence of God, which he described as a quiet, familiar conversation with Him. . . .

People seek for methods of learning to love God. They hope to arrive at it by I know not how many different practices; they take much trouble to remain in the presence of God in a quantity of ways. Is it not much shorter and more direct to do everything for the love of God, to make use of all the labors of one's state in life to show Him that love, and to maintain His presence within us by this communion of our hearts with His? There is no finesse about it; one has only to do it generously and simply. . . .

The prayer time was really taken at both the beginning and the end of my work. At the beginning of my duties I would say to the Lord with confidence, "My God, since You are with me, and since, by Your will, I must occupy myself with external things, please grant me the grace to remain with You, in Your presence. Work with me, so that my work might be the very best. Receive as an offering of love both my work and all my affections."

During my work, I would always continue to speak to the Lord as though He were right with me, offering Him my services and thanking Him for His assistance. And at the end of my work, I used to examine it carefully. If I found good in it, I thanked God. If I noticed faults, I asked His forgiveness without being discouraged, and then went on with my work, still dwelling in Him.

Thus, continuing in this practice of conversing with God throughout each day, and quickly seeking His forgiveness when I fell or strayed, His presence has become as easy and natural to me now as it once was difficult to attain. . . .

Even when he was busiest in the kitchen, it was evident that the brother's spirit was dwelling in God. He often did the work that two usually did, but he was never seen to bustle. Rather, he gave each chore the time that it required, always preserving his modest and tranquil air, working neither slowly nor swiftly, dwelling in calmness of soul and unalterable peace.

In this intimate union with the Lord, our brother's passions grew so calm that he scarcely felt them any more. He developed a gentle disposition, complete honesty, and the most charitable heart in the world. His kind face, his gracious and affable air, his simple and modest manner immediately won him the esteem and the good will of everyone who saw him. The more familiar with him they became, the more they became aware of how profoundly upright and reverent he was.

Despite his simple and common life in the monastery, he did not pretend to be austere or melancholy, which only serves to rebuff people. On the contrary, he fraternized with everyone, and treated his brothers as friends, without trying to be distinguished from them. He never took the graces of God for granted, and never paraded his virtues in order to win esteem, trying rather to lead a hidden and unknown life. Though he was indeed a humble man, he never sought the glory of humility, but only its reality. He wanted no one but God to witness what he did, just as the only reward he expected was God Himself. . . .

Everything was the same to him—every place, every job. The good brother found God everywhere, as much while he was repairing shoes as while he was praying with the community. He was in no hurry to go on retreats, because he found the same God to love and adore in his ordinary work as in the depth of the desert.

Brother Lawrence's only means of going to God was to do everything for the love of Him. He was therefore indifferent about what he did. All that mattered was that he did it for God. It was He, and not the activity, that he considered. He knew that the more the thing he did was opposed to his natural inclination, the greater was the merit of his love in offering it to God. He knew that the pettiness of the deed would not diminish the worth of his offering, because God—needing nothing—considers in our works only the love that accompanies them.

Jo Carr and Imogene Sorley,
Plum Jelly and Stained Glass & Other Prayers

Ah Lord—
    Brother Lawrence said he *"practiced* the presence of God."
Then, yes.
Now? I'm not so sure.
    Could he do so even in the dentist's chair?
    Even in the five o'clock traffic?
Life is considerably more complicated today.
    You know, Lord, this is my excuse.

And yet—Brother Lawrence *practiced* the art of keeping his mind stayed on thee.
And I could, too.
Even in the dentist's chair. What better place! Often the dentist himself walks out and leaves me alone and it is quiet, and peaceful, with none of the I-ought-to-be-up-doing-the-dishes distractions of home. And I *could* use that moment of stillness to center down on thy love. But I don't. I never think of it.

And then, when the dentist comes back, I *still* could practice thy presence, Lord. I certainly can't *talk*, with my mouth full of fingers and tools . . . but I could "think on thee"—and intentionally, at that moment, give thanks for a number of things—including dentists.

Practice thy presence?

Even in the five o'clock traffic? That's certainly no time of peace and quiet. And yet—you are there, too, Lord. And I can focus my grasshopper mind *in-thy-name* on those around me.

They are thy people—beside whom I drive.

Some of them are in a hurry, too. They have worries, problems—like mine—more so?

Ah, Lord, bless them—
and bless me
with thy presence.
Amen.

Sue Monk Kidd, *God's Joyful Surprise*

There is a saying to the effect that work is prayer and prayer is work. How wonderful when we can blend them, giving our work a sense of holiness!

The best place to begin the blending of prayer and work is to form a clear vision of God with us in our work. Our work is God's work. It isn't the type of work we do that makes it holy, but how we do it. "Whatever you do, do all to the glory of God," wrote Paul (1 Cor. 10:31 RSV).

"My job contributes nothing to the kingdom of God," a high school graduate told me one day.

"What do you do?" I asked.

"I work on a piece of tractor machinery as it passes on an assembly line," she said. At first I couldn't think of any response that could help her. Then suddenly it popped into my head.

"You aren't just working on a machine. You're helping to make a tractor that will harvest a field that will help feed the world!"

"Yes, I suppose I am," she said. "I am helping feed the world. I believe I can give myself to that."

Every task, no matter how menial, helps further God's creation. "We may . . . imagine that the creation was finished long ago. But that would be quite wrong. It continues still more magnificently and we serve to complete it by the humblest work of our hands."

This is a very high vision—seeing ourselves as co-creators with God, helping by our labor to transform bit by bit God's creation into His kingdom. At a writers' conference a woman told our group that in some way God was at the tip of her pen. That thought stunned me. I began to view what I was doing very differently. I saw a sacredness in it I'd never glimpsed before.

God is at the tip of our scapels, our screwdrivers, our computer terminals, our dust rags, our pencils and pens. He is with us in our wheelchairs, or on our hospital beds, when all we can do is sit or lie flat. When we envision Him and His purpose in what we do, then we begin to grow aware of His presence in the midst of it. We are able to engage in our inward conversation with Him as we work, naturally, without strain. He becomes our partner, our collaborator.

This secret conversation is fueled by offering our work to God, task by task, moment by moment. We not only do it *with* God, we do it *for* God. At the beginning of each new endeavor, whether it is typing a letter, giving a seminar, or preparing a meal, we might think, "I do this for You." We can refer the least thing to Him. Not only does this sort of dialogue keep us tuned into His presence as we work, it does wonders for the quality of our work and our own peace of mind.

When I first began writing, more than anything I wrote for myself, for my own success and personal enhancement. The first story I ever wrote started as a terrible flop. I had hoped it would draw favorable comments from my writing class. But they said, "There is not much here for a story. It needs lots of work and even then it is doubtful it will ever get published." Being thoroughly stubborn, I refused to give up. One night after rewriting it for the eleventh time, I laid the manuscript on my desk in exhaustion. "God," I prayed, "I give You this story. I will do it for You, not myself."

That was a turning point for me. I discovered that doing my work first and foremost for God was far more satisfying. It lost its compulsive, greedy edge. My writing became more a source of peace and intimacy with God's presence.

When we raise children for God, teach school for God or sell groceries for God, our work draws us to Him. It is not a boring necessity, but a doorway to His presence. I heard Mother Teresa say once in a television interview, "Everything, in that it is for God, becomes beautiful, whatever it may be." Even if we cannot *do* anything—if we are confined to a wheelchair or a bed—we can offer that immobility to God as something for Him to make beautiful.

I try to keep this in mind when I'm doing housework. I am always thinking of something "more important" I could be doing. But of course the stuff has to be done. So I am learning to offer continually even the most menial parts of it to God. *Father, I offer You the task of cleaning this sink.* The truth is, when I clean my sink for God, it sparkles, and I take pleasure in Him as I work. When I clean the sink for myself, I grumble, cut corners and experience the work as drudgery.

A secret dialogue with God—which is nothing more than the lifting and sharing of our thoughts with Him as we work, play, suffer, laugh, rise up, lie down—can envelope our whole day with a pervading sense of God's love and presence. "There is not in the world a kind of life more sweet and delightful than that of a continual conversation with God," wrote Brother Lawrence.

Richard Foster, *Prayer*

Praying the Ordinary

The work of our hands and of our minds is acted out prayer, a love offering to the living God. In what is perhaps the finest line in the movie *Chariots of Fire,* Olympic runner Eric Liddell tells his sister, "Jenny, when I run, I feel his pleasure." This is the reality that is to permeate all vocations, whether we are writing a novel or cleaning a latrine.

It is at the latrine cleaning that many have a problem. It is not hard to see how a Michelangelo or a T. S. Eliot is giving glory to God—theirs are creative vocations. But what about the boring jobs, the unimportant jobs, the mundane jobs. How are those prayer?

Here we must understand the order in the kingdom of God. It is precisely in the "slop-bucket job"—the work that we abhor—where we will find God the most. We do not need to have good feelings or a warm glow in order to do work for the glory of God. All good work is pleasing to the Father. Even the jobs that seem meaningless and mindless to us are highly valued in the order of the kingdom of God. God values the ordinary. If, for the glory of God, you are putting an endless supply of nuts on an endless line of bolts, your work is rising up as a sweet-smelling offering to the throne of God. He is pleased with your labor.

"Aren't you glorifying work a bit too much—you know, Protestant work ethic, and all?" you may be wondering. I think not. Work came before the fall, and the curse of the fall was that work would be "by the sweat of your brow"—that is, the results would not be commensurate with the labor put in. In fact, one of the clearest signs of the grace of God upon us is when the results of our labor are far in excess of the amount of work we do. We glorify God in our labor because we most closely approximate the Creator when we engage in the creative activity of work.

"But what about those who have no jobs, the unemployed and the retired? How do they Pray the Ordinary?" you may ask. We can all work whether we have employable skills or not. Remuneration is not a factor in deciding the value of labor in the kingdom of God. If our abilities or opportunities allow for nothing more than picking up sticks, we are to do so with all our might to the glory of God and the good of our neighbor.

"Can a person live a full, satisfying life that glorifies God without work?" you may question. I do not know how. Certainly all things are possible with God, but I am sure such a thing would be the exception and not the rule. In fact, I value labor as a reflection of the image of God within us so much that my personal conviction is that part of the bliss of heaven will be joyous, creative, productive work.

The Prayer of Action

We are also Praying the Ordinary when we engage in what Jean-Nicholas Grou calls "the prayer of action." "Every action performed in the sight of God because it is the will of God, and in the manner that God wills, is a prayer and indeed a better prayer than could be made in words at such times."

Each activity of daily life in which we stretch ourselves on behalf of others is a prayer of action—the times when we scrimp and save in order to get the children something special; the times when we share our car with others on rainy mornings, leaving early to get them to work on time; the times when we keep up correspondence with friends or answer one last telephone call when we are dead tired at night. These times and many more like them are lived prayer. Ignatius of Loyola notes, "Everything that one turns in the direction of God is prayer."

Then, too, we are Praying the Ordinary when we see God in the ordinary experiences of life. Can we find meaning in the crayon marks on the wall made by the kids? Are they somehow the finger of God writing on the wall of our hearts?

Waiting is part of ordinary time. We discover God in our waiting: waiting in checkout lines, waiting for the telephone to ring, waiting for graduation, waiting for a promotion, waiting to retire, waiting to die. The waiting itself becomes prayer as we give our waiting to God. In waiting we begin to get in touch with the rhythms of life—stillness and action, listening and decision. They are the rhythms of God. It is in the every-day and the commonplace that we learn patience, acceptance, and contentment. Saint Benedict's criterion for allowing a visitor to stay at the monastery is that "he is content with the life as he finds it, and does not make excessive demands . . . but is simply content with what he finds."

I am attracted to this "contentment without excessive demands" because it is the way I would really like to live. In a world in which *Winning Through Intimidation* is the order of the day, I am attracted to people who are free from the tyranny of assertiveness. I am drawn to those who are able to simply meet people where they are, with no need to control or manage or make them do anything. I enjoy being around them because they draw the best out in me without any manipulation whatsoever.

Another way of Praying the Ordinary is by praying throughout the ordinary experiences of life. We pick up a newspaper and are prompted to whisper a prayer of guidance for world leaders facing monumental decisions. We are visiting with friends in a school corridor or a shopping mall, and their words prompt us to lapse into prayer for them, either verbally or silently, as the circumstances dictate. We jog through our neighborhood, blessing the families who live there. We plant our garden, thanking the God of heaven for sun and rain and all good things. This is the stuff of ordinary prayer through ordinary experience.

———✦✦✦———

Marjorie Holmes, *I've Got to Talk to Somebody, God*

PRAYING WHILE SCRUBBING A FLOOR

Thank you for the privilege of scrubbing this floor.
Thank you for the health and the strength to do it.
That my back is straight and my hands are whole.
I can push the mop. I can feel the hard surface under my knees when
    I kneel.
I can grasp the brush and let my energy flow down into it as I erase the
    dirt and make this floor bright and clean.
If I were blind I couldn't see the soil or the patterns of the tile or the
    slippery circles shining.
If I were deaf I couldn't hear the homely cheerful sounds of suds in the
    bucket, the crisp little whisper of brush or mop.
I would miss the music of doors banging and children shouting and the
    steps of people coming to walk across this bright expanse of floor.

Lord, thank you for everything that has to do with scrubbing this floor.
Bless the soap and the bucket and the brush and the hands that do it.
   Bless the feet that are running in right now to track it. This I accept,
   and thank you for.
Those feet are the reason I do it. They are the living reasons for my
   kneeling here—half to do a job, half in prayer.
A floor is a foundation. A family is a foundation. You are our foun-
   dation.
Bless us all, and our newly scrubbed floor.

Noah benShea, *Jacob's Journey*

Jacob [a baker] looked down at his path as if it were the current of a
great river. As he stared into the flow he saw the seemingly unending
line of moments given to him. Then, like a man marking a trail, he
began to put his prayer between the moments, making the common
profound by pausing.

   Using prayer to tie knots in time, Jacob isolated the details that
would pass before others as a stream of events.

   In this way Jacob secured the moments in his life, returned their in-
dividuality, allowed the luster in each of them to be observed, and, appreciated and saved, transformed his moments into a string of pearls.

Augustine

(354–430) Bishop of Hippo in North Africa. Philosopher and Church Father whose ideas greatly influenced the Protestant Reformation.

O Father, light up
the small duties of this day's life:
may they shine
with the beauty of your countenance.
May we believe that glory can dwell
in the commonest task of every day.

David McCasland

Describing how Oswald Chambers's prayer life was influenced by the
personal example of a close friend.

The hills around Dunoon provided brief respites for Chambers, but he craved longer periods when he could walk with his collie, Tweed, and seek renewal in God's creation. During summer breaks, he often traveled a hundred miles north to the Highlands near Fort William, and the home of John Cameron, an old friend.

Cameron pastured sheep on the slopes of Ben Nevis, Britain's highest mountain. Chambers found emotional release in the hard labor of shepherding, and he loved to climb the towering mountain often called "the Ben." . . .

In Chambers' estimation, John Cameron was a man who matched the mountain where he lived. The rugged old bachelor lived simply and gave the bulk of his income to the Lord's work. Cameron entertained hospitably and prayed as regularly and naturally as the sunrise.

[*After receiving the news that his friend and mentor, John Cameron, had died, Chambers wrote in a letter . . .*]

And then old John Cameron. But that hits hard! Few knew him, but I knew him. I remember him on his death-bed in his home on the slopes of Ben Nevis, he could not speak but held out his arms and I bent down and kissed him. The snows were deep not only around him, but on his own head. A stern mountain crag, but the heart of a moss rose was his.

If anyone has felt the tenderness of a rugged old Highlander's embrace and love, they'll know why I thank my God upon my remembrances of old John Cameron. How he knew God! How he talked with God! and how he taught me out on those hills—at midnight, at dawn-light, and at noonday have I knelt before that old veteran in prayer. Truly it was a great goodness of God to allow me to know such men. I learnt a bigger stride, the stride of the mountains of God, with these royal, elemental souls.

Mother Teresa

Interviewed by Dr. Robert Schuller

SCHULLER: AND IF I FOCUS ON JESUS, I WILL KNOW THAT HE BELIEVES IN ME.

Mother Teresa: Exactly. That is why to be a true missionary, we need a deep attachment to Christ. And that's why for us, we have to be deeply, deeply prayerful, and have a real deep love for prayer. We begin the day with meditation, Holy Mass with Holy Communion. And then we end the day with a full service of adoration, and that's something—the greatest gift of God to our society. I don't think I could do what I'm doing if I didn't have those four hours of prayer every day.

SCHULLER: FOUR HOURS?

Mother Teresa: Yes . . . every day.

———

Richard Foster

Interviewed by Jim Castelli in How I Pray

Sometimes I use written prayers, such as the Book of Common Prayer, and other books of writings. I have a class right now in which students are using John Baillie's *Diary of Private Prayers* as a way of leading them into their own prayers. I suppose if I were to list one prayer that is a key prayer for me, it would be the Jesus prayer: "Lord, Jesus Christ, Son of God, have mercy on me, a sinner." That is the most basic prayer, and I use it often. Of course there are many other prayers—the Serenity Prayer, the Saint Francis prayer—that are very good prayers, but personally I like the Jesus prayer.

In one sense we are praying always, but I do have a set time of prayer—perhaps thirty minutes to an hour. And there are other times when I might take a little day of prayer in solitude. Often I'll connect that to the seasons: winter, spring, summer, fall. Or I'll do it in connection with some trip I'm taking: I'll stay a couple of days extra and spend the time in private retreat.

I pray both silently and out loud. Certainly there is silent prayer, the prayer of quiet. I think of Kierkegaard's famous sentence: "A man prayed and first he thought that prayer was talking, but he became more and more quiet until in the end he realized that prayer was listening." Certainly prayer often goes beyond words, but many times words are used. Today I did both. Prayer in silence and then spoken out loud. It doesn't really matter, does it? I mean, God isn't hard of hearing.

Meditation is one of the most basic forms of listening prayer. Usually it's tied to a passage of Scripture. Other times it can move more deeply into what is usually thought of as contemplation, in which, as French author J. N. Grou prayed, "Oh, Divine Master teach me this mute language that says so much." So, there is silence, listening prayer, and meditation. These must be a regular part of our prayer experience because it isn't just a matter of us talking, it's a matter of listening to God's voice in his wondrous, loving, all-embracing silence.

During the experience of prayer I often gain focus, sinking down into the life of God in such a way that I can become comfortable in that posture. And out of that I seek to live my day. I find I am more on target and have a greater sense of confidence and strength in what I am doing, so that I am living the day out of the guidance that prayer gives me.

George Gallup, Jr.

I pray in short bursts but also in longer periods, when I sit quietly and listen. I pray in the morning, at various points during the day, and in bed when I'm reviewing the day and getting set for the next. I pray before business and board meetings. I pray in small groups and at church. I pray with Kinney (my spouse); usually we read something from a book such as Oswald Chambers' *My Utmost for His Highest*.

Andrew Greeley

Prayer has always been important to me. It took me a long time to figure out how to do it and to realize that what works for you is the way you should be praying. No formula for spirituality, however good in theory, is necessarily what you should be doing. It took a rather long time for prayer to become deeply important to me, but it's still not as important as it should be. . . .

Some mornings I get up at four. I do my swim and I do my reflections. This makes a big difference in my day. Prayer is a source of reflection and refreshment and orients the day for me. It doesn't always affect what *happens* during the day, but it always gives an orientation to start off with. . . .

Poetry, art, literature, and music all trigger prayer in me. That's because I'm Catholic; they *should* do that. If they don't, then there's something missing in our personal development. For our religion is sacramental; that is, it believes that God works everywhere in nature. . . .

When I pray, I look for illumination. Surely the things that occur to me as I sit down to write wouldn't have occurred to me *before*; these reflections are from God and are part of the dialogue with God. Now, that doesn't mean that I imagine God whispering in my ear or that I can hear anything in the ordinary sense of hearing. It's just something I know to be true that I didn't know to be true before. Maybe it's the muse, maybe it's an angel, maybe the muses are angels.

PRACTICAL ADVICE

Richard Foster, *Prayer*

I remember well my experiment with "religionless Christianity" . . . I
would seek to live in continuous communion with God for three months
without any outward "props" whatever—no Bible, no liturgy, no
Eucharist, no preaching, no worship services, no set times of prayer,
nothing. God was gracious to me during those ninety days, but far and
away the most important thing I learned was how badly I needed those
"props" to keep me pressing in to the Divine Center. I discovered that
regular patterns of devotion form a kind of skeletal structure upon which
I can build the muscle and tissue of unceasing prayer. Without this outward structure, my internal heart yearnings for God simply do not hold
together. These regular patterns—usually called rituals—are, in fact,
God-ordained means of grace.

———⟨∞⟩———

Oswald Chambers

*(1874–1917) Scottish minister who was converted to Christianity through the preaching of
Charles Spurgeon. Best known as a devotional writer.*

14th: Sunday morn. What a blessed habit I have found my prayer list,
morning by morning, it takes me via the Throne of all Grace straight to
the intimate personal heart of each one mentioned here, and I know that
He Who is not prescribed by time and geography answers immediately.

———⟨∞⟩———

David E. Rosage, *Meeting God in Every Moment*

I love you, O LORD, my strength,
  O LORD, my rock, my fortress, my deliverer. (Ps. 18:2)

This morning I received a letter from a young couple who are very dear
to me. They informed me that their first baby had just been born and
that mother and baby were doing fine. They also included a picture of
the proud father gazing lovingly on mother and child. The announcement said, "The father is recovering quite well."

After reading the announcement, I placed it on my prayer shelf. I
thanked the good Lord for all his creative and providential love, especially
for this young couple. I whispered a little prayer for Gerry and Louise,
asking God to bless them and guide them in rearing their offspring

through the maze of daily living until she reaches her final home in heaven.

My prayer shelf is a very sacred place in my home, almost like a miniature altar. It displays quite an assortment of objects from time to time. These serve as reminders of the presence and power of God operating at every moment in my life.

In front of my prayer shelf is the chair I usually use for my daily prayer time with the Lord. Occupying center stage on the shelf is the Bible. Surrounding the Bible are a number of objects that help me focus my attention on the Lord. They serve as visual aids to remind me of the caring, concerned love of the Lord enveloping me at all times.

On the anniversary of the death of my father or mother, I place their picture on my prayer shelf to remind me to thank God for all they did for me and to praise him for giving me such good parents. When I receive such greeting cards on various occasions, I put them on my miniature altar to stimulate my prayer for the persons who sent them to me.

As I jot down these thoughts, I survey my prayer shelf to take stock of what rests on it at this moment. There is a butterfly that symbolizes the new life Jesus came to give, as he himself said, "I came that they might have life and have it to the full" (John 10:10). Next to it is a rock about the size of my fist. On the open page of the Bible I can read,

I love you, O Lord, my strength,
O Lord, my rock, my fortress, my deliverer.
My God, my rock of refuge,
my shield, the horn of my salvation, my stronghold! (Ps. 18:2–3)

The rock also reminds me that Jesus concluded the Sermon on the Mount with this thought: "Anyone who hears my words and puts them into practice is like the wise man who built his house on rock" (Matt. 7:24).

Next week the collection on my prayer shelf could be totally different, made up of whatever comes my way.

Andrew Murray, *With Christ in the School of Prayer*

(1828–1917) Known for his deep devotional life, Murray was also the most influential leader of the nineteenth-century South African Dutch Reformed Church.

Moses gave neither command nor regulation with regard to prayer: even the prophets say little directly of the duty of prayer; it is Christ who teaches to pray.

The first thing the Lord teaches His disciples is that they must have a secret place for prayer; every one must have some solitary spot where he can be alone with his God. He wants each one to choose for himself the fixed spot where He can daily meet him. That inner chamber, that solitary place, is Jesus' schoolroom. That spot may be anywhere; that spot may change from day to day if we have to change our abode; but that secret place there must be, with the quiet time in which the pupil places himself in the Master's presence, to be by Him prepared to worship the Father. There alone, but there most surely, Jesus comes to us to teach us to pray.

Chester P. Michael and Marie C. Norrisey, *Prayer and Temperament*

All indicators point to a close relationship between our innate temperament and the type of prayer best suited to our needs. Introverts will prefer a form of prayer different from Extroverts. Intuitives approach God from a point of view different from Sensers. Feelers pray in a different way from Thinkers. . . . As we grow in maturity and learn to make good use of all our abilities in functioning and relating, our prayer life should become richer. While we may still prefer the type of prayer that matches our natural temperament, we should familiarize ourselves with the other forms of prayer that have been developed over the centuries.

Romans 8:15 (KJV)

For ye have not received the spirit of bondage again to fear; but ye have received the Spirit of adoption, whereby we cry, Abba, Father.

William Barclay, *A Guide to Daily Prayer*

(1907–1978) Scottish minister and scholar best known for his New Testament commentary series, The Daily Study Bible.

How should we pray? The way in which we ought to pray is settled once and for all by the name which Jesus gave to God, the name by which he enabled us to address God. When Jesus was praying in Gethsemane he addressed God as: Abba, Father. Twice Paul says that that is the way in which the Christian through Christ is able to address God (Rom. 8:15; Gal. 4:6). *Abba* is much more than *father*. *Abba* was the word by which a little Jewish child addressed his father in the privacy and the intimacy of the home circle . . . *Abba* is *Daddy*. This is the way in which we can talk to God. We can talk to God with the same intimacy, and confidence, and trust as a little child talks to his father. Because of what Jesus was, because of what he told us, because of what he did, no one is easier to talk to than God.

All kinds of things are settled by this. We do not need to talk to God in any special kind of religious or theological language. Certainly we do not need to talk to him in Elizabethan and archaic English. That is why in this book I have always used *you* in speaking to God, and not *thou*. We do not need to talk to God in any special position. Kneeling, standing, sitting, lying, it is all the same. As a child runs to his father and tells him everything in the days when he is very young and very innocent and very trusting, so we can talk to God.

It is not that God is any the less God. It is simply that God for us has become the friend of all friends. Once, it is said, a Roman Emperor was celebrating a triumph. He was parading his armies, his captives and his trophies through the streets of Rome. The streets were crowded. At one place on the route there was a little platform where the Empress was sitting with her children. As the Emperor's chariot passed this place the Emperor's little son jumped down, dived through the crowd and was about to run out to the road to his father. One of the Roman legionaries who were lining the pavement stopped the boy. He swung him up in his arms. "You can't do that," he said. "Don't you know who that is? That's the Emperor." The boy looked down at him and laughed. "He may be your Emperor," he said, "but he's my father." God is God but God is *Abba* too.

We must once and for all get rid of the idea that prayer is something stilted and unnatural. It is the most natural thing in the world. It is a child talking to his father, as he did when he was very young.

———— ∽∾∾ ————

W. Bingham Hunter, *The God Who Hears*

Exhaustive research by biblical scholars—particularly J. Jeremias and W. Marchel—has demonstrated that in all the huge literature of ancient Judaism there is not one instance of God being addressed in prayer with the word *abba*. He was called "The Lord Almighty," "The Holy One," "Sovereign of the World" and many other exalted titles, but a word like *abba* was too personal, too familiar and intimate to be appropriate. The Lord was high and lifted up, the incomparable One. He was to be approached with reverence and awe. To call him "Daddy" was unthinkable blasphemy. Yet Jesus prayed like this all the time. . . .

On Jesus' lips *abba* as an address to God in prayer is understandable and perhaps even expected. The amazing and unexpected thing is that he gave . . . his disciples a privilege which previously had been his alone!

Yet to call God "Dear Father" does not seem special to most Christians. Many reading this have grown up, as I did, in communities where we heard God called "Father" from the earliest days of spiritual awareness. We need to be reminded periodically that the privilege of speaking with God so intimately was not given to even the greatest Old Testament saints.

The Pharasaic rabbis of Judaism stretched the Law to astounding limits, but none of them would have dared to call on God in prayer as *abba*. Being too familiar with God was serious business. They tried to kill Jesus for "calling God his own Father" (John 5:18). Yet one of the wonders of the salvation wrought by Jesus' death is the "adoption" into God's family of those who believe (Eph. 1:5). Christians have been made "heirs of God and co-heirs with Christ" (Rom. 8:17), and are now able to approach God without fear as beloved children.

Abba represents the essentials of the new relationship with God which Jesus offered men and women who believe on his name. From the Father's side *abba* implies many things: (1) his mercy, compassion and love for the child; (2) his personal interest in the child and consistent concern for its good; (3) his willingness to provide for the needs of and give protection to the child; and (4) the use of his mature knowledge, judgment and wisdom in guiding and caring for the child. On the child's lips *abba* signifies (1) an implicit willingness to love, honor, and respect the Father; (2) an awareness of dependency on the Father; (3) a sense of confidence in the Father's judgment and trust in his integrity and abilities; and (4) ready obedience to the Father's desires and will, with corresponding acceptance of the Father's right and responsibility to discipline for the child's good. In short, *abba* signifies (1) an implicit willingness to love, honor, and respect the Father; (2) an awareness of dependency on the Father; (3) a sense of confidence in the Father's judgment and trust in his integrity and abilities; and (4) ready obedience to the Father's desires and will, with corresponding acceptance of the Father's right and responsibility to discipline for the child's good. In short, *abba* signifies the essence of what it means to have a personal relationship with God.

William Barclay, *A Guide to Daily Prayer*

Where should we pray? Sometimes the Jews used to say that prayer was not really valid and effective unless it was offered in the Synagogue; but the great Jewish teachers also said that he who prays in his own house and home surrounds it with a wall of iron. The simple answer is that we should pray everywhere. It is quite true that there are certain places in which we are bound to feel closer to God than anywhere else. But, as Stephen said, God does not dwell in temples made with hands (Acts 7:48), and as Whittier, the Quaker poet, put it, the whole round earth is the temple of God.

We can pray anywhere, in the quiet of our own room, or, if we have not got a room of our own, on the street, in the train, on the bus, in some quiet church into which we can slip for a moment. Someone has spoken of what he called "arrow prayers," just words, phrases, half sentences spoken anywhere to God. If God is everywhere, then we can meet him anywhere. Brother Lawrence used to say that he felt just as near to God when he was washing the dirty dishes in the monastery kitchen and going about the tasks of the scullery as ever he did when he was kneeling at the Blessed Sacrament. The set appointment must be kept, but anywhere and everywhere there is a door to the presence of God which no man can ever shut.

Richard Foster, *Prayer*

In *The Saints' Everlasting Rest* Richard Baxter counsels us to seek out the "fittest time for prayer, the fittest place for prayer, and the fittest preparation of heart" for prayer. These constitute the specific fidelities of Covenant Prayer.

The Covenant of Time means a commitment to a *regular* experience of prayer. In his *Rule* Saint Benedict insisted on regularity in prayer because he did not ever want his followers to forget who was in charge. It is an occupational hazard of devout people to confuse their work with God's work. How easy it is to replace "this work is really significant" with "I am really significant." With a profound understanding of this, Benedict would call for prayer at regular intervals throughout the day— right in the middle of apparently urgent and important work. We, too, will find that a commitment to regular prayer will defeat self-importance and the wiles of the devil.

But what is "regular"? That will depend on you: your personality, your needs. The ancient Hebrew pattern was three times a day—morning, afternoon, and evening. Peter and John encountered the lame man because they were going up to the temple at the three o'clock hour of prayer, as was their custom (Acts 3:1). (I know of one group in India that has chimes that ring at ten in the morning and three in the afternoon as a signal for everyone to stop what they are doing and gather up the needs of the community in silent prayer.) Many have found a daily—especially early-morning—regimen especially useful. "O Lord, in the morning you hear my voice," declares the Psalmist (Ps. 5:3).

We must be careful here not to lay impossible burdens upon people. Rural life tends to function around a daily cycle, whereas urban life tends to function around a weekly cycle. In the country there are chores to be done morning and evening—such as milking the cows and feeding the chickens. A daily prayer discipline makes good sense in this context. In urban life, in contrast, everything presses hard toward Friday—"TGIF," as we say—and the weekends are much more discretionary. In this context it might make more sense to order a prayer life around a weekly pattern. Instead of feeling guilty that we cannot set aside time for prayer on a daily basis, perhaps it would be better to devote Saturday mornings, for example, to more extended experiences of prayer and devotional reading. . . .

Once we have made generous latitude for individual differences and schedules, we must firmly discipline ourselves to a regular pattern of prayer. We cannot assume that time will somehow magically appear. We will never *have* time for prayer—we must *make* time. On this score we have to be ruthless with our rationalizations. We must never, for instance, excuse our prayerlessness under the guise of "always living prayerfully." John Dalrymple rightly observes, "The truth is that we only learn to pray all the time everywhere after we have resolutely set about praying some of the time somewhere."

Accountability to others helps immensely. I meet weekly with a small group, and at every gathering each of us answers several questions, the first one being: "What experiences of prayer and meditation have you had this week, and what is your determination for next week?"

Simple, practical decisions can aid us in maintaining our covenant. I like to date each time of prayer in a simple spiral notebook that is always with me. When I travel, I usually plan to use the first leg of the plane flight for worship, prayer, and meditation. One winter I scheduled a three o'clock appointment into my datebook for each working day. I would then leave the office for one hour, drive five minutes to the local zoo, and, with Bible and personal journal in hand, spend fifty minutes on a bench in a lovely indoor rain forest. Most people do not have such discretionary time on the job, but we all have time available to us if we once get the idea.

I hope you know that there is no need to answer the telephone, or the door, for that matter. Archbishop Anthony Bloom tells of his father, who would put a note on his door saying, "Don't go to the trouble of knocking. I am at home but I will not open the door." I have never quite been able to do that, but I have on occasion put a sign on my office that everyone understands—"In Conference with the Boss!"

Be assured of this: everything will try to pull you away from this sacred time. Your phone will ring. Your pen will run dry. Someone will knock at your door. You will suddenly have an urgent need to do something you have left undone for years. In that split second you alone will decide whether you will hold steady in the inner sanctuary of the heart or rush out of the holy place, tyrannized by the urgent. . . .

If the Covenant of Time calls us to constancy, then the Covenant of Place calls us to stability. In his day Saint Benedict saw so many roving prophets without any kind of accountability that he made the vow of stability a central feature of his *Rule*. We, too, need to be anchored somewhere.

The Covenant of Place give us the gift of focus. When I was a new Christian, I used to go out behind the garage each morning and sit on a cinder-block wall with my feet on the trash cans, Bible in hand. This was holy ground. On those days when it was too cold to be outside, I went literally into a closet in our tiny duplex in New Mexico. There found darkness and silence, both of which taught me focus. I urge you, too, to find a place of focus—a loft, a garden, a spare room, an attic, even a designated chair—somewhere away from the routine of life, out of the path of distractions. Allow this spot to become a sacred "tent of meeting." . . .

We are to have the "fittest preparation of heart," says Richard Baxter. Long before anyone knew that body language reveals our innermost feelings, Baxter was urging people to meet God in such an uninhibited way that their deepest feelings could burst forth. We can run, jump, walk, stand, kneel, or lie prostrate on the floor. We can close our eyes bowed in awe and reverence, or we can raise our eyes upward in praise and devotion. We can lift our hands, clap our hands, fold our hands. We can weep, laugh, sing, shout. We can use trumpet, lute, harp, tambourine, strings, pipe, and loud clashing cymbals. We can kneel in silent wonder and adoration.

We can also prepare the heart by cultivating "holy expectancy." With our mind's eye we pass through the outer court and into the inner court. The veil is lifted from our hearts, and we enter the Holy of Holies. The air becomes charged with expectancy. We listen in utter silence for the *Kol Yahweh,* the voice of the Lord.

Another way we make the heart ready to enter the awesome Presence is by disciplining the tongue. How much more fitting to come in absolute silence before the Holy One of eternity than to rush into his presence with hearts and minds askew and tongues full of words. The scriptural admonition is, "The Lord is in his holy temple; let all the earth keep silence before him!" (Hab. 2:20).

Specific preparations can be extremely helpful. The Psalter is the prayerbook of the Church, and I often precede personal prayer with the prayerful reading of a Psalm. My own church tradition is decidedly non-liturgical, which is precisely why at times I use one of the great books of liturgy designed to aid private prayer. Sometimes I have John Baillie cultivate my heart by means of his famous *Diary of Private Prayer,* or I may turn to the lesser-known *Doctor Johnson's Prayers*. At other times I write out my own prayers and pray them as a daily private ritual of heart preparation.

The preparation of your own little sanctuary can draw the heart into worship. I have a friend who lights a candle in her small study whenever she goes to prayer. Fresh flowers can delight both sight and smell. I like to have a cup of coffee in hand whenever I pray in the morning.

I know you have preparations of your own. The idea is to use all the means at our disposal to urge all that is within us into doxology: "Bless the Lord, O my soul, and all that is within me, bless his holy name" (Ps. 103:1).

English Proverb

Prayers should be the key of the day and the lock of the night.

John Baillie, *A Diary of Private Prayer*

(1886–1960) Scottish theologian, writer, and apologist.

Some people find it helpful to begin and end their day with prayer. John Baillie's book *A Diary of Private Prayer* provides the reader with a month of morning and evening prayers, such as these.

Morning

O Lord God, I praise and magnify Thy name that thus Thou hast set Thy seal upon my inmost being, not leaving me to my own poor and petty selfhood or to the sole empire of animal passion and desire, but calling me to be an heir of Thine eternal Kingdom. I bless Thee for that knocking at my heart's door that warns me of Thy waiting presence. I bless Thee for Thy hand upon my life, and for the sure knowledge that, however I may falter and fail, yet underneath are Thine everlasting arms.

O Thou who alone knowest what lies before me this day, grant that in every hour of it I may stay close to Thee. Let me be in the world, yet not of it. Let me use this world without abusing it. If I buy, let me be as though I possessed not. If I have nothing, let me be as though possessing all things. Let me to-day embark on no undertaking that is not in line with Thy will for my life, nor shrink from any sacrifice which Thy will may demand. Suggest, direct, control every movement of my mind; for my Lord Christ's sake. Amen.

Evening

O Divine Love who dost everlastingly stand outside the closed doors of the souls of men, knocking ever and again, wilt Thou not now give me grace to throw open all my soul's doors? To-night let every bolt and bar be drawn that has hitherto robbed my life of air and light and love.

Give me an open ear, O God, that I may hear Thy voice calling me to high endeavour. Too often have I been deaf to the appeals Thou hast addressed to me, but now give me courage to answer, *Here am I, send me.* And when any one of Thy children, my human brothers, cries out in need, give me then an open ear to hear in that cry Thy call to service.

Give me an open mind, O God, a mind ready to receive and to welcome such new light of knowledge as it is Thy will to reveal to me. Let not the past ever be so dear to me as to set a limit to the future. Give me courage to change my mind, when that is needed. Let me be tolerant to the thoughts of others and hospitable to such light as may come to me through them.

Give me open eyes, O God, eyes quick to discover Thine indwelling in the world which Thou hast made. Let all lovely things fill me with gladness and let them uplift my mind to Thine everlasting loveliness. Forgive all my past blindness to the grandeur and glory of nature, to the charm of little children, to the sublimities of human story, and to all the intimations of Thy presence which these things contain.

Give me open hands, O God, hands ready to share with all who are in want the blessings with which Thou hast enriched my life. Deliver me from all meanness and miserliness. Let me hold my money in steward-ship and all my worldly goods in trust for Thee; to whom now be all hon-our and glory. Amen.

———∞∞———

Don Postema, *Space for God*

I used to write in my daily calendar "7–7:30 A.M.—Prayer." But many times I passed that up. It was one more thing to pass by that day. Now I write "7–7:30 A.M—God." Somehow that's a little harder to neglect.

———∞∞———

Robert Munger, "The Living Room," *My Heart—Christ's Home*

This classic of modern devotion uses the image of a home to explore our relationship with Christ. In this short story the young, student con-vert takes Jesus through his home, and room by room we discover some-thing new about our relationship with Christ. In this section, titled "The Living Room," we learn something about how Jesus views our fellowship with Him.

We moved next into the living room. This was a quiet, comfortable room with a warm atmosphere. I liked it. It had a fireplace, sofa, over-stuffed chairs, a bookcase and an intimate atmosphere.

He also seemed pleased with it. He said, "Indeed, this is a delight-ful room. Let's come here often. It's secluded and quiet, and we can have good talks and fellowship together."

Well, naturally, as a young Christian I was thrilled. I couldn't think of anything I would rather do than have a few minutes alone with Christ in close companionship.

He promised, "I will be here every morning early. Meet me here and we will start the day together."

So, morning after morning, I would go downstairs to the living room. He would take a book of the Bible from the bookcase, open it, and we would read it together. He would unfold to me the wonder of God's saving truth recorded on its pages and make my heart sing as he shared all he had done for me and would be to me. Those times together were wonderful. Through the Bible and his Holy Spirit he would talk to me. In prayer I would respond. So our friendship deep-ened in these quiet times of personal conversation.

However, under the pressure of many responsibilities, little by lit-tle, this time began to be shortened. Why, I'm not sure. Somehow I assumed I was just too busy to give special, regular time to be with

Christ. This was not a deliberate decision, you understand; it just seemed to happen that way. Eventually, not only was the period shortened, but I began to miss days now and then, such as during midterms or finals. Matters of urgency demanding my attention were continually crowding out the quiet times of conversation with Jesus. Often I would miss it two days in a row or more.

One morning, I recall rushing down the steps in a hurry to be on my way to an important appointment.

As I passed the living room, the door was open. Glancing in, I saw a fire in the fireplace and Jesus sitting there. Suddenly, in dismay, it came to me, "He is my guest. I invited him into my heart! He has come as my Savior and Friend to live with me. Yet here I am neglecting him."

I stopped, turned and hesitatingly went in. With downcast glance I said, "Master, I'm sorry! Have you been here every morning?"

"Yes," he said, "I told you I would be here to meet with you." I was even more ashamed! He had been faithful in spite of my faithlessness. I asked him to forgive me and he did, as he always does when we acknowledge our failures and want to do the right thing.

He said, "The trouble is that you have been thinking of the quiet time, of Bible study and prayer, as a means for your own spiritual growth. This is true, but you have forgotten that this time means something to me also. Remember, I love you. At a great cost I have redeemed you. I value your fellowship. Just to have you look up into my face warms my heart. Don't neglect this hour if only for my sake. Whether or not you want to be with me, remember I want to be with you. I really love you!"

You know, the truth that Christ wants my fellowship, that he loves me, wants me to be with him and waits for me, has done more to transform my quiet time with God than any other single fact. Don't let Christ wait alone in the living room of your heart, but every day find a time and place when, with the Word of God and in prayer, you may be together with him.

W. Bingham Hunter, *The God Who Hears*

Christians are sometimes told they should rise by at least 6:00 A.M. every morning to pray for thirty minutes. "Jesus got up early to pray and you should be doing it too," we are told. And historical precedent may be used for more clout: "Whenever Martin Luther knew he was going to have a tough day he got up *another* hour earlier so he could pray longer."

Now if you have not been having early morning prayer, all this may depress rather than inspire you.

My encouragement would be to mention that Martin Luther also went to bed about as early as his chickens, and to observe that Jesus also prayed throughout the day, evening and night hours. Our Lord does not come on the air for prayer only between 6:00 and 6:30. Pray when it best fits your schedule. Pick a time you can look forward to rather than dread. Start by praying for as long as you are comfortable. This will probably be longer than you thought, but if it means only five minutes a day, then do it.

And don't feel guilty because you are not yet a great prayer warrior. Warriors are trained; and training takes both time and experience. Luther went through years of structured spiritual training and monastic experience before he developed the prayer habits one so often hears about. Your desire to pray will grow. Those who taste find that the Lord is good. Some day you may find prayer so invigorating that you will agree with the psalmist: "As the deer pants for the water brooks, so my soul pants for Thee, O God. My soul thirsts for God, for the living God" (Ps. 42:1–2 NASB).

Remember also that God, like the rest of us, finds it somewhat less than captivating when you fall asleep on him while talking. Paul seemed to be aiming at this when he urged: "Devote yourselves to prayer, keeping *alert* in it" (Col. 4:2 NASB). And Peter adds, "Be *clear-minded* and self-controlled so that you can pray" (I Pet. 4:7). To communicate effectively you have to think; and to make sense you have to be organized. It is not otherwise with God.

Praying out loud—even though alone—helps some, while using notes, lists and prayer notebooks may help organization and memory. Some find fasting helps their mental acuity, and so they eat after they pray. Those with lower blood sugar levels must eat before they pray. Some people pray in their night clothes while others are fully dressed. If obeying Paul's admonition to "sing . . . with gratitude in your hearts to God" (Col. 3:16) is easiest when you're undergoing the stimulation of a shower, then praise him in the privacy of your bathroom.

The point is to look for the most helpful time of day, find out what will help you get focused and *do* it.

Oswald Chambers, *My Utmost for His Highest*

Get into the habit of dealing with God about everything. Unless in the first waking moment of the day you learn to fling the door wide back and let God in, you will work on a wrong level all day; but swing the door wide open and pray to your Father in secret, and every public thing will be stamped with the presence of God.

———∞———

Jim Castelli, *How I Pray*

Exercise turns out to be a popular time for prayer: [Richard] Foster . . . pray[s] while [he] jog[s]: [Rembert] Weakland prays while using his Nordictrack machine; [Norman] Lear has Saint Francis of Assisi's prayer taped to his treadmill. . . . Exercise seems to provide two elements helpful to prayer: mental privacy and regular breathing. . . .

Music and the arts also help many people pray. [Andrew] Greeley says music and poetry spark prayer in him. . . . Weakland claims the first time he heard Schubert's Fifth Symphony was a religious experience, and [Jane] Redmont says she was converted by Mozart's *Requiem*. [Martin] Marty says the prayerful state he enters while listening to classical music helped him cope with his first wife's death.

———∞———

George Buttrick, *Prayer*

(1892–1980) English philosopher and author who migrated to the United States to become the leader of Madison Avenue Presbyterian Church in New York City.

Which forms of prayer are best? There is no rule of thumb, for the reason that every thumbprint is different and distinct. Some *habit* of prayer is clearly wise, for all life is built on habit; but the habit should be under frequent scrutiny lest it harden into a confining shell. Some *gesture* of prayer is wise. Here also there can be no general prescription. Men have knelt, stood with face upturned, sat haunched with eyes closely focused, and lain prostrate. They have prayed with hands raised to the sky—the early Christians misconstrued the history of that gesture, and adopted it because it seemed to imitate the sufferings of Jesus on the cross—with hands covering the face, with hands bearing gifts, with hands clapping in rhythm, with hands clasped, and with hands close-fisted beating on the breast. These facts warn us against dogmatism, but they testify to the value of *some* gesture-accompaniment in prayer. "Unclasp your fists, and your anger will go," said a wise old counsel. It is too optimistic, but has its truth. "Fold your hands in prayer, or lift them to the sky, and reverence will come," is also, within limits, sage guidance. That is to say, a gesture releases the random energies of the body, and cuts a physical channel through which the spirit may flow. Audible speech has this power in unusual measure: words clarify the vague resolve and themselves carry it into the deed. Again, some *rhythm* in prayer's forms is wise. Hence our "orders of worship" with their changing moods and energies. Speech and silence should both have place, for one is active and the other receptive. Repetition gives deeper and deeper imprint to a prayer, but becomes mere rote unless balanced by newness. So liturgy and "free prayer" each claim place and bestow a mutual good. All prayer's moods, as we have seen, should find their due expression.

⸺ ∞ ⸺

David E. Rosage, *Meeting God in Every Moment*

Kneel to Stand Tall

> *"Here I stand, knocking at the door." (Rev. 3:20)*

After the hubbub of the Christmas festivities settles down, I enjoy taking some time to study the Christmas cards I received. Pondering these cards thoughtfully and reflectively has become a prayerful experience for me.

The last time I did so, I made a new discovery. A large percentage of the cards I received depicted Mary kneeling at the manger of her divine Son in silent reverence, while Joseph, in a standing position, looked on in quiet admiration. It suddenly struck me that these two positions are both splendid prayer postures.

Mary's kneeling position touched me very deeply. As she gazed in awe at her Son, her smiling eyes radiated the love and joy pouring out of her heart. Mary is not merely a young mother lovingly beholding her first-born son, but she is kneeling in recognition of who her Son is. Her silent adoration is indicative of her total submission to the privileged role for which she was chosen. This was the first time that Mary's kneeling posture impressed me so forcefully.

Kneeling is a petitioning posture. We can picture a young man kneeling before a young woman as he asks for her hand in marriage. Kneeling is almost always associated with prayer. It acknowledges God as Creator, Redeemer, and providing Father. It is also a sign of humility. When we kneel, we sacrifice one-third of our height. We want to stand tall before our friends and associates. In prayer we kneel before God so that we can stand tall before men.

Standing is also a proper prayer posture. It is a stance of reverence and respect. It manifests a willingness to be of service. Standing when a special person enters a room is a sign of respect. In the military an enlisted person or even an officer stands at attention when a superior officer is present. A guard stands prepared to protect whatever is entrusted to his custody. I have often wondered if the great prophet Isaiah was standing when he responded to the Lord, "Here I am . . . send me" (Isa. 6:8).

Whatever our prayer posture . . . did Jesus not assure us, "Here I stand, knocking at the door. If anyone hears me calling and opens the door, I will enter his house and have supper with him, and he with me" (Rev. 3:20)?

We need to remember that Jesus is a gentleman. He does not force himself on us but waits for our invitation. We must also note that the latch is on the inside of the door.

Raising Hands

To you I stretch out my hands. (Ps. 88:10)

As I gazed at a perfectly shaped tree, its branches swaying gracefully in the gentle breeze, I was reminded of that verse from Joyce Kilmer's poem entitled "Trees":

"A tree that looks at God all day
and lifts her leafy arms to pray . . ."

The poet touches upon a very meaningful gesture of prayer. For a long time lifting one's hands in prayer was a regular custom, but then it faded into oblivion. Now this prayer posture is becoming common once again.

Raising our arms in prayer is an eloquent way of expressing some dispositions that are essential to sincere prayer. In the first place, lifting our hands with our palms open and upward is a way of expressing our total offering of self to the Lord. The one offering that the Lord desires is that of ourselves, with all that we are and all that we do. Making such an oblation to the Lord enables him to mold and transform us into the kind of person he wants us to be.

Second, hands raised in prayer indicate our willingness to respond to whatever the Lord might ask of us. It is our way of asking the Lord for the grace and help we need to be open and receptive to whatever he wills for us. It is a gesture of acceptance as well as one of giving, leading us into a disposition for humble prayer.

Raising our hands in prayer is also a way of breaking down many of our inhibitions. It opens us to begin expressing ourselves honestly and sincerely.

My good friend Gordon told me that he was very disturbed by people's raising their hands in prayer. He thought it was too emotional and theatrical. In explaining to him the significance of this prayer posture, I pointed out that the priest at Mass often extends his hands in prayer in the same fashion. This is especially apparent at the introductory dialogue at the Preface. The priest says, "Lift up your hearts," and we respond, "We lift them up to the Lord."

I also reminded Gordon that the Psalter is the only book of divinely inspired prayers that we possess. The psalms frequently exhort us to lift our hands in prayer:

> Let my prayer come like incense before you;
>> the lifting up of my hands, like the evening
>>> sacrifice. (Ps. 141:2)

> I stretch out my hands to you;
>> my soul thirsts for you like parched land.
>>> (Ps. 143:6)

> Hear the sound of my pleading, when I cry to you,
>> lifting up my hands toward your holy shrine.
>>> (Ps. 28:2)

> Daily I call upon you, O Lord;
>> to you I stretch out my hands. (Ps. 88:10)

St. Paul adds his own admonition: "It is my wish, then, that in every place the men shall offer prayers with blameless hands held aloft, and be free from anger and dissension" (1 Tim. 2:8).

These are only a few of the mentions in Scripture about this prayer posture. As I write these words, I find myself wanting to raise my hands in prayer. But my old typewriter needs my hands to translate my thoughts onto paper.

———— ∞ ————

Guideposts, *The Miracle of Prayer*

Different ways people in the Bible prayed:

Jeremiah stood before God to pray for his people (Jer. 18:20).

Peter knelt to pray (Acts 9:40).

Nehemiah sat down when he prayed (Neh. 1:4).

Abraham prostrated himself while praying (Gen. 17:3).

Ezekiel prayed in a loud voice (Ezek. 11:13).

Hannah prayed silently to the Lord (1 Sam. 1:13).

Paul prayed and sang in the spirit (1 Cor. 14:15).

David prayed in the morning (Ps. 5:3).

Isaac prayed out in his field in the evening (Gen. 24:63).

Daniel prayed in his house three times a day (Dan. 6:10).

Anna prayed night and day in the temple (Luke 2:37).

———⁂———

Henri Nouwen, *With Open Hands*

There are as many ways to pray as there are moments in life. Sometimes we seek out a quiet spot and want to be alone, sometimes we look for a friend and want to be together. Sometimes we like a book, sometimes we prefer music. Sometimes we want to sing out with hundreds, sometimes only whisper with a few. Sometimes we want to say it with words, sometimes with a deep silence.

———⁂———

Howard Macy, *Rhythms of the Inner Life*

Classic prayers, if we misuse them, can also hinder us, for we may come to think that to pray well—or at all—we must mimic their lofty sentiments and wonderful words. Though we may well learn from them helpful language for prayer, nothing could be further from the truth. As William Penn counsels, "Do not think to overcome the Almighty by the best material put in the aptest phrase. No. One groan, one sigh from a wounded soul, excels and prevails with God." The sublimest prayers of all must not blind us to the fact that real prayer is simple. . . .

What we need is prayer that is real and that flows out of our own lives with authentic words of longing, despair, trust, and praise. Simple, conversational prayer helps bring to life the reality that God is near and not remote.

Effective prayer must also be sincere, for the efficacy of prayer has much more to do with one's relationship to God than with proper technique. The Psalms sharply contrast those who in prayer ". . . outwardly flattered him, and used their tongues to lie to him" (78:36) with those ". . . who call upon him in truth" (145:18 RSV) or "with sincerity." To pray sincerely means to be honest and vulnerable before God, opening ourselves wholeheartedly to this Friend. To put it in the vernacular, it is spilling our guts to God. This is what Thomas Kelly describes when he writes, "Back behind the scenes of daily occupation you offer yourself steadily to God, you pour out all your life and will and love before Him, and try to keep nothing back. Pour out your triumphs before Him. But pour out also the rags and tatters of your mistakes before Him."

———∞———

Richard Foster, *Prayer*

God receives us just as we are and accepts our prayers just as they are. In the same way that a small child cannot draw a bad picture so a child of God cannot offer a bad prayer.

PROVEN METHODS

Silence—Listening to God

Psalm 62:5–6 (NASB)

A psalm of David:

> My soul, wait in silence for God only,
> For my hope is from Him.
> He only is my rock and my salvation,
> My stronghold; I shall not be shaken.

———∞———

Mother Teresa

I always begin my prayer in silence, for it is in the silence of the heart that God speaks. God is the friend of silence—we need to listen to God because it's not what we say but what He says to us and through us that matters.

———∞———

Henri Nouwen, *The Way of the Heart*

Solitude and silence can never be separated from the call to unceasing prayer. If solitude were primarily an escape from a busy job, and silence primarily an escape from a noisy milieu, they could easily become very self-centered forms of asceticism. But solitude and silence are for prayer. The Desert Fathers did not think of solitude as being alone, but as being alone with God. They did not think of silence as not speaking, but as listening to God. Solitude and silence are the context within which prayer is practiced.

Archbishop Anthony Bloom, *Beginning to Pray*

About twenty years ago, soon after my ordination, I was sent before Christmas to an old people's home. There lived an old lady, who died some time later at the age of 102. She came to see me after my first celebration and said "Father, I would like to have advice about prayer." So I said "Oh yes, ask So-and-so." She said "All these years I have been asking people who are reputed to know about prayer, and they have never given me a sensible reply, so I thought that as you probably know nothing, you may by chance blunder out the right thing." That was a very encouraging situation! And so I said "What is your problem?" The old lady said "These fourteen years I have been praying the Jesus Prayer almost continually, and never have I perceived God's presence at all." So I blundered out what I thought. I said "If you speak all the time, you don't give God a chance to place a word in." She said "What shall I do?" I said "Go to your room after breakfast, put it right, place your armchair in a strategic position that will leave behind your back all the dark corners which are always in an old lady's room into which things are pushed so as not to be seen. Light your little lamp . . . and first of all take stock of your room. Just sit, look round, and try to see where you live, because I am sure that if you have prayed all these fourteen years it is a long time since you have seen your room. And then take your knitting and for fifteen minutes knit before the face of God, but I forbid you to say one word of prayer. You just knit and try to enjoy the peace of your room."

She didn't think it was very pious advice but she took it. After a while she came to see me and said "You know, it works." I said "What works, what happens?" because I was very curious to know how my advice worked. And she said "I did just what you advised me to do. I got up, washed, put my room right, had breakfast, came back, made sure that nothing was there that would worry me, and then I settled in my armchair and thought 'Oh how nice. I have fifteen minutes during which I can do nothing without being guilty!' and I looked round and for the first time after years I thought 'Goodness, what a nice room I live in—a window opening onto the garden, a nice shaped room, enough space for me, the things I have collected for years.'" Then she said "I felt so quiet because the room was so peaceful. There was a clock ticking but it didn't disturb the silence; its ticking just underlined the fact that everything was so still and after a while I remembered that I must knit before the face of God, and so I began to knit. And I became more and more aware of the silence. The needles hit the arm rest of my chair, the clock was ticking peacefully, there was nothing to bother about, I had no need of straining myself, and then I perceived that this silence was not simply an absence of noise, but that the silence had substance. It was not absence of something but presence of something. The silence had a density, a richness, and it began to pervade me. The silence around began to come and meet the silence in me." And then in the end she said something very beautiful which I have found later in the French writer Georges Bernanos. She said "All of a sudden I perceived that the silence was a presence. At the heart of the silence there was He who is all stillness, all peace, all poise."

Howard Macy, *Rhythms of the Inner Life*

To approach God with only an incessant stream of words is a filibuster, not prayer.

A. W. Tozer, *The Pursuit of God*

(1897–1963) Without any formal education, Tozer became one of America's most well-known pastor-theologians.

Lord, teach me to listen. The times are noisy and my ears are weary with the thousand raucous sounds which continuously assault them. Give me the spirit of the boy Samuel when he said to Thee, "Speak, for thy servant heareth." Let me hear Thee speaking in my heart. Let me get used to the sound of Thy voice, that its tones may be familiar when the sounds of the earth die away and the only sound will be the music of Thy speaking voice. Amen.

Fulton J. Sheen, *Lift Up Your Heart*

(1895–1979) American Roman Catholic archbishop who authored some fifty books and is best remembered for his radio and television sermons.

One can be impolite to God, too, by absorbing all the conversation, and by changing the words of Scripture from "Speak, Lord, Thy servant hears" to "Listen, Lord, Thy servant speaks." God has things to tell us which will enlighten us—we must wait for Him to speak.

———⚹———

Thomas Merton

(1915–1968) American Trappist monk and prolific writer. His works included sixty books, essays, history, reviews, and poetry. From the sequestered silence of the Abbey of Our Lady of Gethsemani near Bardstown, Kentucky, his life impacted the world.

Keep still, and let Him do some work.

———⚹———

Michel Quoist

THE TELEPHONE

I have just hung up; why did he telephone?
I don't know . . . O! I get it . . .
I talked a lot and listened very little.

Forgive me, Lord, it was a monologue and not a dialogue.
I explained my idea and did not get his;
Since I didn't listen, I learned nothing,
Since I didn't listen, I didn't help,
Since I didn't listen, we didn't communicate.

Forgive me, Lord, for we were connected,
and now we are cut off.

———⚹———

O. Hallesby, *Prayer*

(1879–1961) Norwegian theologian and leader in the resistance against the Nazis who was arrested in 1943 and sent to a concentration camp that was liberated in 1945.

We pray to God. We speak to him about everything we have on our minds both concerning others and ourselves. There come times, not so seldom with me at least, when I have nothing more to tell God. If I were to continue to pray in words, I would have to repeat what I have already said. At such times it is wonderful to say to God, "May I be in Thy presence, Lord? I have nothing more to say to Thee, but I do love to be in Thy presence."

We can spend time in silence together with people whom we know real well. That we cannot do with others. We must converse with them, entertain them either with interesting or profound things as the case may be. But with our own dear ones we can speak freely about common insignificant things. In their presence, too, we can be silent.

It is not necessary to maintain a conversation when we are in the presence of God. We can come into His presence and rest our weary souls in quiet contemplation of Him. Our groanings, which cannot be uttered, rise to Him and tell Him better than words how dependent we are upon Him.

Joan Bel Geddes, *Are You Listening God?*

God: Teach me to let my soul rest, to still my worries and doubts, to stop my constant chatter of questions and protests.

Let me come to you sometimes and just sit quietly, like a mother smiling at her sleeping baby and listening to its soft breathing . . . or like a small child intent on hearing a kitten's purr or a little bird's chirp . . . or as if I were trying to hear a soft breeze moving across a pond, or a leaf dropping onto the grass.

Let me learn to wait patiently and trustingly for you to make things clearer to me.

Teach me to be as calm as a lake after sundown . . . as trusting as a baby in its mother's lap. Teach me to grow gradually, unprotestingly, like a flower . . . to go unresistingly wherever you send me, like an airborne seed obeying the breeze. Teach me to turn always toward you, the very essence of love and of life, the cause of love and life, the nourisher of love and life, the purpose of love and life — the way leaves keep turning toward the life-giving sun.

A. W. Tozer, *The Set of the Sail*

The heart seldom gets hot while the mouth is open. A closed mouth before God and silent heart are indispensable for the reception of certain kinds of truth. No man is qualified to speak who has not first listened.

Psalm 46:10a

A psalm of the Sons of Korah:

> Be still, and know that I am God . . . (NIV)
>
> Cease striving and know that I am God . . . (NASB)
>
> Stand silent! Know that I am God! (*The Living Bible*)

Sherwood E. Wirt, *The Quiet Corner*

Thank You, Father, for this moment of quiet, and for the strength to pick up my tasks again, renewed and refreshed because I have paused to be with You, for the sake of Jesus Christ our Lord. *Amen.*

———— ∞∞∞ ————

Edith Schaeffer, *Common Sense Christian Living*

Now quickly let me warn you: after such a day [a day of peaceful silence] the roof can fall in! It is not a guarantee that the calmness will carry over into an easy evening. The time is really like being in a protected country place, and leaving it to go into the chaos of city traffic. Nothing else is like it in my own life. You will have to try such a time to know what I'm talking about.

———— ∞∞∞ ————

E. M. Bounds

(1835–1913) Methodist minister and devotional writer who served as a pastor in the American South and became a POW during the Civil War.

"I tell the Lord my troubles and difficulties, and wait for Him to give me the answers to them," said one man of God. "And it is wonderful how a matter that looked very dark will in prayer become clear as crystal by the help of God's Spirit. I think Christians fail so often to get answers to their prayers because they do not wait long enough on God. They just drop down and say a few words, and then jump up and forget it and expect God to answer them. Such praying always reminds me of the small boy ringing his neighbor's doorbell, and then running away as fast as he can go."

———— ∞∞∞ ————

A. W. Tozer, *Jesus, Author of Our Faith*

The Quakers had many fine ideas about life, and there is a story from them that illustrates the point I am trying to make. It concerns a conversation between Samuel Taylor Coleridge and a Quaker woman he had met. Maybe Coleridge was boasting a bit, but he told the woman how he had arranged the use of time so he would have no wasted hours. He said he memorized Greek while dressing and during breakfast. He went on with his list of other mental activities—making notes, reading, writing, formulating thoughts and ideas—until bedtime.

The Quaker listened unimpressed. When Coleridge was finished with his explanation, she asked him a simple, searching question: "My friend, when dost thee think?"

God is having a difficult time getting through to us because we are a fast-paced generation. We seem to have no time for contemplation. We have no time to answer God when He calls.

Henri Nouwen, *Reaching Out*

We simply need quiet time in the presence of God. Although we want to make all our time, time for God, we will never succeed if we do not reserve a minute, an hour, a morning, a day, a week, a month or whatever period of time for God and him alone. This asks much discipline and risk taking because we always seem to have something more urgent to do and "just sitting there" and "doing nothing" often disturbs us more than it helps. But there is no way around this. Being useless and silent in the presence of our God belongs to the core of all prayer. In the beginning we often hear our own unruly inner noises more loudly than God's voice. This is at times very hard to tolerate. But slowly, very slowly, we discover that the silent time makes us quiet and deepens our awareness of ourselves and God. Then, very soon, we start missing these moments when we are deprived of them, and before we are fully aware of it an inner momentum has developed that draws us more and more into silence and closer to that still point where God speaks to us.

Brigid E. Herman, *Creative Prayer*

(1875–1923) Widowed at a young age, she gave herself to writing, especially in the field of theology.

As we approach prayer by the spacious antechamber of silence, we come to realize that the first mover is not we, but God. The prayer that rises to our lips as passionate beseeching of a Father's care and sympathy is not an initial pleading; it is rather the response to an advance. Its very passion is inspired by the spirit who broods over the soul's formless waters and brings articulate expression out of a voiceless waste of need. Prayer always begins with God. As the little child learns its first prayers from its mother's lips, the soul learns to pray from God. There is not a half formed aspiration or a heavenward impulse that was not first "inspoken" into the heart by the Spirit who maketh intercession for us. But we so often refuse to come to prayer through the antechamber of silence. We will not wait and listen for the prayers He is waiting to pray in and through us. And the result is a long, weary, discouraging monologue, which grows intolerable as we become aware of our aloneness. . . .

Yet, did we but know it, a recourse to attentive silence would make even these self-willed prayers alive with the reality of the Divine response. The Spirit whom we disregarded in the framing of our prayers is waiting to guide them still, clarifying our vision, deepening our insight, taking of the hidden treasure of Christ and showing it to our [newly opened] eyes. When prayer seems a hallucination, the simple expedient of hushing the soul to silence often serves to assure us, past all doubting, of the reality of our contact with the Unseen. It is upon our willingness to listen and hear God speak that our prayer life from first to last depends. This should be clear when we remember that prayer is the soul's pilgrimage from self to God; and the most effectual remedy for self-love and self-absorption is the habit of humble listening. . . .

If we read the biographies of the great and wise, be they statesmen or priests, teachers or poets, Roman Catholics or Quakers, we shall find that they were men of long silences and deep ponderings. Whatever of vision, of power, of genius there was in their work was wrought in silence. And when we turn to the inner circle of the spiritual masters—the men and women, not necessarily gifted or distinguished, to whom God was "a living, bright reality" which supernaturalized their everyday life and transmuted their homeliest actions into sublime worship—we find that their roots struck deep into the soil of spiritual silence. Living in the world and rejoicing in human relationships, they yet kept a little cell in their hearts whither they might run to be alone with God. . . .

We of today have lost the sure-footed certainty which our spiritual fathers had. We do not claim to have attained; we cannot even be said to press towards the mark, for the mark is often hidden from our dull and wavering eyes. But even though the goal looms dim in the mist and we are not quite certain of the way, we stand wistfully waiting for someone or something to set us on the path.

We wait, but lack the wisdom of them that wait. We wait impatiently, feverishly turning the pages of a hundred guidebooks, making voluble inquiries of this expert and that, embarking upon any and every adventure that tempts our vagrant fancy. We are even violent at times, but with all our violence we do not take the Kingdom by force.

Then, exhausted with our profitless gropings and flutterings, we listen, perchance, to a stray prophet who reminds us that there is such a thing as a divine science of waiting, and that its master key is silence—the deep, full stillness of the expectant soul. "Be still, and know that I am God."

But we hesitate. The vogue of pseudomysticism, with its jargon about recollection, concentration, and "going into the silence," has prejudiced us against the deliberate cultivation of spiritual stillness. And we also hesitate for another and deeper reason. We know that silence is indeed an unexplored realm, peopled with disquieting apparitions and brimful of unguessed terrors for the chance traveller. No one who has honestly tried to still his soul—to wean intellect and will and emotion from their external activity to a concurrent attitude of quiet expectancy—but has sensed possibilities of weird experiences compared to which the most "successful" spiritualistic seance would appear trite and tame.

For we too have sojourned too long in the dusty city of external relationships. We have gazed so fixedly and persistently upon the pageantry of passing things that they have become our only reality. We have lived so deeply in the lives of our neighbors and our community—and in the mere shell of their lives at that—that we have lost track of that mysterious "buried life" of ours which is the only real life we possess. Our very religion has become little more than a vigorous effort to be sociable and communicative. Impulses which should breed resolution in our souls are exhausted in resolutions on paper, and thoughts that should condense to strong purpose evaporate in a moist vapor of small talk. And, as a result, silence of any kind has become difficult. . . .

The other day I chanced to talk to a strong, plain working woman whose mastery over adverse circumstances was little short of heroic. She had much to say concerning the simple habit of silence. "When I was a little girl," she remarked, "my mother taught me that arnica was good for bruised flesh, and silence was good for a bruised soul; and she made me apply both whenever they were needed." The soul that knows how to be silent in the ordinary vicissitudes of life is the soul that will most readily master the art of spiritual quiet and recollection. . . .

The most formidable enemy of the spiritual life, and the last to be conquered, is self-deception; and if there is a better cure for self-deception than silence, it has yet to be discovered. How many of the feverish motions, rooted half in the flesh and half in the nervous system, which we mistake for Divine callings and inspirations would survive the test of silence? We have often been duped by some stirring of surface feeling, or temperamental passion which clothed itself in spiritual garb, when we might have known the truth had we taken our exaltation between our hands, as it were, and put it to the ordeal of silence. . . .

And it is only by the constant, patient effort to attain that stillness in which the voice of God can be heard that we shall ever find rest to our souls. . . .

But how shall we recognize this voice of God, seeing that so many deluding voices call to us in the stillness? To begin with, we must be prepared to find ourselves making mistakes, and not to be discouraged by such mistakes. All life is a pursuit of truth against hazards, and the falsest life of all is that which is forever seeking to guard itself against the risk of imposture. We are sent into the world by the God of brave men that we may, through many mistakes probably, learn to distinguish the voice of the true Shepherd from the voice of "strangers." . . .

So the soul that waits in silence must learn to disentangle the voice of God from the net of other voices—the ghostly whisperings of the subconscious self, the luring voices of the world, the hindering voices of misguided friendship, the clamor of personal ambition and vanity, the murmur of self-will, the song of unbridled imagination, the thrilling note of religious romance. To learn to keep one's ear true to so subtle a labyrinth of spiritual sound is indeed at once a great adventure and a liberal education. One hour of such listening may give us a deeper insight into the mysteries of human nature, and a surer instinct for Divine values, than a year's hard study. . . . That is why the great solitaries always surprise us by their acute understanding of life. Dwelling apart from men, they none the less have a grasp of human nature which the politician and the financier might envy. They are at home among its intricacies, have plumbed both its meanness and its grandeur, and know how to touch its hidden springs of action. And they know man because they know God and have heard his voice. To know God "preeminently" is their distinction, and it may be ours, at the cost of simple, painstaking honesty with our Maker. Prayer of positive, creative quality needs a background of silence, and until we are prepared to practice this silence, we need not hope to know the power of prayer.

W. Bingham Hunter, *The God Who Hears*

If it is one of those days when nothing comes, then tell God, "I want to be alone with you, but I can't think of anything to say." Or open your Bible and read one of David's prayers in the Psalms. Maybe his words will help you find yours. God knows what your day has been like, where your physiology is, where your emotions have been and how much is ahead for you yet. . . .

At the height of his spiritual maturity Paul acknowledged, "we do not know what we ought to pray." But he went immediately on to say, "the Spirit himself intercedes for us with groans that words cannot express. . . . The Spirit intercedes for the saints in accordance with God's will" (Rom. 8:26–27). Jesus himself once prayed, "Now, my heart is troubled, and what shall I say?" (John 12:27). Now Jesus is closer to God than any other, "at the right hand of God . . . interceding for us" (Rom. 8:34). Through the intercession of Jesus and the Spirit, God has provided for our inadequacies.

⸺⧜⸺

Howard Macy, "Waiting," *Rhythms of the Inner Life*

Sometimes I get nearly worn out watching other people become spiritual. They're sincere enough, I'm sure. In fact, the ones that wear me out are usually people who have a new urgency to know God. But in their eagerness, some of them fall into a round of activity that would sap the strength of a marathoner. They go to every Bible study and prayer meeting they can find. They take up church work with a vengeance— teaching Sunday school, working on committees, evangelizing, hunting heretics—whatever the church is doing. And they adopt a stiff regimen of personal disciplines as well. The problem, of course, is not that I get tired of watching, but that they get worn out, too, and often retreat from longing for God into ordinary religion or into nothing at all. They learn too late that seeking must be tempered with waiting, that eagerness must stand in tension with patience.

The devotional masters warn against a double danger in the life with God. The first is complacency, a spiritual sloth for which the life of longing is a cure. The second is "striving," a way of life so filled with religious activity and pious self-will that it drowns out the voice and thwarts the action of God. It is this second danger that the discipline of waiting effectively fights.

Waiting is not simply another religious activity to be added to the rest. Though we have methods to help us—meditation and silence, for example—waiting is more than physical silence. It is a movement of the heart, a stance we take before God. Waiting is an inner acquiescence, releasing our striving and abandoning our lives entirely to the work of God. Quieting our whole selves, we surrender our activity, our plans, and our dreams. When we wait, we yield up our expectations of what God should do, our precious hoards of ritual and doctrine, our social awareness, and our self-concepts. Waiting is totally submitting to God and inviting God to move in our hearts with complete freedom.

Even though waiting is not an outward activity, it is something that we do. It is not leaning back in a rocking chair on the front porch of our hearts, watching with bemused curiosity to see if anything interesting will happen. It is not something we inadvertently fall into, should we ever run out of activities. Instead, we choose to wait. We consciously carve out an inner space of yielded tranquillity. We hush the insistent noises of our hearts.

All of us who have fidgeted through our early experiences with silence or stillness can witness that waiting does not come easily. It requires practice and persistence. As Bernard of Clairvaux put it, "Waiting upon God is not idleness, but work which beats all other work to one unskilled in it." It is a movement of the heart that can be nurtured, however, even to the point where waiting can become a gentle expectancy penetrating the hurly-burly of our days. Indeed, if waiting does not permeate even our busyness, we have not yet learned its ways.

The failure to see waiting as more than mere idleness often obscures its importance. It would be nice to have the luxury of doing nothing, many people think, but they insist that they must press on to more practical aspects of religious life. Blinded by a frantic, misguided pragmatism, they impatiently reject the work of waiting in the life of devotion, even though it is one of the most practical openings to the life with God. It is in waiting that we learn to listen to God. In waiting we become wise enough to reject "staying busy" as a goal in life and learn how better to spend our energies. We learn to see ourselves, our duty, the world, and God more truly, and that is eminently practical. . . .

"Be still, and know that I am God . . . " (Ps. 46:10 RSV), invites the Holy One. *The Jerusalem Bible* translates here, "Pause a while," perhaps capturing more precisely the sense of the Hebrew verb. Drop what you are doing. Take a deep breath. Relax. "Be still, and know that I am God, exalted among the nations, exalted over the earth. . . ."

Often it is in gentle stillness, not in thunderous theophanies, that we can come to know God, overwhelming in both majesty and tenderness. Madame Guyon writes: "The interior life, that is, the inward life of the spirit, is not a place that is taken by storm or violence. That inward kingdom, that realm within you, is a place of peace. It can only be gained by love. . . ."

It is a witness to the spiritual poverty of our culture, for example, that in response to the question, "How are you?" we so often hear the answer, "I'm keeping busy," as if busyness were a guiding spiritual value or an adequate measure of our worth and achievement. Yet the false value of busyness governs many lives and smothers stillness. I find it embarrassingly difficult, for example, to sit still without picking up a book, taking up a task, or in some other way keeping busy. When I attempt to enjoy times of stillness, I find it far too easy to rate myself against colleagues and friends who are praised for productivity won through frenzied labor. Spiritual madness, I observe, *does* have its temporal rewards. Beside lust for activity spring up many other inner noises, including the appetite for material goods, self-doubt, the overbearing need for approval, worry, and other needs and desires that shout insistently within.

Even religious activity can become noise that inhibits the stillness of waiting. . . . Though such activities are helpful in their proper place, some of us, perhaps, should quit chasing after religious books, Bible studies, and noble works of Christian service so that we can stand still to hear God's voice. Religious noise is noise all the same, and it can easily drown out the gentle, steady call of the Holy One. As Kenneth Leech wisely points out: "There is no need to rush around feverishly looking for a prayer life: we need to slow down and look deeply within. What is the point of complaining that God is absent if it is we who are absent from God, and from ourselves by our lack of awareness? . . . "

If we are to build serene inner spaces, we must learn to still the noises that would hinder us. A practical way to begin is to reduce the volume of outward noises, many of which we can control. Simply turn off the radio and television, for example, and use them only selectively, instead of as musical wallpaper. Establish periods of quietness in the home in which the family forgoes conversation and noisy activity. Choose carefully the number and types of voices to which you will listen. An interest in the news, I have found, can easily become obsessive and destroy stillness. One antidote is to read and listen to the news less often. You don't need to hear every newscast in order to be informed. Similarly, don't submit to "news on the hour" headline broadcasts. Their breathless urgency too easily scatters the spirit and skews reality. Plan tasks and appointments so that you can move from one to another without needlessly creating inner hurriedness. By making simple choices like these, we can reduce noise in surprisingly helpful ways.

Even though we don't all control our schedules equally, we all can arrange them to build stillness. Certainly some duties will fall to anyone who has made a commitment to a job, family, church, or other group of people. However, in addition to the time duty requires, many of us feel invaded by an army of "demands" on our time. Friends, the church, the school, the family, the civic club, our special interest, and a hundred more each try to outshout the others as they bid for our energy and attention. In the midst of such a clamor of duty and demand, we must make choices for stillness. A first step is to recognize what, in fact, our duties are. Many of us saddle ourselves with obligations that are not ours and go far beyond what duty requires, often harming ourselves and others. Well-intentioned people who applaud such extra-mile devotion to duty make right choices even harder, but often they are barely aware (and hardly care) that our spirits are withering under the heat of our breakneck pace. Part of the value of waiting is that through it we can learn which duties are real and which are illusory.

We fool ourselves, though, when we simply blame others, for often it is our own weakness that upgrades requests to the status of "demands." Surely some people do pressure us, but more often we twist our own arms with our pride, our lust for activity, or our insatiable need to please others. The things we choose to do are, by and large, worthy enough, but we must learn that we can be tyrannized as easily by the good as by first-rate wickedness. If we are to establish stillness in our lives, then we will have to say no to some good things and to some nice people in order to have it. Ironically, it is waiting for God, which we so seriously jeopardize with calendars crammed full, that can help us learn what to take up and what to turn away.

While we work to reduce the noise around us, we can also actively create places and times of stillness. For example, if we would put it on our calendars and guard it as jealously as any other appointment, many of us could arrange a day, a weekend, or even longer, for a personal retreat. Short of that, however, even little interludes of solitude can leaven the whole day. I find that five minutes of silence scheduled between appointments or before classes brings benefits completely out of proportion to the time spent. Better yet is the centering and stilling effect of taking fifteen minutes alone to stroll under the impressive arches of maples, elms, and cottonwoods. Even lingering quietly for a few extra minutes in the locker room, after playing racquetball, has often refreshed my sense of peace. Whether a week-long retreat to a mountain cabin or a five-minute recess in a bedroom or office, planned times of solitude feed the inner stillness, which can grow to permeate even the most active parts of our lives.

A time-tested way of coming to stillness is to learn the disciplines of meditation and listening prayer (also called "contemplative prayer" and "meditative prayer"). These methods, based on silence and on the expectation that God will come to those who wait, are old and proven practices. The psalmists speak often of meditating, as in "meditating on the Law day and night," and urge practices similar to the historic practice of Christian meditation.

Anne Morrow Lindbergh, *Gift from the Sea*

The problem is not entirely in finding the room of one's own, the time alone, difficult and necessary as that is. The problem is more how to still the soul in the midst of its activities.

Prayerful Contemplation of the Scriptures

Richard Foster, *Prayer*

Allow me to tell you the story of Jim Smith, a former student of mine.
Genuinely bright Jim went on to do graduate work at a prestigious
school on the East Coast. By the second year, however, he was struggling to maintain his spiritual life, and so he decided to take a private
retreat.

He arrived at the retreat house and was introduced to the brother
who was to be his spiritual director for the week. Instantly, Jim was disappointed, for under the brother's cowl he noticed jogging shoes . . .
Adidas jogging shoes! Jim was expecting a bearded sage filled with the
wisdom of the ages, and instead he got a jogging monk!

The brother gave Jim only one assignment: to meditate on the story
of the Annunciation in the first chapter of Luke's Gospel. That was it.
Jim went back to his room and opened his Bible, muttering to himself,
"Birth narrative, I've read it a thousand times." For the first couple of
hours he sliced and diced the passage as any good exegete would do,
coming up with several useful insights that could fit into future sermons.
The rest of the day was spent in thumb-twiddling silence.

The next day Jim met with the brother to discuss his spiritual life. He
asked Jim how things had gone with the assigned passage. Jim shared
his insights, hoping they would impress the monk.

They did not.

"What was your aim in reading the passage?" he asked.

"My aim? To arrive at an understanding of the meaning of the text, I
suppose."

"Anything else?"

Jim paused, "No. What else is there?"

"Well, there is more than just finding out what it says and what it
means. There are also questions, like what did it say to you? Were you
struck by anything? And, most important, did you experience God in
your reading?" The brother assigned Jim the same text for that entire
day, urging him to read it as much with his heart as with his head. All
day Jim tried doing what his spiritual director had instructed, but he
failed repeatedly. By nightfall he practically had the passage memorized,
and still it was lifeless. Jim felt he would go deaf from the silence.

The next day they met again. In despair Jim told the brother that he
simply could not do what was being asked of him. It was then that the
wisdom behind the jogging shoes became evident: "You're trying too
hard, Jim. You're trying to control God. Go back to this passage and this

time be open to receive whatever God has for you. Don't manipulate God; just receive. Communion with him isn't something you institute. It's like sleep. You can't make yourself sleep, but you can create the conditions that allow sleep to happen. All I want you to do is create the conditions: open your Bible, read it slowly, listen to it, and reflect on it."

Jim went back to his room and began reading. Nothing. By noon he shouted out to the ceiling, "I give up! You win!" There was no response, just as he expected. He slumped over the desk and began weeping.

A short time later he picked up his Bible and glanced over the text once again. The words were familiar but somehow different. His mind and heart were supple. The opening words of Mary's response became his words: "Let it be to me . . . let it be to *me*." The words rang round and round in his head. Then God spoke. It was as if a window suddenly had been thrown open and God wanted to talk friend to friend. What followed was a dialogue about the story in Luke, about God, about Mary, about Jim.

The Spirit took Jim down deep into Mary's feelings, Mary's doubts, Mary's fears, Mary's incredible faith-filled response. It was, of course, also a journey into Jim's feelings and fears and doubts, as the Spirit in healing love and gentle compassion touched the broken memories of his past.

Though Jim could barely believe it, the angel's word to Mary seemed to be a word for him as well: "You have found favor with God." Mary's perplexed query was also Jim's question: "How can this be?" And yet it was so, and Jim wept in the arms of a God of grace and mercy.

In the Scripture passage the angel had just informed Mary of her future destiny. What about Jim's future? They talked about this—God and Jim—what might be, what could be. Jim took a prayer walk with God, watching the sun play hide and seek behind the large oak trees to the west. By the time the sun had slipped below the horizon, he was able to utter the prayer of Mary as his own: "Let it be to me according to your word." Jim had just lost control of his life, and in the same moment had found it! . . . "

In Meditative Prayer the Bible ceases to be a quotation dictionary and becomes instead "wonderful words of life" that lead us to *the* Word of Life. It differs even from the study of Scripture. Whereas the study of Scripture centers on exegesis, the meditation upon Scripture centers on internalizing and personalizing the passage. The written Word becomes a living word addressed to us. This is a time not for technical studies or analysis or even the gathering of material to share with others. We are to set aside all tendencies toward arrogance and with humble hearts receive the word addressed to us. Often I find kneeling especially appropriate for this particular time. Dietrich Bonhoeffer says, "Just as you do not analyze the words of someone you love, but accept them as they are said to you, accept the Word of Scripture and ponder it in your heart, as Mary did. That is all. That is meditation. . . ."

Remember, in Meditative Prayer God is always addressing our will. Christ confronts us and asks us to choose. Having heard his voice, we are to obey his word. It is this ethical call to repentance, to change, to obedience that most clearly distinguishes Christian meditation from its Eastern and secular counterparts. In Meditative Prayer there is no loss of identity, no merging with the cosmic consciousness, no fanciful astral travel. Rather, we are called to life-transforming obedience because we have encountered the living God of Abraham, Isaac, and Jacob. Christ is truly present among us to heal us, to forgive us, to change us, to empower us.

———∞∞∞———

Ken Gire, *Windows of the Soul*

A PRAYER OF INTIMACY

Help me, O God,
To treasure all the words in the Scriptures,
   but to treasure them only as they lead to You.
May the words be stepping-stones in finding You,
   and if I am to get lost at all in the search,
      may it not be down a theological rabbit trail,
         or in some briar patch of religious controversy.
If I am to get lost at all,
   grant that it be in Your arms.

———∞∞∞———

Hans Urs von Balthasar, *Prayer*

We must never aim at carrying out a prescribed programme in prayer; as soon as God's word makes its impact, we must leave all the rest and follow it. Once we have grown wings and rise from the ground, the laws of the air and the spirit come into play.

———∞∞∞———

Gemma Galgani

(1878–1903) Italian devotional writer who wrote of her deep spiritual peace in the midst of intense physical pain.

In my prayers, dear Jesus, I am with you wholly.
If I meditate on the cross, I suffer with you.

If I meditate on the resurrection, I rise with you.
So daily I die and rise.

If I walk with you along the hot dusty roads,
I become hot, sweaty, tired, as you surely did.
If I hear you preach, my ears tingle with excitement,
And my heart is pierced by the sharpness of your words.
If I watch you heal people, I can feel your touch,
So my own body trembles at your power.

Let me walk with you during every minute of my life,
Let me constantly be inspired by your words,
Let me daily be renewed by your power,
That I may die to sin and rise to perfect righteousness.

Hans Urs von Balthasar, *Prayer*

In prayer . . . man speaks to a God who has long since revealed Himself
to him in a Word which is so stupendous and all-embracing that it can
never be "past tense"; this Word resounds through all times as a present
reality. The better a man learns to pray, the more deeply he finds that all
his stammering is only an answer to God's speaking to him; this in turn
implies that any understanding between God and man must be on the
basis of God's language. It was God who spoke first, and it is only because God has expressed, "exteriorized," Himself in this way that man
can "interiorize" himself toward God. Just think of the Our Father which
we address to him every day: is not this his own word? Were we not
taught it by the son of God, who is God and the Word of God? . . .

All of a sudden we just *know*: prayer is a conversation in which God's
word has the initiative and we, for the moment, can be nothing more
than listeners. The essential thing is for us to hear God's word and discover from it how to respond to him. His word is the truth, opened up to
us. For there is no ultimate, unquestionable truth in man; he knows this,
as, full of questionings, he looks up to God and sets out toward him.
God's word is his invitation to us to be with him in the truth. We are in
danger of drowning on the open sea, and God's word is the rope ladder
thrown down to us so that we can climb up into the rescuing vessel.
It is the carpet, rolled out toward us so that we can walk along it to
the Father's throne. It is the lantern which shines in the darkness of
the world (a world which keeps silence and refuses to reveal its own
nature); it casts a softer light on the riddles which torment us and encourages us to keep going. Finally, God's word is himself, his most vital,

his innermost self: his only-begotten Son, of the same nature as himself, sent into the world to bring it home, back to him. And so God speaks to us from heaven and commends to us his Word, dwelling on earth for a while: "This is my beloved Son: listen to him" (Matt. 17:5).

Harassed by life, exhausted, we look about us for somewhere to be quiet, to be genuine, a place of refreshment. We yearn to restore our spirits in God, to simply let go in him and gain new strength to go on living. But we fail to look for him where he is waiting for us, where he is to be found: in his Son, who is his Word. Or else we seek for God because there are a thousand things we want to ask him, and imagine that we cannot go on living unless they are answered. We inundate him with problems, with demands for information, for clues, for an easier path, forgetting that in his Word he has given us the solution to every problem and all the details we are capable of grasping in this life. We fail to listen where God speaks: where God's Word rang out in the world once for all, sufficient for all ages, inexhaustible. Or else we think that God's word has been heard on earth for so long that by now it is almost used up, that it is about time for some new word, as if we had the right to demand one. We fail to see that it is we ourselves who are used up and alienated, whereas the word resounds with the same vitality and freshness as ever; it is just as near to us as it always was. "The word is near you, on your lips and in your heart" (Rom. 10:8). We do not understand that once God's word has rung out in the midst of the world, in the fullness of time, it is so powerful that it applies to everyone, addresses everyone, all with equal directness; no one is disadvantaged by distance in space or time. True, there were a few people who became Jesus' earthly partners in dialogue, and we might envy them their good fortune, but they were as clumsy and inarticulate in this dialogue as we and anyone else would have been. In terms of listening and responding to Jesus' real concerns they had no advantage over us; on the contrary, they saw the earthly, external appearance of the Word, and it largely concealed from them the divine interior. "Blessed are those who do not see and yet believe"—and who, perhaps, believe all the more readily for not being able to see. Even the disciples did not understand the true significance of the Word until after the resurrection, and even then many still doubted and evidently failed to understand. Not until after the ascension, at Pentecost, when the Spirit interpreted in them, interiorly, what the Son had explained to them exteriorly, did they really grasp it. So these earthly partners of Jesus were not essentially out of the ordinary. They simply happened to be where anyone else could have been; or, rather: they were where everyone actually *is*. To be sure, Jesus addresses a particular Samaritan woman at the well, but, at the same time, in her, he also addresses every sinner, woman or man. When Jesus sits, tired, at the well's edge, it is not for this one person alone. . . . Therefore, it is not a mere "pious exercise" when, in spirit, I put myself beside this woman and enter into her role. Not only may I play this part: I must play it, for I have long been involved in this dialogue without being consulted. *I* am this dried-up soul, running after the earthly water every day because it has lost its grasp of the heavenly water it is really seeking. Like her I give the same obtuse, groping response to the offer of the eternal wellspring; in the end, like her, I have to be pierced by the Word as it wrings from me the confession of sin. And even then I cannot make this confession in plain language; it has to be supplemented by the grace of the eternal Word and Judge, which—so incomprehensible is his mercy!—actually justifies me and puts me in the right: "You are right in saying, 'I have no husband'; for you have had five husbands, and he whom you now have is not your husband; this you said truly" (John 4:17–18). So it is not at all enough to see the dialogues and encounters presented in the gospel as mere "examples," like the instances of valor in a heroic tale, which a boy reads and feels inspired to emulate. For the Word which became flesh at that particular point in order to speak to us, on whatever particular occasion he addresses us, is concerned with every particular unique occasion; in addressing this repentant sinner he addresses every sinner; in speaking to this woman listening at his feet he is speaking to every listener. Since it is God who is speaking, there can be no historical distance from his word; hence too our attitude to it cannot be merely historical. Instead there is that utter directness which confronted those who met him on the roads of Palestine: "Follow me!" "Go and sin no more!" "Peace be with you! . . . "

It is futile to leaf through the writings of the Old and New Covenants in the hope of coming across truths of one kind or another, unless we are prepared to be exposed to a direct encounter with him, with this personal, utterly free Word which makes sovereign claims upon us. "You search the scriptures, because you think that in them you have eternal life; and it is they that bear witness to me; yet you refuse to come to me that you may have life. If you believed Moses, you would believe me, for he wrote of me. But if you do not believe his writings, how will you believe my words?" (John 5:39–40; 46–47). He gathers up all the words of God scattered throughout the world and concentrates them in himself, the intense focus of revelation. . . . There are also the words strewn throughout creation, stammered and whispered; the words of nature, in macrocosm and microcosm; the words uttered by the flowers and the animals; words of overpowering beauty and of debilitating terror; the words of human existence, in their confusing, myriad forms, laden with both promise and disappointment: all these belong to the one, eternal, living Word who became man for our sakes. . . .

"Behold, as the eyes of servants look to the hand of their master, as the eyes of a maid to the hand of her mistress, so our eyes look to the Lord our God" (Ps. 123:2).

This looking to God is contemplation. It is looking inward into the depths of the soul, and hence beyond the soul toward God. The more contemplation finds God, the more it forgets itself and yet discovers itself in him. This unwavering "beholding," moreover, is also and always a "hearing," because what is beheld is the free and infinite Person who, from the depths of his freedom, can give himself in a way that is ever new, unsuspected and unpredictable. Therefore the word of God is never something finished, to be surveyed like a particular landscape, but it is something new every moment, like water from a spring or rays of light. "And so it is not enough to have received 'insight' and to 'know the testimonies of God,' if we do not continually receive and become inebriated by the fountain of eternal light" (Augustine, *Enarr. in Ps.* 118, XXVI, 6). The lover already knows this; the beloved's face and voice are every moment as new as if he had never seen them before.

Ken Gire, *Windows of the Soul*

A PRAYER FOR GRACE

Thank You, God,

For those moments in my life
    when You opened a window
        and offered a word
            that nourished the hunger in my soul.
Give me the grace to realize
    that these are the words I live by,
        not by bread alone,
            whatever form that bread may take
                however satisfying it may seem at the time.
Give me the grace to live not just reflectively but receptively,
    that I may not only notice when a window is opened
        but also receive what is offered,
            understanding that what is offered
                is my soul's daily bread . . .

Jeanne Guyon, *Experiencing the Depths of Jesus Christ*

(1648–1717) French mystic imprisoned in solitary confinement for four years because of her contemplative writings. Her testimony is recorded in the book Spiritual Torrents, *which became a best-seller for generations. She was branded a heretic for her teaching that justification came by faith in Christ alone.*

I would like to address you as though you were a beginner in Christ, one seeking to know Him. In so doing, let me suggest two ways for you to come to the Lord. I will call the first way "praying the Scripture"; the second way I will call "beholding the Lord" or "waiting in His presence."

"Praying the Scripture" is a unique way of dealing with the Scripture; it involves both reading and prayer.

Here is how you should begin.

Turn to the Scripture: choose some passage that is simple and fairly practical. Next, come to the Lord. Come quietly and humbly. There, before Him, read a small portion of the passage of Scripture you have opened to.

Be careful as you read. Take in fully, gently and carefully what you are reading. Taste it and digest it as you read.

In the past it may have been your habit, while reading, to move very quickly from one verse of Scripture to another until you had read the whole passage. Perhaps you were seeking to find the main point of the passage.

But in coming to the Lord by means of "praying the Scripture," you do not read quickly; you read very slowly. You do not move from one passage to another, not until you have *sensed* the very heart of what you have read.

You may then want to take that portion of Scripture that has touched you and turn it into prayer.

After you have sensed something of the passage and after you know that the essence of that portion has been extracted and all the deeper sense of it is gone, then, very slowly, gently, and in a calm manner begin to read the next portion of the passage. You will be surprised to find that when your time with the Lord has ended, you will have read very little, probably no more than half a page.

"Praying the Scripture" is not judged by *how much* you read but by the *way* in which you read.

If you read quickly, it will benefit you little. You will be like a bee that merely skims the surface of a flower. Instead, in this new way of reading with prayer, you must become as the bee who penetrates into the *depths* of the flower. You plunge deeply within to remove its deepest nectar.

Of course, there is a kind of reading the Scripture for scholarship and for study—but not here. That studious kind of reading will not help you when it comes to matters that are *divine!* To receive any deep, inward profit from the Scripture, you must read as I have described. Plunge into the very depths of the words you read until revelation, like a sweet aroma, breaks out upon you.

I am quite sure that if you will follow this course, little by little you will come to experience a very rich prayer that flows from your inward being.

Let us move now to the second kind of prayer, which I mentioned earlier.

The second kind of prayer, which I described as "beholding the Lord" or "waiting on the Lord," also makes use of the Scripture but it is not actually a time of reading.

Remember, I am addressing you as if you were a new convert. Here is your second way to encounter Christ. And this second way to Christ, although you will be using the Scripture, has a purpose altogether different from "praying the Scripture." For that reason you should set aside a separate time when you can come just to wait upon Him.

In "praying the Scripture" you are seeking to find the Lord in what you are reading, in the very words themselves. In this path, therefore, the content of the Scripture is the focal point of your attention. Your purpose is to take everything from the passage that unveils the Lord to you.

What of this second path?

In "beholding the Lord," you come to the Lord in a totally different way. Perhaps at this point I need to share with you the greatest difficulty you will have in waiting upon the Lord. It has to do with your mind. The mind has a very strong tendency to stray away from the Lord. Therefore, as you come before your Lord to sit in His presence, beholding Him, make use of the Scripture to *quiet your mind.*

The way to do this is really quite simple.

First, read a passage of Scripture. Once you sense the Lord's presence, the content of what you have read is no longer important. The Scripture has served its purpose; it has quieted your mind; it has brought you to Him.

So that you can see this more clearly, let me describe the way in which you come to the Lord by the simple act of beholding Him and waiting upon Him.

You begin by setting aside a time to be with the Lord. When you do come to Him, come quietly. Turn your heart to the presence of God. How is this done? This, too, is quite simple. You turn to Him by *faith.* By faith you believe you have come into the presence of God.

Next, while you are before the Lord, begin to read some portion of Scripture.

As you read, *pause.*

The pause should be quite gentle. You have paused so that you may set your mind on the Spirit. You have set your mind *inwardly*—on Christ.

(You should always remember that you are not doing this to gain some understanding of what you have read; rather, you are reading in order to turn your mind from outward things to the deep parts of your being. You are not there to learn or to read, but you are there to experience the presence of your Lord!)

While you are before the Lord, hold your heart in His presence. How? This you also do by faith. Yes, by faith you can hold your heart in the Lord's presence. Now, waiting before Him, turn all your attention toward your spirit. Do not allow your mind to wander. If your mind begins to wander, just turn your attention back again to the inward parts of your being.

You will be free from wanderings—free from any outward distractions—and you will be brought near to God.

(The Lord is found *only* within your spirit, in the recesses of your being, in the Holy of Holies; this is where He dwells. The Lord once promised to come and make His home within you. (John 14:23) He promised to there meet those who worship Him and who do His will. The Lord *will* meet you in your spirit. It was St. Augustine who once said that he had lost much time in the beginning of his Christian experience by trying to find the Lord outwardly rather than by turning inwardly.)

Once your heart has been turned inwardly to the Lord, you will have an impression of His presence. You will be able to notice His presence more acutely because your outer senses have now become very calm and quiet. Your attention is no longer on outward things or on the surface thoughts of your mind; instead, sweetly and silently, your mind becomes occupied with what you have read and by that touch of His presence.

Oh, it is not that you will think about what you have read, but you will *feed* upon what you have read. Out of a love for the Lord you exert your will to hold your mind quiet before Him.

When you have come to this state, you must allow your mind to rest. How shall I describe what to do next?

In this very peaceful state, *swallow* what you have tasted. At first this may seem difficult, but perhaps I can show you just how simple it is. Have you not, at times, enjoyed the flavor of a very tasty food? But unless you were willing to swallow the food, you received no nourishment. It is the same with your soul. In this quiet, peaceful, and simple state, simply take in what is there as nourishment. . . .

The Lord's chief desire is to reveal Himself to you and, in order for Him to do that, He gives you abundant grace. The Lord gives you the experience of enjoying His presence. He touches you, and His touch is so delightful that, more than ever, you are drawn inwardly to Him.

Ken Gire, "An Intimate Moment with Mary and Joseph,"
Intimate Moments with the Savior

An example of approaching the Scripture in the way Jeanne Guyon suggests.

Scripture (Luke 2: 1–7)

In those days Caesar Augustus issued a decree that a census should be taken of the entire Roman world. (This was the first census that took place while Quirinius was governor of Syria.) And everyone went to his own town to register.

So Joseph also went up from the town of Nazareth in Galilee to Judea, to Bethlehem the town of David, because he belonged to the house and line of David. He went there to register with Mary, who was pledged to be married to him and was expecting a child. While they were there, the time came for the baby to be born, and she gave birth to her firstborn, a son. She wrapped him in cloths and placed him in a manger, because there was no room for them in the inn.

Prayer

Dear Jesus,

Though there was no room for you in the inn, grant this day that I might make abundant room for you in my heart. Though your own did not receive you, grant this hour that I may embrace you with open arms. Though Bethlehem overlooked you in the shuffle of the census, grant me the grace, this quiet moment, to be still and know that you are God. You, whose only palace was a stable, whose only throne was a feeding trough, whose only robes were swaddling clothes.

On my knees I confess that I am too conditioned to this world's pomp and pageantry to recognize God cooing in a manger.

Forgive me. Please. And help me understand at least some of what your birth has to teach—that divine power is not mediated through strength, but through weakness; that true greatness is not achieved through the assertion of rights, but through their release; and that even the most secular of things can be scared when you are in their midst.

And for those times when you yearn for my fellowship and stand at the door and knock, grant me a special sensitivity to the sound of that knock so I may be quick to my feet. Keep me from letting you stand out in the cold or from ever sending you away to some stable. May my heart be warm and inviting, so that when you do knock, a worthy place will always be waiting. . . .

Formal—Liturgical Prayers

Hans Urs von Balthasar, *Prayer*

The liturgy is the service of prayer rendered by the Church to God, whereby, in utter self-oblivion, she seeks only to glorify God in adoration, praise and thanksgiving. These include the prayer of petition, which is an acknowledgment of the void into which the splendour of grace may pour itself, so that the effusion of grace is an inducement to a renewal of praise, adoration and thanks.

———

The Book of Catholic Worship

THE EUCHARISTIC PRAYER—EASTER

Priest: The Lord be with you.
People: AND WITH YOUR SPIRIT.
Priest: Lift up your hearts.
People: WE HAVE LIFTED THEM UP TO THE LORD.
Priest: Let us give thanks to the Lord our God.
People: IT IS RIGHT AND JUST.

It is truly right and just,
proper and helpful toward salvation,
that we always praise you, O Lord,
bur more especially so on this day
(on this night *or* at this season)
when Christ our Pasch was sacrificed.
For he is the true Lamb
who has taken away the sins of the world,
who overcame death for us by dying himself

and who restored us to life by his own resurrection.
Therefore with the Angels and Archangels,
the Thrones and Dominations, and all the militant hosts of heaven,
we continually praise your glory in song, and say:

> HOLY, HOLY, HOLY LORD GOD OF HOSTS.
> HEAVEN AND EARTH ARE FILLED WITH YOUR GLORY.
> HOSANNA IN THE HIGHEST.
> BLESSED IS HE WHO COMES IN THE NAME OF THE LORD.
> HOSANNA IN THE HIGHEST.

Richard Foster, *Prayer*

The intimacy of prayer must be always counterbalanced by the infinite
distance of creature to Creator. . . . The stateliness and formality of the
liturgy help us realize that we are in the presence of *real* Royalty.

The Book of Common Prayer

The Great Litany

To be said or sung, kneeling, standing, or in procession; before the
Eucharist or after the Collects of Morning or Evening Prayer; or sepa-
rately; especially in Lent and on Rogation days.

O God the Father, Creator of heaven and earth,
Have mercy upon us.

O God the Son, Redeemer of the world,
Have mercy upon us.

O God the Holy Ghost, Sanctifier of the faithful,
Have mercy upon us.

O holy, blessed, and glorious Trinity, one God,
Have mercy upon us.

Remember not, Lord Christ, our offenses, nor the offenses of our
forefathers; neither reward us according to our sins. Spare us,
good Lord, spare thy people, whom thou hast redeemed with thy
most precious blood, and by thy mercy preserve us for ever.
Spare us, good Lord.

From all evil and wickedness; from sin; from the crafts and assaults
  of the devil; and from everlasting damnation,
Good Lord, deliver us.

From all blindness of heart; from pride, vainglory, and hypocrisy; from
  envy, hatred, and malice; and from all want of charity,
Good Lord, deliver us.

From all inordinate and sinful affections; and from all the deceits of
  the world, the flesh, and the devil,
Good Lord, deliver us.

From all false doctrine, heresy, and schism; from hardness of heart,
  and contempt of thy Word and commandment,
Good Lord, deliver us.

From lightning and tempest; from earthquake, fire, and flood; from
  plague, pestilence, and famine,
Good Lord, deliver us.

From all oppression, conspiracy, and rebellion; from violence, battle,
  and murder; and from dying suddenly and unprepared,
Good Lord, deliver us. . . .

Eugene Peterson, *Answering God*

We learn to pray by being led in prayer. We commonly think of prayer as
what we do out of our own needs and on our own initiative. We experience a deep longing for God, and so we pray. We feel an artesian gush of
gratitude to God, and so we pray. We are crushed with a truckload of
guilt before God, and so we pray. But in a liturgy we do not take the initiative; it is not our experience that precipitates prayer. Someone stands
in front of us and says, "Let us pray." We don't start it; someone else
starts it, and we fall into step behind or alongside. Our egos are no
longer front and center.

This is so important, for prayer by its very nature is answering speech.
The consensus of the entire Christian community upholds the primacy
of God's word in everything: in creation, in salvation, in judgment, in
blessing, in mercy, and in grace. But in the practice of prayer, inebriated
as we often are by our own heady subjectivity, we boozily set aside the
primacy of God's word and substitute the primacy of our words. We are
so sure that here, at least, we get the first word!

But when we take our place in a worshipping congregation we are not in charge. Someone else has built the place of prayer; someone else has established the time for prayer; someone else tells us to begin to pray. All of this takes place in a context in which the word of God is primary: God's word audible in scripture and sermon, God's word visible in baptism and eucharist. This is the center in which we learn to pray. We do not, of course, remain in this center: lines of praying radiate and lead us outwards. From this center we go to our closets or the mountains, into the streets and the markets, and continue our praying. But it is essential to understand that the prayer goes from the center *outwards;* if we suppose that it proceeds inwards from the convergence of praying individuals we are at cross-purposes with the praying experience of Israel and the church.

The benefit that flows from this is enormous. It more than compensates for the painful (at least it seems so) sacrifice of initiative: we are rescued from the tyranny of our feelings. . . .

But how do we both affirm our feelings and detach ourselves from them? Through liturgy. We pray not when we feel like it but when someone, the pastor, the priest, the "choirmaster"! says, "Let us pray." We lose nothing of our emotions except their tyranny. The gamut of emotions experienced in our human condition is given full expression in the Psalms. We pray through each psalm and hit every note, sound every tone of feeling that we are capable of and learn to be at home with all of them before God. But the feelings do not have the first and controlling word. God does. The feelings are incorporated in the prayers, not the prayers in the feelings. Liturgical prayer misses not a single heartbeat of our emotions, but refuses even a hint of direction from them.

If we insist on maintaining the initiative in prayer, praying when we feel like it according to what we feel we need, we take on a psychic burden that is too much for us. Finally we slump to the ground in exhaustion and give it all up. After a few hours or days or weeks, usually out of guilt, we get up again and give it another try. That is why there is so much intermittent prayer—people who pray in spurts and then lapse, leaving behind them abandoned schemes, failed methods, but always on the lookout for another that will keep them faithful in prayer. It never occurs to them to let the "choirmaster" do that part for them. If we insist on conducting our lives of prayer as a private enterprise, we take on a monumental task that we have no adequate means for carrying out. But the liturgy provides an adequate means. Liturgy depsychologizes prayer. It removes prayer from the control of my emotions, my motivations, my physical energy, and my circumstances.

Spontaneous—Breath Prayers

Richard Foster, *Prayer*

As Christians over the centuries have sought to follow the biblical in-junction to "pray without ceasing," they have developed two fundamental expressions of Unceasing Prayer. The one is more formal and liturgical; the other is more conversational and spontaneous. The first has its origin in the Eastern Christian hesychastic tradition and is usually called aspiratory prayer or breath prayer. The idea has its roots in the Psalms, where a repeated phrase reminds us of an entire Psalm, for example, "O Lord, you have searched me and known me" (Ps. 139:1). As a result, the concept arose of a short, simple prayer of petition that can be spoken in one breath, hence the name "breath prayer.". . .

The most famous of the breath prayers is the Jesus Prayer: "Lord Jesus Christ, Son of God, have mercy on me, a sinner."

Henri Nouwen, *Reaching Out*

In the expression "Lord Jesus Christ, have mercy upon me," we find a powerful summary of all prayer. It directs itself to Jesus, the son of God, who lived, died and was raised for us; it declares him to be the Christ, the anointed one, the Messiah, the one we have been waiting for; it calls him our Lord, the Lord of our whole being: body, mind and spirit, thought, emotions and actions; and it professes our deepest relationship to him by a confession of our sinfulness and by a humble plea for his forgiveness, mercy, compassion, love and tenderness.

Elisabeth Elliot, *Keep a Quiet Heart*

Christians in the Orthodox Church use a prayer called the Jesus Prayer. Sometimes they pray it in the rhythm of breathing, learning in this way almost to "pray without ceasing." The words are simple, but they cover everything we need to ask for ourselves and others: *Lord Jesus Christ, Son of God, have mercy upon us.*

The Lord did not say we should not use repetition. He said we should not use vain repetition. A prayer prayed from the heart of the child to the Father is never vain.

The Very Reverend Kenneth R. Waldron, a priest of both the Ukrainian Orthodox Church and of the Anglican Church, wrote to me of his having had surgery. "The last moment of consciousness before the anaesthetic took over, I heard my surgeon repeating in a whisper: GOSPODI POMILUY, GOSPODI POMILUY, GOSPODI POMILUY [Dr. Waldron put the Russian words into phonetic spelling]—Lord, have mercy on us. . . . It is wonderful to drift off into unconsciousness hearing these words on the lips of the man whose hands you trust to bring you out of your troubles. It is great to have a surgeon who knows how to pray at such a time. Think of the comfort and help that this simple prayer has brought to thousands through the years, a prayer that was a big help to me in January 1982. Some of my hospital friends thought they would not see me alive again, but the good Lord had a bit more work for this old priest to do."

The Jesus Prayer was one my husband Add and I often used together when he was dying of cancer, when we seemed to have "used up" all the other prayers. I recommend it to you.

Anonymous, *The Cloud of Unknowing*

A man or a woman, frightened by a sudden danger of fire, or of death, or whatever else that comes is driven in haste to the height of his spirit and needs to cry or pray for help. How does he cry? Surely not in many words, nor yet in one word of two syllables. Why is that? Surely it is because longer words take too long a time to make plain the urgency of his need and the desperateness of his spirit.

He bursts out with fright in the depths of his spirit and cries out only one little word of one syllable: such a word as this word FIRE, or this word OUT. Just as this little word FIRE stirs and pierces more quickly the ears of his hearers, so does this little word of one syllable pierce the darkness when it is not only cried and thought, but secretly meant in the depth of the spirit, which is the height of the spirit. . . . It pierces the ears of the Almighty God, quicker than any long psalter unmindfully mumbled in the teeth. Therefore it is written that the short prayer pierces heaven.

James Houston, *The Transforming Power of Prayer*

The Cloud of Unknowing, a fourteenth-century Christian classic, called these short prayers "arrows flashed to heaven." It also revealed why these arrows are so effective: . . .

Why does it penetrate heaven, this short little prayer, even of one syllable? Surely because it is prayed with a full heart, in height, depth, length and breadth of spirit of him who prays it. In the height, for it is prayed in all the might of his spirit; in the depth, for in this little syllable is contained all that the spirit knows; in the length, for should it always feel as it does now, it would always cry to God as it now cries; in the breadth, for it would extend to all men what it wills for itself.

J. B. Phillips, Matthew 14:22–31, *The New Testament in Modern English*

Peter's Short Prayer

Directly after this Jesus insisted on his disciples' getting aboard their boat and going on ahead to the other side, while he himself sent the crowds home. And when he had sent them away he went up the hillside quite alone, to pray. When it grew late he was there by himself while the boat was by now a long way from the shore at the mercy of the waves, for the wind was dead against them. In the small hours Jesus went out to them, walking on the water of the lake. When the disciples caught sight of him walking on the water they were terrified. "It's a ghost!" they said, and screamed with fear. But at once Jesus spoke to them. "It's all right! It's I myself, don't be afraid!"

"Lord, if it's really you," said Peter, "tell me to come to you on the water."

"Come on, then," replied Jesus.

Peter stepped down from the boat and did walk on the water, making for Jesus. But when he saw the fury of the wind he panicked and began to sink, calling out, "Lord save me!" At once Jesus reached out his hand and caught him. . . .

Henri Nouwen, *The Way of the Heart*

Our choice of words depends on our needs and the circumstances of the moment, but it is best to use words from Scripture.

This way of simple prayer, when we are faithful to it and practice it at regular times, slowly leads us to an experience of rest and opens us to God's active presence. Moreover, we can take this prayer with us into a very busy day. When, for instance, we have spent twenty minutes in the early morning sitting in the presence of God with the words "The Lord is my Shepherd" they may slowly build a little nest for themselves in our heart and stay there for the rest of our busy day. Even while we are talking, studying, gardening, or building, the prayer can continue in our heart and keep us aware of God's ever-present guidance. The discipline is not directed toward coming to a deeper insight into what it means that

God is called our Shepherd, but toward coming to the inner experience of God's shepherding action in whatever we think, say, or do.

— ❧ —

Breath Prayers

From Psalm 23:

You are my shepherd, Lord. *My* shepherd. One who is always looking out for me. Leading me. Guiding me. Protecting me.

What more could I ask?

I ask that you make me to lie down is some green pasture. You know how much I need the rest.

Lead me beside some place of quiet waters. A place where the rippling sounds can float my cares away. You know how much my soul needs restoring.

You know how weary I am now, Lord, how hungry, how thirsty.

Don't let me stray from the path you are leading me down. You know how prone to wander I am.

I try not to look too far ahead on that path, but you know how anxious I am. I know that somewhere down the path is a dark valley through which I someday must travel.

If I had to go through it alone, I'd be terrified. But I don't have to go through it alone. You will be there. With me. Leading me through it.

Thank you that I don't have to go through life—with all its uncertain shadows—alone. I don't even have to go through today alone. Thank you, dear Shepherd. Where would I be without you?

Especially I ask that you lead me today. I am so worried about . . .

From the New Testament and the Psalms:

- Have mercy on me, O God, a sinner.
- Help me in my unbelief.
- Create in me a clean heart, O God.
- Search me, O God, and know my heart.
- Be gracious to me according to Your lovingkindness.

— ❧ —

Sue Monk Kidd, *God's Joyful Surprise*

In a religious bookstore in Indiana one day I began to talk with Samuel, a wise, spiritual man who managed the store. As our conversation spread from books to the spiritual life, I asked, "What do you think it means to pray without ceasing? It sounds like such an impossible undertaking. Do you think the command is just a hyperbole, an exaggeration to make a point?"

"When you pray always, you don't pray exclusively. You pray simultaneously," he said, gazing at me with dark smiling eyes. "It is to pray when I catalog these books and eat lunch and make change. It is to keep up prayer beneath the surface, lifting my heart to God during all my daily activities."

As I watched Samuel shelving books, smiling and talking with those who entered the store, I could see prayer in his face. It is not moving one's lips, muttering prayers around the clock, or stopping everything else to pray formal prayers. It is praying "simultaneously."

If we define prayer strictly as our talking to God, it will be difficult to come up with a way to pray always while we are concentrating on baby formulas or chemical formulas or driving home in rush hour traffic. Thomas Kelly, however, defined prayer as living concurrently in the level of the world and in the level of God's presence. And when Douglas Steere, a friend of Kelly's, was asked whether it was possible to carry out his friend's call to live in the awareness both of the world and of God's presence, he wrote:

> And old Indian saint gives the identical counsel: "Do all your work then, but keep your mind on God. . . . The tortoise swims about in the waters of the lake, but her mind is fixed to where her eggs are laid on the bank. So, do all the work of the world, but keep your mind on God."

If we can think of prayer like that, as an attitude and attentiveness that permeates our lives, then praying always becomes a possibility. Not a simple, overnight possibility. But possible nonetheless. It is a discipline that can be realized. . . .

The ways of unceasing prayer are about as numerous and unique as the people who practice it. But there is one time-honored way, virtually unknown to lots of Christians, which is becoming, I've discovered, more widespread. I am speaking of the Jesus Prayer.

My introduction to it began on a summer morning on the campus of a seminary. Sandy and I were spending several weeks there while he did some post-graduate study. I had fallen into the habit of taking a walk across the steep green hills on the campus. That morning the sun was beginning to warm the grass, when I came upon an acquaintance of ours sitting cross-legged under a tree, gazing down the hill, apparently deep in thought, a slim paperback in her lap.

"What are you reading that is so engrossing?" I asked.

She looked up and smiled a greeting. "I'm reading about the Jesus Prayer," she said, "even trying to practice it."

"Oh," I muttered, having no idea what she was talking about. I tilted my head to see the book title and said good-bye. Then I walked down the knoll to the seminary bookstore, where I found a copy of *The Way of the Pilgrim*.

That night, while Sandy studied, I sat in bed, reading. The book was the charming narrative of an anonymous Russian peasant in the nineteenth century, who went to church one Sunday and heard a Bible passage urging him to pray constantly. He was overcome with the thought. Pray constantly? Did he hear correctly? He checked his Bible and saw with his own eyes that it is necessary to pray continuously (I Thess. 5:17), to pray in the Spirit on *every* possible occasion (Eph. 6:18) and in *every* place to lift hands of prayer (I Tim. 2:8). A strong and compelling desire took hold of him to discover how to pray always. Since he was a pilgrim, wandering across the steppes of Russia without family and with all his possessions in a small knapsack, he sought someone who could explain the mystery to him.

Finally he met someone along the road who taught him the prayer used by the early church, known as the Jesus Prayer: "Lord Jesus Christ, have mercy on me." He was to pray the prayer as many times as he could during the day, all through his waking moments. The pilgrim acted on the teaching and traveled with the prayer as if it was his friend.

As I read, I found the humble little pilgrim's burning desire for unceasing prayer was rubbing off on me. But how could praying this lovely prayer, taken from Luke's Gospel, lead one to uninterrupted communion with God?

For the pilgrim the transformation came gradually. He learned to correlate the prayer with his breathing, envisioning the prayer entering his heart as he inhaled. The prayer came to life inside of him, like yeast rising slowly and invisibly in the warmth of the dough. It became a self-activating prayer, working itself deeper and deeper into his thoughts until one day he was aware that the prayer had spontaneously moved from his head down into his heart and had begun to pray itself. It prayed in the rhythm of his breathing, in the beating of his heart. "I felt the Prayer, of itself, without any effort on my part, began to function both in my mind and heart; it was active both day and night without the slightest interruption, regardless of what I was doing." He stopped vocalizing the prayer and began to listen to it.

The next morning I sat in the tiny apartment on campus and stared through the window, wondering about the prayer. Was God opening the riches of the prayer to me? How odd that I should come upon the girl cross-legged on the grass and then find this book! Should I try it?

The Jesus Prayer was foreign to me. But so what? Just because something was foreign and beyond my typical way of going about the spiritual life didn't necessarily mean it was wrong. Only that it was new. (What joys in growth I'd missed because of narrow thinking!) "Lord Jesus Christ, have mercy on me," I said a little shyly. Then I said it again. I said it for nearly five minutes, just letting the words happen to me. Below the window I watched the traffic, the squirrels jumping under a tree, students hurrying to class, and I said the prayer blending it with my breathing as the pilgrim had done. "Lord Jesus Christ," on the in-breath . . . "have mercy on me," on the out-breath. I said it slowly, silently finding a rhythm that seemed to slow everything down and focus naturally on Christ.

I have held onto the Jesus Prayer ever since. During those weeks at the seminary I breathed it as much as possible. Of course it was easier there. Bob and Ann were visiting their grandmother, and my typical busy life-style was left back home. There was nothing to do but pray the Jesus Prayer. I walked the hills and prayed it. It was with me so much that if I woke in the night I could reach across the bed and touch it. Oh, the peace of those days!

As the prayer sinks down into one's heart it takes on a life of its own, continuing in the subconscious when one is doing other things, like carrying on a conversation with a friend, washing the car or even sleeping— "I slept, but my heart was awake" (Song of Sol. 5:2 RSV).

"After the words appear to have 'set' in you, then they can be continued behind and between everything else you do during the day," wrote Tilden Edwards. With practice the Jesus Prayer comes to be rooted in your heart and is activated during the day as a living and conscious awareness of Christ.

The words of the prayer are said to hold the gospel within them. "Lord" is a recognition of who rules our lives. It puts everything in the right order. "Jesus Christ" draws before us His presence and His example. Bernard of Clairvaux wrote:

> When I name Jesus, I set before me a man who is meek and humble of heart, kind, prudent, chaste, merciful, flawlessly upright and holy . . . the all-powerful God whose way of life heals me, whose support is my strength. All these re-echo for me at the hearing of Jesus' name.

"Have mercy on me" reminds us of our need for God's grace, and the revelation of that grace in the life and death of Jesus for us. It opens us to receive that grace in ever-widening circles. It even helps us to receive that grace outward to others.

Sometimes the prayer becomes other-directed. It draws up the love in us and directs it toward other people. When passing a stranger on the road one day, I felt the prayer "activate" spontaneously in my heart. "Lord Jesus Christ, have mercy on *him*," I said, breathing the prayer for several blocks.

It can happen, too, with situations. In the midst of talking to a friend who was going through the pain of a rebellious teenage son, the prayer leaped to life. "Lord Jesus Christ, have mercy on this situation." It comes when there are no other words, when you don't know how to pray or what to say.

I have come to think of this prayer as living within me, beating like a heart. It is not in my thoughts all the time. That would be an utter distraction to have it constantly in my heart even when I am unaware of it. It returns during the days, sometimes rising up spontaneously. Other times I call it up when I dress or sit at a stop sign, or wait at the hairdresser. Any place at all we can breathe it in and out, always with gentleness.

When we enter unceasing prayer, we experience God becoming more our center. But the moment we think of ourselves as holier than someone else, more prayerful, more "piped into" God, we have defeated everything. As we attempt to turn to God with an unceasing movement, we do so with all our humanness and fallibility. I imagine with time unceasing prayer can slowly spread before us, becoming the water we walk on day and night. But for most of us, for myself, it is still mostly a trickle I wade about in when I can. But how wondrous even that is!

Anonymous, *The Way of the Pilgrim*
(translated from the Russian by R. M. French)

The events recounted in this book probably took place in Russia after the Crimean War in 1853 but before the Liberation of the Serfs in 1861. Nothing is known of the pilgrim's identity. Somehow the manuscript came into the possession of a monk living on Mount Athos, where the Abbot of St. Michael's Monastery at Kazan found it, copied it, and from his copy a printed version came into existence in Kazan in 1884. Until its publication in 1930, copies were extremely rare and difficult to obtain.

By the grace of God I am a Christian man, by my actions a great sinner, and by calling a homeless wanderer of the humblest birth who roams from place to place. My worldly goods are a knapsack with some dried bread in on my back, and in my breast-pocket a Bible. And that is all. . . .

For a long time I wandered through many places. I read my Bible always, and everywhere I asked whether there was not in the neighbourhood a spiritual teacher, a devout and experienced guide, to be found. . . .

"What do you want of me?" [one such guide] asked.

"I have heard that you are a devout and clever person," said I. "In God's name please explain to me the meaning of the Apostle's words, 'Pray without ceasing.' How is it possible to pray without ceasing? I want to know so much, but I cannot understand it at all."

He was silent for a while and looked at me closely. Then he said: "Ceaseless interior prayer is a continual yearning of the human spirit towards God."

———∞∞∞———

Mother Teresa

You can pray while you work. Work doesn't stop prayer, and prayer doesn't stop work. It requires only that small raising of mind to Him. "I love You, God, I trust You, I believe in You, I need You now." Small things like that. They are wonderful prayers.

PART SIX

WHAT STRUGGLES
DO WE ENCOUNTER
WHEN WE PRAY?

INTRODUCTION

What struggles do we encounter when we pray?

Prayer is a breathing of the soul that acknowledges with every breath the soul's dependence on something other than itself.

But who of us, at some time or another, hasn't had trouble breathing?

Allergies. Asthma. Mowing the yard on a day clinging with humidity. Jogging the track. Catching a plane. Giving birth. Who hasn't struggled to breathe then?

And who of us doesn't struggle now? A child may grow out of her asthma. A teenager may grow out of his allergies. But even as adults, we still live with steep stairways, smoggy freeways, and secondhand smoke.

We still struggle in breathing. And we still struggle in prayer. All of us.

We may have different struggles, but we all struggle.
But maybe if we could just talk about them with each other . . .
we could all breathe a little easier.

THE STRUGGLE OF LEARNING TO PRAY

Ray Stedman, *Jesus Teaches on Prayer*

(1917–1992) Gifted Bible expositor, pastor, and counselor.

It is significant to note that though Jesus never taught his disciples how to preach, he did teach them how to pray.

———— ❧ ————

Donald Whitney, *Spiritual Disciplines for the Christian Life*

Why . . . do so many believers confess that they do not pray as they should? Sometimes the problem is primarily a lack of discipline: Prayer is never planned; time is never allotted just for praying. While lip service is given to the priority of prayer, in reality it always seems to get crowded out by things more urgent.

Often we do not pray because we doubt that anything will actually happen if we pray. Of course, we don't admit this publicly. But if we felt certain of visible results within sixty seconds of every prayer, there would be holes in the knees of every pair of Christian-owned pants in the world! Obviously the Bible never promises this, even though God does promise to answer prayer. Prayer involves communication in the spiritual realm. Many prayers are answered in ways different from what we asked. For a variety of reasons, after we open our eyes we do not always see tangible evidence of our prayers. When we are not vigilant, this tempts us to doubt the power of God through prayer.

A lack of sensing the nearness of God may also discourage prayer. There are those wonderful moments when the Lord seems so near that we almost expect to hear an audible voice. No one needs to be prodded to pray in such times of precious intimacy with God. Usually, though, we don't feel like that. In fact, sometimes we can't *feel* the presence of God at all. While it's true that our praying (as well as all aspects of our Christian living) should be governed by the truth of Scripture rather than our feelings, nevertheless the frailty of our emotions frequently erodes our desire to pray. When the desire to pray is weakened, we can find many other things to do.

When there is little awareness of real need there is little real prayer. Some circumstances drive us to our knees. But there are periods when life seems quite manageable. Although Jesus said, "Apart from me you can do nothing" (John 15:5), this truth hits home more forcefully at some times than at others. In pride and self-sufficiency we may live for days as though prayer were needed only when something comes along that's too big for us to handle on our own. Until we see the danger and foolishness of this attitude, God's expectation for us to pray may seem irrelevant.

When our awareness of the greatness of God and the gospel is dim, our prayer lives will be small. The less we think of the nature and character of God, and the less we are reminded of what Jesus Christ did for us on the Cross, the less we want to pray. While driving today I heard a radio program where the guest, an astrophysicist, spoke of the billions of galaxies in the universe. In only a moment of meditation on this I automatically shifted into praise and prayer. Why? I became newly aware of how great God really is. And when I think of what Christ has saved me from, when I recall the shame He endured so willingly for my sake, when I remember all that salvation means, prayer is not hard. When this kind of thinking is infrequent, meaningful prayer will also be infrequent.

Another reason many Christians pray so little is because they haven't learned about prayer.

If you are discouraged by the command to pray because you feel like you don't know how to pray well, the fact that prayer is learned should give you hope. That means that it's okay to start the Christian life without any knowledge or experience of prayer. No matter how weak or strong your prayer life is right now, you can learn to grow even stronger.

There is a sense in which prayer needs to be taught to a child of God no more than a baby needs to be taught to cry. But crying for basic needs is minimal communication, and we must soon grow beyond that infancy. The Bible says we must pray for the glory of God, in His will, in faith, in the name of Jesus, with persistence, and more. A child of God gradually learns to pray like this in the same way that a growing child learns to talk. To pray as expected, to pray as a maturing Christian, and to pray effectively, we must say with the disciples in Luke 11:1, "Lord, teach us to pray."

If you've ever learned a foreign language you know that you learn it best when you actually have to speak it. The same is true with the "foreign language" of prayer. There are many good resources for learning how to pray, but the best way to learn how to pray is to pray.

Andrew Murray, South African minister and author of *With Christ in the School of Prayer,* wrote, "Reading a book about prayer, listening to lectures and talking about it is very good, but it won't teach you to pray. You get nothing without exercise, without practice. I might listen for a year to a professor of music playing the most beautiful music, but that won't teach me to play an instrument."

The Holy Spirit teaches praying people how to pray better. That's one of the applications of John 16:13 where Jesus said, "But when he, the Spirit of truth, comes, he will guide you into all truth." Just as a plane is guided more easily when it's airborne than when it's on the ground with its engines off, so the Holy Spirit guides us in prayer better when we are airborne in prayer than when we are not.

By Meditating on Scripture

This is one of the most compelling concepts on prayer I've ever learned. Meditation is the missing link between Bible intake and prayer. The two are often disjointed when they should be united. We read the Bible, close it, and then try to shift gears into prayer. But many times it seems as if the gears between the two won't mesh. In fact, after some forward progress in our time in the Word, shifting to prayer sometimes is like suddenly moving back into neutral or even reverse. Instead there should be a smooth, almost unnoticeable transition between Scripture input and prayer output so that we move even closer to God in those moments. This happens when there is a link of meditation in between.

At least two scriptures plainly teach this by example. David prayed in Psalm 5:1, "Give ear to my words, O LORD, consider my sighing." The Hebrew word rendered as "sighing" may also be translated "meditation."

In fact, this same word is used with that meaning in another passage, Psalm 19:14: "May the words of my mouth and the meditation of my heart be pleasing in your sight, O LORD, my Rock and my Redeemer." Notice that both verses are prayers and both refer to other "words" spoken in prayer. Yet in each case meditation was a catalyst that catapulted David from the truth of God into talking with God. In 5:1 he has been meditating and now he asks the Lord to give ear to it and to consider it. In Psalm 19 we find one of the best-known statements about Scripture written anywhere, beginning with the famous words of verse 7, "The law of the Lord is perfect, reviving the soul." This section continues through verse 11 and then David prays in verse 14 as a result of these words and his meditation.

The process works like this: After the input of a passage of Scripture, meditation allows us to take what God has said to us and think deeply on it, digest it, and then speak to God about it in meaningful prayer. As a result, we pray about what we've encountered in the Bible, now personalized through meditation. And not only do we have something substantial to say in prayer, and the confidence that we are praying God's thoughts to Him, but we transition smoothly into prayer with a passion for what we're praying about. Then as we move on with our prayer, we don't jerk and lurch along because we already have some spiritual momentum.

Those who seem to have known this secret best were the English Puritans who lived from 1550 to 1700. Permit me to quote from several Puritan writers, not only to show how remarkably common this now uncommon connection between meditation and prayer was among them, but also to secure its truth firmly into your prayer life. There's much to hold onto in this collection of well-driven nails. . . .

Puritan pastor and Bible commentator Matthew Henry remarked about Psalm 19:14, "David's prayers were not his words only, but his meditations; as meditation is the best preparation for prayer, so prayer is the best issue of meditation. Meditation and prayer go together."

One of the most prolific Puritan preacher-writers was Thomas Manton. In a message on Isaac's meditation in the field (refer to Genesis 24:63), he points directly to meditation as the link between Bible intake and prayer. He wrote,

> Meditation is a middle sort of duty between the word and prayer, and hath respect to both. The word feedeth meditation, and the meditation feedeth prayer. These duties must always go hand in hand; meditation must follow hearing and precede prayer. To hear and not to meditate is unfruitful. We may hear and hear, but it is like putting a

thing into a bag with holes. . . . It is rashness to pray and not to meditate. What we take in by the word we digest by meditation and let out
by prayer. These three duties must be ordered that one may not jostle
out of the other. Men are barren, dry, and sapless in their prayers for
want of exercising themselves in holy thoughts.

William Bates, called "that most classic and cultured of the later Puritan preachers," said, "What is the reason that our desires like an arrow
shot by a weak bow do not reach the mark? but only this, we do not
meditate before prayer. . . .

Among the best of the practical Puritan writings came from the pen
of William Bridge. On meditation he asserted the following:

> As it is the sister of reading, so it is the mother of prayer. Though a
> man's heart be much indisposed to prayer, yet, if he can but fall into
> a meditation of God, and the things of God, his heart will soon come
> off to prayer. . . . Begin with reading or hearing. Go on with medita-
> tion; end in prayer. . . . Reading without meditation is unfruitful;
> meditation without reading is hurtful; to meditate and to read with-
> out prayer upon both, is without blessing. . . .

About two hundred years after the Puritans came the man recognized
as one of the most God-anointed men of prayer ever seen by the world,
George Müller. For two-thirds of the last century he operated an orphanage in Bristol, England. Solely on prayer and faith, without advertising
his need or entering into debt, he cared for as many as two thousand
orphans at a single time and supported mission work throughout the
world. Millions of dollars came through his hands unsolicited, and his
tens of thousands of recorded answers to prayer are legendary.

Anyone who has heard the story of George Müller ponders the secret
of his effectiveness in prayer. Although some argue for one thing as
Müller's "secret" and others argue for another, I believe we must ultimately attribute his unusually successful prayer life to the sovereignty of
God. But if we look for something transferable from his life to ours, my
vote goes for something I've never heard credited as his "secret."

In the spring of 1841, George Müller made a discovery regarding the
relationship between meditation and prayer that transformed his spiritual life. He described his new insight this way:

> Before this time my practice had been, at least for ten years previ-
> ously, as an habitual thing, to give myself to prayer after having
> dressed in the morning. Now, I saw that the most important thing
> was to give myself to the reading of God's Word, *and to meditate on it,*

that thus my heart might be comforted, encouraged, warned, re-proved, instructed; and that thus, by means of the Word of God, *whilst meditating on it,* my heart might be brought into experimental communion with the Lord.

I began therefore to *meditate* on the New Testament from the be-ginning, early in the morning. *The first thing I did,* after having asked in a few words of the Lord's blessing upon His precious Word, *was to begin to meditate on the Word of God,* searching as it were into every verse to get blessing out of it; not for the sake of the public ministry of the Word, not for the sake of preaching on what I had meditated upon, but for the sake of obtaining food for my own soul.

The result I have found to be almost invariably this, that after a few minutes my soul has been led to confession, or to thanksgiving, or to intercession, or to supplication; so that, though I did not, as it were, give myself to prayer, *but to meditation,* yet it turned almost im-mediately more or less to prayer. When thus I have been for a while making confession or intercession or supplication, or have given thanks, I go on to the next words or verse, turning all, as I go on, into prayer for myself or others, as the Word may lead to it, but still con-tinually keeping before me that food for my own soul is the object of my *meditation. The result of this is that there is always a good deal of confession, thanksgiving, supplication, or intercession mingled with my meditation,* and that my inner man almost invariably is even sensibly nourished and strengthened, and that by breakfast time, with rare ex-ceptions, I am in a peaceful if not happy state of heart.

The difference, then, between my former practice and my present one is this: formerly, when I rose, I began to pray as soon as possible, and generally spent all my time till breakfast in prayer, or almost all the time. At all events I almost invariably began with prayer. . . . But what was the result? I often spent a quarter of an hour, or half an hour, or even an hour on my knees before being conscious to myself of having derived comfort, encouragement, humbling of soul, etc.; and often, after having suffered much from wandering of mind for the first ten minutes, or quarter of an hour, or even half an hour, I only then really began to pray.

I scarcely ever suffer now in this way. For my heart being nour-ished by the truth, being brought into experimental fellowship with God, I speak to my Father and to my Friend (vile though I am, and unworthy of it) about the things that He has brought before me in His precious Word. It often now astonishes me that I did not sooner see this point. . . . And yet now, since God has taught me this point, it is as plain to me as anything that the first thing the child of God has to do morning by morning is to obtain food for his inner man.

Now what is food for the inner man? *Not prayer, but the Word of God; and here again, not the simple reading of the Word of God, so that it only passes through our minds, just as water passes through a pipe, but considering what we read, pondering over it and applying it to our hearts. . . .*

I dwell so particularly on this point because of the immense spiritual profit and refreshment I am conscious of having derived from it myself, and I affectionately and solemnly beseech all my fellow believers to ponder this matter. By the blessing of God, I ascribe to this mode the help and strength which I have had from God to pass in peace through deeper trials, in various ways, than I have ever had before; and having now above fourteen years tried this way, I can most fully, in the fear of God, commend it.

How do we learn to pray? How do we learn to pray like David, the Puritans, and George Müller? We learn to pray by meditating on Scripture, for meditation is the missing link between Bible intake and prayer.

By Praying with Others

The disciples learned to pray not only by hearing Jesus teach about prayer, but also by being with Him when He prayed. Let's not forget that the words "Lord, teach us to pray" didn't just come as a random idea. This request followed a time when the disciples accompanied Jesus in prayer (Luke 11:1). In a similar way, we can learn to pray by praying with other people who can model true prayer for us.

And I don't mean just picking up new words and phrases to use in prayer. As with all learning by example, we can acquire some bad habits as well as good ones. I've heard people who never seem to pray an original prayer. Every time they pray they say the same things. And it's obvious they are merely using shiny phrases picked like fruit from the prayers of others here and there throughout the years. Jesus said, "Do not use meaningless repetition" when praying (Matt. 6:7, NASB). These kinds of prayers are rarely from the heart. God is not the audience being addressed. In reality these prayers are offered to impress the other people who are listening.

There are always other believers who can teach us much by praying with them. But we pray with them to learn principles of prayer, not phrases for prayer. One fellow Christian may give biblical reasons to the Lord why a prayer should be answered. Another might show us how to pray through passages of Scripture. By praying with a faithful intercessor we might learn how to pray for missions. Praying regularly with others can be one of the most enriching adventures of your Christian life. Most of the great movements of God can be traced to a small group of people He called together to begin praying.

By Reading about Prayer

Reading about prayer instead of praying simply will not do. But reading about prayer *in addition to* praying can be a valuable way to learn. "As iron sharpens iron," says Proverbs 27:17, "so one man sharpens another." Read the lessons learned by veterans of the trenches of prayer and let them sharpen your weapons of the warfare of prayer. "He who walks with the wise grows wise" is the teaching of Proverbs 13:20. Reading the books of wise men and women of prayer gives us the privilege of "walking" with them and learning the insights God gave them on how to pray.

We've learned from experience how others can see things in a passage of Scripture we cannot, or how they are able to explain a familiar doctrine in a fresh way that deepens our understanding of it. In the same way reading what others have learned about prayer from their study of Scripture and their pilgrimage in grace can be God's instrument of teaching us what we'd never learn otherwise. Who hasn't learned about praying in faith after reading of George Müller's prayer life, or who hasn't been motivated to pray after reading David Brainerd's biography? Hopefully the reading of this chapter on the Discipline of prayer convinces you that you can learn to pray by reading about prayer!

Let me add a word of encouragement. No matter how difficult prayer is for you now, if you will persevere in learning how to pray you will always have the hope of an even stronger and more fruitful prayer life ahead of you.

Joni Eareckson Tada, "Appreciating Prayer," *Glorious Intruder*

Have you ever wondered how people can spend thousands of dollars on a *painting*, of all things?

Or how someone can stand for twenty minutes in front of a Rembrandt in a museum? Or how folks can ooh and ahh over a sculpture or an Ansel Adams photograph?

Do you ever scratch your head and wonder just what people see in art?

Or take music. Does it puzzle you that people buy season tickets to the symphony—and hardly miss a performance? Why do people listen for hours to Bach? And what's so captivating about a Mendelssohn concerto or a Strauss waltz or a Chopin minuet?

Oh sure, you admit they all have their fine points. Art and music are nice to occasionally dabble in, but, come on—how is it that some people go overboard on such things?

If you feel that way . . . I understand. I used to shrug my shoulders toward art and music, too. I suppose I was lacking what they call "appreciation."

But I also remember when that ho-hum, scratch-your-head attitude began to change. It all started when my art teacher sat down with me and started flipping through pages and pages of art books. At almost every page, he would stop and linger over a Monet print or a Cezanne reproduction. He would spend hours discussing the composition and color in a painting by Mary Cassatt.

At first I felt . . . well, bored. But the more I looked and listened, the more I began to appreciate. Spending time with the masters elevated my thinking. I began to see things I had never seen. The more I looked, the more was revealed, and the more I understood.

Now when I see someone stand for long minutes in front of a Rembrandt, I smile and nod my head. I can identify.

If you don't appreciate good art, then go to a museum and start *looking* at good art. If you don't appreciate fine music, go to a concert and *listen* to fine music.

I know people who have a similar struggle when they look at the prayer habits of others. They listen to someone getting all excited about spending a morning talking to the Lord, and can only shake their heads. They will be the first to admit they simply do not appreciate the work of prayer.

Frankly, the only way you and I can develop a real appreciation for prayer is to pray. Prayer itself is an art which only the Holy Spirit can teach.

Pray for prayer.

Pray to be helped in prayer.

Pray until you appreciate prayer.

Like art, like music, like so many other disciplines, prayer can only be appreciated when you actually spend time in it. Spending time with the Master will elevate your thinking. The more you pray, the more will be revealed. You will understand. You will smile and nod your head as you identify with others who fight long battles and find great joy on their knees.

You will appreciate not only the greatness of prayer, but the greatness of God.

———✎———

Eugene Peterson, *Answering God*

Our prayers, whether clumsy or skilled, heretical or orthodox, verbatim from the Psalter or ad-libbed from a sinking ship, get us no merit with God. Nor are the Psalms necessary to validate our prayer as genuine— God hears anything we whisper or shout, say or sing. Right words and correct forms are not prerequisite to a heavenly audience. God is not fastidious in these matters.

All the same, [the Psalms] are necessary. The consensus on this, throughout the church's praying life, is impressive. If we wish to develop in the life of faith, to mature in our humanity, and to glorify God with our entire heart, mind, soul, and strength, the Psalms are necessary. We cannot bypass the Psalms. They are God's gift to train us in prayer that is comprehensive (not patched together from emotional fragments scattered around that we chance upon) and honest (not a series of more or less sincere verbal poses that we think might please our Lord).

The Psalms are necessary because they are the prayer masters. . . .

If we are willfully ignorant of the Psalms, we are not thereby excluded from praying, but we will have to hack our way through formidable country by trial and error and with inferior tools. If we dismiss the Psalms, preferring a more up-to-date and less demanding school of prayer, we will not be without grace, but we will miss the center where Christ worked in his praying. Christ prayed the Psalms—the Christian community was early convinced that he continues praying them through as we pray them: "we recite this prayer of the Psalm in Him, and He recites it in us. . . ."

This is not the latest thing on prayer, but the oldest: the Psalms, obvious and accessible as tools for prayer in the work of faith. . . . I don't mean to suggest that the Psalms are easy: prayer is not easy. But the practice of millions of Christians through centuries of use is adequate proof that we do not have to acquire expertise in the Psalms before we use them; they themselves—prayers that train us in prayer—are the means to proficiency. We don't have to understand a crowbar before we put it to use. Understanding comes with use.

The practice of Christians in praying the Psalms is straightforward: simply pray through the Psalms, psalm by psalm, regularly. John Calvin expressed the consensus of the praying church when he wrote that the

Psalms are "the design of the Holy Spirit . . . to deliver the church a common form of prayer." People who belong to liturgical traditions (Roman Catholic, Eastern Orthodox, Lutheran, Episcopal) have prayer books to guide them through a monthly cycle of praying the Psalms daily. The rest of us can easily mark the Psalms into thirty or sixty daily sections to guide an orderly monthly or bimonthly praying of all the Psalms. That's it: open our Bibles to the book of Psalms and pray them—sequentially, regularly, faithfully across a lifetime. This is how most Christians for most of the Christian centuries have matured in prayer. Nothing fancy. Just do it. The praying itself is deliberate and leisurely, letting (as St. Benedict directed) the motions of the heart come into harmony with the movements of the lips.

Eugene Peterson, *Under the Unpredictable Plant*

Jonah praying from the belly of the fish:

> "I called to the LORD, out of my distress,
>   and he answered me;
> out of the belly of Sheol I cried,
>   and thou didst hear my voice.
> For thou didst cast me into the deep,
>   into the heart of the seas,
>   and the flood was round about me;
> all thy waves and thy billows
>   passed over me.
> Then I said, 'I am cast out
>   from thy presence;
> how shall I again look
>   upon the holy temple?'
> The waters closed in over me,
>   the deep was round about me;
> weeds were wrapped about my head
>   at the roots of the mountains.
> I went down to the land
>   whose bars closed upon me for ever;
> yet thou didst bring up my life from the Pit.
>   O LORD my God.
> When my soul fainted within me.
>   I remembered the Lord;

and my prayer came to thee,
    into thy holy temple.
Those who pay regard to vain idols
    forsake their true loyalty.
But I with the voice of thanksgiving
    will sacrifice to thee;
what I have vowed I will pay.
    Deliverance belongs to the LORD!"
(2:2–9)

So Jonah prayed. *That* Jonah prayed is not remarkable; we commonly pray when we are in desperate circumstances. But there is something very remarkable about the *way* Jonah prayed. He prayed a "set" prayer. Jonah's prayer is not spontaneously original self-expression. It is totally derivative. Jonah had been to school to learn to pray, and he prayed as he had been taught. His school was the Psalms.

The School of the Psalms

Line by line Jonah's prayer is furnished with the stock vocabulary of the Psalms:

- "my distress" from 18:6 and 120:1
- "Sheol" from 18:4–5
- "all thy waves and thy billows passed over me" from 42:7
- "from thy presence" from 139:7
- "upon thy holy temple" from 5:7
- "the waters closed in over me" from 69:2
- "my life from the pit" from 30:3
- "my soul fainted within me" from 142:3
- "into thy holy temple" from 18:6
- "deliverance belongs to the Lord" from 3:8

And more. Not a word in the prayer is original. Jonah got every word—lock, stock, and barrel—out of his Psalms book.

But it is not only a matter of vocabulary, having words at hand for prayer. The form is also derivative. For the last hundred years scholars have given careful attention to the particular form that the psalms take (form criticism) and have arranged them in two large categories, laments and thanksgivings. The categories correspond to the two large conditions in which we humans find ourselves, distress and well-being. Depending on circumstance and the state of our soul, we cry out in pain or burst forth with praise. The categories have subdivisions, each form identifiable by its stock opening, middle, and ending. The rhythms are set. The vocabulary is assigned.

This is amazing. Prayer, which we often suppose is truest when most spontaneous—the raw expression of our human condition without contrivance or artifice—shows up in Jonah when he is in the rawest condition imaginable as *learned*. Our surprise lessens when we consider language itself: we begin with inarticulate cries and coos, but after years of learning we become capable of crafting sonnets. Are infant sounds more honest than Shakespeare's sonnets? They are *both* honest, but the sonnets have far more experience in them. Honesty is essential in prayer, but we are after more. We are after as much of life as possible—*all* of life if possible—brought to expression in answering God. That means learning a form of prayer adequate to the complexity of our lives.

The commonest form of prayer in the Psalms is the lament. It is what we would expect, since it is our commonest condition. We are in trouble a lot, so we pray in the lament form a lot. A graduate of the Psalms School of Prayer would know this form best of all, by sheer force of repetition.

Jonah in the belly of the fish was in the worst trouble imaginable. We naturally expect him to pray a lament. What we get, though, is its opposite, a psalm of praise, in the standard thanksgiving form.

Something important is emerging here: Jonah had been to school to learn to pray, and he had learned his lessons well, but he was not a rote learner. His schooling had not stifled his creativity. He was able to discriminate between forms and chose to pray in a form that was at variance with his actual circumstances. Circumstances dictated "lament." But prayer, while influenced by circumstances, is not determined by them. Jonah, creative in his praying, chose to pray in the form of "praise."

If we want to pray our true condition, our total selves in response to the living God, expressing our feelings is not enough—we need a long apprenticeship in prayer. And then we need graduate school. The Psalms are the school. Jonah in his prayer shows himself to have been a diligent student in the school of Psalms. His prayer is kicked off by his plight, but it is not reduced to it. His prayer took him into a world far larger than his immediate experience. He was capable of prayer that was adequate to the largeness of the God with whom he was dealing.

This contrasts with the prevailing climate of prayer. Our culture presents us with forms of prayer that are mostly self-expression—pouring ourselves out before God or lifting our gratitude to God as we feel the need and have the occasion. Such prayer is dominated by a sense of self. But prayer, mature prayer, is dominated by a sense of God. Prayer rescues us from a preoccupation with ourselves and pulls us into adoration of and pilgrimage to God. . . .

The Psalms are the school for people learning to pray. Fundamentally, prayer is our response to the God who speaks to us. God's word is always first. He gets the first word in, always. We answer. We come to consciousness in a world addressed by God. We need to learn how to answer, really answer—not merely say Yessir, Nosir—our whole beings in response. How do we do this? We don't know the language. We are so underdeveloped in this God-addressed world. We learn well enough how to speak to our parents and pass examinations in our schools and count out the right change at the drugstore, but answering *God?* Are we going to make do by trial and error? Are we going to get by on what we overhear in the streets? Israel and Church put the Psalms into our hands and say, "Here, this is our text. Practice these prayers so that you will learn the full range and the vast depth of your lives in response to God."

For eighteen hundred years virtually every church used this text. Only in the last couple of hundred years has it been discarded in favor of trendy devotional aids, psychological moodbenders, and walks on a moonlit beach. . . .

Augustine called the Psalms a "school." Ambrose provided a livelier metaphor, "gymnasium": in we go for daily workouts, keeping ourselves in shape for a life of spirituality, fully *alive* human beings.

Peter Marshall

(1902–1949) Pastor of New York's Avenue Presbyterian Church. Chaplain of the Senate in the late forties.

Lord, teach us to pray. Some of us are not skilled in the art of prayer. As we draw near to thee in thought, our spirits long for thy Spirit, and reach out for thee, longing to feel thee near. We know not how to express the deepest emotions that lie hidden in our hearts.

Prayer of an Anonymous Confederate Soldier

I asked God for strength that I might achieve;
I was made weak, that I might learn to serve.
  I asked for health, that I might do great things;
    I was given infirmity, that I might do better things.
I asked for wealth, that I might be happy;
I was given poverty, that I might be wise.

I asked for power, that I might earn the praise of men;
I was given weakness, that I might feel the need of God.
I asked for all things, that I might enjoy life;
I was given life, that I might enjoy all things.
I got nothing I asked for, but all I hoped for.
Despite myself, my unspoken prayers were answered.
And I am, among all men, most richly blessed.

THE STRUGGLE OF PRAYING THROUGH SUFFERING

Habakkuk 1:2 (NASB)

How long, O Lord, will I call for help,
And Thou wilt not hear?
I cry out to Thee, "Violence!"
Yet Thou dost not save.

Frederick Douglass, "O God, Save Me"

(1818–1895) Son of a black slave woman and a white slaveholder. Douglass's eloquence and intelligence was divinely matched with a character and passion to form a powerful voice for the abolitionist movement.

Sunday was my only leisure time, I spent this under some large tree, in a sort of beast-like stupor between sleeping and walking. At times I would rise up and a flash of energetic freedom would dart through my soul, accompanied with a faint beam of hope that flickered for a moment, and then vanished. I sank down again, mourning over my wretched condition. I was sometimes tempted to take my life . . . but was prevented by a combination of hope and fear. My sufferings, as I remember them now, seem like a dream rather than like a stern reality.

Our house stood within a few rods of the Chesapeake Bay, whose broad bosom was ever white with sails from every quarter of the habitable globe. Those beautiful vessels, robed in white, and so delightful to the eyes of freemen, were to me so many shrouded ghosts, to terrify and torment me with thoughts of my wretched condition. I have often, in the deep stillness of a summer's Sabbath, stood all alone upon the banks of that noble bay, and traced, with saddened heart and tearful eye, the countless number of sails moving off to the mighty ocean. The sight of these always affected me powerfully. My thoughts would compel utterance; and there, with no audience but the Almighty, I would pour out my soul's complaint in my rude way with an apostrophe to the multitude of ships.

"You are loosed from your moorings, and free. I am fast in my chains, and am a slave! You move merrily before the gentle gale, and I sadly before the bloody whip. You are freedom's swift-winged angels, that fly around the world; I am confined in bonds of iron. O, that I were free! O, that I were one of your gallant decks, and under your protecting wing. Alas! betwixt me and you the turbid waters roll. Go on, go on; O, that I could also go! Could I but swim! If I could fly! O, why was I born a man, of whom to make a brute! The glad ship is gone: she hides in the dim distance. I am left in the hell of unending slavery. O, God, save me! God, deliver me! Let me be free!"

Fannie Woods, "A Slave Mother's Doleful Prayer"

We stopped at this boarding house. This was our first night's stop after leaving Wilmington [Delaware]. The keeper of the boarding house tried to buy Fannie Woods' baby, but there was a disagreement regarding the price. About five the next morning we started on. When we had gone about half a mile a colored boy came running down the road with a message from his master, and we were halted until his master came bringing a colored woman with him, and he bought the baby out of Fannie Woods' arms. As the colored woman was ordered to take it away I heard Fannie Woods cry, "Oh God, I would rather hear the clods fall on the coffin lid of my child than to hear its cries because it is taken away from me." She said, "good bye, child." We were ordered to move on, and could hear the crying of the child in the distance as it was borne away by the other woman, and I could hear the deep sobs of a broken hearted mother. We could hear the groans of many as they prayed for God to have mercy upon us, and give us grace to endure the hard trials through which we must pass.

Psalm 57 (*The Message*)

A psalm of David, when he hid in a cave from Saul:

> Be good to me, God—and now!
>   I've run to you for dear life.
> I'm hiding out under your wings
>   until the hurricane blows over.
> I call out to High God,
>   the God who holds me together.

He sends orders from heaven and saves me,
    he humiliates those who kick me around.
God delivers generous love,
    he makes good on his word.

I find myself in a pride of lions
    who are wild for a taste of human flesh;
Their teeth are lances and arrows,
    their tongues are sharp daggers.

Jeff Stetson, "Why, Jesus?!"

Sermon preached after tragedy; from an unpublished play:

This church has never before been so full and, yet, I as your pastor, have never felt this empty. In these past few days, I have prayed for the strength and the courage that would enable me to deliver a message to you of love and hope built out of ashes of despair and upon the dead bodies of these four innocent little girls. . . . I have screamed to Jesus the question, "Why," and I have listened for a response that could help me here today but, my brothers and sisters, perhaps my heart was too weak, or my faith not strong enough, for no response came. . . . And, so, I stand before you this afternoon, still waiting, still asking, "Why," still praying for *faith* which has been severely tested by the sacrifice and blood of our delicate young children who should be here to dream, to laugh, to discover, to learn, to experience, to wonder, to do *all* of the things that children have a *right* to do, protected from the insanity of a world driven *mad* by the hatred and evil of men who deny Jesus as quickly as they accept faith. (He looks carefully and slowly at his congregation.) I know, some of you are here with violence and revenge in your hearts. (He points to some members.)

You young brothers dressed in the militancy of our times sitting in anger, backs erect, jaws tightened, fists clenched, ready and willing to correct that which can never be corrected. What do I say to you to change your minds, to touch you with a greater vision, to turn you again from thoughts of destruction and lead you toward the road of compassion and forgiveness? What do I say, sweet Jesus, to these grieving parents, who want only to hold their children again, to guide them to safety, to protect them from the wickedness that destroyed them in the place where we worship your father, murdered them in the very house of God! What can I say to this congregation, who suffers with them, who now fear for their own children, who may be the next to be violated on this hallowed? (He seems desperate and lost.)

Dear Lord, master of life, what can you say to me, that will restore a purpose to what I do, and a belief in what I speak to these your devoted servants? I have never asked you for a sign before, I have never *begged* you to answer questions that my faith was once strong enough to push aside. But, Jesus, I *was not ready* for this test. I was not prepared for this, your greatest challenge. I cannot go on without an answer to this question which burns a hole inside of me, that shakes my very foundation, that makes me curse restraint, and has given me cause to doubt my own capacity to believe. WHY, IN THIS HOUSE, WHERE WE OFFER OUR DEVOTION TO YOU? WHY, THESE CHILDREN WHO WANTED ONLY TO SERVE YOU, THAT PRAYED TO YOU WHILE THEIR PRECIOUS LIMBS WERE BEING BLOWN APART AND CRUSHED BENEATH THE WEIGHT OF FALLEN DREAMS AND BROKEN PROMISES? WHY? Why, in your holy and sacred name did you allow barbarism and evil to enter this church and make a mockery of *all* that we hold dear, to shatter goodness, to destroy hope, to torture the faithful who now live only to mourn the dead? WHY, TAKE OUR CHILDREN AND LEAVE US MEMORIES OF WHAT COULD HAVE BEEN BUT NO LONGER CAN BE? Why death instead of dreams, why lifelessness instead of laughter, why sorrow instead of the serenity of our children's smiles? WHY!? (His voice and spirit are now all but broken.)

Why these children, who never had a chance to let life touch them fully, to know the answer of life before confronted with the question of death? Why? (He searches his congregation for an answer that does not come.)

Do you have an answer? . . . Do *any* know why we are gathered in this place? . . . You? . . . Or you? . . . Sisters, is there no hint of an answer? . . . Brother, is there no clue? . . . No whisper to silence the wonder? . . . Then, are we not surely lost? (He lifts his head to heaven, cries softly, then screams.)

Why?

Barbara Von Der Heydt, *Candles Behind the Wall*

The Christian Church in Russia suffered intense, brutal persecution from the Communist regime.

"The KGB watched all Christians. . . ." Anyone who became a deacon or a pastor was visited by KGB agents, who attempted to persuade the individual to "cooperate." Specially schooled interrogators would alternate between cajoling and threatening to try to get what they wanted. "Frightened Christians agreed to cooperate. It doesn't mean they did so willingly—they did so out of fear. Some came to the church in tears later and asked for forgiveness."

But Christians under pressure often responded in exactly the opposite way that their persecutors intended. As Jakob Janzen, a member of an unregistered Baptist congregation, explains it, "They wanted to destroy the church, but during those times the congregation was stronger than ever. They held together like never before. And they prayed more often than ever. At home our children didn't pray a prayer they had learned by rote; they prayed from the heart with their own words: 'Lord, give our father strength.' The result brought our children, and us, closer to God."

Richard Foster, "Praying Through Chronic Pain," *Prayers from the Heart*

O Lord, my God, I do not ask for the pain to go away. I've prayed that prayer a thousand times over, and the pain remains with me. But I'm not angry about it. I'm not even disappointed anymore. I've come to terms with my pain.

No, my prayer is much more basic, much more simple. I ask, O God, for help in getting through this day. It's difficult because I've lost the ability to care.

God, what's hardest of all is that no one understands my experience of pain. If I had a broken leg, they could understand. But my pain is too hidden for them to understand. And because they cannot understand, they doubt my experience, and when they doubt my experience, they doubt me. And their doubts make me doubt myself, and when I doubt myself, it is hard to get through the day.

Maybe Lord, the pain is all in my head like everyone says. Even those closest to me think that though they've learned not to say it. Jesus, do you think that too?

Meaning has long since fled my life. What purpose is there in all this pain? Why am I here on this earth? What am I supposed to do with my life? These questions mock me.

I don't know who I am anymore, but whoever I am, O Lord, you know that I am Thine.

Amen.

Migrant Worker

As recorded by Robert Coles in Migrants, Sharecroppers, Mountaineers

Last year we went to a little church in New Jersey—we were picking mostly beans and radishes—and I was afriad we'd all be put in jail, the whole family, and it was because of what my husband did. We had all our children there, the baby included. The Reverend Jackson was there, I can't forget his name, and he told us to be quiet, and he told us how glad we should be that we're in this country, because it's Christian, and not "godless." Then my husband went and lost his temper; something happened to his nerves, I do believe. He got up and started shouting, yes sir. He went up to Reverend Mr. Jackson and told him to shut up and never speak again—not to us, the migrant people. He told him to go on back to his church, wherever it is, and leave us alone and don't be standing up there looking like he was so nice to be doing us a favor.

Then he did the worst thing he could do: he took the baby, Annie, and he held her right before his face, the minister's, and he screamed and shouted and hollered at him, that minister, like I've never before seen anyone do. I don't remember what he said, the exact words, but he told him that here was our little Annie, and she's never been to a doctor, and the child is sick . . . and we've got no money, not for Annie or the other ones or ourselves.

Then he lifted Annie up, so she was higher than the reverend, and he said why doesn't he go and pray for Annie and pray that the growers will be punished for what they're doing to us, all the migrant people. . . . And then my husband began shouting about God and His neglecting us while He took such good care of the other people all over.

Then the reverend did answer—and that was his mistake, yes it was. He said we should be careful and not start blaming God and criticizing Him and complaining to Him and like that, because God wasn't supposed to be taking care of the way the growers behave and how we live, here on this earth. "God worries about your *future*"; that's what he said, and I tell you, my husband near exploded. He shouted about 10 times to the reverend, "Future, future, future." Then he took Annie and near pushed her in the reverend's face and Annie, she started crying, poor child, and he asked the reverend about Annie's "future" and asked him what he'd do if he had to live like us, and if he had a "future" like ours. Then he told the reverend he was like all the rest, making money off us, and he held our Annie as high as he could, right near the cross, and told God He'd better stop having the ministers speaking for Him, and He should come and see us for Himself, and not have the "preachers"—he kept calling them the "preachers"—speaking for Him. . . .

He stopped after he'd finished talking about the "preachers" and he came back to us, and there wasn't a sound in the church, no sir, not one you could hear—until a couple of other men said he was right, my husband was, and so did their wives say so . . . and everyone clapped their hands and I felt real funny.

Daniel Coker, *Prayers from a Pilgrim's Journal*

(1780–1846) One of the first ministers of the A.M.E. church. He served as a missionary in West Africa.

Prayer at Sherbro Island, Saturday, March 18, 1820

We have anchored about twenty or thirty miles from Sherbro island. The sand has a handsome appearance, looks level. I have to labour between hope and fear as to our reception. At this moment the language of my heart is, while I write and look at the vast tracts of land in sight,—Oh God! is there not for us a place whereon to rest the soals [soles] of our feet? Will not Africa open her bosom, and receive her weeping and bleeding children that may be taken from slave ships or come from America?

> When will Jehovah hear our cries?
> When will the sun of freedom rise?
> When will for us a Moses stand,
> And bring us out from Pharaoh's hand?

Exodus 2:23–25 (NASB)

Now it came about in *the course* of those many days that the king of Egypt died. And the sons of Israel sighed because of the bondage, and they cried out; and their cry for help because of their bondage rose up to God.

So God heard their groaning; and God remembered His covenant with Abraham, Isaac, and Jacob.

And God saw the sons of Israel, and God took notice *of them*.

William Donnel Watley,
"O God, I Get So Tired of Racism Wherever I Go"

O God, as a black man, I get exceedingly tired and so filled up with confronting and fighting racism, that formidable foe. It passes its poison from one generation to another. It has polluted all of the wellsprings of the nation's institutional life. More widespread than the drug scourge, more explosive than nuclear weapons, more crippling than germ warfare—racism has washed up on the shores of every nation of every continent.

O God, I get tired of racism wherever I go—abroad and at home. From stores that let me know that I have gotten "out of place"; from looks of fear that my black manly presence engenders in some; from small insults to major offenses; from polite, subtle, condescending paternalism or maternalism to outright, open hostility; from insulting jokes about my intelligence to curiosity about alleged black sexual prowess from caricatures and stereotypes to the "you are the exception" syndrome—racism rears its many heads and shows its various faces all the time.

Yet as I bow before you, O God, I pledge to you, to my ancestors who sacrificed greatly so that I might enjoy whatever rights and privileges—however limited or circumscribed—are mine to experience, and to my children and to their children that I will keep up the noble fight of faith and perseverance. I will not go back to the back of the bus. I will not accept the invincibility of racism and the inviolability of its mythical sacred precepts.

I know that greater is the One that is in me than the one that is in the world. May that Spirit's presence and power direct and inspire me now and evermore until victory is won for my people, and all people, and until the kingdoms of this world become the kingdom of our Lord and of his Christ. Amen.

Acts 7:54–60 (*The Message*)

The Apostle Stephen becomes the first martyr of the Church:

> At that point they went wild, a rioting mob of catcalls and whistles and invective. But Stephen, full of the Holy Spirit, hardly noticed—he only had eyes for God, whom he saw in all his glory with Jesus standing at his side. He said, "Oh! I see heaven wide open and the Son of Man standing at God's side!"
>
> Yelling and hissing, the mob drowned him out. Now in full stampede, they dragged him out of town and pelted him with rocks. The ringleaders took off their coats and asked a young man named Saul to watch them.
>
> As the rocks rained down, Stephen prayed, "Master Jesus, take my life." Then he knelt down, praying loud enough for everyone to hear, "Master, don't blame them for this sin"—his last words. Then he died.

Julian of Brioude

(Third century) Believed to have been a soldier converted to Christianity in Gaul who surrendered himself to authorities and was beheaded during a local persecution. This was his last prayer.

I have been too long
    in this world of strife;
I would be with Jesus.

Dietrich Bonhoeffer, *Letters and Papers from Prison*

Written Christmas 1943 in a Nazi concentration camp.

O God, early in the morning do I cry unto Thee.
Help me to pray, and to think only of Thee.
I cannot pray alone.
In me there is darkness,
But with Thee there is light.

I am lonely,
    but Thou leavest me not.
I am feeble in heart,
    but Thou leavest me not.
I am restless,
    but with Thee there is peace.
In me there is bitterness,
    but with Thee there is patience.
Thy ways are past understanding,
    but Thou knowest the way for me.

Lord Jesus Christ,
Thou wast poor, and in misery,
    a captive and forsaken as I am.
Thou knowest all man's distress;
Thou abidest with me when all others have deserted me;
Thou wilt not forget me, Thou seekest me.
Thou willest that I should know Thee and turn to Thee.
Lord, I hear Thy call and follow Thee;
do Thou help me. . . .

I would remember before Thee
    all my loved ones,

my fellow prisoners,
and all who in this house perform their hard service.
Lord have mercy.
Restore my liberty and enable me so to live that I may
    answer before Thee and before the world.

Lord, whatsoever this day may bring,
Thy name be praised.
Be gracious unto me and help me.
Grant me strength to bear whatsoever Thou dost send,
And let not fear overrule me.
I trust Thy grace, and commit my life wholly into Thy
    Hands.
Whether I live or whether I die, I am with Thee
And Thou art with me,
    O my Lord and my God.
Lord, I wait for Thy salvation,
    and for the coming of Thy Kingdom. *Amen.*

Edwin Robertson, *The Shame and the Sacrifice*

[Dietrich] Bonhoeffer was hanged in the early hours of Monday morning, 9 April 1945. Only one eyewitness has told the story of that last hour. No story of his life is complete without this last witness of Bonhoeffer to a man who knew nothing about him and who would never understand his theology. He was the camp doctor and, writing ten years after the event, he could not forget it:

On the morning of that day between five and six o'clock the prisoners, among them Admiral Canaris, General Oster, General Thomas and Councillor of the German Surpreme Court Sack, were taken from their cells, and the verdicts of the court martial read out to them. Through the half-open door in one room of the huts I saw Pastor Bonhoeffer, before taking off his prison garb, kneeling on the floor praying fervently to God. I was most deeply moved by the way this lovable man prayed, so devout and so certain that God heard his prayer. At the place of execution, he again said a short prayer and then climbed the steps to the gallows, brave and composed. His death ensued after a few seconds. In almost fifty years that I worked as a doctor, I have hardly ever seen a man die so entirely submissive to the will of God.

Fox's Book of Martyrs

Polycarp, the venerable bishop of Smyrna, hearing that persons were seeking for him, escaped, but was discovered by a child. After feasting the guards who apprehended him, he desired an hour in prayer, which being allowed, he prayed with such fervency, that his guards repented that they had been instrumental in taking him. He was, however, carried before the proconsul, condemned, and burnt in the market place. . . .

It has been said that the lives of the early Christians consisted of "persecution above ground and prayer below ground." Their lives are expressed by the Coliseum and the catacombs. Beneath Rome are the excavations which we call the catacombs, which were at once temples and tombs. The early Church of Rome might well be called the Church of the Catacombs. There are some sixty catacombs near Rome, in which some six hundred miles of galleries have been traced, and these are not all. These galleries are about eight feet high and from three to five feet wide, containing on either side several rows of long, low, horizontal recesses, one above another like berths in a ship. In these the dead bodies were placed and the front closed, either by a single marble slab or several great tiles laid in mortar. . . . When the Christian graves have been opened, the skeletons tell their own terrible tale. Heads are found severed from the body, ribs and shoulder blades are broken, bones are often calcined from fire.

—∞∞∞—

Arthur Bennett

THE VALLEY OF VISION

Lord, High and Holy, Meek and Lowly,
Thou hast brought me to the valley of vision,
    where I live in the depths, but see Thee in the heights;
    hemmed in by mountains of sin I behold Thy glory.

Let me learn by paradox
    that the way down is up,
    that to be low is to be high,
    that the broken heart is the healed heart,
    that the contrite spirit is the rejoicing spirit,
    that the repenting soul is the victorious soul,
    that to have nothing is to possess all,
    that to bear the cross is to wear the crown,
    that to give is to receive,

that the valley is the place of vision.
Lord, in the daytime stars can be seen from deepest wells,
   and the deeper the wells the brighter thy stars shine;
Let me find thy light in my darkness,
   thy life in my death,
   thy joy in my sorrow,
   thy grace in my sin,
   thy glory in my valley.

―――∽∞∾―――

Matthew 26:36–44 (NIV)

Christ praying in Gethsemane immediately before His arrest and crucifixion:

> Then Jesus went with his disciples to a place called Gethsemane,
> and he said to them, "Sit here while I go over there and pray." He
> took Peter and the two sons of Zebedee along with him, and he began
> to be sorrowful and troubled. Then he said to them, "My soul is over-
> whelmed with sorrow to the point of death. Stay here and keep watch
> with me."
>
> Going a little farther, he fell with his face to the ground and prayed,
> "My Father, if it is possible, may this cup be taken from me. Yet not
> as I will, but as you will."
>
> Then he returned to his disciples and found them sleeping.
> "Could you men not keep watch with me for one hour?" he asked
> Peter.
>
> "Watch and pray so that you will not fall into temptation. The
> spirit is willing, but the body is weak."
>
> He went away a second time and prayed, "My Father, if it is not
> possible for this cup to be taken away unless I drink it, may your will
> be done."
>
> When he came back, he again found them sleeping, because their
> eyes were heavy. So he left them and went away once more and prayed
> the third time, saying the same thing.

―――∽∞∾―――

Hebrews 5:7–8 (NASB)

> In the days of his flesh, [Jesus] offered up both prayers and supplications
> with loud crying and tears to the One able to save Him from death, and
> He was heard because of His piety.

Although He was a Son, He learned obedience from the things which He suffered.

THE STRUGGLE OF ENDURING GOD'S HIDDENNESS

Inscription on the Walls of a Cellar in Cologne, Germany, Where Jews Hid from Nazis

I believe in the sun even when it is not shining.
I believe in love even when feeling it not.
I believe in God even when He is silent.

W. Bingham Hunter, *The God Who Hears*

No thinking Christian will be able to evade the issue of God's silence and inactivity in the face of suffering. On some days we may find prayer impossible. Pain, anguish and grief can become so consuming that there is nothing left over to pray with. There *are* periods when the emotional insult of evil, injustice and destruction leave us emotionally, intellectually and spiritually numb.

Psalm 13:1–2 (NASB)

A psalm of David:

How long, O Lord? Wilt Thou forget me forever?
How long wilt Thou hide Thy face from me?
How long shall I take counsel in my soul,
Having sorrow in my heart all the day? . . .

E. M. Bounds

(1835–1913) Methodist minister and devotional writer who served as a pastor in the American South and became a POW during the Civil War.

To go through the motion of praying is a dull business, though not a hard one. To say prayers in a decent, delicate way is not heavy work. But to pray really, to pray till hell feels the ponderous stroke, to pray till the iron gates of difficulties are opened, till the mountains of obstacles are removed, till the mists are exhaled and the clouds are lifted, and the sunshine of a cloudless day brightens—this is hard work, but it is God's work and man's best labor. Never was the toil of hand, head and heart less spent in vain than when praying. It is hard to wait and press and pray, and hear no voice, but stay till God answers.

W. Bingham Hunter, *The God Who Hears*

The Silence of God

Almost a century ago Sir Robert Anderson [wrote:]

> Society, even in the great centres of our modern civilisation, is all too like a slave-ship, where, with the sounds of music and laughter and revelry on the upper deck, there mingle the groans of untold misery battened down below. Who can estimate the sorrow and suffering and wrong endured during a single round of the clock?
>
> From the old days of Pagan Rome right down through the centuries of so-called "Christian" persecutions, the untold millions of the martyrs, the best and purest of our race have been given up to violence and outrage and death in hideous forms. The heart grows sick at the appalling story, and we turn away with a dull but baseless hope that it may be in part at least untrue. But the facts are too terrible to make exaggeration in the record of them possible. Torn by wild beasts in the arena, torn by men as merciless as wild beasts, and far more hateful, in the torture chambers of the Inquisition, His people have died, with faces turned to heaven, and hearts upraised in prayer to God; but the heaven has seemed as hard as brass, and the God of their prayers as powerless as themselves or as callous as their persecutors! . . .

God Makes Evil into Good

Some Christians believe that God always turns evil into good. Alvera Mickelsen deals with this question, relating it to the death of John the Baptist:

> There is no clue as to why God permitted John to be beheaded in a silly display of power by Herod. So far as we know, Jesus did not tell his disciples either that a great good would result from it, or that they should "praise the Lord" for the tragedy. He just went away alone to mourn John's death. . . .

WHAT STRUGGLES DO WE ENCOUNTER WHEN WE PRAY? 259

When an innocent child (or John the Baptist) is murdered, that is *evil*. Yes, God can, and often does, bring good results (conversions, family reconciliations, and so on) from such horrible events. But no parent would choose to let his child be cruelly murdered *so that* these "good things" would result. Friends who have faced tragic losses are not usually comforted by well-meaning friends who tell them "someday you will understand God's reasons."

The facts are that God does not make evil into good. Evil remains evil no matter how much good God may eventually be pleased to reveal.

Romans 8:28 does not say that God makes all things good, but rather that "in all things God works for the good of those who love him." Confidence in God's love, presence and providence does not require that we deny the objective reality of evil or say that pain really does not hurt. Jesus delighted in doing God's will, but he did not delight to go to the cross. The text says that Jesus "for the joy set before him *endured* the cross" (Heb. 12:2). . . .

There is too much agony in Gethsemane to believe the Savior was "just praising the Lord" on the Mount of Olives. Luke 22:44 says he was in anguish and sweat profusely. Hebrews 5:7 says he cried. He asked for the help of friends who failed him (Mark 14:32), and he needed the help of an angel to continue (Luke 22:43). If our Lord and Master could be deeply distressed and troubled in the face of sin and evil, if he could say, "My soul is overwhelmed with sorrow to the point of death" (Mark 14:33–34), if he could cry . . . then why is it that we Christians continue to pretend—in the name of living the abundant or victorious life—that somehow it is good for bad things to happen and that dark is really light from God's point of view? . . .

So What's This Got to Do with Prayer?

I do not think we Christians can begin to pray effectively for ourselves or others in pain until we are honest. Because of our creatureliness, much, if not most, human suffering seems meaningless. Our conjectures about why people hurt obscure the fact that *we simply don't know why*. It may seem helpful to suppose that God is doing or will do something good in these circumstances. But the truth is that we, like Job and the mothers of Bethlehem, usually don't know what is going on. What we know is that it hurts.

What we must stop doing is trying to be God, who *can* figure things out, and admit that we are creatures who cry. There is no victory in that (pagan) stoicism which says, "Smile even though it hurts; remember your testimony." Such attitudes are a victory for deception and spiritual schizophrenia. . . . Read the Psalms again. Notice how honest David is when he prays, admitting his anguish, sorrow, grief and affliction (Ps. 31:7, 9–10). We need not pretend to enjoy pain and anguish in order to be found faithful and pray effectively. . . .

Truly victorious Christians are those who admit their humanness *and* who admit the emotional insult of God's apparent silence when we suffer. They submit themselves to others and their Creator with tears on their faces. Such Christians can pray like Jesus, "Not as I will, but as thou wilt." Jesus was heard, we are told in Hebrews 5:7, because of his "godly fear" (RSV) or "reverent submission" (NIV). He was not heard because he whistled in the dark. Jesus' words showed his unconditional trust *in the midst* of fear and pain. In his *Psalms of My Life,* Joseph Bayly [who endured the death of each of his three sons] writes this prayer:

> I cry tears
> to you Lord
> tears
> because I cannot speak.
> Words are lost
> among my fears
> pain
> sorrows
> losses
> hurts
> but tears
> You understand
> my wordless prayer
> You hear.
> Lord
> wipe away my tears
> all tears
> not in distant day
> but now here.

When we stop pretending with ourselves, one another and with our Lord, this is the sort of prayer which comes forth.

Corrie ten Boom

(1892–1983) Imprisoned by the Nazis for sheltering Jews, Corrie survived Ravensbruck concentration camp and her life and ministry became the embodiment of Christ's forgiveness.

When the train goes through a tunnel and the world gets dark, do you jump out? Of course not. You sit still and trust the engineer to get you through.

Job 23:2b–4, 8–9 (NASB)

His hand is heavy despite my groaning.
"Oh that I knew where I might find Him,
That I might come to His seat!
I would present my case before Him
And fill my mouth with arguments. . . .
Behold, I go forward but He is not *there*,
And backward, but I cannot perceive Him;
When He acts on the left, I cannot behold *Him*;
He turns on the right, I cannot see Him."

Archbishop Anthony Bloom, *Beginning To Pray*

At the outset there is, then, one very important problem: the situation of one for whom God seems to be absent. . . . Obviously I am not speaking of a real absence—God is never really absent—but of the *sense* of absence which we have. We stand before God and we shout into an empty sky, out of which there is no reply. We turn in all directions and He is not to be found. What ought we to think of this situation? . . .

If you look at the relationship in terms of *mutual* relationship, you will see that God could complain about us a great deal more than we about Him. We complain that He does not make Himself present to us for the few minutes we reserve for Him, but what about the twenty-three and a half hours during which God may be knocking at our door and we answer "I am busy, I am sorry" or when we do not answer at all because we do not even hear the knock at the door of our heart, of our minds, of our conscience, of our life. So there is a situation in which we have no right to complain of the absence of God, because we are a great deal more absent than He ever is.

John Baillie

(1886–1960) Scottish theologian, writer, and apologist.

And if still I cannot find thee, O God, then let me search my heart and know whether it is not rather I who am blind than thou who art obscure. . . .

———∞∞∞———

Philip Yancey, *Disappointment With God*

Is God Hidden?

To get the full emotional impact of Job's plight, I winnowed the book's speeches for Job's own words. I expected to find him complaining about his miserable health and lamenting the loss of his children and fortune; but to my surprise Job had relatively little to say about those matters. He focused instead on the single theme of God's absence. What hurt Job most was the sense of crying out in desperation and getting no response. I had heard that same feeling described by many suffering people, perhaps best by C. S. Lewis, who wrote these words in the midst of deep grief after his wife's death from cancer:

> Meanwhile, where is God? This is one of the most disquieting symptoms. When you are happy, so happy that you have no sense of needing Him . . . you will be—or so it feels—welcomed with open arms. But go to Him when your need is desperate, when all other help is vain, and what do you find? A door slammed in your face, and a sound of bolting and double bolting on the inside. After that, silence. You may as well turn away. The longer you wait, the more emphatic the silence will become.

Above all else, Job demanded a chance to plead his case before God. His friends' pieties he shook off like a dog shaking off fleas. He wanted the real thing, a personal appointment with God Almighty. Despite what had happened, Job could not bring himself to believe in a God of cruelty and injustice. Perhaps if they met together, at least he could hear God's side of things. But God was nowhere to be found. Job heard only the whining cant of his friends and then a dreadful, vacuous sound. The door slammed in his face. . . .

Human longing for the actual presence of God may crop up almost anywhere. But we dare not make sweeping claims about the promise of God's intimate presence unless we take into account those times when

God seems absent. C. S. Lewis encountered it, Job encountered it
. . . at some point nearly everyone must face the fact of God's hiddenness.

The cloud of unknowing can descend without warning, sometimes at
the very moment we most urgently desire a sense of God's presence. A
South African minister, the Reverend Allan Boesak, was thrown in jail
for speaking against the government. He spent three weeks in solitary
confinement, almost constantly on his knees, praying for God to set him
free. "I do not mind telling you," he later related to his congregation,
"that this was the most difficult moment of my life. As I knelt there, the
words couldn't come anymore and there were no more tears to cry." His
experience was one common to blacks in South Africa: they pray, they
weep, they wait, and still they provoke no answer from God.

Some would argue that God does not hide. One religious bumper
sticker reads, "If you feel far from God, guess who moved?" But the guilt
implicit in the slogan may be false guilt: the Book of Job details a time
when, apparently, it was God who moved. Even though Job had done
nothing wrong and pled desperately for help, God still chose to stay hidden. (If you ever doubt that an encounter with God's hiddenness is a
normal part of the pilgrimage of faith, simply browse in a theological library among the works of the Christian mystics, men and women who
have spent their lives in personal communion with God. Search for one,
just one, who does not describe a time of severe testing, "the dark night
of the soul.")

For those who suffer, and those who stand beside them, Job offers up
an important lesson. The doubts and complaints . . . are valid responses,
not symptoms of weak faith—so valid, in fact, that God made sure the
Bible included them all. One does not expect to find the arguments of
God's adversaries—say, Mark Twain's *Letters from the Earth* or Bertrand
Russell's *Why I Am Not a Christian*—bound into the Bible, but nearly
all of them make an appearance, if not in Job, then in the Psalms or
Prophets. The Bible seems to anticipate our disappointments, as if God
grants us in advance the weapons to use against him, as if God himself
understands the cost of sustaining faith.

And, because of Jesus, perhaps he does understand. At Gethsemane
and Calvary in some inexpressible way God himself was forced to con-
front the hiddenness of God. "God striving with God" is how Martin
Luther summarized the cosmic struggle played out on two crossbeams
of wood. On that dark night, God learned for himself the full extent of
what it means to feel God-forsaken.

Job's friends insisted that God was not hidden. They brought up reminders—dreams, visions, past blessings, the splendors of nature—of how God had proved himself to Job in the past. "Don't forget in the darkness what you learned in the light," they chided. And those of us who live after Job have even more light: the record of fulfilled prophecy, and the life of Jesus. But sometimes all insights or "proofs" will fail. Mere memory, no matter how pleasant, will not deaden pain or loneliness. Perhaps, for a time, all verses of Scripture and all inspirational slogans will likewise fail.

Three Responses

I know too well my own instinctive response to the hiddenness of God: I retaliate by ignoring him. Like a child who thinks he can hide from adults by holding a chubby hand over his eyes, I try to shut God out of my life. If he won't reveal himself to me, why should I acknowledge him?

The Book of Job gives two other responses to such disappointment with God. The first was shown by Job's friends, who were scandalized by his assaults on the most basic tenets of their faith. Job's profound disappointment with God did not match their theology. They saw a clear-cut choice between a man who claimed to be just and a God they knew to be just. The very idea of Job demanding an audience with God! Suppress your feelings, they told him. We know for a fact that God is not unjust. So stop thinking that! Shame on you for the outrageous things you're saying!

The second response, Job's, was a rambling mess, a jarring counterpoint to his friend's relentless logic. "Why then did you bring me out of the womb?" he demanded of God. "I wish I had died before any eye ever saw me." Job lashed out in a protest he knew to be futile, like a bird repeatedly hurling itself against a windowpane. He had few sound arguments, and even admitted that his friend's logic sounded right. He wavered, contradicted himself, backtracked, and sometimes collapsed in despair. This man renowned for his righteousness railed against God: "Turn away from me so I can have a moment's joy before I go to the place of no return, to the land of gloom and deep shadow."

And which of the two responses does the book endorse? Both parties needed some correction, but after all the windy words had been uttered, God ordered the pious friends to crawl repentantly to Job and ask him to pray on their behalf.

One bold message in the Book of Job is that you can say anything to God. Throw at him your grief, your anger, your doubt, your bitterness, your betrayal, your disappointment—he can absorb them all. As often as not, spiritual giants of the Bible are shown *contending* with God. They prefer to go away limping, like Jacob, rather than to shut God out. In this respect, the Bible prefigures a tenet of modern psychology: you can't really deny your feelings or make them disappear, so you might as well express them. God can deal with every human response save one. He cannot abide the response I fall back on instinctively: an attempt to ignore him or treat him as though he does not exist. That response never once occurred to Job.

The Big Picture

Freedom to express feelings is not the only lesson from Job, however. The "behind the curtain" view of proceedings in the unseen world shows that an encounter with the hiddenness of God may badly mislead. It may tempt us to see God as the enemy and to interpret his hiddenness as a lack of concern.

Job concluded just that: "God assails me and tears me in his anger." Those of us in the audience know that Job was mistaken. For one thing, the prologue makes the subtle but important distinction that God did not personally cause Job's problems. He permitted them, yes, but the account of The Wager presents Satan, not God, as the instigator of Job's suffering. In any event, God was surely not Job's enemy. Far from being abandoned by God, Job was getting direct, almost microscopic scrutiny from him. At the very moment Job was pleading for a courtroom trial to present his case, he was actually participating in a trial of cosmic significance—not as the prosecuting attorney jabbing his finger at God, but as the main witness in a test of faith.

By no means can we infer that our own trials are, like Job's, specially arranged by God to settle some decisive issue in the universe. But we can safely assume that our limited range of vision will in similar fashion distort reality. Pain narrows vision. The most private of sensations, it forces us to think of ourselves and little else.

From Job, we can learn that much more is going on out there than we may suspect. Job felt the weight of God's absence; but a look behind the curtain reveals that in one sense God had never been more present. In the natural world, human beings only receive about 30 percent of the light spectrum. (Honeybees and homing pigeons, can, for example, detect ultraviolet light waves invisible to us.) In the supernatural realm, our vision is even more limited, and we get only occasional glimpses of that unseen world.

An incident in the life of another famous Bible character makes this same point in a very different way. The prophet Daniel had a mild—mild in comparison with Job's—encounter with the hiddenness of God. Daniel puzzled over an everyday problem of unanswered prayer: why was God ignoring his repeated requests? For twenty-one days Daniel devoted himself to prayer. He mourned. He gave up choice foods. He swore off meat and wine, and used no lotions on his body. All the while he called out to God, but received no answer.

Then one day Daniel got far more than he bargained for. A supernatural being, with eyes like flaming torches and a face like lightning, suddenly showed up on a riverbank beside him. Daniel's companions fled in terror. As for Daniel, "I had no strength left. My face turned deathly pale and I was helpless." When he tried talking to the dazzling being, he could hardly breathe.

The visitor proceeded to explain the reason for the long delay. He had been dispatched to answer Daniel's very first prayer, but had run into strong resistance from "the prince of the Persian kingdom." Finally, after a three-week standoff, reinforcements arrived and Michael, one of the chief angels, helped him break through the opposition.

I will not attempt to interpret this amazing scene of the universe at war, except to point out a parallel to Job. Like Job, Daniel played a decisive role in the warfare between cosmic forces of good and evil, though much of the action took place beyond his range of vision. To him, prayer may have seemed futile, and God indifferent; but a glimpse "behind the curtain" reveals exactly the opposite. Daniel's limited perspective, like Job's, distorted reality.

What are we to make of Daniel's angelic being who needed reinforcements, not to mention the cosmic wager in Job? Simply this: the big picture, with the whole universe as a backdrop, includes much activity that we never see. When we stubbornly cling to God in a time of hardship, or when we simply pray, more—much more—may be involved than we ever dream. It requires faith to believe that, and faith to trust that we are never abandoned, no matter how distant God seems.

At the end, when he heard the Voice from the whirlwind, Job finally attained that faith. God reeled off natural phenomena—the solar system, constellations, thunderstorms, wild animals—that Job could not begin to explain. *If you can't comprehend the visible world you live in, how dare you expect to comprehend a world you cannot even see!* Conscious of the big picture at last, Job repented in dust and ashes.

C. S. Lewis, *A Grief Observed*

(1898–1963) Christian apologist, Oxford scholar, and author.

When I lay . . . questions before God I get no answer. But a rather special sort of "No answer." It is not the locked door. It is more like a silent, certainly not uncompassionate, gaze. As though He shook His head not in refusal but waiving the question. Like, "Peace, child; you don't understand."

Matthew 27:33–46 (NASB)

The crucifixion of Jesus.

And when they had come to a place called Golgotha, which means Place of a Skull, they gave Him wine to drink mingled with gall; and after tasting it, He was unwilling to drink. And when they had crucified Him, they divided up His garments among themselves, casting lots; and sitting down, they *began* to keep watch over Him there. And they put up above His head the charge against Him which read, "THIS IS JESUS THE KING OF THE JEWS." At that time two robbers were crucified with Him, one on the right and one on the left. And those passing by were hurling abuse at Him, wagging their heads, and saying, "You who *are going to* destroy the temple of God, come down from the cross." In the same way the chief priests also, along with the scribes and elders, were mocking *Him,* and saying, "He saved others; He cannot save Himself. He is the King of Israel; let Him now come down from the cross, and we shall believe in Him. "HE TRUSTS IN GOD; LET HIM DELIVER *Him* NOW, IF HE TAKES PLEASURE IN HIM; for He said, 'I am the Son of God.'" And the robbers also who had been crucified with Him were casting the same insult at Him.

Now from the sixth hour darkness fell upon all the land until the ninth hour. And about the ninth hour Jesus cried out with a loud voice, saying, "ELI, ELI, LAMA SABACHTHANI?" that is, "MY GOD, MY GOD, WHY HAST THOU FORSAKEN ME?"

Richard Foster, *Prayer*

Prayer of the Forsaken

There is no more plaintive or heartfelt prayer than the cry of Jesus: "My God, My God, why hast thou forsaken me?" (Matt. 27:46b, KJV). Jesus' experience on the cross was, of course, utterly unique and unrepeatable, for he was taking into himself the sin of the world. But in our own way you and I *will* pray this Prayer of the Forsaken if we seek the intimacy of perpetual communion with the Father. Times of seeming desertion and absence and abandonment appear to be universal among those who have walked this path of faith before us. We might just as well get used to the idea that, sooner or later, we, too, will know what it means to feel forsaken by God.

The old writers spoke of this reality as *Deus Absconditus*—the God who is hidden. Almost instinctively you understand the experience they were describing, do you not? Have you ever tried to pray and felt nothing, saw nothing, sensed nothing? Has it ever seemed like your prayers did no more than bounce off the ceiling and ricochet around an empty room? Have there been times when you desperately needed some word of assurance, some demonstration of divine presence, and you got nothing? Sometimes it just seems like God is hidden from us. We do everything we know. We pray. We serve. We worship. We live as faithfully as we can. And still there is nothing . . . nothing! It feels like we are "beating on Heaven's door with bruised knuckles in the dark," to use the words of George Buttrick.

I am sure you understand that when I speak of the absence of God, I am talking about not a true absence but rather a *sense* of absence. God is always present with us—we know that theologically—but there are times when he withdraws our consciousness of his presence.

But these theological niceties are of little help to us when we enter the Sahara of the heart. Here we experience real spiritual desolation. We feel abandoned by friends, spouse, and God. Every hope evaporates the moment we reach for it. Every dream dies the moment we try to realize it. We question, we doubt, we struggle. Nothing helps. We pray and the words seem empty. We turn to the Bible and find it meaningless. We turn to music and it fails to move us. We seek the fellowship of other Christians and discover only backbiting, selfishness, and egoism.

The biblical metaphor for these experiences of forsakenness is the desert. It is an apt image, for we do indeed feel dry, barren, parched. With the Psalmist we cry out, "I call all day, my God, but you never answer" (Ps. 22:2). In fact, we begin to wonder if there is a God to answer.

These experiences of abandonment and desertion have come and will come to all of us. Therefore, it is good to see if anything helpful can be said as we face the barren wasteland of God's absence.

A Major Highway

The first word that should be spoken is one of encouragement. We are on not a rabbit trail but a major highway. Many have traveled this way before us. Think of Moses exiled from Egypt's splendor, waiting year after silent year for God to deliver his people. Think of the Psalmist's plaintive cry to God, "Why have you forgotten me?" (Ps. 42:9). Think of Elijah in a desolate cave keeping a lonely vigil over wind and earthquake and fire. Think of Jeremiah lowered down into a dungeon well until he "sank in the mire." Think of Mary's solitary vigil at Golgotha. Think of those solitary words atop Golgotha, "My God, My God, why . . . why . . . why?"

Christians down through the centuries have witnessed the same experience. Saint John of the Cross named it "the dark night of the soul." An anonymous English writer identified it as "the cloud of unknowing." Jean-Pierre de Cassade called it "the dark night of faith." George Fox said simply, "When it was day I wished for night, and when it was night I wished for day." Be encouraged—you and I are in good company.

In addition, I want you to know that to be faced with the "withering winds of God's hiddenness" does not mean that God is displeased with you, or that you are insensitive to the work of God's Spirit, or that you have committed some horrendous offense against heaven, or that there is something wrong with you, or anything. Darkness is a definite experience of prayer. It is to be expected, even embraced. . . .

Anatomy of an Absence

Allow me to share with you one time when I entered the Prayer of the Forsaken. By every outward standard things were going well. Publishers wanted me to write for them. Speaking invitations were too numerous and too gracious. Yet through a series of events it seemed clear to me that God wanted me to retreat from public activity. In essence God said, "Keep quiet!" And so I did. I stopped all public speaking, I stopped all writing, and I waited. At the time this began, I did not know if I would ever speak or write again—I rather thought I would not. As it turned out, this fast from public life lasted about eighteen months.

I waited in silence. And God was silent too. I joined in the Psalmist's query: "How long will you hide your face from me?" (Ps. 13:3). The answer I got: nothing. Absolutely nothing! There were no sudden revelations. No penetrating insights. Not even gentle assurances. Nothing.

Have you ever been there? Perhaps for you it was the tragic death of a child or spouse that plunged you into the desolate desert of God's absence. Maybe it was a crisis in marriage or vocation, or a failure in business. It may have been none of these. There may have been no dramatic event at all—you simply slipped from the warm glow of intimate communion to the icy cold of . . . nothing. At least "nothing" is how it feels . . . well, actually there is no feeling at all. It is as if all feelings have gone into hibernation. (You see how I am struggling for the language to describe this experience of abandonment, for words are fragmentary approximations at best, but if you have been there, you understand what I mean.)

As I mentioned earlier, this discipline of silence lasted some eighteen months. It ended finally and simply with gentle assurances that it was time to reenter the public square.

The Purifying Silence

As best I can discern, the silence of God month after weary month was a purifying silence. I say "as best I can discern" because the purifying was not dramatic or even recognizable at the time. It was a little like when you do not realize that a child has grown at all until you measure her against the mark on the hallway doorjamb from last year.

Saint John of the Cross says that . . . purifications occur in the dark night of the soul. . . . The first involves stripping us of dependence upon *exterior results*. We find ourselves less and less impressed with the religion of the "big deal"—big buildings, big budgets, big productions, big miracles. Not that there is anything wrong with big things, but *they* are no longer what impress us. Nor are we drawn toward praise and adulation. Not that there is anything wrong with kind and gracious remarks, but *they* are no longer what move us.

Then, too, we become deadened to that impressive corpus of religious response to God. Liturgical practices, sacramental symbols, aids to prayer, books on personal fulfillment, private devotional exercises—all of these become as mere ashes in our hands. Not that there is anything wrong with acts of devotion, but *they* are no longer what fascinate us.

The final stripping of dependence upon exterior results comes as we become less in control of our destiny and more at the mercy of others. Saint John calls this the "Passive Dark Night." It is the condition of Peter, who once girded himself and went where he wanted but in time found that others girded him and took him where he did not want to go (John 21:18–19).

For me the greatest value in my lack of control was the intimate and ultimate awareness that I could not manage God. God refused to jump when I said, "Jump!" Neither by theological acumen nor by religious technique could I conquer God. God was, in fact, to conquer me.

The second purifying of Saint John involves stripping us of dependence upon *interior results*. This is more disturbing and painful than the first purification because it threatens us at the root of all we believe in and have given to ourselves to. In the beginning we become less and less sure of the inner workings of the Spirit. It is not that we disbelieve in God, but more profoundly we wonder what kind of God we believe in. Is God good and intent upon our goodness, or is God cruel, sadistic, and a tyrant?

We discover that the workings of faith, hope, and love become themselves subject to doubt. Our personal motivations become suspect. We worry whether this act or that thought is inspired by fear, vanity, and arrogance rather than faith, hope, and love.

Like a frightened child we walk cautiously through the dark mists that now surround the Holy of Holies. We become tentative and unsure of ourselves. Nagging questions assail us with a force they never had before. "Is prayer only a psychological trick?" Does evil ultimately win out?" "Is there any real meaning in the universe?" "Does God really love me?"

Through all of this, paradoxically, God is purifying our faith by threatening to destroy it. We are led to a profound and holy distrust of all superficial drives and human strivings. We know more deeply than ever before our capacity for infinite self-deception. Slowly we are being taken off of vain securities and false allegiances. Our trust in all exterior and interior results is being shattered so that we can learn faith in God alone. Through our barrenness of soul God is producing detachment, humility, patience, perseverance.

Most surprising of all, our very dryness produces the habit of prayer in us. All distractions are gone. Even all warm fellowship has disappeared. We have become focused. The soul is parched. And thirsty. And this thirst can lead us to prayer. I say "can" because it can also lead us to despair or simply to abandon the search.

The Prayer of Complaint

This brings us to the issue of what we do during these times of abandonment. Is there any kind of prayer in which we can engage when we feel forsaken? Yes—we can begin by praying the Prayer of Complaint. This is a form of prayer that has been largely lost in our modern, sanitized religion, but the Bible abounds with it.

The best way I know to relearn this time-honored approach to God is by praying that part of the Psalter traditionally known as the "Lament Psalms." The ancient singers really knew how to complain, and their words of anguish and frustration can guide our lips into the prayer we dare not pray alone. They expressed reverence *and* disappointment: "God whom I praise, break your silence" (Ps. 109:1, JB). They experienced dogged hope *and* mounting despair: "I am here, calling for your help, praying to you every morning: why do you reject me? Why do you hide your face from me?" (Ps. 88:13–14, JB). They had confidence in the character of God *and* exasperation at the inaction of God: "I say to God, my rock, 'Why have you forgotten me?'" (Ps. 42:9).

The Lament Psalms teach us to pray our inner conflicts and contradictions. They allow us to shout out our forsakenness in the dark caverns of abandonment and then hear the echo return to us over and over until we bitterly recant of them, only to shout them out again. They give us permission to shake our fist at God one moment and break into doxology the next.

Short Darts of Longing Love

A second thing we can do when we are buffeted by the silence of God is to beat upon the cloud of unknowing "with a short dart of longing love." We may not see the end from the beginning, but we keep on doing what we know to do. We pray, we listen, we worship, we carry out the duty of the present moment. What we learned to do in the light of God's love, we also do in the dark of God's absence. We ask and continue to ask even though there is no answer. We seek and continue to seek even though we do not find. We knock and continue to knock even though the door remains shut.

It is this constant, longing love that produces a firmness of life orientation in us. We love God more than the gifts God brings. Like Job, we serve God even if he slays us. Like Mary, we say freely, "Here am I, the servant of the Lord; let it be with me according to your word" (Luke 1:38). This is a wonderful grace.

Trust Precedes Faith

I would like to offer one more counsel to those who find themselves devoid of the presence of God. It is this: wait on God. Wait, silent and still. Wait, attentive and responsive. Learn that trust precedes faith. Faith is a little like putting your car into gear, and right now you cannot exercise faith, you cannot move forward. Do not berate yourself for this. But when you are unable to put your spiritual life into drive, do not put it into reverse; put it into neutral. Trust is how you put your spiritual life in neutral. Trust is confidence in the character of God. Firmly and deliberately you say, "I do not understand what God is doing or even where God is, but I know that he is out to do me good." This is trust. This is how to wait.

I do not fully understand the reasons for the wildernesses of God's absence. This I do know: while the wilderness is necessary, it is never meant to be permanent. In God's time and in God's way the desert will give way to a land flowing with milk and honey. And as we wait for that promised land of the soul, we can echo the prayer of Bernard of Clairvaux, "O my God, deep calls unto deep (Ps. 42:7). The deep of my profound misery calls to the deep of Your infinite mercy."

Psalm 88 (NIV)

A psalm of the sons of Korah:

> O Lord, the God who saves me,
>   day and night I cry out before you.
> May my prayer come before you;
>   turn your ear to my cry.
>
> For my soul is full of trouble
>   and my life draws near the grave.
> I am counted among those who go down to the pit;
>   I am like a man without strength.
> I am set apart with the dead,
>   like the slain who lie in the grave,
> whom you remember no more,
>   who are cut off from your care.
>
> You have put me in the lowest pit,
>   in the darkest depths.
> Your wrath lies heavily upon me;
>   you have overwhelmed me with all your waves.
>
> You have taken from me my closest friends
>   and have made me repulsive to them.
> I am confined and cannot escape;
>   my eyes are dim with grief.
>
> I call to you, O Lord, every day;
>   I spread out my hands to you.
> Do you show your wonders to the dead?
>   Do those who are dead rise up and praise you?
> Is your love declared in the grave,
>   your faithfulness in Destruction?
> Are your wonders known in the place of darkness,
>   or your righteous deeds in the land of oblivion?

But I cry to you for help, O Lord,
  in the morning my prayer comes before you.
Why, O Lord, do you reject me
  and hide your face from me?

From my youth I have been afflicted and close to death;
  I have suffered your terrors and am in despair.
Your wrath has swept over me;
  your terrors have destroyed me.
All day long they surround me like a flood;
  they have completely engulfed me.
You have taken my companions and loved ones from me;
  the darkness is my closest friend.

———⊗⊗⊗———

Harriet A. Jacobs, "A Piteous Prayer to a Hidden God"

(1813–1897) Famous fugitive slave who wrote Incidents of the Life of a Slave Girl, *one of the classic slave narratives of the nineteenth century.*

I well remember one occasion when I attended a Methodist class meeting. I went with a burdened spirit, and happened to sit next [to] a poor, bereaved mother, whose heart was still heavier than mine. The class leader was the town constable—a man who bought and sold slaves, who whipped his brethren and sisters of the church at the public whipping post, in jail or out of jail. He was ready to perform that Christian office any where for fifty cents. This white-faced black-hearted brother came near us, and said to the stricken woman, "Sister, can't you tell us how the Lord deals with your soul? Do you love him as you did formerly?"

She rose to her feet, and said, in piteous tones, "My Lord and Master, help me! My load is more than I can bear. God has hid himself from me, and I am left in darkness and misery." Then, striking her breast, she continued, "I can't tell you what is in here! They've got all my children. Last week they took the last one. God only knows where they've sold her. They let me have her sixteen years, and then—O! O! Pray for her brothers and sisters! I've nothing to live for now. God make my time short!"

She sat down, quivering in every limb.

———⊗⊗⊗———

C. S. Lewis, *Screwtape Letters*

The following advice is from the imaginative correspondence between a mentoring devil named Uncle Screwtape and his demon nephew named Wormwood. The "Enemy" referred to in their letters is God.

My Dear Wormwood,

. . . You must have often wondered why the Enemy does not make more use of His power to be sensibly present to human souls in any degree He chooses and at any moment. But you now see that the Irresistible and the Indisputable are the two weapons which the very nature of His scheme forbids Him to use. Merely to override a human will (as His felt presence in any but the faintest and most mitigated degree would certainly do) would be for Him useless. He cannot ravish. He can only woo. For His ignoble idea is to eat the cake and have it; the creatures are to be one with Him, but yet themselves; merely to cancel them, or assimilate them, will not serve. He is prepared to do a little overriding at the beginning. He will set them off with communications of His presence which, though faint, seem great to them, with emotional sweetness, and easy conquest over temptation. But He never allows this state of affairs to last long. Sooner or later He withdraws, if not in fact, at least from their conscious experience, all those supports and incentives. He leaves the creature to stand up on its own legs—to carry out from the will alone duties which have lost all relish. It is during such trough periods, much more than during the peak periods, that it is growing into the sort of creature He wants it to be. Hence the prayers offered in the state of dryness are those which please Him best. . . .

Your affectionate uncle,
Screwtape

Ken Gire, "Windows of the Wilderness," *Windows of the Soul*

OLD TESTAMENT TYPOLOGY IN
MATTHEW'S AND LUKE'S TEMPTATION NARRATIVES
A Thesis
Presented to
the Faculty of the Department of Semitic Languages
and Old Testament Exegesis
Dallas Theological Seminary

In Partial Fulfillment
of the Requirements for the Degree
Master of Theology

by
Kenneth Paxton Gire, II
April 4, 1978

That was the first page of my master's thesis, which was also the last page of my four years of theological education. It has the proper form, proper margins, and a proper "Introduction," which reads:

The purpose of this thesis is to exegetically establish a typological correspondence between Israel and her wilderness testings and Christ and His wilderness testings and between Adam and Christ. The temptation narratives of Matthew and Luke will be used as a focus of exegesis. The goal is twofold: first, to explicate a theory of typology; second, to exegete the temptation narratives to uncover the author's intention. It will be demonstrated that a studied attempt is made to compare and contrast Christ with Israel in Matthew and Christ with Adam in Luke.

It sounds like I know what I'm talking about, doesn't it? And with the first page full of single-spaced footnotes, it looks like I know what I'm talking about. Certainly after four years of theological education, I should know what I'm talking about.

There was only one problem.

As of April 4, 1978, I had never been through a wilderness that even remotely resembled the one about which I had written with such authority. Yet a month later, in the ceremonious turn of a tassel, I became a "Master of Theology."

At other graduation ceremonies I have attended over the years, I have heard, as I'm sure you have heard, someone at sometime or another extol the poem "Invictus," by W. E. Henley.

It matters not how strait the gate,
How charged with punishments the scroll,
I am the master of my fate:
I am the captain of my soul.

Being the captain of our soul, like going off to sea, has always been something of a romantic theme in literature. And, as we send off graduates from the safe harbors of higher education to the high seas of whatever vocational course they have charted for their lives, Henley's poem, as we wave from the dock, seems the most appropriate thing to say.

Until their ship hits a reef.

Then what do we say?

Every man for himself? Cling for dear life to whatever's left floating? Hope for dear life that some other captain will come to your rescue? Dog-paddle for shore?

A captain whose ship is dashed against the rocks is no more the master of his fate than I was a master of theology. But it took my life running aground before I realized that. When it did, I found myself washed up on a lonely stretch of shore where the only way back to civilization was by land, land that led through an uncertain and unsafe wilderness.

When I graduated from seminary, I pushed off from the dock, having charted a course to teach in a secular university and write during the summers, though I had no formal education in writing and didn't know what I would write about. The course quickly and unexpectedly changed. As I was being turned down by every institution of higher learning to which I applied, I helped start [a] small rural church. . . .

After two years there, I felt a gentle wind filling my sails, and something in the wind—Was it the Spirit of God?—telling me it was time to start writing. That's when I attempted my first book, a short children's novel about a year in the lives of a set of twins, a boy and a girl, one of whom was mentally handicapped.

Writing the book was an exhilarating experience, and when I finished, I began rearranging deck chairs to accommodate this sprawling passion that had boarded my life. I left the church and took a job selling oil-field equipment, hoping to earn enough money so I could take off some time to continue writing. After two-and-a-half years selling pumping units and sucker rods, I was able to do that. It was a dream come true. I moved our family to east Texas to the town of Nacogdoches, where every day I walked to the college library and wrote from eight to five.

My ship had come in.

What I didn't know was that it had come in on its way to running aground. As its hull scraped the shoals, I discovered that the writing life was not the romantic cruise the travel brochures made it out to be but, rather, one jarring rejection after another.

It was a painfully introspective time for me, trying to get a grip on my elusive craft, trying to find out who I was, which proved equally elusive, and trying to support a wife and four kids on the words I put on 8½" x 11" sheets of paper.

For two years nothing sold. Two years of going to work every day and never coming home with a paycheck. Someone once said that writing is the only profession in which one can make no money without looking ridiculous. But at the end of two years, if I wasn't looking that way, I was certainly feeling that way.

When our savings ran out, we liquidated our IRA, sold a car and some furniture. When that money ran out, we put our house up for sale. It seemed like the appropriate, however improvident, next step. Was it?

Was it walking by faith or just wishing upon a star? Was I being steadfast or just stubborn? I couldn't tell. I was determined to write and to make a living at it. Was I too determined? Or not determined enough? I didn't know.

It was a recessionary time in Texas when we tried to sell our house, and houses weren't selling. I hung wallpaper to make ends meet. So many times I would come home from work with sore knees and a sunken heart, feeling so foolish for squandering our security on pipe dreams and return postage for publishers.

I kept a journal of those times, my thoughts clinging to some passages from the Bible, a few stanzas of poetry, an occasional scene from a movie, anything. But going into my third year of clinging, I was tired and starting to lose my grip.

Jan. 22, 1985, Nacogdoches

It is so discouraging being on the outside. With no job and no material security and everyone else seeming so ordered and established. Adrift. Cut loose from any moorings & far from harbor. It is a dizzy and sick feeling. A lonely feeling. I hate it.

Fe. 20, 1985, Nacogdoches

I have come to a point of emotional and spiritual exhaustion. Drained dry, a drop of life at a time. I can no longer read my Bible, feeling forsaken. I can no longer pray, feeling ignored. It is a great hurt. If God is truly a great God, he can love me even though I can no longer look into His face or call out to Him in prayer. If He cannot, then my prayers and devotions are ill-spent anyway, and my time is better used elsewhere.

Nov. 26, 1985, Nacogdoches

I don't know who is wrestling against me, God or Satan, but whoever it is, I surrender. . . . I have done everything in my power to serve Him in the way I feel most qualified and effective. I have depleted all my material resources, my prayers, my energies, my heart. I don't know what else I can do. I've given all I can give. And now I give up. . . . He has stripped me of all my self-worth, my self-respect, and now I stand naked, impotent, and ashamed before Him. . . . Today, someone has won a victory. I don't know if it is God or Satan—but I know who lost—me.

During those last days in Nacogdoches, as I was trying to figure out what God wanted from me, I came across a passage of Scripture that I noted in my journal.

April 9, 1985, Nacogdoches

Though the fig tree does not bud
    and there are no grapes on the vines,
though the olive crop fails
    and the fields produce no food,
though there are no sheep in the pen
    and no cattle in the stalls,
yet I will rejoice in the LORD,
    I will be joyful in God my Savior.
The Sovereign LORD is my strength;
    he makes my feet like the feet of a deer,
    he enables me to go on the heights.
(Hab. 3:17–19)

I couldn't rejoice during those days. My faith wasn't that strong. But I could believe, from the budding azaleas and hydrangeas emerging from the east Texas winter, that there was at least the hope of something emerging from my life as well. As I look back on it, that passage was a window of the soul, revealing what God wanted from me. He wanted me to trust that spring would follow winter. To live by faith, not by sight. And to have Him, not success, be the source of my joy.

Six months later the house finally sold, and my wife's parents let us move into a vacant farmhouse they owned in Poolville, Texas. For the next year we lived off the equity of the house we had sold. I continued to write. And I continued to tell myself that spring would come. But it didn't. It was so humiliating to face friends and relatives and have to answer well-meaning questions like, "How's the writing going?"—all the while knowing it wasn't going anywhere, but having trouble admitting that to myself, let alone, to anybody else.

To protect myself from the embarrassment of those encounters, I withdrew. To Poolville. There I was—there we all were, all six of us—in the middle of nowhere. With no savings, no retirement fund, no home of our own, no job, no medical insurance—and no future. Or so it seemed. There were snakes outside the house, scorpions inside, and the scorn of the Texas sun glaring down on us. Or was it the scorn of God? I didn't know.

I couldn't understand, when I felt so passionately about writing, worked so diligently, sacrificed so completely, why nothing was working out. Where was God in all this? Why wasn't He helping me? I needed His help, wanted His help, asked for His help. Didn't He hear the words I prayed, see the tears I cried, understand the confusion I felt? Didn't He care?

In Ernest Hemingway's book *The Old Man and the Sea,* he expressed something of what I felt when he described what it was like for a fish on the other end of a fishing line. "The punishment of the hook is nothing. The punishment of hunger, and that he is against something that he does not comprehend, is everything."

Suddenly I found myself against a God who baited me and then set the hook. But it was not the punishment of the hook. That was nothing. It was the hunger in my soul, and that I was against something, or something was against me, that I did not comprehend. That was everything.

As physical hunger intensifies with the absence of food, so spiritual hunger intensifies with the absence of God. That is why the wilderness plays such an important role in our lives, as it did in the lives of Moses, David, Elijah, Job. The wilderness is where we experience prolonged periods of God's absence. For me, that was Poolville. For you, it may be Los Angeles or Odessa, General Motors or graduate school. For me, it was a crisis brought on by a change of careers. For you, it may be a crisis brought on by cancer or divorce or some other struggle.

Whatever the wilderness, wherever the wilderness, it is in that wilderness where we learn that we do not live by bread alone but by every word that proceeds from the mouth of God, that His word is not only the most natural food for our soul but the most necessary.

I will never forget how hungry I was for some word from Him to let me know that He saw me stranded there in Poolville, that He heard my prayers, and, most of all, that He cared. I will never forget, too, how He fed me. Through a small window in our front door, something like manna was offered me, I believe, by the hand of God.

I jotted down the experience in my journal.

Jan 6, 1986, Poolville

A family of stray cats (a mother & three kittens) has sought refuge from the cold underneath the pier-and-beam foundation of our house. They are timid & fearful, scared of coming too close to us in spite of our gentle efforts at coaxing them. Every night I leave some food out with some milk. As I peek through the blinds of the front porch door, I see them cautiously approach their daily allotment, ears erect, eyes darting. They are cold and scared and, I suppose, the world has shown them little kindness—if not outright cruelty.

As I bend the blind, looking down on them as they eat, I feel a certain kindred spirit with them—the cold, the scared, the abandoned—and I hope that somewhere God is bending a blind to look down on me.

Every night I watched as one by one, a tentative step at a time, the gray-and-white kittens came out. I tried to lure them into the house by opening the door and leaving a trail of food for them to follow, hoping they would come just far enough in so I could close the door and catch one. But they were too wary for that.

So one day at dusk I put a big cardboard box in front of the crawl space opening with some cat food at the end of it. I waited. And waited. And finally . . . the sound of a tentative paw. Then another. Step by scratchy step. Until the kitten reached the end of the box. And then I flipped it over.

Gotcha!

I brought the box inside. We all gathered around the square rim of cardboard, nosing down for a good look. I put on a pair of leather work gloves and picked up the ball of brindled fluff. The kitten didn't move. Not a muscle. Not a whisker. It was as lifeless as a stuffed animal.

After we oohed and aahed over it a while, I put it in the bathroom with a saucer of milk and some food and closed the door so it could get used to the foreign surroundings. An hour or so later I came back. As soon as I opened the door, the kitten shot to a corner of the tiled bathroom and wedged itself there. It arched its back and hissed, taking a swipe at me with its paw when I approached. With my gloved hand, I reached for it. It slashed at the glove and bit into the leather, making all sorts of fierce little sounds, spitting, hissing, its eyes wild with anger.

What the kitten didn't know was that all I wanted to do was to draw it close, to give it a safe and warm place in our house, feed it so it didn't have to hunt down its food. I wanted to take care of it, give it a better life, pet it, and look after it. That's all. I didn't want to hurt it. But how would a kitten born in the wild know that?

Suddenly I realized.

I was that kitten. Scared stiff one minute; spitting mad the next. Was that what God was wanting to do with me? Draw me close? Give me shelter, food, look after me? But the shelter I was wanting was the security of a job, not the security of His arms. The food I was wanting was from the grocery store, not from His hand. And I could look after myself—thank you very much —I just needed a break, that was all.

The God who now held me in the clutches of His hand was so foreign to the God I had once held in mine. Was it His face I was scratching at, His hand I was biting?

That image of the scared kitten stayed with me, and softened me. I didn't want to scratch and bite anymore. I was through fighting. But not crying. Every day as the sun set in the expansive Texas sky, I cried out to God to give me my life back, to rescue me from the wilderness. He taught me that the way out of the wilderness was on a road paved with tears.

The road led to southern California—and a job. Of all the jobs I had applied for, it was the only one that said yes. And it was a writing job. I couldn't believe it. Someone was actually paying me to do what I loved.

The fig tree had budded.
Spring had come.
Finally.

When I first listened to the call of God to write, little did I realize it was a call to the wilderness. But it was there, not seminary, that God prepared me to be a writer. The wilderness was a place of panic, of humiliation, of uncertainty, of loneliness and desperation. All of which were necessary for me to experience if I was to be the writer I needed to be, wanted to be, prayed to be. How could I know the feelings of the desperate if I had not been desperate myself? How could I know the feelings of the poor if I had not been poor myself? How could I know the feelings of the confused if I had not been confused myself? Or depressed myself? Or abandoned?

Seminary prepared me to use my gift. The wilderness prepared me to live my life. And it will prepare you to live yours. But your wilderness will be different from mine. And the windows you will be shown will be different from the ones shown to me. The education of the wilderness is not standardized, like seminary. It is individualized, for you and you alone as it was for me and me alone. For each and every one who enters the wilderness, what is shown them is for their eyes and their eyes only. For their ears. And for their heart.

Something about that is like being on the frontier with all its risks and uncertainties. And that's a little unsettling.

"We don't like risk," said Howard Macy, "and even though the frontiers of spiritual growth require it, we prefer to avoid it. Not only would we like to have the frontiers of the spirit scouted out for us, we would also like to have the frontier fully tamed and settled, like a new suburban development with well-lighted streets and sewers installed, established zoning codes, houses built and finished save for seeding the lawn and planting the shrubs, shopping centers nearby, and adequate police protection. No pioneering for us—no danger from the dark wild, no felling trees or clearing boulders so that we can plant a subsistence garden, no climbing mountain passes or fording swollen streams. We prefer comfortable safety to risk."

Seminary was the suburbs of my spiritual life.

It was a safe neighborhood where I could learn about God and the Bible and the spiritual life. I could choose my own well-lighted course of study, and, within the established limits of evangelical zoning codes, I could landscape at least a portion of my curriculum. I could choose morning classes or ones in the afternoon. Choose to have summers off or take summer school and lighten my load in the fall. I could even choose the topic for my thesis.

All of this, and, if I paid the tuition, showed up for classes, did the required work, I would become in four years a master of theology.

It was all so safe.

And safe is what we all really want to be, isn't it? It was what the children wanted to be in C. S. Lewis's *The Lion, the Witch and the Wardrobe,* when they first heard that the true king of Narnia was a lion.

[Susan asks the Beavers.] "Is he—quite safe? I shall feel rather nervous about meeting a lion."

"That you will, dearie, and no mistake," said Mrs. Beaver, "if there's anyone who can appear before Aslan without their knees knocking, they're either braver than most or else just silly."

"Then he isn't safe?" said Lucy.

"Safe?" said Mr. Beaver. "Don't you hear what Mrs. Beaver tells you? Who said anything about safe? Course he isn't safe. But he's good."

The wilderness taught me theology and how incapable I was of ever becoming its master. There was nothing safe or systematic about it. No syllabus, no class notes, no textbook. At the beginning, I didn't know how long the course would last or what tuition I would have to pay before it was over. I disagreed with my teacher, sometimes angrily, sometimes disrespectfully. I complained about the course load and wanted to drop the class. But it was a required course, I was to discover, not an elective, and this was the only time it was being offered. I raised my hand, waved my hand, persistently, but my questions were not acknowledged, let alone, answered. At least, not in my time or on my terms.

The wilderness was my thesis. It was where I had to prove to myself who God really is. It was all original research. No quotes from secondary sources. I had to write it a painful word at a time, a puzzling paragraph at a time, page after page, until my thesis was proved. There was no proper form to follow. All the margins were off; the spacing, erratic; the pages, out of sequence. It was a mess.

But it was *my* mess.

And out of it came the message of my life, or at least, the beginnings of it. And now I am able to know from my own life—not somebody else's—who God really is.

As the emerging nation of Israel left the wilderness, where they had wandered for the past forty years, and crossed the Jordan River into the Promised Land, they were shown a window revealing the purpose for those disorienting years. That window is preserved for our viewing in Deuteronomy 8. The first thing they were shown was that it was God who had led them into the wilderness. It wasn't Moses or Aaron or simply their own inept sense of direction. It was also important for them to see *why* He had led them there—"to humble them, to test them, and to do good to them in the end." (v. 16)

To do good to them in the end.

"Course he isn't safe," was the conclusion I reached in the wilderness. "But he's good."

A PRAYER FOR TRANSFORMATION

Help me, O God,

To realize the role the wilderness plays
    in my continuing education.
Thank You that even in the wilderness there are windows,
    revealing what You want from me,
    showing that You care,
    and clarifying, when I look back,
    what You were doing in my life.
Thank You, God, for the wild and untamed theology
    You have taught me in the wilderness,
    and for the assurance that,
    though You are not safe,
    you are good . . .

Francois Chagneau

IN MY SOLITUDE

I am alone
On the road I travel,
On the road you take me,
Drawing me on with a force
That exceeds all human demands.

I am alone
And I feel this solitude
Like a deeply open wound
In the depths of my being.
All those who surround me
Are only shadowy figures,
Vanishing furtively
At the sound of my appeal.
They flee and disappear
When I try to approach them.
And the time is coming
When I will settle into this solitude
And it will be my lone companion.

I do not know from where
This solitude comes to me.
Does it come from you?
Is it the only road
Where I will discover you
And find at last your truth?
Or does it come from other men
Who refuse to give me love
And thus drive me deeper down
Into a life of cold indifference?
Or does it come from me
Repulsing other human beings
As I try to draw them to me?

I walk, O Lord, in solitude
And the silence resounds in my ears
More loudly than the shouts of men.
I walk, O Lord, in solitude,
Plunging deeper into it
As I journey on to you,
My Lord and God.

———— ❧ ————

Richard Foster, *Prayers from the Heart*

A PRAYER IN DARKNESS

God, where are you?
    I beg, I plead . . . and you do not answer.
    I shout, I yell . . . and get nothing.

Break your silence, O God.
  Speak to me!
  Teach me!
  Rebuke me!
  Strike me down!
  But do not remain silent.
The God who is mute. Is that who you are?

You have revealed yourself as the speaking God—our
communicating Cosmos.
You pointed Abraham to a city whose builder and maker was God.
You revealed your divine name to Moses.
You spoke with clarity
  to David,
  to Ruth,
  to Esther,
  to Isaiah,
  to Ezekiel,
  to Daniel,
  to Mary,
  to Paul,
  and a host of
  others.
Why are the heavens made of iron for me?

Job, I know, experienced you as the hidden God. And Elijah held a
  lonely vigil over earthquake, wind, and fire. Me, too.

O God of wonder and of mystery, teach me by means of your wondrous,
  terrible, loving, all-embracing silence.
Amen.

----- ∞ -----

W. E. Biederwolf

(1867–1939) American Presbyterian evangelist and scholar.

If Jacob's desire had been given him in time to get a good night's sleep,
he might never have become the prince of pray-ers we know today. If
Hannah's prayer for a son had been answered at the time she set for herself, the nation might never have known the mighty man of God it found
in Samuel. Hannah wanted only a son, but God wanted more. He
wanted a prophet, and a saviour, and a ruler for His people. Someone

said that "God had to get a woman before He could get a man." This woman He got in Hannah precisely by delaying the answer to her prayer, for out of the discipline of those weeks and months and years there came a woman with a vision like God's, with tempered soul and gentle spirit and a seasoned will prepared to be the kind of a mother for the kind of a man God knew the nation needed.

Catherine Marshall, *Adventures in Prayer*

And let us not be weary in well doing: for in due season we shall reap, if we faint not.

Waiting seems to be a kind of acted-out prayer that is required more often and honored more often than I could understand until I saw what remarkable faith-muscles this act develops. For isn't it true that waiting demands patience, persistence, trust, expectancy—all the qualities we are continually beseeching God to give us?

THE STRUGGLE OF
DEALING WITH UNANSWERED PRAYER

Psalm 22:1–2 (NASB)

A psalm of David:

My God, my God, why hast Thou forsaken me?
Far from my deliverance are the words of my groaning.
O my God, I cry by day, but Thou dost not answer;
And by night, but I have no rest.

W. Bingham Hunter, *The God Who Hears*

Sure, I know, there *are* lots of thrilling answers to prayer. We can read about powerful petition in dozens of books and articles every year and see supersupplicators almost every month on TV. But all this only increases the heartache, guilt and frustration of those who feel they can't, or are afraid to, take prayer seriously. It is hard to rejoice with those who rejoice . . . if you feel you have to cry alone. When is the last time you felt free to "share" your tremendous *unanswered* prayer? I am convinced that a huge, but largely secret, group of Christians genuinely longs to know both God and themselves better and are weary of having to sing "It is well with my soul" with their fingers crossed.

St. John of the Cross

(1542–1591) Spanish mystic who wrote a number of prayers, but his most noted work is The Dark Night of the Soul.

Why Are You Waiting?

Lord God, my beloved, if you still remember my sins, and so withhold the blessing for which I yearn, I beg you either to punish me as I deserve, or to have mercy on me. If you are waiting for me to behave well and do good to others, then give me the strength and the will to act as you want.

Why are you waiting? Why do you delay in pouring out the love for which I yearn? How can I behave well and love others, if you do not strengthen and guide me? How can I be worthy of you, if you do not make me worthy? How can I rise up to you, if you do not raise me up?

Surely you will not take from me the grace which you gave me in your dear Son Jesus Christ? Surely the love which he revealed to all mankind will be granted to me? Why are you waiting?. . .

I give you my life, my all! Why are you waiting to receive it?

Philip Yancey, *Disappointment with God*

I have known Meg for more than a decade. She is a devout Christian, a pastor's wife, and a very fine writer. Yet I cannot think of Meg without feeling a stab of grief.

The Woodsons had two children—Peggie and Joey—both born with cystic fibrosis. Peggie and Joey stayed skinny no matter how much food they ate. They coughed constantly and labored to breathe—twice a day Meg had to pound on their chests to clear out mucus. They spent several weeks each year in a local hospital, and both grew up knowing they would probably die before reaching adulthood.

Joey, a bright, happy, all-American boy, died at the age of twelve. Peggie defied the odds by living much longer. I joined Meg in desperate prayers for Peggie. Although we knew of no recorded miraculous healings of cystic fibrosis, we prayed for healing anyway. Peggie survived several health crises in high school and went away to college. She seemed to grow stronger, not weaker, and our hopes rose that she would find healing after all.

But there was no miracle: Peggie died at the age of twenty-three. And that night in my basement office I came across the letter Meg had written to me after Peggie's death.

I find myself wanting to tell you something of how Peggie died. I don't know why except that the need to talk about it is so compelling and, since I refuse to put my friends here through it more than once, I have run out of people to tell.

The weekend before she went into the hospital for the last time, Peggie came home all excited about a quotation from William Barclay her minister had used. She was so taken with it that she had copied it down on a 3 x 5 card for me: "Endurance is not just the ability to bear a hard thing, but to turn it into glory." She said her minister must have had a hard week, because after he read it he banged the pulpit and then turned his back to them and cried.

After Peggie had been in the hospital for a while and things were not going well, she looked around at all the paraphernalia of death to which she was attached. Then she said, "Hey, Ma, remember that quotation?" And she looked around again at all the tubes, stuck the tip of her tongue out of the corner of her mouth, nodded her head, and raised her eyes in excitement at the experiment to which she was committing herself.

Her commitment held as long as her awareness of anything in the real world held. Once, the president of her college came to see her and asked if there was anything specific he could pray for. She was too weak to talk, but nodded to me to explain the Barclay quote and ask him to pray that her hard time would be turned into glory.

I was sitting beside her bed a few days before her death when suddenly she began screaming. I will never forget those shrill, piercing, primal screams. Nurses raced into the room from every direction and surrounded her with their love. "It's okay, Peggie," one said. "Jeannie's here."

The nurses stroked her body. Eventually with their words and their touches they soothed her (though as time went on and the screaming continued, they could not). I've rarely seen such compassion. Wendy, Peggie's special nurse-friend, tells me there isn't a nurse on the floor who does not have at least one patient she would give one of her lungs to save if she could.

So, it's against this background of human beings falling apart—nurses can only stay on that floor so long—because they could not do more to help, that God, who could have helped, looked down on a young woman devoted to Him, quite willing to die for Him to give Him glory, and decided to sit on His hands and let her death top the horror charts for cystic fibrosis deaths.

I tell you, Philip, it does not help to talk of the good that results from pain. Nor does it help to talk of God almost always letting the physical process of disease run its course. Because if He ever intervenes, then at every point of human suffering He makes a decision to intervene or not, and in Peggie's case His choice was to let C.F. rip. There are moments when my only responses are grief and an anger as violent as any I have ever known. Nor does expressing it dissipate it.

Peggie never complained against God. It was no pious restraint: I don't think it ever occurred to her to complain. And none of us who lived through her death with her complained at the time either. We were upheld. God's love was so real, one could not doubt it or rail against its ways.

If I've been telling you all this in an effort to come to some kind of resolution to the problem of Peggie's and my pain, perhaps I've been brought once again to the only thing that helps me experience God's love: His stroking, His "I'm here, Meg." But, again I wonder, how could He be in a situation like that and sit on His hands?

As I think of it, I've never expressed all this to anyone before, for fear of disturbing someone's faith. Don't think you must say anything to "make me feel better." But thanks for listening. Most people have no idea how much that helps.

After reading Meg's letter, I could not work anymore that evening.

Lamentations 3:1–18 (NIV)

The prophet Jeremiah:

> I am the man who has seen affliction
>   by the rod of his wrath.
> He has driven me away and made me walk
>   in darkness rather than light;
> indeed, he has turned his hand against me
>   again and again, all day long.

He has made my skin and my flesh grow old
    and has broken my bones.
He has besieged me and surrounded me
    with bitterness and hardship.
He has made me dwell in darkness
    like those long dead.

He has walled me in so I cannot escape;
    he has weighed me down with chains.
Even when I call out or cry for help,
    he shuts out my prayer.
He has barred my way with blocks of stone;
    he has made my paths crooked.
Like a bear lying in wait,
    like a lion in hiding,
he dragged me from the path and mangled me
    and left me without help.
He drew his bow
    and made me the target for his arrows.

He pierced my heart
    with arrows from his quiver.
I became the laughingstock of all my people;
    they mock me in song all day long.
He has filled me with bitter herbs
    and sated me with gall.

He has broken my teeth with gravel;
    he has trampled me in the dust.
I have been deprived of peace;
    I have forgotten what prosperity is.
So I say, "My splendor is gone
    and all that I had hoped from the Lord."

C. S. Lewis, *The World's Last Night*

Prayer is not a machine. It is not magic. It is not advice offered to
God. . . .

It would be even worse to think of those who get what they pray for
as a sort of court favorites, people who have influence with the throne.
The refused prayer of Christ in Gethsemane is answer enough to that.

And I dare not leave out the hard saying which I once heard from an experienced Christian: "I have seen many striking answers to pray and more than one that I thought miraculous. But they usually come at the beginning: before conversion, or soon after it. As the Christian life proceeds, they tend to be rarer. The refusals, too, are not only more frequent; they become more unmistakable, more emphatic."

Does God then forsake just those who serve Him best? Well, he who served Him best of all said, near His tortured death, "Why hast thou forsaken me?" When God becomes man, that Man, of all others, is least comforted by God, at His greatest need. There is a mystery here which, even if I had the power, I might not have the courage to explore. Meanwhile, little people like you and me, if our prayers are sometimes granted, beyond all hope and probability, had better not draw hasty conclusions to our own advantage. If we were stronger, we might be less tenderly treated. If we were braver, we might be sent, with far less help, to defend far more desperate posts in the great battle.

---

2 Corinthians 12:8–10 (NIV)

The Apostle Paul:

> Three times I pleaded with the Lord to take [a thorn in my flesh, a messenger of Satan] away from me. But he said to me, "My grace is sufficient for you, for my power is made perfect in weakness." Therefore I will boast all the more gladly about my weaknesses, so that Christ's power may rest on me. That is why, for Christ's sake, I delight in weaknesses, in insults, in hardships, in persecutions, in difficulties. For when I am weak, then I am strong.

Anonymous, *Some Pray and Die*

I wish that people would stop writing about people who pray on rafts and get rescued. *Because they don't all get rescued.*

We had prayed together before the altar, a young pilot and his chaplain. Then he had climbed into his ship and flown away toward the desert with God's blessing and peace in his heart. But I must tell my story as I saw it. It had a sad ending, in a way; for the plane crashed and the young pilot was killed. Only those who believe in certain things as he did could see the part that wasn't sad. He was in God's grace. He was prepared. He was ready to meet death, and that is not sad but glorious.

Is there such a thing as getting the "breaks" in prayer? What about the fellows who pray regularly, but get killed regularly? What was wrong with their prayers? That's why I'm beginning to get a little touchy about all these stories of successful raft-praying. That's why I wish people would stop writing about the soldiers who pray and have their prayers answered by *not* getting killed. Why do all the other soldiers seem to get the wrong answer?

What I want to know is this: what sort of an extra-special, super-powered prayer is needed to make everything turn out the way you want it? That sounds facetious, almost irreverent, but I'm serious. I really want to know. I'm an Army chaplain, and I could use some special prayers with my men—and, heaven knows, we need them badly at times. Because the fact is there are always more men who pray to come back than there are men who get back. Quite a lot more. What is the deciding factor?

The thing for all of us to remember is this: someone else does the answering. Prayer must be distinguished from a monologue. Prayer is always a dialogue. Prayers are answered by God. Otherwise you are only talking to yourself, and that's not good. What you have in mind may not be what God has in mind. If you ask Him something, you must be ready and willing to take what He gives. Without that as a basis of understanding the whole business becomes ridiculous.

That is why I am about to become famous as the apostle to those whose prayers get answers they don't expect. That is why I am a bit depressed by the writings of those who try to get other people to pray by telling them that you get what you want. People must learn to want what they get. There is a real danger that "success stories" in prayer may act as a boomerang. They tend to create a false impression that God saves some and lets the others go. If all the rubber rafts were picked up, of course, there wouldn't be any problem. I may be a little stubborn about this, but I can't help thinking of all the men who pray and don't come back.

So when I talk to soldiers about prayer I try to tell them that they must be adults. God expects us to be men. Only children demand a happy ending to every story. How old must we be before we begin to realize that even prayer can't get us everything we want, unless the thing we want is right for us to have? For grown-ups know only too well that there is much of life which appears to have an unhappy ending. It needn't be unhappy unless we make it so.

But to end my little story of last spring—the one about the young pilot who was killed. If anyone deserved to live, it was he. For he wasn't one of these fellows who forget God until the bad moment comes, and then begin to pray hysterically. His practice of prayer had small reference to a panic-stricken emergency, for he prayed daily and well.

He flew the Atlantic to Africa, alone. But before he had been in a foreign land 24 hours he had found a chaplain and a chapel. Early in the morning he was there, kneeling at the altar. This to him was home. As he said his prayers, he thanked God for many things—for having been born in a good land, for having parents who taught him to love God. For himself he asked little, save that he might repay the debt, that he might stay in God's good grace.

What if he did ask that he might be allowed to live? I should think it very strange of him if he hadn't for he had everything to live for. But I am sure that what he asked for most of all was strength to face whatever might lie ahead. If it were the gift of lengthened life, he would live it well. If it were the call of sudden death, he would take it like a man. Surely God must know about such things.

After all I have said about being adult in our prayers, I am ashamed to confess that it was I, not he, who fell back upon the childish praying. As he knelt quietly at the altar, so fine and young and full of promise, I secretly asked for him a happy ending.

Let him have long life and a happy ending. "He shall give his angels charge over thee, to keep thee: and in their hands they shall bear thee up." *Hold him up. Don't let him fall.*

What was wrong with my prayers? I asked myself as I stood by the fearful wreckage of the plane he had tried so bravely to bring safely in. Other people's prayers are answered. What's the matter with ours?

Who gets the breaks in prayers? Nobody. There is no such thing. We get what God in His infinite love and foreknowledge sees fit to give. That's not always the same as getting what we want. But it ought to be. . . .

John Polkinghorne, *Science and Providence*

Canon John Gunstone tells of how, in a prayer group, he heard of a woman in her thirties who was suffering from terminal cancer. She lived far away from Manchester, where he worked, and he did not know her. A little later he decided he ought to write to her, but as he began to do so he was seized by the conviction that he did not need to do so because they would meet the next day. He was due to preach at a church forty miles away from where the woman was living. As he sat down to lunch before the service, he asked his host if he knew the woman. He said that he did not but she and her husband had written to him, out of the blue, to ask if it would be permissible for them to come to the Eucharist for healing which was Gunstone's reason for being there. After the service a couple made their way to him. "Are you Philip and Heather?" he asked. They were astonished to be greeted by name and John Gunstone explained the remarkable sequence of events which had led to their meeting. It seemed that God's hand was in the encounter and Gunstone was moved to say "Heather, I believe the Lord has arranged this meeting so that we can anoint you and pray for your healing." She answered that she believed that too. Within three months she was dead. John Gunstone tells us that "For a long time afterwards I avoided being involved in the ministry of healing. Over and over again I wanted to say with the psalmist 'Has God forgotten to be merciful?'"

Psalm 77:1–12 (NIV)

A psalm of Asaph:

I cried out to God for help;
  I cried out to God to hear me.
When I was in distress, I sought the Lord;
  at night I stretched out untiring hands
  and my soul refused to be comforted

I remembered you, O God, and I groaned;
  I mused, and my spirit grew faint.
You kept my eyes from closing;
  I was too troubled to speak.
I thought about the former days,
  the years of long ago;
I remembered my songs in the night.
  My heart mused and my spirit inquired:

"Will the Lord reject forever?
  Will he never show his favor again?
Has his unfailing love vanished forever?
  Has his promise failed for all time?
Has God forgotten to be merciful?
  Has he in anger withheld his compassion?"

Then I thought, "To this I will appeal:
  the years of the right hand of the Most High."

I will remember the deeds of the Lord;
>   yes, I will remember your miracles of long ago.
I will meditate on all your works
>   and consider all your mighty deeds.

Philip Yancey, *Where Is God When It Hurts?*

As a freshman at the University of Washington, Brian set a national collegiate freshman mark of 15'8". By his sophomore year, he was ranked the No. 1 pole-vaulter in the world by track magazines. He found himself among the world's great athletes. The year was 1963. John Kennedy was president, and beating the Russians a national pastime. It looked as if the U.S. had a winner in Brian Sternberg, and world attention focused on the nineteen-year-old.

The season of 1963 ushered in unbelievable success. Brian made sports headlines every week. Undefeated in outdoor competition, he set an American record in indoor competition. Then that spring he set his first world mark with a vault of 16'5".

In quick succession Brian racked up new records of 16'7" and 16'8" and captured both the NCAA and AAU titles. . . .

Everything changed on July 2, three weeks after Brian's last world record. Now, well over a decade later, Brian Sternberg still competes, but in a far more lonely and desperate contest. There have been no more vaults.

The Accident

The ordeal began when he grabbed his sweater and yelled, "I'm going to limber up at the pavilion, mom." He drove across the river to the University of Washington and began a gymnastics warm-up. The U.S. track team was readying for a tour to Russia, and Brian's practice time was now preciously indispensable. This is the way Brian described what happened next:

> If there is ever a frightening moment in trampolining, it is just as you leave the trampoline bed, on your way up. At that moment, even the most experienced gymnast sometimes gets a sensation of panic, for no good reason, that does not disappear until he is down safe on the bed again. It hit me as I took off. I got lost in midair and thought I was going to land on my hands and feet, as I had done several times before when the panic came. Instead I landed on my head.
>
> I heard the crack in my neck, then everything was gone. My arms and legs were bounding around in front of my eyes, but I couldn't feel

them moving. Even before the bouncing stopped, I was yelling, "I'm paralyzed," in as loud a voice as I could, which was pretty weak because I had practically no lung power. The paralysis was affecting my breathing.

There was nothing I could do. I couldn't move. It scared me at first, but then, for some reason, the panic disappeared. I told the people looking down at me, "Don't move me, especially don't move my neck." At one point, when I started losing my power to breathe and could feel myself passing out, I remember telling a buddy about mouth-to-mouth resuscitation: "Do everything, but don't tilt my head back."

Real anguish hit me a couple of times while we waited for the doctor. It was not physical pain: I just broke from the thought of what had happened to me. But at the time I was thinking only about the near future. I had not begun to think about the possibility of never walking again.

For the next eight weeks Brian lay strapped onto a Foster frame, a steel-and-canvas device nicknamed "the canvas sandwich." It was hinged at both ends, and every few hours a nurse would flip Brian upside down, preventing bedsores and other complications. . . .

Three months after the accident is the time Brian dates his awakening as a Christian. His brooding had taught him several things. He realized that if he ever walked again it would have to be with God's help. No amount of straining could budge his limbs. If there was dead nerve fiber in his spinal cord, it would have to be remade, and medicine could not do that. He also knew that his faith in God couldn't be a bargain: "You heal me, God, and I'll believe." He had to believe because God was worthy of his faith. He took that risk and committed his life to Jesus Christ.

Brian began a prayer that has not ended. Scores, hundreds, thousands of times he's asked God the same request. Everything about his life reminds him that the prayer has not been answered. He's prayed with bitterness, with pleading, with desperation, with the highest longing. Others have prayed—small clusters of athletes, churches, college students. Always the same prayer; never the answer Brian wants and believes in.

Less than a year after the accident, Brian ended the *Look* magazine article with this quote: "Having faith is a necessary step toward one of two things. Being healed is one of them. Peace of mind, if healing doesn't come, is the other. Either one will suffice." But Brian has a different view now. To him there's only one option—complete healing.

Brian's World

What could feed a faith enough to survive a decade of suffering? Over the years, some who first claimed healing for Brian have changed their prayers. But not the Sternbergs. Were they stubborn or superhuman? I wondered as I drove to their Seattle home. Others had warned me: "It's strange—they just won't accept Brian's condition.". . .

What strikes a visitor first is how totally Brian depends on other people for his life. If left alone for forty-eight hours, he would die. Orderlies from high schools and Seattle Pacific bathe him, give him medication, feed him, hold glasses of water for him. Brian has always fought against this dependence, but he has no choice. His body lies exactly where the orderly last placed it.

Brian's head is of normal size, but the rest of his body has shrunk due to muscle atrophy. He can now make some motions with his arms. He can hit switches, turn knobs with difficulty, even type with a special contraption that holds back all but one finger. . . .

The Miracle That Won't Come

Brian is the first to admit the progress he has made. But now more than ever, he does not accept his condition. He has one hope and one prayer—for total healing. He tells that to every visitor. Medically, he needs a miracle—time has done little, and his chances of natural recovery have steadily diminished.

The worst part is the pain. It's as if Brian's body is in revolt. The pain comes from within and spreads invisibly throughout his whole body, like the pain machine from George Orwell's 1984 that tapped right into the central nervous system. Taken at a single moment, it's enough to knock a strong man howling across the floor. To Brian, it's a horrible routine. . . .

After the first shock, which lasted almost six months, the Sternbergs were flooded with genuine expressions of hope and support. Many believed Brian would recover. It had to be God's will, they said, for such a young, talented guy to walk again. Brian has met with famous Christians known for their healing powers, but he still suffers. At one point, Christian leaders from seven different denominations met in his room, praying and anointing him with oil. Everyone was moved, everyone believed, but nothing happened.

For comfort and guidance the Sternbergs turned to the Bible. They had talked to pastors and theologians of every stripe; they had read all the books on why God allows suffering. As they read, they became even more convinced Brian would be healed.

"What we found," says Mrs. Sternberg, "was that God loves. No, it's more than that. God is love. All around us people were telling us to accept this tragedy as what God must want for us. But the Jesus we saw in the Bible came to bring healing. Where there was hurt, He touched and made well. He never cursed or afflicted people. Jesus was God's language to man. What God is, Jesus lived. Has God's language changed? Does our son's condition contradict what God revealed as Himself?

"People would say to us, 'Well, look at the good that has come of this tragedy. Perhaps God in His wisdom knew Brian would stray away from Him, and so He allowed this to happen.' But the God we found in the New Testament was a God who respected man so much He gave us freedom, even to rebel against Him. The Holy Spirit, we believe, is a gentleman. He suggests and woos, but never forces."

Other Christians who have met extreme suffering have found comfort in learning to accept what is and work from there. Obviously, God doesn't enjoy watching us suffer. But somehow He does permit it. The Sternbergs, though, aren't satisfied with acceptance.

"To put it bluntly," Mrs. Sternberg continues, "I don't think God is very happy with Brian's condition either. God's will as seen in the Bible is a full, abundant life. It's wholeness, health—not the body Brian's trapped in.

"God's will. You can use it as the pious period to every question mark. But God is mysterious and deep. We can never learn too much about Him. We can't stop searching with God and become fatalists, saying, 'I know God's will has been done.' I never read about Jesus saying to a blind man, 'Sorry, buddy, I wish I could help, but God is trying to teach you something, so get used to it.' When Jesus saw a blind man, He healed. And He taught us to pray for God's will to 'be done on earth as it is in heaven.'"

She pauses. The words are strong, and they come with a background of pain few others have felt.

She presses her chin in her hands. "In this life, we don't know the full answers to any questions. We take a lot on faith. My husband and I and Brian cling most strongly to God's love. If something—like the accident—doesn't tally with God's love, we look elsewhere. We know it's not from Him.

"I don't know why Brian's not on his feet yet. I believe God is all-powerful, but I also believe He's limited Himself. Satan is strong. And I think it's to Satan's great advantage to keep us incapacitated. Anything to keep us from wholeness. He'll exploit our weakness, like a boxer jabbing again and again at a sore jaw or bloody eye. He doesn't quit."

As she talked of the battle between good and evil, I thought of Satan's attacks on Jesus while He was on earth—a slaughter of babies, temptations, betrayal, and finally death. Good Friday must have seemed victorious from Satan's viewpoint. Yet God transformed the awful, grisly death of His own Son into His greatest victory.

In smaller, more subtle ways He has used Brian's tragedy, too—bringing Brian Sternberg and hundreds more to Himself. Yet will He crash through with a resounding turn of the tables wiping out the tragedy with a healing as He had wiped out death with a resurrection? The Sternbergs are staking everything on this hope.

Mrs. Sternberg continues, "No one in Brian's condition has ever walked. No one. Yet we still believe. I have no idea when God will heal Brian. It's conceivable this particular battle will not be won here on earth. Some people you pray for are healed. Some aren't in this world. But that doesn't change God's desire for wholeness—body, mind, and spirit.

"We won't give up. We're like doctors searching for a cure; we won't stop investigating. We think it pleases God for us to persevere."

Luke 18:1–8a (KJV)

And he spake a parable unto them to this end, that men ought always to pray, and not to faint;

Saying, There was in a city a judge, which feared not God, neither regarded man:

And there was a widow in that city; and she came unto him, saying, Avenge me of mine adversary.

And he would not for a while: but afterward he said within himself, Though I fear not God, nor regard man;

Yet because this widow troubleth me, I will avenge her, lest by her continual coming she weary me.

And the Lord said, Hear what the unjust judge saith.

And shall not God avenge his own elect, which cry day and night unto him, though he bear long with them?

I tell you that he will avenge them speedily.

George MacDonald

(1824–1905) Poverty-stricken Scottish pastor, poet, and novelist whose works profoundly influenced C. S. Lewis.

In the very structure of the parable [the Lord] seems to take delay for granted, and says notwithstanding, "He will [avenge] them speedily!"

The reconciling conclusion is that God loses no time, though the answer may not be immediate.

He may delay because it would not be safe to give us at once what we ask: we are not ready for it. To give ere we could truly receive would be to destroy the very heart and hope of prayer, to cease to be our Father. The delay itself may work to bring us nearer to our help, to increase the desire, perfect the prayer, and ripen the receptive condition.

Again, not from any straitening in God, but either from our own condition and capacity, or those of the friend for whom we pray, time may be necessary to the working out of the answer. God is limited by regard for our best; our best implies education; in this we must ourselves have a large share; this share, being human, involves time. And perhaps, indeed, the better the gift we pray for, the more time is necessary to its arrival.

To give us the spiritual gift we desire, God may have to begin far back in our spirit, in regions unknown to us, and do much work that we can be aware of only in the results. . . .

To [avenge] speedily must mean to make no delay beyond what is absolutely necessary, to begin the moment it is possible to begin. Because the Son of Man did not appear for thousands of years after men began to cry out for a Savior, shall we imagine He did not come the first moment it was well He should come? Can we doubt that to come a moment sooner would have been to delay, not to expedite, His kingdom? For anything that needs a process, to begin to act at once is to be speedy. God does not put off like the unrighteous judge; He does not delay until irritated by the prayers of the needy. He will hear while they are yet speaking; yea, before they call He will answer.

———∞∞∞———

C. S. Lewis, Excerpts from *Letters to Malcolm* and *Christian Reflections*

I see you won't let me off. And the longer I look at it the less I shall like it. I must face—or else explicitly decline—the difficulties that really torment us when we cry for mercy in earnest. I have found no book that helps me with them all. I have so little confidence in my own power to tackle them that, if it were possible, I would let sleeping dogs lie. But the dogs are not sleeping. They are awake and snapping. We both bear the marks of their teeth. That being so, we had better share our bewilderments. By hiding them from each other we should not hide them from ourselves.

The New Testament contains embarrassing promises that what we pray for with faith we shall receive. Mark XI:24 is the most staggering. Whatever we ask for, believing that we'll get it, we'll get. No question, it seems, of confining it to spiritual gifts; *whatever* we ask for. No question of a merely general faith in God, but a belief that you will get the particular thing you ask. No question of getting either it or else something that is really far better for you; you'll get precisely it. And to heap paradox on paradox, the Greek doesn't ever say "believing that you *will* get it." It uses the aorist . . . which one is tempted to translate "believing that you *got* it. . . ."

How is this astonishing promise to be reconciled (a) With the observed facts? and (b) With the prayer in Gethsemane, and (as a result of that prayer) the universally accepted view that we should ask everything with a reservation ("if it be Thy will")?

As regards (a), no evasion is possible. Every war, every famine or plague, almost every death-bed, is the monument to a petition that was not granted. At this very moment thousands of people in this one island are facing as a *fait accompli* the very thing against which they have prayed night and day, pouring out their whole soul in prayer, and, as they thought, with faith. They have sought and not found. They have knocked and it has not been opened. "That which they greatly feared has come upon them."

But (b), though much less often mentioned, is surely an equal difficulty. How is it possible at one and the same moment to have a perfect faith—an untroubled or unhesitating faith as St. James says (1:6)—that you will get what you ask and yet also prepare yourself submissively in advance for a possible refusal? If you envisage a refusal as possible, how can you have simultaneously a perfect confidence that what you ask will not be refused? If you have that confidence, how can you take refusal into account at all?

It is easy to see why so much more is written about worship and contemplation than about "crudely" or "naïvely" petitionary prayer. That may be—I think they are—nobler forms of prayer. But they are also a good deal easier to write about.

As regards the first difficulty, I'm not asking why our petitions are so often refused. Anyone can see in general that this must be so. In our ignorance we ask what is not good for us or for others, or not even intrinsically possible. Or again, to grant one man's prayer involves refusing another's. There is much here which it is hard for our will to accept but nothing that is hard for our intellect to understand. The real problem is different; not why refusal is so frequent, but why the opposite result is so lavishly promised. . . .

Dare we say that when God promises "You shall have what you ask" He secretly means "You shall have it if you ask for something I wish to give you"? What should we think of an earthly father who promised to give his son whatever he chose for his birthday and, when the boy asked for a bicycle gave him an arithmetic book, then first disclosing the silent reservation with which the promise was made?

Of course the arithmetic book may be better for the son than the bicycle, and a robust faith may manage to believe so. That is not where the difficulty, the sense of cruel mockery, lies. The boy is tempted, not to complain that the bicycle was denied, but that the promise "of anything he chose" was made. So with us. . . .

I have no answer to my problem, though I have taken it to about every Christian I know, learned or simple, lay or clerical, within my own Communion or without. . . .

One thing seems to be clear to me. Whatever else faith may mean (that is, faith in the granting of the blessing asked . . .) I feel quite sure that it does not mean any state of psychological certitude such as might be—I think it sometimes is—manufactured from within by the natural action of a strong will upon an obedient imagination. The faith that moves mountains is a gift from Him who created mountains. . . .

But some discomfort remains. I do not like to represent God as saying, "I will grant what you ask in faith" and adding, so to speak, "Because I will not give you the faith—not that kind—unless you ask what I want to give you." Once more, there is just a faint suggestion of mockery, of goods that look a little larger in the advertisement than they turn out to be. Not that we complain of any defect in the goods: it is the faintest suspicion of excess in the advertisement that is disquieting. But at present I have got no further. I come to you, reverend Fathers, for guidance. How am I to pray this very night?

Lamentations 3:19–32 (NIV)

The prophet Jeremiah:

> I remember my affliction and my wandering,
>   the bitterness and the gall.
> I well remember them,
>   and my soul is downcast within me.
> Yet this I call to mind
>   and therefore I have hope:
>
> Because of the Lord's great love we are not consumed,
> for his compassions never fail.
> They are new every morning;
> great is your faithfulness.
> I say to myself, "The Lord is my portion;
> therefore I will wait for him."

The Lord is good to those whose hope is in him,
    to the one who seeks him;
it is good to wait quietly
    for the salvation of the Lord.
It is good for a man to bear the yoke
    while he is young.

Let him sit alone in silence,
    for the Lord has laid it on him.
Let him bury his face in the dust—
    there may yet be hope.
Let him offer his cheek to one who would strike him,
    and let him be filled with disgrace.

For men are not cast off
    by the Lord forever.
Though he brings grief, he will show compassion,
    so great is his unfailing love.

THE STRUGGLE OF
WRESTLING WITH OUR HUMANITY

The Struggle of Reluctance

C. S. Lewis, *Letters to Malcolm*

Well, let's now at any rate come clean. Prayer is irksome. An excuse to
omit it is never unwelcome. When it is over, this casts a feeling of relief
and holiday over the rest of the day. We are reluctant to begin. We are
delighted to finish. While we are at prayer, but not while we are reading
a novel or solving a cross-word puzzle, any trifle is enough to distract us.

And we know that we are not alone in this. . . .

The odd thing is that this reluctance to pray is not confined to periods of dryness. When yesterday's prayers were full of comfort and exaltation, today's will still be felt as, in some degree, a burden.

Now the disquieting thing is not simply that we skimp and begrudge
the duty of prayer. The really disquieting thing is it should have to be
numbered among duties at all. For we believe that we are created "to
glorify God and enjoy Him forever." And if the few, the very few minutes

we now spend on intercourse with God are a burden to us rather than a delight, what then? . . . What can be done *for*—or what should be done *with*—a rose-tree that *dislikes* producing roses? Surely it ought to want to. . . .

If we were perfected, prayer would not be a duty, it would be delight. Some day, please God, it will be. The same is true of many other behaviours which now appear as duties. If I loved my neighbour as myself, most of the actions which are now my moral duty would flow out of me as spontaneously as song from a lark or fragrance from a flower. Why is this not so yet? Well, we know, don't we? Aristotle has taught us that delight is the "bloom" on an unimpeded activity. But the very activities for which we were created are, while we live on earth, variously impeded: by evil in ourselves or in others. Not to practice them is to abandon our humanity. To practice them spontaneously and delightfully is not yet possible. This situation creates the category of duty . . . morality, the Law. A schoolmaster, as St. Paul says, to bring us to Christ. We must expect no more of it than of a schoolmaster; we must allow it no less. I must say my prayers to-day whether I feel devout or not; but that is only as I must learn my grammar if I am ever to read the poets.

But the school-days, please God, are numbered. There is no morality in Heaven. The angels never knew (from within) the meaning of the word *ought*, and the blessed dead have long since gladly forgotten it. . . .

I am therefore not really deeply worried by the fact that prayer is at present a duty, and even an irksome one. That is humiliating. It is frustrating. . . . But we are still only at school.

The Struggle of Emotional Ups and Downs

Henri Nouwen, "Ebb and Flow"

Dear Lord, today I thought of the words of Vincent van Gogh: "It is true there is an ebb and flow, but the sea remains the sea." You are the sea. Although I experience many ups and downs in my emotions and often feel great shifts and changes in my inner life, you remain the same. Your sameness is not the sameness of a rock, but the sameness of a faithful lover. Out of your love I came to life; by your love I am sustained, and to your love I am always called back. There are days of sadness and days of joy; there are feelings of guilt and feelings of gratitude; there are moments of failure and moments of success; but all of them are embraced by your unwavering love.

My only real temptation is to doubt in your love, to think of myself as beyond the reach of your love, to remove myself from the healing radiance of your love. To do these things is to move into the darkness of despair.

O Lord, sea of love and goodness, let me not fear too much the storms and winds of my daily life, and let me know that there is ebb and flow but that the sea remains the sea.

The Struggle of Dryness

Andrew Murray, *With Christ in the School of Prayer*

(1828–1917) Known for his deep devotional life, Murray was also the most influential leader of the nineteenth-century South African Dutch Reformed Church.

Christians often complain that private prayer is not what it should be. They feel weak and sinful, the heart is cold and dark; it is so if they have so little to pray, and in that little no faith or joy. They are discouraged and kept from prayer by the thought that they cannot come to the Father as they ought or as they wish. Child of God! listen to your Teacher. He tells you that when you go to private prayer your first thought must be: The Father is in secret, the Father waits me there. Just because your heart is cold and prayerless, get you into the presence of the loving Father. As a father pitieth his children, so the Lord pitieth you. Do not be thinking of how little you have to bring God, but of how much He wants to give you. Just place yourself before, and look up into, His face; think of His love, His wonderful, tender, pitying love. Just tell Him how sinful and cold and dark [it] all is: it is the Father's loving heart [that] will give light and warmth to yours. O do what Jesus says: Just shut the door, and pray to thy Father which is in secret. Is it not wonderful? to be able to go alone with God, the infinite God. And then to look up and say: My Father! . . .

———❧———

Friedrich von Hügel, *The Life of Prayer*

(1852–1925) British Roman Catholic philosopher, writer, and spiritual director.

Spiritual dryness is indeed inevitable in the life of prayer; we will be much helped to bear these desert stretches, by persistent recognition— hence also, indeed especially, in our times of fervour—of the normality and the necessity of such desolation. We will thus come to treat desolation in religion as we treat the recurrence of the night within every twenty-four hours of our physical existence; or as bodily weariness at the end of any protracted exertion in our psychic life. When desolation is actually upon us, we will quietly modify, as far as need be, the kind and the amount of our prayer—back, say, from prayer of quiet to ordinary meditation, or to vocal prayer—even to but a few uttered aspirations. And, if the desolation is more acute, we will act somewhat like the Arab caravans behave in the face of a blinding sandstorm in the desert. The men dismount, throw themselves upon their faces in the sand; and there they remain, patient and uncomplaining, till the storm passes, and until, with their wonted patient endurance, they can and do continue on their way.

C. S. Lewis, *Letters to Malcolm*

I have a notion that what seems our worst prayers may really be, in God's eyes, our best. Those, I mean, which are least supported by devotional feeling and contend with the greatest disinclination. For these, perhaps, being nearly all will, come from a deeper level than feeling. In feeling there is so much that is really not ours—so much that comes from weather and health or from the last book read. One thing seems certain. It is no good angling for the rich moments. God sometimes seems to speak to us most intimately when He catches us, as it were, off our guard. Our preparations to receive Him sometimes have the opposite effect. Doesn't Charles Williams say somewhere that the altar must often be built in one place in order that the fire from heaven may descend *somewhere else?*

Guigo the Carthusian

(Twelfth century) Monk and contemplative.

A GRAPE, A WELL, A SPARK, A SEED

Lord, how much juice you can squeeze from a single grape.
How much water you can draw from a single well. .
How great a fire you can kindle from a tiny spark.
How great a tree you can grow from a tiny seed.
My soul is so dry that by itself it cannot pray;
Yet you can squeeze from it the juice of a thousand prayers.
My soul is so parched that by itself it cannot love;

Yet you can draw from it boundless love for you and for my neighbour.
My soul is so cold that by itself it has no joy;
Yet you can light the fire of heavenly joy within me. My soul is so feeble
    that by itself it has no faith;
Yet by your power my faith grows to a great height.
Thank you for prayer, for love, for joy, for faith;
Let me always be prayerful, loving, joyful, faithful.

The Struggle of Knowing What to Pray For

Larry Dossey, M.D., *Healing Words*

Growing up in Texas, I was continually astonished by the bizarre ways
people used prayer. In autumn hundreds of cities and towns all over the
state would passionately engage in the Friday night ritual of high school
football. As part of the pregame ceremony, opposing teams would gather
in their respective locker rooms and huddle for the team prayer, in
which the earnest young gladiators would pray to the same God for victory and for help in reducing their opponents to smithereens. How could
both team's prayers possibly be answered?

   This perverse use of prayer is not, of course, confined to football-
crazed Texans. Prayers by opposing teams for victory are universal. Most
recently, in the Persian Gulf war, Americans prayed to God for aid in de-
feating Iraq, while the Iraqis were simultaneously beseeching Allah to
exterminate the Western infidels. What's a God to do?

Abraham Lincoln

(1809–1865) Sixteenth president of the United States.

Second Inaugural Address, March 4, 1965, given to a war-torn nation.
In contrast to the anxious and fearful audience that heard Lincoln's first
address, this audience responded with quiet reverence, and at the end of
the speech many of their eyes streamed with tears.

   On the occasion corresponding to this four years ago, all thoughts
   were anxiously directed to an impending civil war. All dreaded it. All
   sought to avoid it. . . . Both parties deprecated war, but one of them

would make war rather than let it perish, and war came. . . . Neither party expected the magnitude or duration which it has already attained. . . . Both read the same Bible and pray to the same God. Each invokes His aid against the other. It may seem strange that any man should dare to ask a just God's assistance in wringing bread from the sweat of other men's faces; but let us judge not, that we be not judged. The prayer of both should not be answered; that of neither has been answered fully, for the Almighty has His own purposes. . . . Fondly do we hope, fervently do we pray, that this mighty scourge of war may speedily pass away. . . .

With malice toward none, with charity for all, with firmness in the right, as God gives us to see the right, let us strive on to finish the work we are in, to bind up the nation's wounds, to care for him who shall have borne the battle, and for his widow and orphans; to do all which may achieve and cherish a just and a lasting peace among ourselves and with all nations.

The Struggle of Persistence

W. Bingham Hunter, *The God Who Hears*

Two things these days thwart persistent prayer. The first is our time orientation. Persisting in prayer is not popular anymore because there isn't time to do it. Who can wait for God to get around to responding? If you want to trust God for more than instant answers, you may have to change the way you live. It's hard, very hard, for Christians who are used to instant pudding, instant credit, and instant replay to wait for anything . . . even God.

The second complicating factor is misunderstanding. Persistence and importunity are *not* methods we adopt to convince a reluctant God that we are serious; nor must we pray long—through a period of discipline— so we will appreciate the value of God's blessing. Persistence often does provide a time of waiting during which we can evaluate our motives and obtain the counsel of others. But we persist in prayer primarily as an expression of our *complete dependency* on God for all aspects of our existence. Persistence and importunity affirm our recognition of the reality that apart from God we can do nothing. Persistence flows from the certainty of our creaturely helplessness and the logical conviction that God *alone* can help. "Whom," says prayer persistence and importunity, "have I in heaven but you?" (Ps. 73:25).

Persistence is an act of humility as well as an expression of faith. This attitude is diametrically opposite the popular notion that if we are importunate over a long enough period, God will eventually see the strength of our desire and respond. That is manipulation. It says, "Look at me; Look At Me; LOOK AT ME!" while humility says, "I'm looking to you; I'm looking to You; I'm looking to YOU." The point? Great faith in God *always* expresses itself in humble acknowledgment of dependency.

The Struggle of Impatience

Thomas Merton, *Contemplative Prayer*

(1915–1968) American Trappist monk and prolific writer. His works included sixty books, essays, history, reviews, and poetry. From the sequestered silence of the Abbey of Our Lady of Gethsemani near Bardstown, Kentucky, his life impacted the world.

Many people who have a few natural gifts and a little ingenuity tend to imagine that they can quite easily learn, by their own cleverness, to master the methods—one might say the "tricks"—of the spiritual life. The only trouble is that in the spiritual life there are no tricks and no short cuts. Those who imagine that they can discover special gimmicks and put them to work for themselves usually ignore God's will and his grace. They are self-confident and even self-complacent. They make up their minds that they are going to attain to this or that, and try to write their own ticket in the life of contemplation. They may even appear to succeed to some extent. . . . One cannot begin to face the real difficulties of the life of prayer and meditation unless one is first perfectly content to be a beginner and really experience himself as one who knows little or nothing, and has a desperate need to learn the bare rudiments. Those who think they "know" from the beginning will never, in fact, come to know anything.

People who try to pray and meditate above their proper level, who are too eager to reach what they believe to be "a high degree of prayer," get away from the truth and from reality. In observing themselves and trying to convince themselves of their advance, they become imprisoned in themselves. Then when they realize that grace has left them they are caught in their own emptiness and futility and remain helpless. . . .

We do not want to be beginners. But let us be convinced of the fact that we will never be anything else but beginners, all our life!

The Struggle of Complacency

A. W. Tozer, *The Pursuit of God*

(1897–1963) Without any formal education, Tozer became one of America's most well-known pastor-theologians.

How tragic that we in this dark day have had our seeking done for us by our teachers. Everything is made to center upon the initial act of "accepting" Christ . . . and we are not expected thereafter to crave any further revelation of God to our souls. . . .

In the midst of this great chill there are some, I rejoice to acknowledge, who . . . turn away with tears to hunt some lonely place and pray, "O God, show me thy glory." They want to taste, to touch with their hearts, to see with their inner eyes the wonder that is God.

I want deliberately to encourage this mighty longing after God. The lack of it has brought us to our present low estate. The stiff and wooden quality about our religious lives is a result of our lack of holy desire.

The Struggle of Fatigue

C. S. Lewis, *Letters to Malcolm*

And, talking of sleepiness, I entirely agree with you that no one in his senses, if he has any power of ordering his own day, would reserve his chief prayers for bed-time—obviously the worst possible hour for any action which needs concentration. The trouble is that thousands of unfortunate people can hardly find any other. Even for us, who are the lucky ones, it is not always easy. My own plan, when hard pressed, is to seize any time, and place, however unsuitable, in preference to the last waking moment. On a day of traveling—with, perhaps, some ghastly meeting at the end of it—I'd rather pray sitting in a crowded train than put it off till midnight when one reaches a hotel bedroom with aching head and dry throat and one's mind partly in a stupor and partly in a whirl. On other, and slightly less crowded, days a bench in a park, or a back street where one can pace up and down, will do.

The Struggle of Transparency

Henri Nouwen, *With Open Hands*

Often you will catch yourself wanting to receive your loving God by putting on a semblance of beauty, by holding back everything dirty and spoiled, by clearing just a little path that looks proper. But that is a fearful response—forced and artificial. Such a response exhausts you and turns your prayer into torment.

———

O. Hallesby, *Prayer*

(1879–1961) Norwegian theologian and leader in the resistance against the Nazis who was arrested in 1943 and sent to a concentration camp that was liberated in 1945.

The idea is deeply imbedded in all of us that we can by means of our prayers influence God and make Him interested in us, good to us, and kindly disposed toward us, so as to give us what we ask of Him. . . . Among the heathen, prayer is looked upon as a means whereby someone can win the favor of the gods and move them to give away some of their divine surplus.

The same thought flashes upon us frequently when we pray, without our thinking a great deal about it. We feel that there is something God must see in us before He can answer our prayer. We think that He must find an earnest, urgent, burning desire within us in the event that we are praying for something for ourselves. And if we are interceding on behalf of others, we think that He must find a hearty and spiritual solicitude for them in our prayers if He is to hear us. For this reason our prayers often become a soul-exertion by means of which we endeavor to produce within ourselves attitudes which will make an impression upon God.

You have undoubtedly noticed that most of us even change our tone of voice when we pray to God. We adopt a peculiar, pleading, tearful tone of voice. With some it is pure affectation. But this is certainly not the case with most people. It is with them a naive, unaffected, genuine expression of Old Adam's views of God and prayer: When God hears how great our needs is, and how urgent it is for us to receive that for which we are praying, He will likely be moved to such an extent that He will yield and let us have it!

A complete revolution with reference to this will take place in our prayer life as soon as the Spirit has taught us to pray in the name of

Jesus. He will teach us plainly that what we lack in fervency, solicitude, love and faith are not the things which prevent us from being heard and answered when we pray. These things merely reveal our helplessness. And helplessness is . . . fundamental in prayer. . . .

When Jesus hears our prayers and intervenes in our distress, He does so because . . . His love toward us is free and unmerited, and because He by His suffering and death has purchased and won for us all that we need. And He is now ready at all times to give us these things. He waits only for one thing, and for this He must wait, and that is for us to ask Him to help us. For Jesus will not and cannot force Himself into our distress. We ourselves must open unto Him. And that is the only purpose that our prayers should serve.

Joan Bel Geddes, *Are You Listening God?*

If it's true that God hates hypocrisy more than God hates almost anything, then it's good that I am being honest with God and not giving "false worship." You can't honor Truth with lies.

The Struggle of Intimacy

William Barry, *Paying Attention to God*

Let us, for a moment, reflect on how friendships grow in intimacy. The more of ourselves we reveal to another, the more we develop intimacy. A close friend may intuit what I feel or desire, but if I am hesitant to express my feelings or desires to him or her, we have a problem of intimacy. The issue is not one of knowledge, but of trust and transparency. Intimacy requires growing transparency. I let go of some of my defenses in order to let the other see me as I am.

With regard to God, people often say, "There's no need to tell him how I feel or what I desire because he knows already." What is in question is not God's knowledge but my trust in him, my willingness to be as transparent as I can be before him. Do I *want* him to see me as I am? If I wish to grow in intimacy with God, therefore, it may be necessary that I tell him how I feel and what I really want—not to increase his knowledge, but to draw closer to him.

Thus, the naked expression of what we really want may be a necessary step toward intimacy. It may be that we do not grow in intimacy with God because we cannot or do not or will not tell him what we feel and desire. It has been my experience that stiltedness and boredom in prayer are often broken when a person can say that he is angry at God for a loss or a suffering, that she is disappointed at not having a desire fulfilled, that he wants to experience God's presence and is frustrated and angry at the felt distance. What is at stake are not "answers" to life's difficulties or more clarity about God's purposes, but intimacy. . . .

If we take the Old and New Testaments seriously, God has freely committed himself to intimacy with us, an intimacy of parent to child, of lover to beloved, of friend to friend. One could read the Bible as a testament of God's dogged determination to convince us of the seriousness of *his* desire for a relationship of intimacy with us as a people and as individuals. Perhaps some of our problems in prayer stem from our unwillingness or inability to believe God. It may not be too whimsical to think of God as a frustrated lover who cannot seem to get through to us that he really does love us and want our intimate friendship. . . .

We know what happens in a close relationship when one party gets very angry at the other because of a real or apparent injustice but suppresses the expression of the anger because of fear of the loss of the relationship or for some other reason. Conversations between them grow more polite and bland because to touch on serious issues would require opening up the raw wound. The injured party may harbor hopes that the other will notice that something is wrong and beg forgiveness. If the two people are lucky, the injured party gradually loses sight of the grievance, and they begin to share at deeper levels. But the unhealed wound may fester and be opened up again by a chance remark. The relationship may never move to the deeper levels that seemed possible before the injury. Because the injured party did not want to risk losing "everything," i.e., the whole relationship, the relationship may be doomed to stagnation.

The same dynamic often operates in our relationship with God, that is, in our prayer. The suppression of anger or rage at God or of anxiety about the justice and meaning of life may create a gulf between us and God in our experience. He may seem "a million miles away" just when we need him most. Our prayers to God become perfunctory and ritualistic, much as with a friend who has hurt us conversation tends to be about the weather or other banalities. Words are used to fill up the time. With God we may rationalize the experience of distance with ideas about God's sovereign freedom, about his difference from us, or about the "dark night" as a testing ground. We forget that the saints were able to tell God that they did not like the way he seemed to be treating them. Even if it is the dark night sent by God to purify me, I may not like it and, if I trust God, can tell him so. Ultimately, what keeps us from being honest with our human friends as well as with God is our fear that honesty will destroy the relationship. No wonder God seems "a million miles away.". . .

If we understand prayer as personal relationship and follow through on the consequences of that definition, then we will find that strong emotions, even strongly negative or painful emotions, are not foreign to prayer. Indeed, they are the stuff of prayer as they are of any relationship. Just as we human beings do not know how deep our trust and love of one another is until we open up our dark sides, so too we will not know how deep the mutual love and trust is between God and us until we let him see us as we are.

The Struggle of Self-Centeredness

Leslie Weatherhead

Dear Lord, forgive me in that so much of my religion is concerned with myself. I want harmony with thee. I want peace of mind. I want health of body—and so I pray.

Forgive me, for I have made thee the means and myself the end.

I know it will take long to wean me from this terrible self-concern, but O God, help me, for hell can be nothing else but a life on which self is the centre.

Joseph Bayly, *Psalms of My Life*

A PSALM FOR PALM SUNDAY

King Jesus
why did you choose
a lowly ass
to carry you
to ride in your parade?
Had you no friend

who owned a horse
—a royal mount with spirit
fit for a king to ride?
Why choose an ass
small unassuming
beast of burden
trained to plow
not carry kings.

King Jesus
why did you choose
me
a lowly unimportant person
to bear you
in my world today?
I'm poor and unimportant
trained to work
not carry kings
—let alone the King of kings
and yet you've chosen me
to carry you in triumph
in this world's parade.
King Jesus
keep me small
so all may see
how great you are
keep me humble
so all may say
Blessed is he who cometh in the name
of the Lord
not what a great ass he rides.

The Struggle of Surrendering Self

William Barry, *Paying Attention to God*

I have periodically run into people who . . . speak about very positive religious experiences which are followed inexplicably by period of avoiding prayer, and they are puzzled by the sequence. In one instance, a person on retreat told me of four periods of prayer in one day which were very heart-warming and moving as he felt how much the Lord loved him and enjoyed his company. The next day of retreat he decided that he had better use the prayer times to make plans for his apostolic work after retreat. It was only when we looked at how his prayer had shifted that he realized that he was running away from the positive experience of the day before.

Such experiences seem to occur to people who are serious enough about the spiritual life and their relationship with the Lord to pray regularly and see a spiritual director. In other words, they are not neophytes in prayer. I began to formulate the idea that something in us could not brook too much intimacy with God. . . .

Could this be it then, that what we most deeply yearn for we most deeply fear? When we are united with God, we see reality whole, and we are not the center of it. This "vision" is deeply gratifying and reassuring at one level and deeply threatening at another. Moreover, we fear the loss of self in surrendering to God, and this even though our continual experience of encounters with God indicates the paradoxical opposite: that the closer we are united with God the more ourselves we are. The patriarchs and prophets of Israel discovered this paradoxical truth, Jesus carried the experience to its zenith, and holy women and men down through the ages have witnessed to the same truth. We ourselves have had inklings of the truth in our experience. Nevertheless, despite all the evidence, we continually back off as if from a precipice over an abyss. . . .

What can one do now? It seems so much a part of the human condition to fear what one most wants, namely union with God, that one despairs of overcoming the resistance. . . .

Perhaps we can take a leaf from the Alcoholics Anonymous program which encourages the alcoholic to take one day, one hour, one step at a time and to admit to God one's helplessness to save oneself. We express to God our profound desire to encounter and trust him and our almost as profound fear of doing so and ask his help to overcome our ambivalence—and keep overcoming it.

Moreover, we need to keep reminding ourselves that as long as we are alive, this strain of resistance will also be alive. I am reminded of the chicken pox virus which lodges in a nerve cell of the spinal column after the disease has run its course. At any moment it can break out in the very irritating and painful rash called shingles. There is nothing one can do to get rid of the virus strain. So too with the strain of resistance described here. No wonder that saints could realize how deeply sinful they were, the closer they came to God.

The Struggle of Busyness

Eugene Peterson, *The Contemplative Pastor*

I want to do the original work of being in deepening conversation with the God who reveals himself to me and addresses me by name. I don't want to dispense mimeographed hand-outs that describe God's business; I want to witness out of my own experience. I don't want to live as a parasite on the first-hand spiritual life of others, but to be personally involved with all my senses, tasting and seeing that the Lord is good.

I know it takes time to develop a life of prayer: set-aside, disciplined, deliberate time. It isn't accomplished on the run, nor by offering prayers from a pulpit or at a hospital bedside. I know I can't be busy and pray at the same time. I can be active and pray; I can work and pray; but I cannot be busy and pray. I cannot be inwardly rushed, distracted, or dispersed. In order to pray I have to be paying more attention to God than to my clamoring ego. Usually, for that to happen there must be a deliberate withdrawal from the noise of the day, a disciplined detachment from the insatiable self.

The Struggle of Distractions

John Donne, *Eighty Sermons*

(1573–1631) *First and greatest of the Metaphysical poets. His life was deeply marked by suffering and sickness. Most well-known line, "Ask not for whom the bell tolls; it tolls for thee."*

I throw myself down in my chamber, and I call in, and invite God, and his Angels thither, and when they are there, I neglect God and his Angels, for the noise of a fly, for the rattling of a coach, for the whining of a door.

Warren Wiersbe, *Classic Sermons on Prayer*

"The Power of Prayer" by R. A. Torrey

We do not live in a praying age. . . .

We live in an age of hustle and bustle, of man's efforts and man's determination, of man's confidence in himself and in his own power to achieve things, an age of human organization and human machinery, human push and human scheming, and human achievement, which in the things of God means no real achievement at all.

I think it would be perfectly safe to say that the church of Christ was never in all its history so fully, so skillfully and so thoroughly and so perfectly organized as it is today. Our machinery is wonderful; it is just perfect, but alas, it is machinery without power; and when things do not go right, instead of going to the real source of our failure, our neglect to depend on God and look to God for power, we look around to see if there is not some new organization we can get up, some new wheel that we can add to our machinery. We have altogether too many wheels already. . . .

I believe that the devil stands and looks at the church today and laughs in his sleeve as he sees how its members depend on their own scheming and power of organization and skillfully devised machinery. "Ha, ha," he laughs, "you may have . . . your costly church edifices, your multi-thousand-dollar church organs, your brilliant university-bred preachers, your high-priced choirs . . . your immense men's Bible classes, yes, and your Bible conferences, and your Bible institutes, and your special evangelistic services, all you please of them; it does not in the lest trouble me, if you will only leave out of them the power of the Lord God Almighty sought and obtained by the earnest, persistent, believing prayer that will not take no for an answer." But when the devil sees a man or woman who really believes in prayer, who knows how to pray, and who really does pray, and, above all, when he sees a whole church on its face before God in prayer, "he trembles" as much as he ever did, for he knows that this day in that church or community is at an end.

Carmen Bernos de Gasztold, *Prayers from the Ark, the Creatures' Choir*

Prayers from the Ark is a collection of fanciful prayers from the animals on Noah's ark, most of which were written during the German occupation of France, where the author was living in impoverished conditions. From her freezing bedroom she wrote these prayers that reflect much about human nature. This one by the butterfly particularly illustrates the problem of distractions when we pray.

PRAYER OF THE BUTTERFLY

Lord!
Where was I?

Oh yes! This flower, this sun,
thank you! Your world is beautiful!
This scent of roses . . .
Where was I?
A drop of dew
rolls to sparkle in a lily's heart.
I have to go . . .
Where? I do not know!
The wind has painted fancies
on my wings.
Fancies . . .
Where was I?
Oh yes! Lord,
I had something to tell you:
Amen.

———⊂∞⊃———

A. W. Tozer, *The Pursuit of God*

Lord, teach me to listen. The times are noisy and my ears are weary
with the thousand raucous sounds which continuously assault them.
Give me the spirit of the boy Samuel when he said to Thee, "Speak, for
thy servant heareth." Let me hear Thee speaking in my heart. Let me get
used to the sound of Thy voice, that its tones may be familiar when the
sounds of earth die away and the only sound will be the music of Thy
speaking voice. Amen.

———⊂∞⊃———

Thomas Merton, *Seeds of Contemplation*

Prayer and love are learned in the hour when prayer has become impossible and your heart has turned to stone.

If you have never had any distractions you don't know how to pray.
For the secret of prayer is a hunger for God and for the vision of God, a
hunger that lies far deeper than the level of language of affection. And
a man whose memory and imagination are persecuting him with a crowd
of useless or even evil thoughts and images may sometimes be forced to
pray far better, in the depths of his murdered heart, than one whose
mind is swimming with clear concepts and brilliant purposes and easy
acts of love.

That is why it is useless to get upset when you cannot shake off
distractions. In the first place, you must realize that they are often

unavoidable in the life of prayer. The necessity of kneeling and suffering submersion under a tidal wave of wild and inane images is one of the standard trials of the contemplative life. If you think you are obliged to stave these things off by using a book and clutching at its sentences the way a drowning man clutches at straws, you have the privilege of doing so, but if you allow your prayer to degenerate into a period of simple spiritual reading you are losing a great deal of fruit. You would profit much more by patiently resisting distractions and learning something of your own helplessness and incapacity. And if your book merely becomes an anesthetic, far from helping your meditation it has ruined it altogether.

One reason why you have distractions is this. The mind and memory and imagination only work, in meditation, in order to bring your will into the presence of its object, which is God. Now when you have practised meditation for a few years, it is the most spontaneous thing in the world for the will to settle down to its occupation of obscurely and mutely loving God as soon as you compose yourself for prayer. Consequently the mind and memory and imagination have a real job to do. The will is busy and they are unemployed. So, after a while, the doors of your subconscious mind fall ajar and all sorts of curious figures begin to come waltzing about on the scene. If you are wise you will not pay any attention to these things: remain in simple attention to God and you keep your will peacefully directed to Him in simple desire, while the intermittent shadows of this annoying movie go about in the remote background. If you are aware of them at all it is only to realize that you refuse them.

The kind of distractions that holy people most fear are generally the most harmless of all. But sometimes pious men and women torture themselves at meditation because they imagine they are "consenting" to the phantasms of a lewd and somewhat idiotic burlesque that is being fabricated in their imagination without their being able to do a thing to stop it. The chief reason why they suffer is that their hopeless efforts to put a stop to this parade of images generates a nervous tension which only makes everything a hundred times worse.

If they ever had a sense of humor, they have now become so nervous that it has abandoned them altogether. Yet humor is one of the things that would probably be most helpful at such a time.

There is no real danger in these things. The distractions that do harm are the ones that draw our will away from its profound and peaceful occupation with God and involve it in elaborations of projects that have been concerning us during our day's work. We are confronted by issues that really attract and occupy our wills and there is considerable danger that our meditation will break down into a session of mental letter writing or sermons or speeches or books or, worse still, plans to raise money to take care of our health.

It will be hard for anyone who has a heavy job on his shoulders to get rid of these things. They will always remind him of what he is, and they should warn him not to get too involved in active work, because it is no use trying to clear your mind of all material things at the moment of meditation, if you do nothing to cut down the pressure of work outside that time.

But in all these things, it is the will to pray that is the essence of prayer, and the desire to find God and to see Him and to love Him is the one thing that matters. If you have desired to know Him and love Him you have already done what was expected of you, and it is much better to desire God without being able to think clearly of Him, than to have marvelous thoughts about Him without desiring to enter into union with His will.

———⊗∞⊗———

Don Postema, *Space for God*

A father and his son, travelling together in a wagon,
    came to the edge of the forest.
Some bushes, thick with berries,
    caught the child's eye.
"Father," he asked, "may we stop a while
    so that I can pick some berries?"
The father was anxious to complete his journey,
    but he did not have it in his heart
    to refuse the boy's request.
The wagon was called to a halt,
    and the son alighted to pick the berries.

After a while,
    the father wanted to continue on his way.
But his son had become so engrossed in berry-picking
    that he could not bring himself to leave the forest.
"Son!" cried the father, "we cannot stay here all day!
    We must continue our journey!"
Even the father's pleas were not enough
    to lure the boy away.
What could the father do?
Surely he loved his son no less
    for acting so childishly.

He would not think of leaving him behind—
    but he really did have to get going on his journey.

Finally he called out:
    "You may pick your berries for a while longer,
    but be sure you are still able to find me,
    for I shall start moving slowly along the road,
As you work, call out 'Father! Father!'
    every few minutes, and I shall answer you.
As long as you can hear my voice,
    know that I am still nearby.
But as soon as you can no longer hear my answer,
    know that you are lost,
    and run with all your strength to find me!"

E. M. Bounds

Too busy to pray gives religion a Christian burial, it is true, but kills it nevertheless.

Fulton J. Sheen, *Lift Up Your Heart*

(1895–1979) American Roman Catholic archbishop who authored some fifty books and is best remembered for his radio and television sermons.

St. Augustine says, *Amor pondus meum;* love is the law of gravitation. All things have their center. The schoolboy finds it hard to study, because he does not love knowledge as much as athletics. The businessman finds it hard to think of heavenly pleasures because he is dedicated to the filling of his "barn." The carnal-minded find it difficult to love the spirit because their treasure lies in the flesh. Everyone becomes like that which he loves: if he loves the material, he becomes like the material; if he loves the spiritual, he is converted into it in his outlook, his ideals, and his aspirations. Given this relationship between love and prayer, it is easy to understand why some souls say: "I have no time to pray." They really have not, because to them other duties are more pressing; other treasures more precious; other interests more exhilarating.

PART SEVEN

WHAT DIFFERENCE DOES PRAYER MAKE IN OUR LIVES?

INTRODUCTION

What difference does prayer make in our lives?

If Tennyson was right, all the difference in the world.

"For more things are wrought by prayer than this world dreams of."

If he was right, maybe prayer is what brought down the Berlin wall and broke up the Communist Bloc. Maybe prayer is what brought down the wall of your heart, and the wall of mine. Maybe prayer is what broke up the bad relationship we were in. Or what started the good one we're in now.

Maybe prayer, or the lack of it, is why we ended up where we are. Or why we are even here at all.

Who knows?

But if Tennyson was right, and "the whole round earth is every way bound by gold chains about the feet of God," then our sovereign God is a sovereign in chains, forged from the seemingly inconsequential links of our prayers.

That should make a difference not only in our prayers . . . but in our lives.

It Empowers Us to Fulfill the Great Commandment

Richard Foster, quoted in How I Pray by Jim Castelli

Of necessity, love of God eventuates in love of neighbor. The two great commandments really are one. Prayer *always* has a social dimension to it. Prayer, to be real prayer, does not take us out of the world; it sends us *into* the world and excites our endeavors to heal the world.

It Changes Lives

An Unknown Christian, The Kneeling Christian

Many of us will recall the wonderful things that God did for Korea a few years ago, entirely in answer to prayer. A few missionaries decided to meet together to pray daily at noon. At the end of the month one brother proposed that, "as nothing had happened," the prayer meeting should be discontinued. "Let us each pray at home as we find it convenient," said he. The others, however, protested that they ought rather to spend even more time in prayer each day. So they continued the daily prayer meeting for four months. Then suddenly the blessing began to be poured out. Church services here and there were interrupted by weeping and confessing of sins. At length a mighty revival broke out. At one place during a Sunday evening service the leading man in the church stood up and confessed that he had stolen one hundred dollars in administering a widow's legacy. Immediately conviction of sin swept the audience. That service did not end till 2 o'clock on Monday morning. God's wondrous power was felt as never before. And when the Church was purified, many sinners found salvation.

Multitudes flocked to the churches out of curiosity. Some came to mock, but fear laid hold of them, and they stayed to pray. Among the "curious" was a brigand chief, the leader of a robber band. He was convicted and converted. He went straight off to the magistrate and gave himself up. "You have no accuser," said the astonished official, "yet you accuse yourself! We have no law in Korea to meet your case." So he dismissed him.

It Produces Character

Eugene Peterson, *Under the Unpredictable Plant*

We become what we are called to be by praying.

It Equips Us for Spiritual Warfare

E. M. Bounds

(1835–1913) Methodist minister and devotional writer who served as a pastor in the American South and became a POW during the Civil War.

The closet is not an asylum for the indolent and worthless Christian. It is not a nursery where none but babes belong. It is the battlefield of the Church; its citadel; the scene of heroic and unearthly conflict. The closet is the base of supplies for the Christian and the Church. Cut off from it there is nothing left but retreat and disaster. The energy for work, the mastery over self, the deliverance from fear, all spiritual results and graces, are much advanced by prayer. The difference between the strength, the experience, the holiness of Christians is found in the contrast in their praying.

William Barclay, *A Guide to Daily Prayer*

(1907–1978) Scottish minister and scholar best known for his New Testament commentary series, The Daily Study Bible.

Prayer is not escape; prayer is the way to conquest. Prayer is not flight; prayer is power. Prayer does not deliver a man from some terrible situation; prayer enables a man to face and to master the situation. When Jesus prayed that the bitter cup of the Cross might pass from him, that cup was not taken away from him. He had to drain it to its last agonizing dregs. But he was enabled to come through the Cross and to emerge on the other side of it in triumph. So often people pray to be delivered from a problem, to be rescued from a situation, to be saved from a disaster, to be spared a sorrow, to be healed from a sickness, to be freed from a mental or a physical agony. Sometimes, it is true, that deliverance comes; but far more often the answer is that we are given the strength which is not our strength to go through it, and to come out at the other side of it, not simply as a survivor, but with a faith that is strengthened and deepened and a mind and a life and a character which are purified and ennobled. Prayer does not provide a means of running away from the human situation; prayer provides a way of meeting the human situation.

It Motivates Us to Serve

Henri Nouwen, *Show Me the Way*

Prayer and action, therefore, can never be seen as contradictory or mutually exclusive. Prayer without action grows into powerless pietism, and action without prayer degenerates into questionable manipulation. If prayer leads us into a deeper unity with the compassionate Christ, it will always give rise to concrete acts of service. And if concrete acts of service do indeed lead us to a deeper solidarity with the poor, the hungry, the sick, the dying, and the oppressed, they will always give rise to prayer. In prayer we meet Christ, and in him all human suffering. In service we meet people, and in them the suffering Christ.

It Transforms Us

E. M. Bounds

"One night alone in prayer," says [Charles] Spurgeon, "might make us new men, changed from poverty of soul to spiritual wealth, from trembling to triumphing." We have an example of it in the life of Jacob. Afore time the crafty shuffler, always bargaining and calculating, unlovely in almost every respect, yet one night in prayer turned the supplanter into a prevailing prince, and robed him with celestial grandeur. From that night he lives on the sacred page as one of the nobility of heaven. Could not we, at least now and then, in these weary earth-bound years, hedge about a single night for such enriching traffic with the skies? What, have we no sacred ambition? Are we deaf to the yearnings of divine love? Yet, my brethren, for wealth and for science men will cheerfully quit their warm couches, and cannot we do it now and again for the love of God and the good of souls? Where is our zeal, our gratitude, our sincerity? I am ashamed while I thus upbraid both myself and you. May we often tarry at Jabbok and cry with Jacob, as he grasped the angel—

'With thee all night I mean to stay,
And wrestle till the break of day.'

It Impacts Our Attitude

George MacDonald

(1824–1905) Poverty-stricken Scottish pastor, poet, and novelist whose works profoundly influenced C. S. Lewis.

There are some who would argue for prayer, not on the ground of any possible answer to be looked for, but because of the good to be gained in the spiritual attitude of the mind in praying. There are those even who, not believing in any ear to hear, any heart to answer, will yet pray. They say it does them good; they pray to nothing at all, but they get spiritual benefit.

I will not contradict their testimony. So needful is prayer to the soul that the mere attitude of it may encourage a good mood.

It Gives Understanding

Eleana Silk

Prayer life, if it's intense and regular, helps you to deal with those people that you come in contact with who are very angry. When you go to the grocery store and the clerk is really nasty, if you're grounded in a good prayer life, that person will disturb you, but not to the point of making you angry as well. So a good prayer life is a defense against the difficulties that other people are having. Someone can come in the office and yell and scream at you, but you know that they've had a bad day and you look at it from a different point of view because you realize that not everyone is going to offer up everything every day to God.

There are going to be times when we're going to fall and we're going to be angry and we're going to offend and say things that we don't mean. But prayer gives you a greater respect for the person, for the identity of the person in front of you. Rather than treating everyone like numbers or bodies that pass in the day, you want to stop—even if you're very busy— and look on the face of the other person and pay attention. If that person is angry, prayer makes you try to understand why they're angry, to say a word to calm their anger.

It Promotes Physical and Psychological Health

Alexis Carrel, *Light From Many Lamps*

(1873–1944) Nobel Prize-winning surgeon.

Prayer is not only worship; it is also an invisible emanation of man's worshipping spirit—the most powerful form of energy that one can generate. The influence of prayer on the human mind and body is as demonstrable as that of secreting glands. Its results can be measured in terms of increased physical buoyancy, greater intellectual vigor, moral stamina, and a deeper understanding of the realities underlying human relationships.

If you make a habit of sincere prayer, your life will be very noticeably and profoundly altered. Prayer stamps with its indelible mark our actions and demeanor. A tranquillity of bearing, a facial and bodily repose, are observed in those whose inner lives are thus enriched. . . .

Prayer is a force as real as terrestrial gravity. As a physician, I have seen men, after all other therapy has failed, lifted out of disease and melancholy by the serene effort of prayer. It is the only power in the world that seems to overcome the so-called "laws of nature"; the occasions on which prayer has dramatically done this have been termed "miracles." But a constant, quieter miracle takes place hourly in the hearts of men and women who have discovered that prayer supplies them with a steady flow of sustaining power in their daily lives.

Debbie Warhola, "The Power of Prayer in Healing,"
Gazette Telegraph, March 16, 1996

Since recorded history, ill people of various faiths have pointed to their own prayers and the prayers of others as the power that aided their recovery and healed their broken bodies. Alternative medicine also has long touted the benefits of balancing the mind and body through prayer, positive thinking, meditation, yoga or other techniques.

Now, the traditional medical community is beginning to take note as well. Scientific studies confirming that religious commitment has a positive effect on health are getting the attention of physicians, psychiatrists and managed health-care companies around the nation.

More than 200 recent studies regarding the connection between spirituality and health published in medical and psychiatric journals were discussed at a conference in Boston in December.

Sponsored by Harvard Medical School, the conference focused on scientific evidence that prayer can heal illness and prolong life. Nearly 1,000 doctors, nurses, researchers and clergy attended. Among the citings:

In 1988, a study of 392 patients in a coronary care unit in a San Francisco hospital compared recovery rates of patients who were being prayed for (without their knowledge) to patients who were not. The 192 patients who had been prayed for had fewer cases of congestive heart failure, less pneumonia, fewer heart attacks, less intubation (the process of inserting tubes into organs to admit air) and less need for antibiotics.

In a study of 91,909 people in rural Maryland, weekly churchgoers had fewer deaths than non-attenders—50 percent fewer from heart disease, 74 percent fewer from cirrhosis, 56 percent fewer from pulmonary emphysema and 53 percent fewer from suicides.

Men age 55 and older who ranked religion as "very important" in their lives had lower diastolic blood pressure than those who said that faith was "somewhat" or "not important."

The Harvard conference would have been unthinkable a decade ago, said Herbert Benson, president of Harvard's Mind/Body Medical Institute and author of a book on meditation, because the medical community used to see spirituality as having little if any practical use in health care.

Not so today.

"If spirituality were a drug, we wouldn't be able to make it fast enough," he said.

Common sense explains part of [the] correlation between health and prayer: People who pray and attend church regularly tend to have fewer vices that can affect their health than people without strong religious commitments.

But Dr. Brian Olivier believes prayer has the power to help heal people, as well as lead them to healthy lifestyles.

Olivier, a local physician in family practice, has been praying with his patients for years.

"It's a discretionary area that is available to patients who request that I pray with them," says Olivier, a Christian. "We pray for God's intervention, for him to work through me so I can gain wisdom.

"But I can't second-guess what God's going to do. In the ultimate outcome, God's plan may include suffering and death, and not healing. So I think it's hard to capsulate and quantify answers to prayer."

Richard Foster, "Healthy Skepticism and Wholesome Faith," *Prayer*

You may remain skeptical about Healing Prayer. That is not all bad—there are some people in our day who could profit from a little healthy skepticism.

Saint Augustine was that way. He doubted the validity of Healing Prayer, stating in his early writings that Christians should not look for the continuance of the healing gift. But in 424 A.D. a brother and sister came to his town of Hippo, seeking healing of convulsive seizures. They came every day to Augustine's church to pray for healing. Nothing happened until the second Sunday before Easter. The young man was in the crowded church, praying. Augustine was still in the vestibule, ready for the processional, when the young man fell down as if dead. People nearby were seized with fear, but the next moment he got up and stood staring back at them, perfectly normal and fully cured.

Augustine took the young man home for dinner, and they talked at length. Slowly Augustine's skepticism began to crumble before the witness of this young man. Finally, on the third day after Easter Augustine had the brother and sister stand on the choir steps, where the whole congregation could see them—one quiet and normal, the other still trembling convulsively—while he read a statement from the young man. He then had everyone sit down, and he began a sermon on healing. Augustine was, however, interrupted by shouts from the congregation, for the young woman had also fallen to the ground and was instantaneously healed. Once more she stood before the people, and in Augustine's own words, "Praise to God was shouted so loudly that my ears could scarcely stand the din."

All this happened while Augustine was writing his magnum opus, *The City of God,* so he devoted one of the final sections to the miracles of healing occurring in his own diocese. He described how he set up a process for recording and authenticating miracles, for "once I realized how many miracles were occurring in our own day . . . [I saw] how wrong it would be to allow the memory of these marvels of divine power to perish from among our people. It is only two years ago that the keeping of records was begun in Hippo and already, at this writing, we have nearly seventy attested miracles."

May we, like Augustine, be able to trade in our healthy skepticism for wholesome faith as we witness the humble testimony of those who receive the healing touch of God.

Mark 9:24 (NASB)

A desperate father's response to Jesus' words, "All things are possible to him who believes."

"I do believe; help me in my unbelief."

Mark 5:22–42 (NIV)

A healing and a resurrection:

> Then one of the synagogue rulers, named Jairus, came there. Seeing Jesus, he fell at his feet and pleaded earnestly with him, "My little daughter is dying. Please come and put your hands on her so that she will be healed and live." So Jesus went with him.
>
> A large crowd followed and pressed around him. And a woman was there who had been subject to bleeding for twelve years. She had suffered a great deal under the care of many doctors and had spent all she had, yet instead of getting better she grew worse. When she heard about Jesus, she came up behind him in the crowd and touched his cloak, because she thought, "If I just touch his clothes, I will be healed." Immediately her bleeding stopped and she felt in her body that she was freed from her suffering.
>
> At once Jesus realized that power had gone out from him. He turned around in the crowd and asked, "Who touched my clothes?"

"You see the people crowding against you," his disciples answered, "and yet you can ask, 'Who touched me?' "

But Jesus kept looking around to see who had done it. Then the woman, knowing what had happened to her, came and fell at his feet and, trembling with fear, told him the whole truth. He said to her, "Daughter, your faith has healed you. Go in peace and be freed from your suffering."

While Jesus was still speaking, some men came from the house of Jairus, the synagogue ruler. "Your daughter is dead," they said. "Why bother the teacher any more?"

Ignoring what they said, Jesus told the synagogue ruler, "Don't be afraid; just believe."

He did not let anyone follow him except Peter, James and John the brother of James. When they came to the home of the synagogue ruler, Jesus saw a commotion, with people crying and wailing loudly. He went in and said to them, "Why all this commotion and wailing? The child is not dead but asleep." But they laughed at him.

After he put them all out, he took the child's father and mother and the disciples who were with him, and went in where the child was. He took her by the hand and said to her, *"Talitha koum!"* (which means, "Little girl, I say to you, get up!"). Immediately the girl stood up and walked around (she was twelve years old). At this they were completely astonished.

Catherine Marshall, "The Enigma of Healing," *Something More*

Most of us feel no need of facing the question, "Does God heal directly today?" until we are personally confronted with some physician's blunt finality: "There's nothing more we can do."

Those were the precise words my friend Sandra was hearing so incredulously that night—February 8, 1966. I did not learn of this sequence of events until later when Sandra Ghost (now a close friend. Yes, her name really is Ghost) shared it with me. Arriving at the hospital room where her little son lay, Sandy had encountered Dr. Gallo.

"Mrs. Ghost, there's been no improvement in Kent's condition since this afternoon," the distinguished looking, dark-haired doctor told her. "No question of the diagnosis—a cerebral hemorrhage. He's still in deep coma."

Over his shoulder Sandra could see the slight form of her two-year-old son, usually unable to stay still for an instant. Now there wasn't a flicker of movement anywhere—from his toes to his blond head.

Dr. Gallo asked gently, "You did call your husband in Louisville?"

"Yes, I did. Bill caught the first plane possible. He should be here at ten o'clock."

"I must warn you. . . . Kent may not hold on until your husband gets here. Mrs. Ghost, you may go in now." He paused. "There's nothing more we can do."

The words spoken so slowly for emphasis struck Sandra like a physical blow. Their impact detached some part of her mind and sent her thoughts spinning backward to that first day when she and Kent, his hand clinging so tightly to hers, had walked through the front door of the National Institute of Health on the outskirts of Washington, D.C. What relief she had felt! To think that his great research arm of the United States Government had been willing to take on their son's case of acute lymphocytic leukemia. Why, this place was one of medicine's frontiers. In these vast government buildings they were finding answers. Surely, she told herself, only God could have made the connection between the Ghost family in Louisville, Kentucky, and NIH. Therefore, the fine and compassionate doctors on Two-East (the leukemia unit) would discover the key to the healing of Kent's leukemia.

And in the two months since, the doctors had indeed proved themselves compassionate. In fact, the warmth of everyone around NIH —laboratory technicians, housekeeping detail, clean-up crews, and Mr. Botts, the gentle black elevator operator who "God-blessed" all his passengers—had steadily reassured her.

So how could Dr. Gallo be saying so seriously, "There's nothing more we can do"? For what he meant was, "Kent is going to die and I can't prevent his death. Medicine, science, the best we know, has no further resources to give you."

Her thoughts reeled and staggered. "But that can't be! This is the twentieth century. I—Sandra Ghost—am a twentieth-century woman. I have relied on science. Science can do *anything*."

But she only stared at the doctor, nodded her head, and murmured, "Thank you, Doctor." For an instant she watched the physician's back retreating down the long corridor almost at a trot, as though eager to be away. Then she hurried to Kent's room.

This was Intensive Care with Di-Gi on duty, a nurse whom Sandra had learned to know well during the two months. Every ten minutes Di-Gi was taking vital signs: would Kent respond to the beam of light flashed directly into his eyes? Any sign of consciousness by grip or response? Any change in temperature? Blood pressure?

But there was no visible response—none at all. Her child was so still and so white, his legs so limp. Almost the smell of death was in this room. Was Sandra imagining it? No, this was no illusion; she saw it in the nurse's eyes.

Sandy kept a grip on her emotions through two of the ten-minute periods. Then she broke down, sobbing quietly.

Di-Gi understood. "Some black coffee would help," she suggested, "help me too. Why don't you go down to the Snack Shop for two cups?"

The distraught mother realized the nurse was using psychology on her, but she also knew that some activity would help. "Sure," Sandra agreed, "good idea."

On Sandy's return from the Snack Shop, she was surprised to see Mr. Botts running the elevator; it was rare to see him on night duty, rarer still for her to be the only passenger. As the doors slid shut and the elevator mounted, Mr. Botts asked as he always did, "And how's my little man?"

This time the question brought quick tears to Sandra's eyes. She shifted the sack with its two steaming cartons of coffee to her left hand in order to grope for her handkerchief. "Mr. Botts, Kent's bad. He's—not expected to live." Then from deep inside her came a request that she was surprised to hear herself making, "Will you—would you pray for Kent?"

At that moment they arrived at the second floor and the elevator doors opened. Sandra was no more than three steps into the hallway when she heard Mr. Botts's voice behind her. "Get back on the elevator, would you? Let's pray *now*. Please get back on."

Wordlessly, Sandra obeyed. The elevator doors shut, only this time Mr. Botts left the elevator stationary at the second floor.

"Lord Jesus," he prayed, "I ask you to heal this child as you healed me when the doctors told me I would never walk again. The Church prayed and You heard their prayers, and there's nothing wrong with me now. I ask You to do for this child what You did for me since the Good Book says, 'God is no respecter of persons.'

"Lord, enter this little boy's body. Heal Kent, Lord, and let him walk again. And Lord Jesus, give Kent's mother here Your strength. She needs it so much. . . ."

Was there more of the prayer? Sandy could never remember, only that she was aware of God's love in that elevator as she had never before felt it. And wasn't it odd that during what had seemed to her a long stretch of time, no one had rung for the elevator? Fumbling for words, she tried to thank Mr. Botts. Then she ran left down the corridor and through the double swinging doors to Kent's room. As she went, she glanced at her wrist watch—six minutes before nine.

"Any change?" she asked the nurse.

Di-Gi shook her head. "No change."

As the two women sipped coffee, Di-Gi talked. Sandra discovered one reason for this nurse's special depth of compassion. She had been through trouble too: her mother and her younger sister had died in an automobile wreck just two months before. Sandra wondered why Di-Gi was not angry with God or bitter. She had the feeling that the nurse knew Him.

As they talked, two sets of vital signs were taken. At the third, Di-Gi seemed startled and made no attempts to hide it. "His blood pressure! Coming down fast, toward normal."

Almost immediately, Kent stirred in the bed. His eyes fluttered open. Recognizing his mother, he turned toward her, "Mommy, I'm thirsty."

Di-Gi restrained her excitement long enough to finish taking all the vital signs and recheck them, then she ran for the doctor on duty. He made it to Kent's room in record time.

By the time Bill Ghost arrived from the airport, Kent was fully conscious, sitting up in bed, sipping a soft drink through a straw, anticipating his Dad's coming.

During the night hours Kent continued to improve. The next day, February 9, Dr. Robert Gallo appeared to be in sharp disagreement with the battery of neurologists. Though the parents at NIH are always considered part of the "medical team" for their own child, the Ghosts were surprised to hear the physicians openly discussing their differences: Dr. Gallo could not possibly have been correct in his diagnosis, the neurologists insisted; no patient could recover from a cerebral hemorrhage as quickly as Kent Ghost had.

Dr. Gallo stood his ground. Yes, he reiterated, his diagnosis had been correct. He had performed the requisite spinal tap. Nor had a vein been punctured during the tap, thus accounting for blood in the test tube.

Finally the neurologists would not be appeased unless they performed another spinal tap, so Kent was wheeled away to a treatment room. There Dr. Gallo was vindicated: yes, the little boy had had a brain hemorrhage.

Two days later, Kent was riding the rocking horse in the playroom at NIH, unaware of the doctors and nurses who kept drifting by the playroom door, staring at him. . . . "Can you believe that's Kent Ghost?" Between his turns on the rocking horse, he would ride Mr. Botts's elevator up and down, down and up, and each time a jubilant Mr. Botts would pat "his little man's" head, make gleeful remarks or hum under his breath, all the time looking as though he possessed a secret too marvelous to contain.

It Makes Us More Accepting

Richard Foster, quoted in *How I Pray* by Jim Castelli

People who really pray—not people who just analyze prayer or dissect it, but who actually *do* it—become more loving, more sensitive to other people. I've watched this happen, and I think I'm reflecting not only my own experience but the experience of many other people. Prayer enlarges our ability to embrace other people. The class I'm teaching right now, for example, is an incredibly cross-cultural group. We have Afro-Americans, we have Anglos, we have Koreans, we have Japanese, we have Latinos. The mix is wonderful and because these people pray, their hearts are enlarged toward one another, even with all the cultural differences.

It Summons Help from Heaven

Acts 12:1-17 *(The Message)*

That's when King Herod got it into his head to go after some of the church members. He murdered James, John's brother. When he saw how much it raised his popularity ratings with the Jews, he arrested Peter—all this during Passover Week, mind you—and had him thrown in jail, putting four squads of four soldiers each to guard him. He was planning a public lynching after Passover.

All the time that Peter was under heavy guard in the jailhouse, the church prayed for him most strenuously.

Then the time came for Herod to bring him out for the kill. That night, even though shackled to two soldiers, one on either side, Peter slept like a baby. And there were guards at the door keeping their eyes on the place. Herod was taking no chances!

Suddenly there was an angel at his side and light flooding the room. The angel shook Peter and got him up: "Hurry!" The handcuffs fell off his wrists. The angel said, "Get dressed. Put on your shoes." Peter did it.

Then, "Grab your coat and let's get out of here." Peter followed him, but didn't believe it was really an angel—he thought he was dreaming.

Past the first guard and then the second, they came to the iron gate that led into the city. It swung open before them on its own, and they were out on the street, free as the breeze. At the first intersection the angel left him, going his own way. That's when Peter realized it was no dream. "I can't believe it—this really happened! The Master sent his angel and rescued me from Herod's vicious little production and the spectacle the Jewish mob was looking forward to."

Still shaking his head, amazed, he went to Mary's house, the Mary who was John Mark's mother. The house was packed with praying friends. When he knocked on the door to the courtyard, a young woman named Rhoda came to see who it was. But when she recognized his voice— Peter's voice!—she was so excited and eager to tell everyone Peter was there that she forgot to open the door and left him standing in the street.

But they wouldn't believe her, dismissing her, dismissing her report. "You're crazy," they said. She stuck by her story, insisting. They still wouldn't believe her and said, "It must be his angel." All this time poor Peter was standing out in the street, knocking away.

Finally they opened up and saw him—and went wild! Peter put his hands up and calmed them down. He described how the Master had gotten him out of jail. . . .

Kelsey Tyler, *Heaven Hears Each Whisper*

Three-year-old Randy Scogin marched across the yard and toward the back door of his family's house in Houston, Texas. He pulled a toy dog on wheels behind him. The air was particularly humid that Sunday afternoon in June 1975, and the child found his mother inside talking on the telephone to her sister. She glanced at the boy and he waved, his brown eyes sparking with adventure.

"Bye, Mommy," he said. "I'm going to Bo-Bo's house."

Marilyn, twenty-nine, smiled at the child. "Okay, Randy, have fun."

Bo-Bo, the children's grandmother, lived five miles away, and Marilyn knew Randy would never really consider such a thing. The boy was playing a game of make-believe, as he had so many other times, and Marilyn felt at ease as she continued her conversation and watched the child disappear into the backyard.

Fifteen minutes later Marilyn hung up the telephone and sauntered outside to round up Randy and his six-year-old brother, Rusty. The older child was sitting in a frustrated heap, having given up his attempt to fly a kite on such a still summer day. The temperature was rising, and Marilyn wanted the children to come inside before they were affected by the heat.

"No wind, huh?" she said, bending over and fingering the limp kite.

Rusty shook his head and sighed.

"Well, it's getting too hot out here. Let's go inside and have some cold lemonade." She stood up and glanced around the yard. "Where's Randy?"

Rusty gathered his kite and shrugged as he struggled to his feet. "He was pulling that little dog, but he's been gone for a while."

"Rusty, go ask the neighbors if they've seen him." Marilyn took the kite from her oldest son, and the boy set off running. "Hurry back!" she shouted.

Marilyn flew across the yard into the house and fought back a wave of panic. Certainly the child was in the house, perhaps taking a nap with the boys' father. But inside, Marilyn searched closets and bedrooms, and finally found Harold sleeping alone.

"Harold, wake up!" she said, her voice frantic. "Randy's missing."

Harold's eyes flew open, and together he and Marilyn searched the house and yard again. Rusty returned from checking with the neighbors and announced that no one had seen Randy that afternoon.

"What's the last thing you remember him saying or doing?" Harold asked, fully awake and filled with concern.

Marilyn ran her fingers nervously through her hair. "I was on the phone with my sister and Randy told me he was going to Bo-Bo's house. I thought he was just playing and I said okay."

Marilyn and Harold exchanged a sickening look. Thirty minutes had passed since Randy's disappearance. If their son had attempted the five-mile walk to his grandmother's house by himself, he could have been kidnapped or hit by a car. Most frightening of all, he could be anywhere at all because the child was too young to have any sense of direction.

Immediately Marilyn ran to the telephone and called her mother.

"Randy's lost," she said breathlessly, closing her eyes and forcing herself to concentrate. "He left here half an hour ago and he said he was going to your house."

Five miles away, the older woman's face turned white. "He'll never make it! Even if he knows the way, there's two busy streets between your house and mine," she murmured. "Marilyn, stay there. I'll leave right now and check every street on the way. Don't worry, we'll find him or I'll know the reason why."

"Thanks, Mom." There were tears in Marilyn's eyes as she handed the telephone to Harold. She felt rooted to the spot as she watched him frantically dial the local police station. . . .

As Harold spoke, Marilyn could no longer stand still. Every moment that passed meant that Randy could be getting run over or picked up by a stranger. She struggled to breathe, suffocated by the feeling of help-lessness.

On the verge of hysteria, she grabbed the car keys. "I'll be back!" she shouted as she ran out the door and climbed into their family sedan.

Covering her face with her hands, she began to pray. "Please, God. Please watch over Randy and lead me to him." Then she started the car and set out to find him.

Marilyn and Harold were deeply faithful Christians and had been all their lives. Together they had taught their boys to pray and trust God in any situation where they felt they needed help. But a few months be-fore, Marilyn's father died of cancer, and since then she had felt none of the joy that usually accompanied her faith. She had even tried letting go of her sorrow by counting her blessings, but she was still left feeling sad and empty.

Now, as she raced through the streets in her neighborhood, she was keenly aware of how precious life was and how desperately she wanted to find her son and hold him close again. She circled the block sur-rounding her house and branched out into the spring Shadows Subdivision, driving up one street and down another. But there was no sign of Randy.

"Please, God," she whispered aloud. "Please take care of him and lead me to him."

Suddenly the cloud of sorrow lifted and she knew how very blessed she was, the mother of two beautiful children and married to a loving, faithful man who cherished her and the boys. If only she could find Randy, Marilyn knew she would never take these—God's greatest bless-ings —for granted again.

Marilyn continued to search intently along dozens of streets, but when fifteen minutes passed she decided to return home for an update. Perhaps Randy had come home or maybe the police knew something. She swerved into the driveway and saw that her mother still had not ar-rived. Racing inside, she found Harold and Rusty waiting by the tele-phone.

"The police know nothing." Harold's voice was wracked with hysteria and his eyes were filled with tears. "They can't file a missing person's re-port until Randy's been missing twenty-four hours."

"Isn't there anything they can do?" Marilyn's voice rose anxiously.

"They said they'll look for him and call us if they get any news."

Harold hung his head and began crying. "Not Randy," he shouted through his tears, "Not my Randy!"

At that instant Marilyn's mother arrived, and ran into the house wide-eyed. "Have you find him yet?"

"No." Marilyn turned and headed for the door with her mother in tow. "Listen . . . I'm getting in that car and I'm not coming back until we find our baby. . . ."

"Pray, Mother," Marilyn implored as she hurried across the yard toward the driver's door of the car. "Please pray."

Together the women set out along the same streets they'd already searched, working their way out from the Scogin house in every possible direction. As they drove they prayed aloud.

"Please lead us to him and please, God, please protect him." Marilyn's tears streamed down her face. "Please, God," she added, her voice barely a whisper. "He's only three years old. . . ."

Nearly two hours after the boy had disappeared and more than a mile from their house, the women turned onto a busy street and saw a three-some on the sidewalk half a block ahead. A tall, slim, dark-haired woman and a younger, blond woman were walking together a few feet behind a boy with curly hair wearing a green and yellow sunsuit. The child was pulling a dog behind him.

"Randy!" Marilyn screamed, and sped up, pulling alongside the trio and quickly parking her car. "My sweet Randy. Thank you, God. Thank you."

"Randy!" Marilyn shouted toward the threesome as she stepped out of the car. The women and the little boy stopped and watched as Marilyn and her mother ran toward them. Relieved and sobbing, Marilyn fell to her knees next to Randy and pulled him tightly to her, stroking his hair and closing her eyes.

"Randy, oh, Randy," she cried into his curly hair. "Thank you, God."

"Hi, Mommy. Hi, Bo-Bo!" Randy smiled easily, calm and unaffected by his adventure away from home.

Standing back, careful not to interrupt the reunion, the women who had been trailing behind the boy smiled.

"He's okay, ma'am," the older woman said softly. "He fell into a ditch back there a ways. There was a bit of water in it and we helped him out. We've been following him ever since so he wouldn't get hurt."

Marilyn nodded, still clinging tightly to the child. "Thank you so much," she said, wiping at her tears and looking Randy over to be sure he was all right.

The woman continued, "He said he lived in the shadows."

Marilyn uttered a short laugh and sniffled loudly. She and Harold had recently been trying to teach Randy his address and that he lived in the Spring Shadows Subdivision, but all that had stuck with the boy was the word "shadows."

"Anyway," the woman said, "he seemed to know where he was going."

Marilyn nodded . . . She swept the boy into her arms and thanked the women once more for their help. Then, fresh tears of relief streaming down her cheeks, she and her mother raced home to share the good news with the others.

Back at the house Marilyn ran inside with Randy in her arms and passed him to his crying father. "We found him walking a mile from here. Two women were walking behind him, watching out for him."

"Oh, thank you, dear Lord. Thank you," Harold said, his body flooded with relief as he hugged the boy close.

At that instant Marilyn realized something.

"Mother, we forgot to offer those women a ride home. They followed Randy all that way and I'm sure they have a long walk ahead of them." She grabbed her keys once more. "Come on, let's go find them."

Leaving Randy with his father and brother, Marilyn and her mother got into the car and returned to the spot where only minutes earlier they'd found Randy. When they turned onto the street Marilyn checked her watch. Only about four minutes had passed since they had left the women, but now as Marilyn looked up the street, there was no one in sight. As it was a long stretch of roadway without any cross streets, Marilyn was confused.

"That's strange," she muttered aloud. "No one could walk that fast. I wonder where they went."

Her mother was puzzled, too. "Let's keep looking," she said. "Maybe if we drive the length of the street we'll find them resting somewhere."

For nearly fifteen minutes Marilyn and her mother drove back and forth on the street looking carefully for the women who had so kindly watched over Randy.

"I feel so badly," Marilyn said. "They were so nice to look after Randy and then I didn't even offer them a ride home."

"Oh well," her mother finally said. "I guess they got home some other way."

There was silence for a moment.

"Mother," Marilyn said, her voice suddenly curious. "You don't think they might have been angels, do you?"

"Oh, Marilyn, come now. They were just friendly neighbors doing a kind deed."

"You're right," Marilyn said, turning the car back toward home. "Well, whoever they were, they were an answer to our prayers, that's for sure."

Back home, Marilyn hugged Randy close once more and tousled his hair. Rusty and Harold and Marilyn's mother gathered around the boy so that the family formed a circle.

"We were worried about you, Randy," Marilyn said softly.

"I know, Mommy. I won't walk off anymore."

"That's good," Harold said.

Marilyn smiled and took the boy's hand in hers. "Listen, Randy, remember those ladies who helped you and stayed with you?"

The child nodded. "Yes, Mommy. They were strangers."

"But you weren't afraid of them, were you?"

"No, they were nice."

Harold nodded, "Yes, they looked after you. Did they tell you their names?"

"They told me they were from God," Randy said simply.

There was a pause as his family leaned closer, curious expressions on their faces.

Randy looked up at his mother. "What's an angel, Mommy?"

The adults stared at the child for a moment, and then exchanged a knowing look as goose bumps rose up on each of their arms. Quietly, and with a greater understanding than at any time in his life, Harold directed his family to form a circle and hold hands; then he closed his eyes and bowed his head. When he spoke his voice was filled with awe.

"Dear God, we do not know your ways and we do not pretend to have the answers. But somehow today we know that you brought about divine intervention in the life of our little Randy. Thank you for hearing our prayers and bringing him home safely.

"God." Harold paused, his voice choked with emotion. "Thank you for the simple faith of our children. And thank you for your angels. In Jesus' name, amen."

It Rallies God's Protection for Others

Brent Haggerty, "The Amazing Impact of One Committed Intercessor"

Florence Delano was a member of the church in which I grew up in Houlton, Maine. While I was at Nyack College in the mid–1970s, letters from my mother would often contain the comment, "Florence Delano was asking about you in church today, Brent. She wants you to know that she's praying for you."

During the time I attended seminary and did my missionary home service requirement in Ohio, my mother's letters often bore the same message from Florence, "Brent, I want you to know I'm praying for you." Florence also prayed for my relatives who were also engaged in Christian service.

After my family and I went to France for language study, we began receiving letters personally from Florence, beautiful letters, usually on one sheet of paper filled on both sides with words of encouragement, admonition, and exhortation. "Brent, keep your eyes fixed on Jesus. He's the One who called you to Africa. He has given you a task to do there. Regardless of how discouraged you may be, forge ahead." And at the end of each letter, she would write, "Brent and Susan, I just want you to know, I'm upholding you before the Lord in prayer."

During the first three years of our work in Burkina Faso, we seemed to live in a bubble of isolation, with no major health problems. Then suddenly that bubble burst. We started having one problem after another. One of the children would get sick with sores, fevers, scrapes and bruises, diarrhea—things that cause a parent to be anxious. That one would get better, but the second child would get sick and then get better while the third one would get sick and then get better, just in time for the first one to get sick again. It was like this for nearly six months.

In the midst of all that chaos, Susan developed an infection in her big toe, causing it to swell to twice its normal size. Many times I saw tears streaming down her face. It was hindering her housework, her family life, and her ministry.

Along with the children's problems and my wife's trouble, I fell ill. We got discouraged. I will never forget what my wife said one day: "Brent, I'm tired of being sick. I'm tired of seeing my children sick. I'm tired of you being sick. Oh, I wish we could get on a plane and go home."

At that time, my sister and her husband were in language study in France. She was pregnant and developed thyroid problems. The baby came a month early, developed a bronchial problem, and nearly died.

While those problems were going on in France and Burkina Faso, my brother, Brian, a missionary in Gabon, had trouble with one of his children who was in boarding school. Ben contracted cerebral malaria, and became nearly comatose.

In the middle of all this, my sister and her family arrived in Africa. We talked about the nitty-gritty of life on the mission field. Then my sister brought something to my attention. "Brent," she said, "you have been struggling with health problems in Burkina and you are at your wit's end. We nearly lost our son in France, and Brian almost lost Ben in Gabon. Do you realize all of this happened only weeks after Florence Delano passed away?"

It Can Avert Tragedy

Kelsey Tyler, *Heaven Hears Each Whisper*

David Moore had never flown before, but that Sunday night in July 1971, when he was offered the opportunity to fly from Texas to North Carolina to see his wife and infant daughter, David didn't hesitate.

"What time do we leave?" he asked his friend, Henry Gardner. The man was a local crop duster and he owned a small Cessna 180. He had planned to take a sightseeing trip the next day, and was willing to go out of his way to see that David and his family were reunited. The past nine weeks had been especially traumatic for the Moore family, and Gardner wanted to do what he could to help.

The trouble began when David, twenty-four, and Florence, twenty-one, his wife, discovered that her mother was dying of cancer. The sick woman lived in Hendersonville, North Carolina—at least a two-day drive from Yoakum, Texas, where the young couple and their infant daughter lived. The situation was especially difficult because David had recently been named pastor of Hebron Baptist Church, a position which required his presence—especially on Sundays.

"We'll work out a schedule," David assured his wife, "so that we can spend as much time as possible in North Carolina."

The staff at Hebron Baptist was completely understanding, and arranged for David to take a partial leave of absence. As long as Florence's mother was ill, David could be gone during the week and then home for the Sunday morning service.

The couple decided that Florence and their daughter would stay in North Carolina while David drove the weekly commute to Texas. Nine times David made the round-trip trek before he began feeling the strain of the routine.

"I need to rest," he admitted to Florence one evening as he was preparing to return to Texas once again.

"Honey, why don't you take the bus?" She was worried about his long hours on the road. "That way you can sleep, or catch up on your plans for Sunday, and it won't be so hard on you."

David thought for a moment. "Good idea," he said, rubbing his tired eyes. "And you could have the car so you'd have some way to get around if you need to."

He boarded a passenger bus late that week determined to spend the next two days resting. Instead, the trip was a nightmarish forty-six hours of crying babies, constant stops, and loud conversations. His family was on a tight budget, and he could not afford to fly. But David was more exhausted than ever before, and he decided he'd rather walk back to North Carolina, or hitchhike the highways, than ride another bus for two straight days.

Over the weekend, Henry Gardner's daughter—a member of Hebron Baptist Church—caught wind of David's need to find a way back to North Carolina. She told her father, and on Sunday night Henry called with his offer.

"It's a small plane, but smooth as honey in the air," Henry said. "You can be my navigator."

In the recesses of his mind David felt a slight wave of anxiety course through his body. He had always been wary of small planes, and expected that when the time came for him to fly it would be on a jumbo jet. He pushed aside his momentary fears and cleared his throat.

"I've never done any navigating," he said with a laugh. "But I'd be willing to fly the plane myself if it meant getting back to my family."

David met Henry the next day at a small airport outside town. The morning was beautiful, clear, and without any trace of bad weather.

"Looks like we picked a good day to hit the skies," Henry said, easily shifting his body into the cockpit.

David sized up the tiny aircraft and silently, almost unconsciously, whispered a prayer: *Lord, guide us as we go and please get us there safely.*

For the first half hour the craft flew easily through the clear skies, but as they neared Houston they entered a thick fog.

"No problem," Henry said, pointing out the windshield. "You can see the Houston radio towers there above the fog. If we keep our eyes on them we'll know where we are. Besides, we have aviation maps on board. Everything will be fine."

For a while, it looked as if Henry would be right. Then, when the plane was just outside Jackson, Mississippi, the fog worsened so that the plane became cocooned in a cloud with no visibility whatsoever.

Almost at the same time, the plane's radio and instruments died. Suddenly, the men could no longer see anything on the ground, and because of the instrument failure they couldn't monitor the fuel or talk to people in the control tower.

David may have been inexperienced at flying, but he did not need a pilot's license to know that they were in grave danger. His thoughts turned to his pretty young wife and their sixteen-month-old daughter. The couple was in the process of adopting the child, and they were expecting to sign the final papers any time. *Please, God, help us,* he prayed silently, his hands clenched and his face white with terror. *Please, get us through this safely.*

At that moment they flew through a clearing in the fog and caught a glimpse of the small Jackson airport just below. Henry maneuvered the craft through the opening in the clouds and smoothly down onto the runway.

"Thank God," David whispered as the men climbed out of the plane and Henry began tinkering with the fuse box. A burned-out fuse had caused the instrument failure, and Henry replaced it while David telephoned Florence.

"Listen, honey," David told Florence, "we're running late because of bad weather. Meet me at the Asheville Airport about an hour later than we planned."

"Is everything okay? With the plane, I mean?" she asked. David could hear how Florence was trying to control the concern in her voice.

"It's fine," he said, sounding more confident than he felt. "I love you, honey. See you in a few hours."

As they climbed back in the craft, David again uttered a silent prayer: *You got us this far, God. Please see us through safely to North Carolina.*

In less than an hour the men were back in the sky, enjoying the fact that the sun had come out and the conditions were once again clear. By the time they flew over Atlanta, Georgia, David's fears had nearly disappeared and he began looking forward to being with his family.

Then, as the plane passed Greenville, South Carolina, the fog appeared once more, and almost instantly engulfed the small craft in a dense, suffocating blanket of gray. Moments later they approached a mountain range, and David watched as Henry struggled to clear it safely.

"After these mountains it should be sunny again," David said, struggling to convince himself as much as Henry. "There's never fog in this area."

But that afternoon there was indeed fog, and it was so thick the men could see nothing past the plane's windshield. The airport wasn't far away, and Henry immediately contacted the Asheville Airport for assistance.

"We're closed because of fog," the air traffic controller informed Henry. "We have no capability for instrument landing. Return to Greenville and land there."

"I can't," Henry said, a tinge of panic creeping into his voice. "We're almost out of fuel. We don't have enough to fly back to Greenville."

For a moment, the cockpit was eerily silent. They had no visibility, and David's eyes fell on the fuel gauge and the needle, which danced dangerously over the letter E. Again he silently prayed, struggling to control his terror: *Please, God, get us out of these clouds safely.*

Finally, a different voice broke the silence: "Okay. We'll get the ground crew ready. Come in on an emergency landing."

David clutched the sides of his seat, his eyes wide in disbelief. There was no way they could make an emergency landing when visibility between the plane and the control tower was completely cut off by the fog.

Henry's voice snapped David to attention.

"Get the aviation maps."

David opened them instantly, and Henry estimated their location. According to the map, they should be directly above the airport. Gradually, Henry began to descend through the fog toward the ground. As he did, the voice of the controller entered the cockpit.

"Pull it up! Pull it up!"

Henry responded immediately, just as both men saw a split in the fog. They were not over the airport as they had thought. Instead they were over a busy interstate highway, and had missed an overpass bridge by no more than five feet.

David felt his heart thumping wildly, and he was struck by the certainty of one thing. Short of divine intervention, there was no way they would escape their grave situation alive.

At that instant, the controller's voice broke the silence once again. "If you will listen to me, I'll help you get down," he said.

Henry released a pent-up sigh. "Go ahead. I'm listening."

David closed his eyes momentarily and prayed, begging God to guide them safely through the fog onto the ground.

Meanwhile, the controller began guiding Henry toward a landing.

"Come down a little. Okay, a little more. Not that much. All right, now over to the right. Straighten it out and come down a little more."

The calm, reassuring voice of the controller continued its steady stream of directions, and Henry, intent on the voice, did as he was instructed. The trip seemed to take an eternity, and David wondered whether he would see his wife and daughter again. "Please, God," he whispered. "Get us onto the ground, God. Please."

The controller continued. "Raise it a little more. Okay, you're too far to the left. That's right. Now lower it a little more. All right, you're right over the end of the runway. Set it down. Now!"

Carefully responding just as he was told, Henry lowered the plane, and when he was a few feet from the ground the runway came into sight. As the plane touched down, David saw Florence standing nearby waiting for him, and his eyes filled with tears of relief and gratitude.

The two men looked at each other and without saying a word, they bowed their heads and closed their eyes. "Thank you, God," David said, his voice choked with emotion. "Thank you for sparing our lives today. And thank you for listening."

Henry picked up the plane's radio and contacted the control tower. "Hey, I just want to thank you so much for what you did. We couldn't have made it without those directions. You probably saved our lives."

There was a brief pause. "What are you talking about?" the controller asked. He had a different voice this time, and he was clearly confused. "We lost all radio contact with you when we told you to return to Greenville."

Goose bumps rose up on David's arms, and he watched as Henry's face went blank in disbelief. "You *what?*" he asked.

"We never heard from you again and we never heard you talking to us or to anyone else," the controller said. "We were stunned when we saw you break through the clouds right over the runway. It was a perfect landing."

David and Henry looked at each other in a way that needed no words. If the Asheville controller hadn't been in contact with them through the emergency landing, who had? Whose calm, clear voice had filled the cockpit with the directions that saved their lives?

It Affects Our Destiny

Mark Link, *Decision*

Irmgard Wood lived in Stuttgart, Germany, during World War II. One morning her mother and sisters saw an American plane catch fire and fall from the sky. Instinctively, they prayed for the pilot, even though he was an American.

Years later the Wood family migrated to the United States. Irmgard's mother got a job in a hospital in the San Fernando Valley in California. One day a patient detected her German accent and asked her whereabouts she lived in Germany. "Stuttgart," she replied.

"Stuttgart!" said the patient. "I almost got killed in Stuttgart. One morning during World War II, my plane caught fire and fell from the sky. Somebody must have really been praying for me that day."

That story recalls the words of the British poet Alfred Lord Tennyson: "More things are wrought through prayer than this world dreams of."

———— ✇ ————

Alfred Lord Tennyson, "The Passing of Arthur"

IDYLLS OF THE KING

More things are wrought by prayer
Than this world dreams of. Wherefore, let thy voice
Rise like a fountain for me night and day.
For what are men better than sheep or goats
That nourish a blind life within the brain,
If, knowing God, they lift not hands of prayer
Both for themselves and those who call them friend?
For so the whole round earth is every way
Bound by gold chains about the feet of God.

———— ✇ ————

Martin Luther

(1483–1546) Theologian, teacher, and writer who ignited the Reformation.

Prayer is a powerful thing, for God has bound and tied Himself thereto.

———— ✇ ————

Joan Winmill Brown, *Wings of Joy*

Many years ago in a small, poverty-stricken house in London, there lived a hard-working woman. Her back was bent from years of standing day after day over a washtub, this being her only source of income. As she worked, she constantly prayed for her son who later was to run away to sea while only a teenager. She was aware that the Lord answers prayer and with this faith she never gave up hope that her son would one day give his life to Him. After she died her prayers were answered and her son, by then a slave trader, became the "sailor preacher" of London. John Newton brought thousands of men to Christ. His hymn "Amazing Grace," which has been sung by Christians all over the world, is today as meaningful as when he sat down and wrote the words—words which were his testimony of the grace and forgiveness of God.

John Newton's words reached a skeptical man of great learning named Thomas Scott, who had avowed he did not need a Saviour. Later Scott's writings led scores of people to the Lord, including William Cowper. Cowper's poetry and prose in turn touched so many, one being

William Wilberforce, the British statesman who went on to work so vigilantly for the abolition of slavery.

The chain of influence goes on as people read and are inspired by the words of these men. Little did John Newton's mother dream that the prayers for her son would be used by the Lord to go on and on touching so many lives for Him!

Eugene Peterson, *Under the Unpredictable Plant*

Herbert Butterfield, the Oxford historian of modern history, is convinced that what Christians do in prayer is the most significant factor in the shaping of history—more significant than war and diplomacy, more significant than technology and art. . . .

It Brings Down the Power of Heaven

Ray Stedman, *Jesus Teaches on Prayer*

(1917–1992) Gifted Bible expositor, pastor, and counselor.

Prayer is a powerful thing.

"Prayer has already divided seas and rolled up flowing rivers, it has made flinty rocks gush into fountains, it has quenched flames of fire, it has muzzled lions, disarmed vipers and poisons, it has marshaled the stars against the wicked, it has stopped the course of the moon and arrested the sun in its race, it has burst open iron gates and recalled souls from eternity, it has conquered the strongest devils and commanded legions of angels down from heaven. Prayer has bridled and chained the raging passions of men and destroyed vast armies of proud, daring, blustering atheists. Prayer has brought one man from the bottom of the sea and carried another in a chariot of fire to heaven." That is not mere hyperbole, that is historical fact. Prayer has done a great many other things as well. It is an awesome, mighty force in the world of men.

Eugene Peterson, *Reversed Thunder*

The prayers which had ascended, unremarked by the journalists of the day, returned with immense force—in George Herbert's phrase, as "reversed thunder." Prayer reenters history with incalculable effects. Our earth is shaken daily by it.

It Opens a Door for Spiritual Activity

A. W. Tozer, *Tragedy in the Church*

(1897–1963) *Without any formal education, Tozer became one of America's most well-known pastor-theologians.*

All of the advertising we can do will never equal the interest and participation in the things of God resulting from the gracious answers to the prayers of faith generated by the Holy Spirit.

Billy Graham

People often ask the renowned evangelist, "What is the secret of your evangelistic crusades?"

His reply: There are three secrets: (1) prayer; (2) prayer; (3) prayer.

Robert Bakke, "Prayer: God's Catalyst for Revival"

Throughout church history men and women of God have felt constrained to summon believers to united prayer. . . . The eternal work of God requires it—even waits for it.

In the 16th and 17th centuries, the church floundered under dead orthodoxy. Appealing to the example of the early church, evangelical leaders developed a movement of "prayer societies" as a foundation to spiritual awakening. The societies were small cells of Christians meeting in homes every two weeks or so, to seek God for a general, extraordinary blessing upon the church. The prayer cells proliferated and by the beginning of the 18th century were found in most evangelical settings—whether churches, schools, or colleges. Tens of thousands of Christians were involved. The cells were especially attractive to students. Cotton Mather, son of Harvard's great president, Increase Mather, aggressively organized the prayer cells in the American colonies.

Meanwhile, Count Nicholas Von Zinzendorf gathered an incredibly diverse group of Christians (Catholics, Lutherans, Calvinists, etc.) from across Europe. He was able to forge and sustain their union as a single movement (the Moravians) only when he called his community to a lifestyle of united praying. In prayer, God made Zinzendorf's crowd of "one mind." Not only were the hearts of these disparate believers melded into a single community, but their united prayers also launched an international missionary thrust that presaged the modern missionary movement. For over 100 years Moravians prayed 24 hours a day for God's blessing on His church and the advancement of Christ's kingdom to the ends of the earth. The history of the church changed.

These movements of united prayer were largely responsible for the Great Awakening (1725–1740) when God lit America, England, and parts of Europe with a brilliant conflagration of Pentecostal grace. Millions of men, women, and children were swept into the kingdom and great international figures were thrust to the forefront of Christendom (e.g., John Wesley, George Whitefield, and Jonathan Edwards). . . .

Out of this massive international 18th-century awakening came another design for united prayer that would weave itself into the fabric of the evangelical world—with profound effect. The new plan was launched by Scottish Presbyterians; embraced by Congregationalists Jonathan Edwards, David Brainerd, and Timothy Dwight; Anglicans John Wesley and George Whitefield; Baptists Andrew Fuller, Isaac Backus, and William Carey; and countless others. Called "The Concert of Prayer," this plan would become one of the most powerful schemes since the Reformation. For nearly 150 years the concert prevailed.

On a monthly or quarterly basis, Christians from every denominational stripe gathered in their communities, rotating among participating local churches, to pray for the outpouring of God's Spirit on the church and the advancement of Christ's kingdom. Some neighborhood churches prayed together for more than 100 years.

From the concert sprang hundreds of missionary societies, evangelistic efforts, and works of benevolence. It was at a concert of prayer in Northamptonshire, England, that William Carey experienced the call of God to India. The concert of prayer was also the foundation of the Second Great Awakening, called "America's Pentecost" or the revival of 1800, the most powerful religious episode in United States history. The concert was the common denominator of three massive international awakenings, the modern missionary movement, and hundreds of local revivals.

Today schemes of united prayer are being born in every quarter of the church—in the West, to be sure, but especially around the earth. The weekly, monthly, quarterly rhythms of the international concert of prayer are being resurrected, but dozens of other plans and strategies for prayer are flourishing, too. Prayer cells, like Neighborhood Houses of Prayer, are echoing the movements of past years. In extraordinary ways God is stirring up His people to seek Him, pouring out upon them a spirit of prayer. God's people are rediscovering not only the power of prayer, but the potency of union. As both the Scriptures and church history indicate, we can expect neighborhoods and nations to be changed as prevailing, united prayers move the hand of God.

———— ∞∞∞ ————

John F. DeVries, "Prayer Can Change a City, One Neighborhood at a Time," *Pray!* magazine, 1996

Goa, India—An Indian mission reports that in spite of repeated attempts to plant house churches in Goa over the past 20 years, as of August 1994, they only have eight small, struggling churches in the city.

A team of Brazilian intercessors comes to Goa in the summer of 1994, rents a house, and prays for 12 months. They do not engage in any witnessing, literature distribution, or church planting. They simply pray for an entire year.

In the two months after they leave, the Indian mission plants 18 new house churches in this no longer resistant city!

Grand Rapids, MI, USA—Four single women in the inner city decide to pray for their drug-ridden, gang-infested neighborhood by forming a neighborhood house of prayer. Within a few weeks, four teens are prayed out of a gang. A week later, while praying, the young women decide they should "stop praying" and visit these teens. That night they lead all four of them to Christ and later get them involved in a discipleship program in their church.

Lansing, MI, USA—A Michigan State University student decides to form a "dormitory house of prayer" in February of 1995 and offers to pray for fellow students each week. The response is so positive that within two months houses of prayer spread to seven other dorms, and a witch is prayed out of a dorm coven and comes to Christ. Christian agencies working on campus unite during the summer with the goal of having a dormitory house of prayer in every dorm by December 1, 1995. They beat their goal by one month.

It Transforms the Spiritual Landscape

The Story of the Man Who Planted Trees

The story of Elzeard Bouffler, a shepherd in the French Alps, who Jean Giono met in 1913.

At that time, because of careless deforestation, the mountains around Provence, France, were barren. Former villages were deserted because their springs and brooks had run dry. The wind blew furiously, unimpeded by foliage.

While mountain climbing, Giono came to a shepherd's hut, where he was invited to spend the night.

After dinner Giono watched the shepherd meticulously sort through a pile of acorns, discarding those that were cracked or undersized. When the shepherd had counted out 100 perfect acorns, he stopped for the night and went to bed.

Giono learned that the 55-year-old shepherd had been planting trees on the wild hillsides for over three years. He had planted 100,000 trees, 20,000 of which had sprouted. Of those, he expected half to be eaten by rodents or die due to the elements, and the other half to live.

After World War I, Giono returned to the mountainside and discovered incredible rehabilitation: there was a veritable forest, accompanied by a chain reaction in nature. Water flowed in the once-empty brooks. The ecology, sheltered by a leafy roof and bonded to the earth by a mat of spreading roots, became hospitable. Willows, rushes, meadows, gardens, and flowers were birthed.

Giono returned again after World War II. Twenty miles from the lines, the shepherd had continued his work, ignoring the war of 1939 just as he had ignored that of 1914. The reformation of the land continued. Whole regions glowed with health and prosperity.

Giono writes, "On the site of the ruins I had seen in 1913 now stand neat farms. . . . The old streams, fed by the rains and snows that the forest conserves, are flowing again. . . . Little by little, the villages have been rebuilt. People from the plains, where land is costly, have settled here, bringing youth, motion, the spirit of adventure."

Those who pray are like spiritual reforesters, digging holes in barren land and planting the seeds of life. Through these seeds, dry spiritual wastelands are transformed into harvestable fields, and lifegiving water is brought to parched and barren souls.

A CLOSING PRAYER

MICHAEL LEUNIG, *The Prayer Tree*

Let us live in such a way
That when we die
Our love will survive
And continue to grow.
Amen

RECOMMENDED READING

Listed in order of recommendation.

Foster, Richard. *Prayer*. San Francisco, CA: HarperSanFrancisco, 1992.

An in-depth look at prayer in all its variations, from spontaneous breath-prayers to formal liturgical prayer. from a deep well of trained insight, compassion, and practical experience that will deepen your experience with God.

Macy, Howard. *Rhythms of the Inner Life*. Old Tappan, NJ: Fleming H. Revell Company, 1988.

Using the Psalms as its starting point, it deals with different themes in the spiritual life, ranging from despair to celebration. Presently out of print, but a truly outstanding book if you can find it.

Peterson, Eugene H. *Answering God*. San Francisco, CA: Harper & Row Publishers, San Francisco, 1989.

Welcome to the prayer-school of the Psalms. Eugene Peterson will be your spiritual guide, and we would be hard-pressed to find anyone better qualified to walk us through this rich and time-honored method of prayer.

Hunter, Bingham W. *The God Who Hears*. Downers Grove, IL: InterVarsity Press, 1986.

You'll like Bingham Hunter's approach to the most important of subjects. He's fearless about tackling the tough issues surrounding prayer and he does so with a touch of humor and a ton of practical insight.

Balthasar, Hans Urs von. *Prayer*. New York: Sheed & Ward, 1961.

This book has tutored many in the way of prayer. It is not an easy read, but it is rich. Read it slowly. Listen carefully. And come back to it often.

Lewis, C. S. *Letters to Malcolm: Chiefly on Prayer*. New York: Harvest/Harcourt Brace Jovanovich, 1964.

A classic discussion on prayer, framed in the literary form of personal correspondence. The advice contained in Lewis' letters is as readable as it is practical.

Baillie, John. *A Diary of Private Prayer*. New York: Charles Scribner's Sons, 1977.

An intimate daily devotional whose morning and evening prayers will touch your heart and guide you to the heart of God.

Holmes, Marjorie. *I've Got to Talk to Somebody, God*. Garden City, NY: Doubleday & Company, Inc., 1969.

A patchwork of prayer embroidered with honest and heartfelt feelings. The author's homespun warmth comes through on every page, and, by example, shows the reader how to stitch the scraps of everyday events into a covering of prayer.

White, John. *Daring To Draw Near*. Downers Grove, IL: InterVarsity Press, 1977.

Draw near and listen to Abraham plead, watch Jacob wrestle, hear David confess, agonize as Jesus prays through the pain of His crucifixion. John White doesn't tell you about prayer, he helps you to hear, see, touch, taste, and feel it by examining some of the most intense moments of prayer recorded in the Scriptures.

An Unknown Christian. *The Kneeling Christian*. Grand Rapids, MI: Zondervan Publishing House, 1986.

Filled with a number of illustrative quotes and inspiring anecdotes, this practical primer on prayer answers such questions as "What is prayer?" "Does God always answer prayer?" and "How shall I pray?"

Brother Lawrence. *The Practice of the Presence of God*. Springdale, PA: Whitaker House, 1982.

And who was Brother Lawrence? A Pastor? Teacher? Bishop? President? No, a cook, that's all. A lowly monastery cook. Yet he understood something that pastors, teachers, bishops, and presidents have all wanted to understand and practice—intimate and unbroken fellowship with God. Have a seat at the kitchen table and listen as this humble cook explains how to experience God in the daily routines of your life.

Bonhoeffer, Dietrich. *Life Together*. New York and Evanston: Harper & Row Publishers, 1954.

Bonhoeffer opens the door for the reader to enter his "underground seminary" in Nazi Germany and cultivate a deeper intimacy with Christ through silence, solitude, and prayer. This book is primarily about community, how it is formed and nurtured, and it is in this context that the discussions on prayer are set.

PERMISSIONS

READER'S REFERENCE

A quick reference tool for finding quotes and original sources for further reading.
Each listing provides page(s) found in this book—author, title of the original source (publisher information, and copyright date) followed by the page(s) quoted from the original source.

A
Adler, Bill
p. 56—Bill Adler, *Dear Lord* (Nashville,
Tennessee: Thomas Nelson, Inc., 1982).
Ambrose of Milan
p. 71—in *The HarperCollins Book of
Prayers*, comp. by Robert Van de Weyer
(New York: HarperCollins Publishers,
1993), 24–25.
Amon Ra, hymn to the sun god
p. 52—in *Tongues of Fire*, comp. by
Grace H. Turnbull (Baltimore: The Johns
Hopkins Press, 1941), 59.
Anonymous
p. 49—Prostitute in "Why We Pray," *Life*,
March 1994, 59.
p. 62—Attributed to an aged seventeenth-century nun in *Eerdman's Book of
Famous Prayers*, comp. by Veronica
Zundel (Grand Rapids, Michigan: Wm.
B. Eerdmans Publishing Company,
1983), 53.
p. 90—Prayer for grace.
p. 116—Prayer of forgiveness.
p. 180—English Proverb in *Distilled
Wisdom*, comp. and ed. by Alfred Armand
Montapert (Englewood Cliffs, New
Jersey: Prentice-Hall, Inc., 1964), 279.

p. 220—*The Cloud of Unknowing*
(New York: Harper & Brothers, 1948),
46–47.
p. 226—*The Way of the Pilgrim*, translated from the Russian by R. M. French
(New York: The Seabury Press, 1965),
1–2.
p. 244—Confederate Soldier. Cited in
Moments of Transcendence, ed. by Rabbi
Dov Peretz Elkins (Northvale, New
Jersey: Jason Aronson Inc.), 144.
p. 257—Inscription on the walls of a cellar in Cologne, Germany, where Jews hid
from Nazis, in *The Passover Haggadah*,
ed. by Nahum N. Glatzer (New York:
Schocken Books Inc., 1981), xxvi.
p. 292—"Some Pray and Die" in *Essays
on Prayer* (Downers Grove, Illinois: InterVarsity Press, 1968), 69–72.
p. 327—An Unknown Christian, *The
Kneeling Christian* (Grand Rapids,
Michigan: Zondervan Publishing House,
1986), 33.
Anselm of Canterbury
p. 105—in *The HarperCollins Book of
Prayers*, comp. by Robert Van de Weyer
(New York: HarperCollins Publishers,
1993), 34–35.

p. 147—in *Challenge* by Mark Link (Valencia, California: Tabor Publishing, 1988), 49.

p. 148—in *The HarperCollins Book of Prayers*, comp. by Robert Van de Weyer (New York: HarperCollins Publishers, 1993), 32.

Aquinas, Thomas
p. 38—as told by Peter Calo in *The Soul Afire*, ed. by H. A. Reinhold (Garden City, New York: Doubleday & Company, 1973), 58.

p. 72—in *The HarperCollins Book of Prayers*, comp. by Robert Van de Weyer (New York: HarperCollins Publishers, 1993), 362–363.

p. 122—in *Graces* by June Cotner (San Francisco, HarperSanFrancisco: 1994), 8.

Askew, Eddie
p. 13—Eddie Askew, *A Silence and a Shouting* (London: The Leprosy Mission International), 6–7.

Augustine
p. 9—in *Prayer* by Richard Foster (San Francisco: HarperSanFrancisco, 1992), 1.

p. 23—in *Wings of Joy*, comp. and ed. by Joan Winmill Brown (Old Tappan, New Jersey: Fleming H. Revell Company, 1977), 54.

p. 25—in *Lord Hear Our Prayer*, comp. by Thomas McNally and William G. Storey (Notre Dame, Indiana: Ave Maria Press, 1978), 67.

p. 72—in *The HarperCollins Book of Prayers*, comp. by Robert Van de Weyer (New York: HarperCollins Publishers, 1993), 43.

p. 97—in *Speaking to God* by Nancy Benvenga (Notre Dame, Indiana: Ave Maria Press, 1993), 17.

p. 110—Augustine, *Confessions* (New York: Oxford University Press, 1991), 6.

p. 134—in *The HarperCollins Book of Prayers*, comp. by Robert Van de Weyer (New York: HarperCollins Publishers, 1993), 44–45.

p. 140—in *Speaking to God* by Nancy Benvenga (Notre Dame, Indiana: Ave Maria Press, 1993), 86.

p. 168—in *Lord Hear Our Prayer*, comp. by Thomas McNally and William G. Storey (Notre Dame, Indiana: Ave Maria Press, 1978), 65.

B
Babylonian Prayer
p. 52—in *Tongues of Fire*, comp. by Grace H. Turnbull (Baltimore: The Johns Hopkins Press, 1941), 93–94.

Baillie, John
p. 127—John Baillie, *A Diary of Private Prayer* (New York: Charles Scribner's Sons, 1949), 9.

p. 180—John Baillie, *A Diary of Private Prayer* (New York: Charles Scribner's Sons, 1949), 21, 63.

p. 262—in *A Diary of Prayer* by Elizabeth Gouge (New York: Coward-McCann, Inc., 1966), 34.

Bakke, Robert
p. 354—"Prayer: God's Catalyst for Revival," *Pray!* magazine preview issue (Colorado Springs, Colorado: The Navigators, 1996), 8–9.

Balthasar, Hans Urs von
p. 12—Hans Urs von Balthasar, *Prayer* (Great Britain: Geoffrey Chapman Ltd., 1961), 11.

p. 206—Hans Urs von Balthasar, *Prayer* (Great Britain: Geoffrey Chapman Ltd., 1961), 108.

p. 207—Hans Urs von Balthasar, *Prayer* (Great Britain: Geoffrey Chapman Ltd., 1961), 14–19, 24–25.

p. 215—Hans Urs von Balthasar, *Prayer* (Great Britain: Geoffrey Chapman Ltd., 1961), 88.

Barclay, William
p. 101—in *Speaking to God* by Nancy Benvenga (Notre Dame, Indiana: Ave Maria Press, 1993), 75–76.

p. 174—William Barclay, *A Guide to Daily Prayer* (New York: Harper & Row, 1962), 11–12.

p. 177—William Barclay, *A Guide to Daily Prayer* (New York: Harper & Row, 1962), 13–14.

p. 329—William Barclay, *A Guide to Daily Prayer* (New York: Harper & Row, 1962), 15–16.

Barry, William A.
p. 313—William Barry, *Paying Attention to God* (Notre Dame, Indiana: Ave Maria Press, 1990), 21–23, 28–30.

p. 316—William Barry, *Paying Attention to God* (Notre Dame, Indiana: Ave Maria Press, 1990), 33–36.

Chadwick, Samuel
p. 26—in *A Treasury of Prayer*, comp.
and cond. by Leonard Ravenhill (Minneapolis, Minnesota: Bethany House
Publishers, 1961), 186.

Chagneau, Francois
p. 284—in *The HarperCollins Book of
Prayers*, comp. by Robert Van de Weyer
(New York: HarperCollins Publishers,
1993), 99–100.

Chambers, Oswald
p. 10—Oswald Chambers, *My Utmost
For His Highest* (Burlington: Welch Publishing Company, Inc., 1963), 176.
p. 15—Oswald Chambers, *My Utmost
For His Highest* (Burlington: Welch Publishing Company, Inc., 1963), 106.
p. 25—in *Oswald Chambers: Abandoned
to God* by David McCasland (Nashville,
Tennessee: Discovery House Books,
1993), 71.
p. 27—in *Oswald Chambers: Abandoned
to God* by David McCasland (Nashville,
Tennessee: Discovery House Books,
1993), 110.
p. 94—Oswald Chambers, *My Utmost
For His Highest* (Burlington: Welch Publishing Company, Inc., 1963), 259.
p. 101—in *Oswald Chambers: Abandoned
to God* by David McCasland (Nashville,
Tennessee: Discovery House Books,
1993), 109–110.
p. 142—Oswald Chambers, *My Utmost
For His Highest* (Burlington: Welch Publishing Company, Inc., 1963), 57.
p. 145—Oswald Chambers, *My Utmost
For His Highest* (Burlington: Welch Publishing Company, Inc., 1963), 27.
p. 172—in *Oswald Chambers: Abandoned
to God* by David McCasland (Nashville,
Tennessee: Discovery House Books,
1993), 120.
p. 184—Oswald Chambers, *My Utmost
For His Highest* (Burlington: Welch Publishing Company, Inc., 1963), 173.

Channing, William Henry
p. 92—in *Moments of Transcendence,
Inspirational Readings for Yom Kippur*, ed.
by Rabbi Dov Peretz Elkins (Northvale,
New Jersey: Jason Aronson Inc., 1992),
268.

Chiang Kai-shek, Madame
p. 39—*Wings of Joy*, comp. and ed. by
Joan Winmill Brown (Old Tappan, New

Jersey: Fleming H. Revell Company,
1977), 49.

China
p. 63—in *The World At One in Prayer*, ed.
by Daniel J. Fleming (New York: Harper
& Brothers, 1942), 43.

Chrysostom, St. John
p. 30—in *The Harper Religious and Inspirational Quotation Companion*, comp. and
ed. by Margaret Pepper (New York: Harper
and Row, Publishers, Inc., 1989), 326.

Cohen, Barbara
p. 130—*Yussel's Prayer*, retold by Barbara
Cohen (New York: Lothrop, Lee &
Shepard Books, 1981).

Cohen, Leonard
p. 12—"F.," in "Beautiful Losers," sct. 18
(1970) as quoted in *The Columbia Dictionary of Quotations* (New York: Columbia University Press, 1993), 722.

Coker, Daniel
p. 251—in *Conversations with God* by
James Melvin Washington (New York:
HarperCollins, 1994), 23.

Coleridge, Samuel Taylor
p. 26—"The Ancient Mariner" in *The
Harper Religious and Inspirational Quo-
tation Companion*, comp. and ed. by
Margaret Pepper (New York: Harper and
Row Publishers, Inc., 1989), 326.

Cranmer, Thomas
p. 109—in *The Book of Common Prayer*
according to the use of the Protestant
Episcopal Church (Greenwich, Connecticut: Seabury Press, 1953), 75.

Cyprian of Carthage
p. 71—in *The HarperCollins Book of
Prayers*, comp. by Robert Van de Weyer
(New York: HarperCollins Publishers,
1993), 121.

Cyril of Jerusalem, St.
p. 31—in *Lord Hear Our Prayer*, comp.
by Thomas McNally and William G.
Storey (Notre Dame, Indiana: Ave Maria
Press, 1978), 46.

D

DeVries, John F.
p. 102—"Prayer Can Change a City, One
Neighborhood at a Time," *Pray!* Prayer
Resource Guide (Colorado Springs,
Colorado: The Navigators, 1996), 8–9.
p. 356—"Prayer Can Change a City, One
Neighborhood at a Time," *Pray!* Prayer

York: Doubleday & Company, Inc., 1969), 7–8.

p. 85—Marjorie Holmes, *I've Got to Talk to Somebody, God* (Garden City, New York: Doubleday & Company, Inc., 1969), 29–30.

p. 167—Marjorie Holmes, *I've Got to Talk to Somebody, God,* "Praying While Scrubbing a Floor" (Garden City, New York: Doubleday & Company, Inc., 1969), 30–31.

Hoste, Dr.

p. 41—as told by Edith Schaeffer in *Common Sense Christian Living* by Edith Schaeffer (Nashville, Tennessee: Thomas Nelson, Inc., Publishers, 1983), 211.

Hough, Lee

p. 59—Lee Hough (previously unpublished prayer), June 1996.

Houston, James

p. 17—James Houston, *The Transforming Power of Prayer* (Colorado Springs, Colorado: NavPress, 1996), 5.

p. 23—James Houston, *The Transforming Power of Prayer* (Colorado Springs, Colorado: NavPress, 1996), 63.

p. 220—James Houston, *The Transforming Power of Prayer* (Colorado Springs, Colorado: NavPress, 1996), 110.

Huebsch, Bill

p. 24—Bill Huebsch, *A New Look at Prayer* (Mystic, Connecticut: Twenty-Third Publications, 1991), 19.

Hügel, Friedrich von

p. 306—in *The Choice Is Always Ours,* ed. by Dorothy Berkley Phillips, co-ed. by Elizabeth Boyden Howes and Lucille M. Nixon (New York: HarperCollins, 1960), 245.

Hugo, Victor

p. 34—*Les Miserables,* pt. 4, bk. 5, ch. 4, 1862, as quoted in *The Columbia Dictionary of Quotations* by Robert Andrews (New York: Columbia University Press, 1993), 723.

Hunter, W. Bingham

p. 11—W. Bingham Hunter, *The God Who Hears* (Downers Grove, Illinois: InterVarsity Press, 1986), 173.

p. 151—W. Bingham Hunter, *The God Who Hears* (Downers Grove, Illinois: InterVarsity Press, 1986), 81.

p. 175—W. Bingham Hunter, *The God Who Hears* (Downers Grove, Illinois: InterVarsity Press, 1986), 97–98.

p. 183—W. Bingham Hunter, *The God Who Hears* (Downers Grove, Illinois: InterVarsity Press, 1986), 73–74.

p. 199—W. Bingham Hunter, *The God Who Hears* (Downers Grove, Illinois: InterVarsity Press, 1986), 75–76.

p. 257—W. Bingham Hunter, *The God Who Hears* (Downers Grove, Illinois: InterVarsity Press, 1986), 85.

p. 258—W. Bingham Hunter, *The God Who Hears* (Downers Grove, Illinois: InterVarsity Press, 1986), 85–91.

p. 287—W. Bingham Hunter, *The God Who Hears* (Downers Grove, Illinois: InterVarsity Press, 1986), 11–12.

p. 309—W. Bingham Hunter, *The God Who Hears* (Downers Grove, Illinois: InterVarsity Press, 1986), 170–171.

Hyde, John

p. 157—in *The Kneeling Christian* by An Unknown Author (Grand Rapids, Michigan: Zondervan Publishing House, 1986), 60.

I

Ignatius of Loyola, St.

p. 140—in *Speaking to God* by Nancy Benvenga (Notre Dame, Indiana: Ave Maria Press, 1993), 89–90.

Ireland (Northern)

p. 66—in *Children's Prayers from Around the World* (New York: William H. Sadlier, Inc., 1981), 11.

J

Jacobs, Harriet A.

p. 274—in *Conversations with God* by James Melvin Washington (New York: HarperCollins, 1994), 45.

Japan

p. 65—in *The World At One in Prayer,* ed. by Daniel J. Fleming (New York: Harper & Brothers, 1942), 58–59.

John of the Cross, St.

p. 146—in *The HarperCollins Book of Prayers,* comp. by Robert Van de Weyer (New York: HarperCollins Publishers, 1993), 213.

p. 288—in *The HarperCollins Book of Prayers,* comp. by Robert Van de Weyer (New York: HarperCollins Publishers, 1993), 214–215.

Julian of Brioude
p. 253—in *Prayers of the Martyrs* by
Duane W. H. Arnold (Grand Rapids,
Michigan: Zondervan, 1991), 103.

K

Kagawa, Dr. Toyohiko
p. 66—in *The World At One in Prayer*, ed.
by Daniel J. Fleming (New York: Harper
& Brothers, 1942), 61.
Kempis, Thomas à
p. 33—in "Renewed Day by Day" by A. W.
Tozer (Vol. 1, Jan. 10.)
p. 73—in *The Oxford Book of Prayer*, ed.
by George Appleton (New York: Oxford
University Press, 1985), 92–93.
Ken, Thomas
p. 124—in *The Gift of Prayer*, comp. and
ed. by Jared T. Kieling (New York: The
Continuum Publishing Co., 1995), 25.
Kenya
p. 64—in *My Favorite Prayers* by Norman
Vincent Peale (New York: HarperCollins,
1993), 86.
Kidd, Sue Monk
p. 163—Sue Monk Kidd, *God's Joyful
Surprise* (New York: Guideposts Associates, Inc., 1987), 218–220.
p. 222—Sue Monk Kidd, *God's Joyful
Surprise* (New York: Guideposts Associates, Inc., 1987), 206–207, 220–224.

L

Lacedaemonian Prayer to Zeus
p. 53—in *Tongues of Fire*, comp. by
Grace H. Turnbull (Baltimore: The Johns
Hopkins Press, 1941), 97.
Lavender, John Allan
p. 27—John Allen Lavender, *Why Prayers
are Unanswered* (Wheaton, Illinois: Tyn-
dale House Publishers, Inc., 1980), 51.
Law, William
p. 14—William Law, *A Serious Call to a
Devout and Holy Life* (Grand Rapids,
Michigan: Baker Book House, 1977),
138.
Lear, Norman
p. 50—in *How I Pray* by Jim Castelli
(New York: Random House, 1994),
82–83.
Lessing, Gotthold
p. 118—in *The Treasure Chest*, ed. by
Charles L. Wallis (New York: Harper &
Row, 1965), 213.

Leunig, Michael
p. 59—Michael Leunig, *The Prayer Tree*
(Australia: HarperCollinsPublishers,
1973).
p. 359—Michael Leunig, *The Prayer Tree*
(Australia: HarperCollinsPublishers,
1973).
Lewis, C. S.
p. 6—C. S. Lewis, *The World's Last Night*
(New York: Harcourt Brace Jovanovich,
Inc., 1960), 8.
p. 17—C. S. Lewis, *Letters to Malcolm:
Chiefly on Prayer* (New York: Harcourt
Brace Jovanovich, Inc., 1964), 81.
p. 26—C. S. Lewis, *Letters to Malcolm:
Chiefly on Prayer* (New York: Harcourt
Brace Jovanovich, Inc., 1964), 28.
p. 30—C. S. Lewis, *Letters to Malcolm:
Chiefly on Prayer* (New York: Harcourt
Brace Jovanovich, Inc., 1964), 22.
p. 48—C. S. Lewis, *Surprised by Joy*
(New York: Harcourt Brace Jovanovich,
Inc., 1955), 225, 228–229.
p. 54—C. S. Lewis, *Letters to Malcolm:
Chiefly on Prayer* (New York: Harcourt
Brace Jovanovich, Inc., 1964), 23.
p. 89—in *The Joyful Christian*, selected
readings from C. S. Lewis (New York:
Macmillan Publishing Co., Inc., 1977),
87–88.
p. 106—in *The Quotable Lewis*, ed. by
Wayne Martindale and Jerry Root
(Wheaton, Illinois: Tyndale House Pub-
lishers, Inc., 1989), 491.
p. 115—C. S. Lewis, *Letters to Malcolm:
Chiefly on Prayer* (New York: Harcourt
Brace Jovanovich, Inc., 1964),
106–107.
p. 116—C. S. Lewis, *Letters to Malcolm:
Chiefly on Prayer* (New York: Harcourt
Brace Jovanovich, Inc., 1964), 27.
p. 127—C. S. Lewis, *Letters to Malcolm:
Chiefly on Prayer* (New York: Harcourt
Brace Jovanovich, Inc., 1964), 91.
p. 267—C. S. Lewis, *A Grief Observed*
(New York: HarperSanFrancisco, 1961),
81.
p. 274—C. S. Lewis, *The Screwtape
Letters* (Old Tappan, New Jersey:
Fleming H. Revell Company, 1976),
50–51.
p. 291—C. S. Lewis, *The World's Last
Night* (New York: Harcourt Brace
Jovanovich, Inc., 1960), 10–11.

p. 301—C. S. Lewis, *Letters to Malcolm: Chiefly on Prayer* (New York: Harcourt Brace Jovanovich, Inc., 1964), 57–59.

p. 301—C. S. Lewis, *Christian Reflections*, ed. by Walter Hooper (Grand Rapids, Michigan: Wm. B. Eerdmans, 1967), 149–151.

p. 304—C. S. Lewis, *Letters to Malcolm: Chiefly on Prayer* (New York: Harcourt Brace Jovanovich, Inc., 1964), 113--116.

p. 307—C. S. Lewis, *Letters to Malcolm: Chiefly on Prayer* (New York: Harcourt Brace Jovanovich, Inc., 1964), 116–117.

p. 311—C. S. Lewis, *Letters to Malcolm: Chiefly on Prayer* (New York: Harcourt Brace Jovanovich, Inc., 1964), 16–17.

Lincoln, Abraham
p. 28—in *The International Dictionary of Thoughts,* comp. by John P. Bradley, Leo F. Daniels, Thomas C. Jones (Chicago: J. G. Ferguson Publishing Company, 1969), 577.

p. 74—in *My Favorite Prayers* by Norman Vincent Peale (New York: HarperCollins, 1993), 90.

p. 308—in *A Treasury of the World's Great Speeches,* sel. & ed. by Houston Peterson (New York: Simon & Schuster, Inc., 1965), 523–524.

Lindbergh, Anne Morrow
p. 203—Anne Morrow Lindbergh, *Gift from the Sea* (New York: Pantheon Books, Inc., 1955), 51.

Link, Mark
p. 49—a story of a prisoner in *Decision* by Mark Link (Allen, Texas: Tabor Publishing, 1988), 71.

p. 351—a story of a World War II pilot in *Decision* by Mark Link (Allen, Texas: Tabor Publishing, 1988), 113.

Lucado, Max
p. 79—Max Lucado, *The Applause of Heaven* (Dallas, Texas: Word Publishing, 1990), 59–64.

Luther, Martin
p. 40—as told by E. M. Bounds in *A Treasury of Prayer,* comp. and cond. by Leonard Ravenhill (Minneapolis, Minnesota: Bethany House Publishers, 1961), 69–70.

p. 68—as told by E. M. Bounds in *A Treasury of Prayer,* comp. and cond. by Leonard Ravenhill (Minneapolis, Minnesota: Bethany House Publishers, 1961), 100.

p. 73—in *The Oxford Book of Prayer,* ed. by George Appleton (New York: Oxford University Press, 1985), 53.

p. 137—in *Prayers Across the Centuries,* ed. by Vinita Hampton Wright (Wheaton, Illinois: Harold Shaw Publishers, 1993), 87.

p. 352—in *The Gift of Prayer,* comp. and ed. by Jared T. Kieling (New York: The Continuum Publishing Co., 1995), 2.

M

McCasland, David
p. 25—David McCasland, *Oswald Chambers: Abandoned to God* (Nashville, Tennessee: Discovery House Books, 1993), 71.

p. 168—David McCasland, *Oswald Chambers: Abandoned to God* (Nashville, Tennessee: Discovery House Books, 1993), 74, 112.

MacDonald, George
p. 6—in *George MacDonald,* ed. by C. S. Lewis (London: William Collins Sons & Co. Ltd., 1946), p. 154.

p. 28—in *George MacDonald Creation in Christ,* ed. by Rolland Hein (Wheaton, Illinois: Harold Shaw Publishers, 1976), 337.

p. 111—in *Keep a Quiet Heart* by Elisabeth Elliot (Ann Arbor, Michigan: Servant Publications, 1995), 116.

p. 143—in *George MacDonald Creation in Christ,* ed. by Rolland Hein (Wheaton, Illinois: Harold Shaw Publishers, 1976), 328.

p. 300—in *George MacDonald Creation in Christ,* ed. by Rolland Hein (Wheaton, Illinois: Harold Shaw Publishers, 1976), 329–330.

p. 330—in *George MacDonald Creation in Christ,* ed. by Rolland Hein (Wheaton, Illinois: Harold Shaw Publishers, 1976), 327–328.

Macy, Howard
p. 7—Howard Macy, *Rhythms of the Inner Life* (Old Tappan, New Jersey: Fleming H. Revell Company, 1988), 125.

p. 8—Howard Macy, *Rhythms of the Inner Life* (Old Tappan, New Jersey: Fleming H. Revell Company, 1988), 124–125.

p. 14—Howard Macy, *Rhythms of the Inner Life* (Old Tappan, New Jersey: Fleming H. Revell Company, 1988), 132.

p. 48—Howard Macy, *Rhythms of the Inner Life* (Old Tappan, New Jersey: Fleming H. Revell Company, 1988), 26–27.

p. 189—Howard Macy, *Rhythms of the Inner Life* (Old Tappan, New Jersey: Fleming H. Revell Company, 1988), 132–133.

p. 192—Howard Macy, *Rhythms of the Inner Life* (Old Tappan, New Jersey: Fleming H. Revell Company, 1988), 51.

p. 200—Howard Macy, *Rhythms of the Inner Life* (Old Tappan, New Jersey: Fleming H. Revell Company, 1988), 41–43, 45–50.

Manning, Brennan

p. 9—Brennan Manning, *Abba's Child* (Colorado Springs, Colorado: NavPress, 1994), 39.

p. 109—Brennan Manning, *The Ragamuffin Gospel* (Portland, Oregon: Multnomah Press, 1990), 143.

Marshall, Catherine

p. 287—Catherine Marshall, *Adventures in Prayer* (Old Tappan, New Jersey: Fleming H. Revell Co., 1975), 44–45.

p. 335—*The Inspirational Writings of Catherine Marshall* (New York: Inspirational Press, 1974), 157–161.

Marshall, Eric, and Stuart Hample

p. 55—*Children's Letters to God,* comp. by Eric Marshall and Stuart Hample (New York: Pocket Books, 1966).

p. 83—*Children's Letters to God,* comp. by Eric Marshall and Stuart Hample (New York: Pocket Books, 1966).

p. 86—*Children's Letters to God,* comp. by Eric Marshall and Stuart Hample (New York: Pocket Books, 1966).

Marshall, Peter

p. 244—in *The HarperCollins Book of Prayers,* comp. by Robert Van de Weyer (New York: HarperCollins Publishers, 1993), 249.

Mello, Anthony de

p. 110—a story of Perugin, an Italian painter of the Middle Ages in *Taking Flight* by Anthony de Mello (New York: Bantam Doubleday Dell Publishing Group, Inc., 1988), 22.

p. 145—a story of Akbar, the Moghul Emperor, and a peasant woman in *Taking Flight* by Anthony de Mello (New York: Bantam Doubleday Dell Publishing Group, Inc., 1988), 30–31.

Merton, Thomas

p. 193—in *A Seven Day Journey with Thomas Merton* by Esther de Waal (Ann Arbor, Michigan: Servant Publications, 1992), 44.

p. 310—Thomas Merton, *Contemplative Prayer* (New York: Doubleday, 1969), 36–37.

p. 320—Thomas Merton, *Seeds of Contemplation* (Norfolk, Connecticut: New Directions Books, 1949), 140–143.

Michael, Chester P., and Marie C. Norrisey

p. 157—a southern rural minister in *Prayer and Temperament* by Chester P. Michael and Marie C. Norrisey (Charlottesville, Virginia: The Open Door Inc., 1984), 32.

p. 174—Chester P. Michael and Marie C. Norrisey, *Prayer and Temperament* (Charlottesville, Virginia: The Open Door Inc., 1984), 16.

Michelangelo

p. 73—in *One Prayer at a Time,* ed. by F. Forrester Church and Terrence J. Mulry (New York: Macmillan Publishing Company, 1989), 22.

Migrant farmhand mother

p. 250—in *Migrants, Sharecroppers, Mountaineers* by Robert Coles, M.D. (Boston: Little Brown and Company, 1971), 612–614.

Montgomery, James

p. 5—in *Space for God* by Don Postema (Grand Rapids, Michigan: CRC Publications, 1983), 25.

Moody, D. L.

p. 29—in *Every Knee Shall Bow,* comp. and ed. by Joan Winmill Brown (Minneapolis, Minnesota: Grason, 1978), 108.

More, St. Thomas

p. 88—in *Lord Hear Our Prayer,* comp. by Thomas McNally and William G. Storey (Notre Dame, Indiana: Ave Maria Press, 1978), 33.

Muhammad

p. 53—in *Tongues of Fire,* comp. by Grace H. Turnbull (Baltimore: The Johns Hopkins Press, 1941), 99.

Minnesota: Bethany House Publishers, 1961), 101.

S

Sales, St. Francis de
p. 30—in *The Harper Religious and Inspirational Quotation Companion,* comp. and ed. by Margaret Pepper (New York: Harper and Row Publishers, Inc., 1989), 327.

Schaeffer, Edith
p. 33—Edith Schaeffer, *Common Sense Christian Living* (Nashville, Tennessee: Thomas Nelson, Inc., Publishers, 1983), 205.
p. 39—Edith Schaeffer, *Common Sense Christian Living* (Nashville, Tennessee: Thomas Nelson, Inc., Publishers, 1983), 211.
p. 41—Edith Schaeffer, *Common Sense Christian Living* (Nashville, Tennessee: Thomas Nelson, Inc., Publishers, 1983), 211.
p. 97—Edith Schaeffer, *Common Sense Christian Living* (Nashville, Tennessee: Thomas Nelson, Inc., Publishers, 1983), 214–215.
p. 130—Edith Schaeffer, *Common Sense Christian Living* (Nashville, Tennessee: Thomas Nelson, Inc., Publishers, 1983), 207–208.
p. 195—Edith Schaeffer, *Common Sense Christian Living* (Nashville, Tennessee: Thomas Nelson, Inc., Publishers, 1983), 212.

Senter, Ruth
p. 18—Ruth Senter, "I Don't Believe in Prayer If . . . " (*Campus Life Magazine,* November 1995), 33.

Shapiro, Rabbi Phineas
p. 30—in *The Word* by Noah benShea (New York: Random House, 1995), 22.

Sheen, Fulton J.
p. 27—Fulton J. Sheen, *Lift Up Your Heart* (Garden City, New York: Doubleday & Company, Inc., 1955), 184.
p. 192—Fulton J. Sheen, *Lift Up Your Heart* (Garden City, New York: Doubleday & Company, Inc., 1955), 193.
p. 323—Fulton J. Sheen, *Lift Up Your Heart* (Garden City, New York: Doubleday & Company, Inc., 1955), 188.

Shuttleworth, Reverend Canon

p. 134—Reverend Canon Shuttleworth, *Self-Culture for Young People,* vol. X, editor-in-chief, Andrew Sloan Draper (New York, Twentieth Century Self Culture Association, 1907), 174.

Silk, Eleana
p. 330—in *How I Pray* by Jim Castelli (New York: Random House, 1994), 156–157.

Sill, Edward Rowland
p. 110—"The Fool's Prayer" by Edward Rowland Sill in *One Hundred and One Famous Prayers,* comp. by Roy J. Cook (Chicago: The Cable Company, 1929), 159–160.

Smith, Sallie
p. 58—Prayers of Slave Children (Sallie Smith) in *Conversations with God* by James Melvin Washington (New York: HarperCollins, 1994), 67.

Solzhenitsyn, Aleksandr
p. 75—in *Prayers Across the Centuries,* ed. by Vinita Hampton Wright (Wheaton, Illinois: Harold Shaw Publishers, 1993), 143–144.

Spurgeon, Charles
p. 85—as told by An Unknown Author in *The Kneeling Christian* (Grand Rapids, Michigan: Zondervan Publishing House, 1986), 79–80.

Stanford, Susan, with David Hazard
p. 101—in *The Christian Speaker's Treasury* by Ruth A. Tucker (New York: Harper and Row, 1989), 266–267.

Stedman, Ray C.
p. 231—Ray Stedman, *Jesus Teaches on Prayer* (Waco, Texas: Word Books, Publisher, 1975), 113.
p. 353—Ray Stedman, *Jesus Teaches on Prayer* (Waco, Texas: Word Books, Publisher, 1975), 99.

Steindl-Rast, Brother David
p. 16—Brother David Steindl-Rast, *Gratefulness, the Heart of Prayer* (Ramsey, New Jersey: Paulist Press, 1984), 39–40.

Stetson, Jeff
p. 247—in *Conversations with God* by James Melvin Washington (New York: HarperCollins, 1994), 280–281.

Stevenson, Robert Louis
p. 44—in *Prayers,* Robert Louis Stevenson, as told by his wife (Avenel, New Jersey: Gramercy Books, 1995).

p. 112—in *Prayers*, Robert Louis Stevenson, as told by his wife, (Avenel, New Jersey: Gramercy Books, 1995).

Stewart, James S.
p. 141—in *Every Knee Shall Bow*, comp. and ed. by Joan Winmill Brown (Minneapolis, Minnesota: Grason, 1978), 110.

Story of the Man Who Planted Trees, The
p. 356—Jean Giono, the story of Elzeard Bouffler in *Leadership Journal*, Spring 1993: Vol. XIV, Number 2, 48.

Stuart, Queen Mary
p. 89—in *Lord Hear Our Prayer*, comp. by Thomas McNally and William G. Storey (Notre Dame, Indiana: Ave Maria Press, 1978), 32–33.

T

Tada, Joni Eareckson
p. 238—Joni Eareckson Tada, *Glorious Intruder* (Portland, Oregon: Multnomah Press, 1989), 40–41.

Taylor, Hudson
p. 32—in *Hudson Taylor's Spiritual Secret* by Howard and Geraldine Taylor (Grand Rapids, Michigan: Discovery House Publishers, 1990), 17.

Taylor, Jeremy
p. 25—*The Rule and Exercises of Holy Living*, ch. 4, sct. 7, 4th ed., 1654, as quoted in *The Columbia Dictionary of Quotations* (New York: Columbia University Press, 1993), 723.

Temple, William
p. 128—in *The Oxford Book of Prayer*, ed. by George Appleton (New York: Oxford University Press, 1985), 3.

Tennyson, Alfred Lord
p. 352—Alfred Lord Tennyson, *Idylls of the King*, "The Passing of Arthur" (New York: Dell Publishing Co., Inc., 1967), 155.

Teresa of Ávila
p. 74—in *A Life of Prayer* by St. Teresa of Avila, abridged and ed. by James M. Houston (Portland, Oregon: Multnomah Press, 1983), 27–28.
p. 125—*The HarperCollins Book of Prayers*, comp. by Robert Van de Weyer (New York: HarperCollins Publishers, 1993), 349.
p. 128—*The HarperCollins Book of Prayers*, comp. by Robert Van de Weyer (New York: HarperCollins Publishers, 1993), 346.

Teresa of Calcutta, Mother
p. 75—*The HarperCollins Book of Prayers*, comp. by Robert Van de Weyer (New York: HarperCollins Publishers, 1993), 351.
p. 91—Mother Teresa, *Words To Love By* (Notre Dame, Indiana: Ave Maria Press, 1983), 47.
p. 140—in *Eerdman's Book of Famous Prayers*, comp. by Veronica Zundel (Grand Rapids, Michigan: Wm. B. Eerdmans Publishing Company, 1983), 99.
p. 169—"Mother Teresa: Looking to Jesus," an interview with Dr. Schuller, *Possibilities Magazine* May/June 1989, 9.
p. 190—Mother Teresa, *A Simple Faith* (New York: Random House, Inc., 1995), 7.
p. 227—in *Love, A Fruit Always in Season*, sel. and ed. by Dorothy S. Hunt (San Francisco: Ignatius Press, 1987), 79–80.

Thompson, Francis
p. 47—"The Hound of Heaven" in *The Literature of England* by George K. Anderson et al. (Dallas: Scott, Foresman and Company, 1953), 981.

Thurman, Howard
p. 139—in *Conversations with God* by James Melvin Washington (New York: HarperCollins, 1994), 182.

Torrey, R. A.
p. 318—in *Classic Sermons on Prayer*, comp. by Warren Wiersbe (Grand Rapids, Michigan: Kregel Publications, Inc., 1987), 88–90.

Tozer, A. W.
p. 24—A. W. Tozer, *Of God and Men* (Harrisburg, Pennsylvania: Christian Publications, 1960), 52.
p. 28—A. W. Tozer, *God Tells the Man Who Cares* (Harrisburg, Pennsylvania: Christian Publications, 1970), 60–61.
p. 29—A. W. Tozer, *The Divine Conquest* (New York: Fleming H. Revell, 1950), 22.
p. 32—A. W. Tozer, *Jesus, Our Man in Glory* (Camp Hill, Pennsylvania: Christian Publications, 1987), 104–105.
p. 33—A. W. Tozer, *The Root of the Righteous* (Harrisburg, Pennsylvania: Christian Publications, 1955), 105–106.
p. 146—A. W. Tozer, *The Pursuit of God* (Camp Hill, Pennsylvania: Christian Publications, Inc., 1982), 15.

p. 147—A. W. Tozer, *Faith Beyond Reason* (Camp Hill, Pennsylvania: Christian Publications, 1989), 44–45.

p. 148—A. W. Tozer, *The Pursuit of God* (Camp Hill, Pennsylvania: Christian Publications, Inc., 1982), 18.

p. 192—A. W. Tozer, *The Pursuit of God* (Camp Hill, Pennsylvania: Christian Publications, Inc., 1982), 82–83.

p. 194—A. W. Tozer, *The Set of the Sail* (Camp Hill, Pennsylvania: Christian Publications, 1986), 15.

p. 195—A. W. Tozer, *Jesus, Author of Our Faith* (Camp Hill, Pennsylvania: Christian Publications, 1988), 46.

p. 311—A. W. Tozer, *The Pursuit of God* (Camp Hill, Pennsylvania: Christian Publications, Inc., 1982), 16–17.

p. 320—A. W. Tozer, *The Pursuit of God* (Camp Hill, Pennsylvania: Christian Publications, Inc., 1982), 82–83.

p. 354—A. W. Tozer, *Tragedy in the Church* (Camp Hill, Pennsylvania: Christian Publications, Inc., 1990), 8.

Trueblood, Elton

p. 32—Elton Trueblood, *The New Man For Our Time* (New York: Harper & Row, 1970), 60.

Truth, Sojourner

p. 103—in *Conversations with God* by James Melvin Washington (New York: HarperCollins, 1994), 55.

Tyler, Kelsey

p. 93—Kelsey Tyler, *Heaven Hears Each Whisper* (New York: The Berkley Publishing Group, 1996), 4–5.

p. 98—Kelsey Tyler, *Heaven Hears Each Whisper* (New York: The Berkley Publishing Group, 1996), 21–25.

p. 340—Kelsey Tyler, *Heaven Hears Each Whisper* (New York: The Berkley Publishing Group, 1996), 27–34.

p. 347—Kelsey Tyler, *Heaven Hears Each Whisper* (New York: The Berkley Publishing Group, 1996), 121–127.

U

Underhill, Evelyn

p. 123—Evelyn Underhill, *The Love of God,* ed. by the Right Rev. Lumsden Barkway, D.D., and Lucy Menzies, D.D. (New York: Morehouse-Barlow Co., 1976), 134, 136, 138.

V

Vining, Elizabeth Gray

p. 24—Elizabeth Gray Vining, *The World in Tune* (New York: Harper & Brothers Publishers, 1954), 40.

p. 66—Elizabeth Gray Vining, *The World in Tune* (New York: Harper & Brothers Publishers, 1954), 68.

W

Wangerin, Walter Jr.

p. 156—Walter Wangerin, *Reliving the Passion* (Grand Rapids, Michigan: Zondervan Publishing House, 1992), 65–66.

Warhola, Debbie

p. 332—Debbie Warhola, *The Gazette Telegraph,* "The Power of Prayer in Healing" (Colorado Springs, Colorado: Saturday, March 16, 1996), Section F, p. F/1.

Watley, William Donnel

p. 251—in *Conversations with God* by James Melvin Washington (New York: HarperCollins, 1994), 266.

Weatherhead, Leslie

p. 104—in *One Prayer at a Time,* ed. by F. Forrester Church and Terrence J. Mulry (New York: Macmillan Publishing Company, 1989), 15.

p. 315—in *The HarperCollins Book of Prayers,* comp. by Robert Van de Weyer (New York: HarperCollins Publishers, 1993), 382.

Wesley, John

p. 42—as told by E. M. Bounds in *A Treasury of Prayer,* comp. and cond. by Leonard Ravenhill (Minneapolis, Minnesota: Bethany House Publishers, 1961), 100.

p. 42—as told by Warren Wiersbe in *Walking with the Giants* by Warren Wiersbe (Grand Rapids, Michigan: Baker Book House Company, 1976), 280.

Wiersbe, Warren

p. 40—*Classic Sermons on Prayer,* comp. by Warren W. Wiersbe (Grand Rapids, Michigan: Kregel Publications, 1987), 24.

Wirt, Sherwood E.

p. 195—in *Wings of Joy,* comp. and ed. by Joan Winmill Brown (Old Tappan, New Jersey: Fleming H. Revell Company, 1977), 51.

Whitney, Donald
  p. 10—Donald Whitney, *Spiritual Disciplines for the Christian Life* (Colorado Springs, Colorado: NavPress, 1991), 65.
  p. 231—Donald Whitney, *Spiritual Disciplines for the Christian Life* (Colorado Springs, Colorado: NavPress, 1991), 65–74.
Wilberforce, William
  p. 43—as told by E. M. Bounds in *A Treasury of Prayer,* comp. and cond. by Leonard Ravenhill (Minneapolis, Minnesota: Bethany House Publishers, 1961), 119.
Woods, Fannie
  p. 246—in *Conversations with God* by James Melvin Washington (New York: HarperCollins, 1994), 41.
Wouk, Herman
  p. 29—Herman Wouk, *This Is My God* (Garden City, New York: Doubleday & Company, Inc., 1959), 110.
Wyon, Olive
  p. 149—Olive Wyon, *The School of Prayer,* "White Birds" as quoted in *Illus-trations Unlimited,* ed. by James Herrett (Wheaton, Illinois: Tyndale House Publishers, 1988), 425–427.

Y
Yancey, Philip
  p. 262—Philip Yancey, *Disappointment with God* (Grand Rapids, Michigan: Zondervan Publishing House, 1988), 231–237.
  p. 288—Philip Yancey, *Disappointment with God* (Grand Rapids, Michigan: Zondervan Publishing House, 1988), 156–159.
  p. 296—Philip Yancey, *Where Is God When It Hurts?* (Grand Rapids, Michigan: Zondervan Publishing House, 1977), 100–102, 104–108.

Z
Zimbabwe
  p. 63—in *The World At One in Prayer,* ed. by Daniel J. Fleming (New York: Harper & Brothers, 1942), 109.